THE BUNKER FAMILY ENG & CHANG, THEIR WIVES AND THEIR CHILDREN.

*****

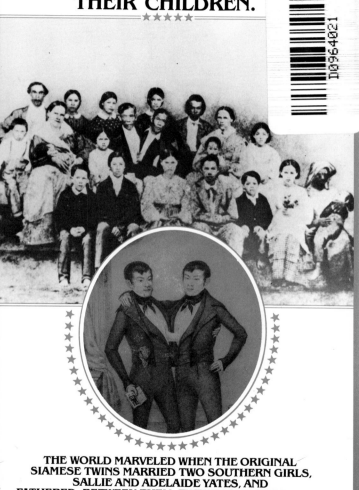

THE WORLD MARVELED WHEN THE ORIGINAL SIAMESE TWINS MARRIED TWO SOUTHERN GIRLS, SALLIE AND ADELAIDE YATES, AND FATHERED, BETWEEN THEM, TWENTY-ONE CHILDREN...

THE WEDDING
OF TWO AND TWO

The wedding took place, beneath a bower of roses, on Thursday, April 13, 1843, in the two-story private residence of a well-to-do farmer named David Yates. It was a double wedding—the two brothers, naturalized American citizens, were marrying two native-born southern sisters.

First, Mr. C. Bunker, age thirty-two, took Miss Adelaide Yates, age nineteen, for his wife, for better or for worse, to love and to cherish until death did them part. Next, Mr. E. Bunker, age thirty-two, took Miss Sarah Yates, age twenty, for his wife.

The only problem was that when Miss Adelaide Yates accompanied Mr. C. Bunker to their nuptial bed she took with her not only her newly wed husband but also her brother-in-law, Mr. E. Bunker.

And when Miss Sarah Yates prepared to enjoy her honeymoon with her husband, Mr. E. Bunker, she would share the same problem . . .

Bantam Books by Irving Wallace and Amy Wallace
THE BOOK OF LISTS (with David Wallechinsky)
THE TWO

Bantam Books by Irving Wallace
Ask your bookseller for books you have missed
THE FAN CLUB
THE MAN
THE PEOPLE'S ALMANAC #2 (with David Walle-
chinsky)
THE R DOCUMENT
THE SUNDAY GENTLEMAN

★★★★★

THE TWO

A BIOGRAPHY

★★★★ BY ★★★★

IRVING WALLACE

★★★★ AND ★★★★

AMY WALLACE

★★★★★

BANTAM BOOKS · TORONTO · NEW YORK · LONDON

NEW YORK

THE TWO
A Bantam Book

PRINTING HISTORY
Simon and Schuster edition published March 1978
Bantam edition / January 1979

ISBN 0–553–12160–X

Published simultaneously in the United States and Canada

*Bantam Books are published by Bantam Books, Inc. Its trade-
mark, consisting of the words "Bantam Books" and the por-
trayal of a bantam, is Registered in U.S. Patent and Trademark
Office and in other countries. Marca Registrada. Bantam
Books, Inc., 666 Fifth Avenue, New York, New York 10019.*

PRINTED IN THE UNITED STATES OF AMERICA

For Sylvia
With love and thanks
IRVING AND AMY

For Bob
With love
AMY

PICTURE CREDITS

CONTENTS

What therefore God hath joined together, let not man put asunder.

—*St. Matthew, 19:6*

THE
TWO

CHAPTER
1

Enter the Double Boys

The year 1843 was not a notable year for news in the United States. The occupant of the White House, the nation's tenth President, was fifty-three-year-old John Tyler, who had taken office only two years earlier upon the death of William Henry Harrison. The most exciting event on his agenda was the dedication of a monument at Bunker Hill, where Daniel Webster delivered the keynote address. Members of Congress had bestirred themselves long enough to vote a $30,000 appropriation for the testing of the newly invented telegraph. Dorothea Dix, reformer, published a Memorial attacking the treatment of the insane in the twenty-six states. Edgar Allan Poe won a $100 newspaper prize for his short story "The Gold Bug," and William Hickling Prescott brought out his popular *History of the Conquest of Mexico*. John Frémont was in Kansas City mounting an expedition to explore the Oregon country. William Miller and his Millerites were preparing for the end of the world. In Nauvoo, Illinois, the Mormon prophet Joseph

1

Smith announced that he had received a revelation that sanctioned polygamy for true believers.

The most provocative news story of the year, as it turned out, one that would stimulate international interest and inquiry, was a brief marriage ceremony held in an obscure corner of the state of North Carolina.

The wedding took place, beneath a bower of roses, on Thursday, April 13, 1843, in the two-story private residence of a well-to-do farmer named David Yates, located on Mulberry Farm six miles northwest of the town of Wilkesboro. It was a double wedding—the two brothers, naturalized American citizens, were marrying two native-born Southern sisters—and the Reverend James L. Davis, a minister of the Methodist Church, conducted the ceremony.

First, Mr. C. Bunker, age thirty-one, took Miss Adelaide Yates, age nineteen, for his wife, for better or for worse, to love and to cherish until death did them part.

Next, Mr. E. Bunker, age thirty-one, took Miss Sarah Yates, age twenty, for his wife, for better or for worse, to love and to cherish until death did them part.

The only problem—indeed, the factor that made the occasion international news—was that when Miss Adelaide Yates accompanied Mr. C. Bunker to their home nearby at Trap Hill and then to their nuptial bed, she took with her not only her newly wed husband but also her brother-in-law, Mr. E. Bunker.

And when Miss Sarah Yates prepared to enjoy her honeymoon with her husband, Mr. E. Bunker, she knew that she would have to share it alongside her brother-in-law, Mr. C. Bunker.

If the marriages were solemnized until death did them part, it did not alter the simple, inexorable fact that in life the grooms also could not part, then or ever after. For Mr. C. Bunker and Mr. E. Bunker, who had married the Yates sisters that April day in 1843, were none other than Mr. Chang Bunker and Mr. Eng Bunker—Chang and Eng, the world-renowned original Siamese Twins.

Although distinctly two persons, Chang and Eng had been united as one in their conception and had remained united in the thirty-two years since their birth. On their wedding day they stood joined by a thick fleshy ligament resembling an arm, five to six inches long and eight inches in circumference, that connected them at the base of their chests. Adelaide and Sarah Yates were definitely two separate and normal young women, two of the six children of a five-hundred-pound mother (renowned in the community for her weight, most likely due to a glandular malfunction) and a prosperous Baptist father.

Despite the problem of the two husbands being one and the two wives being two, the marriages of the Siamese Twins to Adelaide and Sarah Yates lasted almost thirty-one years—and produced a total of twenty-one children.

At the time of their marriage, the Siamese Twins were world-famous. Until the appearance of Phineas T. Barnum's twenty-five-inch-tall Tom Thumb the year before, the Siamese Twins had been the earth's stellar show-business attraction. For fourteen years they had been a focus of attention for the press and had attracted enthusiastic audiences throughout most of the United States, the British Isles, France, Holland, and Belgium. They had been called by a contemporary writer "the eighth wonder of the world."

Yet at the time of their marriages—surely few marriages in world history, before or since, have been as incredible as these—not many could imagine that the bizarre saga of the Siamese Twins was just at its beginning.

For Chang and Eng, the actual beginning had occurred thirty-two years earlier, halfway around the world in a distant and exotic land named Siam, which would forever be known for three of its products—the Siamese white elephant, the Siamese cat, and the Siamese Twins.

◆— ◆— ◆—

They were born on May 11, 1811, on a bamboo mat in a small houseboat afloat on the river in the village of Meklong, located sixty miles west of Bangkok, the capital of Siam.

Their mother's name was Nok, and she was three-quarters Chinese and one-quarter Siamese. Their father, a fisherman named Ti-eye, was fully Chinese, born and raised in his native land, from which he had migrated to Siam. A Westerner who later met Nok described her as being "about five feet seven inches in height, well formed, with large hips, and, for her country, a strong woman. . . . She was thirty-five years of age when her twins were born." Nok already had four children. The twins increased the brood to six. There would be nine in all before the father died.

The mother informed an American visitor later "that she suffered no greater inconvenience at their birth than at those of her other children; that they were born with the head of one between the legs of the other, and as infants were rather small."

Once delivered, they lay compactly fitted together but facing in opposite directions, and this excited some wonder among the attending midwives and neighbors. Wonder soon gave way to joy that they were twins (in a land where a woman's prestige was enhanced by the number of children she bore), that they were well formed, that their first sounds proved they were alive and healthy. Immediately, a midwife prepared to right the one who had come out head first, and to separate them and bathe them—but suddenly it was observed that they could not be separated.

It was unbelievable, a sight that had never been witnessed before by any of those present. Nok's newborn twins were bound together, were joined breastbone to breastbone by a short, flexible, fleshy band or ligament. The two were two yet one.

Consternation. Fright, even horror, at this monstrosity. No hands touched them.

Nok, it appeared, was a no-nonsense mother. What-

ever their condition at birth, they were still her newborn sons. They lay before her, their connecting
band twisted by their manner of birth, continuing to
utter their earliest cries of life. Nok untwisted them,
straightened the band until they were face to face.
Then she bathed them.

Shortly after, Nok and her husband gave the
twins their names. The one on the twins' own left
was named Chang, and the one on the right was
named Eng. In the years to follow, many Westerners
would speculate on the meaning of their names. The
most common belief was that Chang meant "left" and
that Eng meant "right" in the Siamese, or Thai, language. This interpretation was discredited in later
years. More than six decades later, Dr. William H.
Pancoast, a surgeon teaching at Philadelphia's Jefferson Medical College who examined the bodies of the
twins after their death, became curious about their
names and reported his findings:

> I have examined in the Astor Library, of New York,
> a copy of the celebrated dictionary of the Siamese lan-
> guage, *Dictionarium linguae Thai sive Siamiensis*, by
> Monseigneur J. B. Pallegoix, Bishop of Mallo, etc.
> Therein are numerous translations of the words Eng
> and Chang, but in no place do they signify right and
> left. In the Siamese language, words spelt exactly in the
> same way may have an entirely different signification
> according to the accompanying accent. Thus, by a dif-
> ferent pronunciation, a word is made to do service for
> various meanings. Of all the different significations of
> Chang that of "unsavory, tasteless," seem alone ap-
> plicable. This justifies the statement which has been
> made, that the twins were not originally called Eng
> and Chang to distinguish them as right and left, but
> that the names were given them to express their natural
> characteristics. Eng was ever the stronger and healthier
> of the two, and of a pleasant disposition; Chang was ir-
> ritable, and less amiable. With this understanding of
> their peculiarities, the names seem much more ap-
> propriate, and were probably given for this rea-
> son.

However, the most likely explanation exists in a passage in a Thai textbook, *Famous Thai People:*

> Their mother called them "In" and "Jun" . . . In and Jun were the names of a certain kind of local fruit growing on trees. When the fruit was raw, it was green, and we called it In fruit, and when the fruit was ripe it was yellow, and we called it Jun fruit. Since to Europeans the pronunciation of these two words was not familiar, they pronounced them Eng-Chang.

Word of the twins' unnatural birth spread through Siam like wildfire, from Meklong to stately Bangkok, and then to outlying villages. Among savants, and some royalty, the abnormal union was regarded as a bad omen, perhaps heralding the destruction of the country, possibly even the world. Two verdicts were reached. One came from several of the nation's leading medical practitioners, who believed that if the twins could be separated, the evil they symbolized would be eliminated. The other came from Rama II, the all-powerful king of Siam. He decided that to avert disaster, the infants Chang and Eng must be put to death.

The Siamese medical doctors of the period, mostly of Chinese origin, were an unorthodox lot by Western standards. An Edinburgh newspaper dismissed them, saying: "Their medicine is as rude as their other sciences. One process of cure is laying the patient flat on the floor and trampling him under foot." Several of these local practitioners came forward to entreat Nok to allow Chang and Eng to be separated. According to a pamphlet published about the twins in New York in 1853:

"Most suggestions offered in the case of the twins were absurd beyond the power of description. One venerable [Siamese] leech proposed hanging them across a fine cat-gut cord, like a pair of saddle-bags, estimating that this would, in time, work its way entirely through the connecting ligature, by degrees, allowing the severed parts time to heal as it progressed. Another advised cutting them apart with a red-hot wire." Yet another Siamese doctor advised they be sawed apart, and still another suggested the ligament be burned.

All of this sagacious advice the mother Nok resisted, dreading the pain that would be imposed on her sons, and eventually the doctors gave up and went their ways to trample on other afflicted patients.

King Rama II's sentence of death was a momentary whim, and he failed to act upon it. He had inherited the throne only two years before the birth of the twins, and he was known to be a compassionate, thoughtful, quiet man possessed of creative gifts. He had a reputation as a poet, and once had collaborated with the leading court poets to produce the Thai version of the Hindu epic *Ramayana*. Not only did he promote arts and letters, but he instigated the construction of magnificent buildings which he designed himself and for which he personally sculpted decorations. It was said that upon learning that the twins were maturing as healthy and vigorous youngsters and would one day be able to earn their keep—and assured by now that their advent had not doomed the kingdom—he formally retracted his original death sentence and left the twins alone.

Yet another factor may have influenced the king. Quite possibly one of his advisers or scholars had acquired some medical literature from the West and learned that while xiphophagic, or joined, twins had occurred throughout history, their births had not signaled national disasters. These medical records cited around one hundred joined twins. The year 945 saw the birth of the Armenian Twins, united at the abdomen. When an effort was made to separate them, one died immediately, the other three days later. In the year 1100, two sisters, Mary and Eliza Chulkhurst, were born in the hamlet of Biddenden, Kent, England. The girls were joined at the hips and possibly at the shoulders. Known as the Biddenden Maids, they lived to the age of thirty-four, leaving twenty acres of land to the church upon their death. Part of the rent from this land was to be spent each

Easter to distribute cakes bearing the twins' images to itinerants and the poor.

Around 1475, the Scottish Brothers were born near Glasgow. The boys were joined at the back, two persons from the waist up, one person from the waist down. They were protected by the king of the Scots, James III, educated and raised at court, and lived to the age of twenty-eight. In 1689, there were joined twins born in Basle, held together by a ligament one inch long and five inches in diameter. At risk of life, a celebrated doctor named Fatio operated upon them. Employing six surgical wires, Dr. Fatio successfully separated them. In 1701, there were the Hungarian Sisters, Helen and Judith, whose bodies were welded together back to back, with only one pair of legs for the two of them. Helen and Judith spent their early years being exhibited in fairs across England, Holland, Germany, and Italy, but at the age of nine they were placed in a convent. The pair survived until the age of twenty-two.

If King Rama II was indeed told about these births, and had learned that none of them was followed by a natural calamity, it would explain why he permitted Chang and Eng to escape death.

To understand the original attitude of the king and his medical practitioners toward the birth of Chang and Eng, one must understand the country of Siam as it was in the year 1811. At that time, Siam—which had become a nation in the sixth century—was an independent kingdom located in southeastern Asia, due south of China, with Burma bordering it to the west, and Cochin China as its neighbor to the east. For more than a thousand years, the nation's rulers called their country "Sayam"—or Siam—in communications with the outside world. But to the people themselves, the country was known as Muang T'ai—"land of the Thai race"—which became "Thailand" in discussions with foreigners. (Not until 1939 did the then-regent of Siam officially decree that the nation would thereafter be known, to foreigners and natives alike, as Thailand.)

Siam was a feudal kingdom of over five million persons in 1811. Under King Rama II the land was divided up among the nobility—lords and princes who, in turn, leased their acres to impoverished tenant farmers. Every male Siamese over twenty was ordered by law to toil on these farms, mostly rice paddies, three months out of every year, just as every male over twenty was expected to serve six months in the Thai army, a portion of that time without pay.

One group of citizens was exempt from these onerous duties—the Chinese immigrants who had become subjects of the Siamese king. About 310,000 citizens of Siam were Chinese, and the Chinese males over twenty were excused from farm labor and military conscription so long as each paid a tax of three dollars every three years for such exemption. The reason for this favoritism went back to an ancient time when Siam had been subjugated by neighboring Burma. There had then arisen in the ranks of the conquered Siamese army a Chinese-born soldier named Piatac, who had rallied and organized the Siamese fighting men, led a revolt against the Burmese, driven the invaders out, reestablished Siam's independence, and made himself king of the newly free country, establishing Bangkok as his capital.

Piatac had given his fellow Chinese in Siam special privileges, and these privileges were still perpetuated under King Rama II. One of the beneficiaries of this traditional largess was the Chinese father of Chang and Eng.

King Rama II ruled his land as an absolute monarch. His ornate Royal Palace, surrounded by a two-mile wall, was located sixty miles west of the village where the twins were born, in Bangkok (which in Thai means Village of Wild Plums), a city built largely on piles and floating pontoons and with a population of about 400,000. In the palace were the king's family, his aides and statesmen, his servants, numbering three thousand persons in all. Since polygamy was the custom, practiced mostly by the wealthy, King Rama II had a harem of seven hundred wives and con-

cubines. This harem, and that of his successor, King
Rama III, was modest compared to the seraglio of
the latter's successor, King Rama IV, better known to
history as King Mongut. After Mongut attained the
throne in 1851 and opened Siam to the West, he filled
his harem with nine thousand wives and concubines, thirty of whom gave him sixty-seven children.

All of this was attested to by Mrs. Anna H. Leonowens, an English woman from Wales who as a twen-
ty-seven-year-old widow had come to Bangkok to tu-
tor King Mongut's vast brood of children. After five
years in the king's palace. Mrs. Leonowens departed
to write two best-selling books, *The English Governess at the Siamese Court* and *The Romance of the
Harem.* The first book became famous in the next century when it served as the basis for another book,
Anna and the King of Siam by Margaret Landon, and
a play and motion picture that were both called *The
King and I.* "Polygamy—or, properly speaking, con-
cubinage—and slavery are the curses of the country,"
Mrs. Leonowens wrote in her second book. "The
number of concubines is limited only by the means of
the man. As the king is the source of all wealth and
influence, dependent kings, princes, and nobles, and
all who would seek the royal favor, vie with each
other in bringing their most beautiful and accomplished daughters to the royal harem. . . . Woman is
the slave of man."

King Rama II kept his country isolated from the
West. At the beginning of his reign, the only foreigners admitted were Chinese, Portuguese, and Dutch
traders. But in his later years he did admit a handful
of English and American traders. According to Jesse
Franklin Graves, an American jurist who was close
to the twins during most of their adult life, "The
people of Siam have a great attachment to their country and their feeling of nationality is so strong that
they look upon all foreigners except the Chinese with
suspicious hatred and contempt, holding themselves
to be vastly superior to the people of every other
nation."

The masses of the people were erratically educated and poorly read. The few popular books were "written on slips of palm-leaf, with an iron style, a black powder being thrown over the impression to render it legible. These slips are from a foot to a foot and a half long. To bring a volume together, they are tied up in small bundles, richly gilded and painted on the edges, and placed in an envelope of silk or cotton cloth."

Almost the entire population of Siam was guided by religion and superstition. Basically, the people were Buddhists, but a few innovations had been added, such as a belief in a single creator known as the Golden Supreme. While the people subsisted peacefully on rice and fish, and chewed betel, and dwelt in poverty, the priests lived in comfort in magnificently decorated temples.

Justice was primitive. The fate of the accused in a trial was usually determined by some ordeal. Typically, when a man accused of a crime was brought to trial, he was ordered to pluck a large stone out of a pot of boiling water. Afterward his hands were wrapped in bandages and these were not removed for three days. If on the fourth day his hands showed burn marks, he was declared guilty of the crime. If his hands showed no burns, he was declared innocent and freed.

This was the world in which Chang and Eng, called the Chinese Twins by their neighbors, grew to maturity. Their immediate world, however, was much more limited. Their home remained a bamboo house, the roof thatched with palm leaves, set on a raft secured to the bank of a branch of the Meklong River. There were several small rooms in the house, with a table set outside the front door from which their father sold his catch of fish as well as various small articles of merchandise.

Above the river bank rose the village of Meklong, described by a visitor, Sir John Bowring, as "a populous and beautiful city, with its floating bazaars, fine pagodas and gardens, and a population of ten thousand, the largest proportion of which are Chinese. There is a considerable fortification for the defence of the place. The soil is remarkably fertile, and the salt-pits produce enough to supply the whole kingdom. Both sides of the river are peopled and cultivated."

As infants, the Chinese Twins were delicate and constricted, held face to face by their common ligament. They remained objects of intense curiosity. Townfolk who had heard of the strange birth came to see them, and visitors from afar sometimes lined the river bank for a glimpse of them. Gradually, as they grew and the villagers became used to seeing them, the crowds of curious onlookers thinned, and eventually disappeared altogether.

Their mother Nok was determined that they should grow up as normally as possible, and she neither ignored the twins nor pitied and overprotected them. She was matter-of-fact about them, and treated the two much as she treated her other children.

One of the first difficulties they faced was in learning to walk. An American pamphlet described their initial efforts: "Any one who has ever seen two inebriated men, with locked arms, endeavoring to proceed in a fixed direction, may form some idea of their earliest efforts; but their mother has remarked that, after once becoming accustomed to the task of maintaining a proper center of gravity, their advance in the practice of pedestrianism was truly astonishing."

In one of their first forays alone, they were toddling along the river bank when they were attracted by the music from a floating theater gliding by. They started toward it, and went tumbling straight into the river, from which they were rescued "by the crew of an aquatic laundry."

In their childhood, they were always attentive to music and theatrical performances. Among their fondest memories in later years was a magical night when they were taken to view a Siamese play. The play was not a written play—in Siam, based on no

more than a thread of a story, the actors made up
their own dialogue. It was a romantic play recounting
the adventures of a remote historical prince in love
and war, and the story was filled with the feats of
tumblers, jugglers, sword-swallowers, fire-eaters. The
twins never forgot it.

Soon they were not only walking firmly, but were
running with ease. Their favorite sport was to leave
their floating home, scramble to the summit of a nearby hill, wrap their arms around each other tightly,
and roll down the hill shouting with laughter.

The twins learned to anticipate and coordinate
their movements, like a practiced dance team, but
sometimes there were accidents. One day they raced
toward a low fence and attempted to leap over it together. As they left the ground, one lagged a split
second behind the other. They came down hard,
their connecting ligament straddling the top of the
fence, and one twin was left hanging on each side of
it. They dangled there until one had the strength to
haul himself over the top to join the other. But the
ligament that bound them had been badly bruised,
and both were ill for several days.

During all of this, they had grown quite strong.
Now when they played rough games with the neighborhood children, they were always confident. Once
one of them remarked that, since there were two of
them to one of everyone else, they should do everything twice as well as their friends.

The river was their father's life and part of their
own lives, too. Quickly, they learned to swim in tandem, and they learned to handle a boat. Their father,
like many others dependent on the river, had a small
spare craft tied to the houseboat, which was used for
fishing and travel. In a short time the twins, too, were
using the boat, standing at the stern, each plying one
oar.

This strenuous physical activity, which was constantly encouraged by their mother, began to affect
their joining band. Gradually, the connecting ligament stretched, from four inches to five and a half

inches, so that soon they moved away from their face-to-face position and were able to walk almost side by side, their arms around each other's shoulders.

There were occasional problems of health and of temperament. At the age of six they were ill for two weeks with smallpox, but they overcame that successfully. They had caught it on the same day, and recovered on the same day.

More serious was the matter of their opposing temperaments. Chang, the slightly shorter of the pair, who stood on their own left, was the dominant member of the two and the more quick-tempered. Eng was more agreeable, compliant, docile. In disagreements, Eng usually gave in and thus avoided trouble. But on one occasion, in a heated argument, Eng refused to give in. Then, for the first and only time in their childhood, they began to hit one another. The fight grew more violent, until their mother came between them. The situation was critical. They could not be pulled apart and sent off to different rooms, for they were held together, with their anger, only inches from one another. Their mother lectured them, reasoned with them, explained that their condition made any more fights impossible. They must learn to tolerate each other, take turns at placating and compromising. Without such self-control, they would not survive their physical bondage to one another. The lesson was not lost on them.

By the time they were seven, Chang and Eng had received their first schooling. According to an American pamphlet: "At an early age they received the usual amount of teaching given to the middling classes, and learned to read and write their native language with tolerable proficiency."

They grew up completely at the age of eight.

It was 1819, and it was in that year that disaster struck their close-knit family. A cholera epidemic swept through all of Southeast Asia, and it hit the village of Meklong full force. Long after, Chang and Eng would recount the devastation to their American friend Judge Graves, and he would note their impression of the disaster in his unpublished biography of the twins:

"The cholera came upon the inhabitants of Meklong in the most malignant form; no precaution would prevent it; no remedies, relieve or cure it. The victims died suddenly; the living were unable to bury the dead; the bodies were thrown into the river; the sluggish water did not remove the putrid mass; stench arose from the water."

The twins' family at the outset of the horror numbered eleven—the two parents and their nine children. Almost immediately three of the children died. In short weeks, two more children succumbed to the plague, and the father, Ti-eye, lay seriously ill. And then, finally, he died, too.

When the cholera epidemic abated, only five of them were left. The mother Nok was alive, as were an older brother named Noy and an older sister whose name is not known—and Chang and Eng themselves.

The dead siblings had long since been removed, and what remained was the father's funeral, an event that could never be erased from the twins' minds.

Although only eight, Chang and Eng trailed after their mother, brother, and sister into the courtyard of the Buddhist temple. The coffin that held the body of their father rested on a bier covered with cloth, six feet above the ground. The coffin itself was draped with a crimson cloth woven with gold. Above the bier was a canopy of white—the color of mourning—and the canopy was festooned with fragrant flowers.

Soon there was the sound of music, as Siamese flutes, drums, and gongs began to play together. Nearby, in the courtyard, a Buddhist priest appeared in a shed to read aloud a prayer, while on a low platform at his feet sat a group of women holding lighted tapers.

When the prayer was done, the priest, accompanied by several other priests, moved slowly toward the coffin. Chang and Eng watched as the priests lifted a strip of cloth that was attached to the head of their father's coffin. The cloth was cut by the priests, and pieces of it were handed to Nok, to Noy, to the sister, and to Chang and Eng.

Now the priests lifted the coffin and moved it inside the temple. Chang and Eng were told that temple attendants were washing and purifying their father's corpse.

Meanwhile, combustibles were being thrown on the bier. At last the priests reappeared carrying the body, which they placed gently on the bier. A priest passed out lighted tapers to the mourners, then returned to the bier and set fire to it. He signaled for the mourners to put their burning tapers to the funeral pyre also. Soon flames surrounded it, licking upward toward the sky, engulfing the twins' father in a blaze of red.

And then it was over, the cremation ended, their father gone forever.

Nok made the final expected ceremonial gesture. She turned toward the pressing group of beggars who had gathered from the village and went among them distributing alms.

It had been an impressive ceremony, a necessary one, but a woefully expensive one. Its cost depleted all of Nok's small savings. The family was penniless, and without a father to support it. Chang and Eng would never be young again.

Mourning could be of only short duration. For the survivors to continue to survive, they had to eat, and to eat they had to find an immediate means of livelihood.

Nok at first undertook to extract and make oil from cocoa nuts, but it was slow and difficult work, too difficult for the children to help her with, and too much to do by herself. She gave this up, and by some desperate means managed to collect notions, which she placed for sale on the outdoor table of the house-boat. This brought some small income, but not enough. It was then that young Chang and Eng realized that they must go to work, become family providers, and from that time on, for the rest of their lives, they rarely had surcease from work.

Their father had been a fisherman. They decided to be fishermen, too. They found a job with a successful fisherman on the river and helped him with his catch, but after a while they felt that they could do better going into business for themselves. With the extra money they had acquired, they bought a small boat and began to fish on their own. Their income increased.

Presently, they determined to go into something even more profitable. They would become, as they themselves called it, "merchants." They would buy various goods cheap, ferry them to the floating marketplace, and sell them at a profit. Thus, between the ages of ten and thirteen, the twins engaged in trade and made money. Three factors worked for them. They possessed an innate shrewdness at bargaining. As the Chinese Twins, bound together by a band of flesh, they aroused the sympathy and interest of others. And, because of their handicap, the government did not tax them as it taxed other peddlers, and so they could sell cheaper than their competitors.

Soon they were able to support the family, as well as set aside small savings. However, life was not without its occasional problems. One night, while tied in with a small armada of boats manned by other merchants, they moved down a canal toward the Meklong River. With the coming of morning, one merchant discovered that some of his most valuable goods—parcels of peacock tail feathers—had been stolen during the night. The victim did not know who had done it, but he knew the crime had been committed by someone in the group. Immediately, he summoned the authorities. Everyone, including Chang and Eng, was arrested and brought before the district chief. Like the others, the twins gave testimony and pleaded not guilty. Since the court could not uncover the culprit by ordinary means, the chief pronounced that a trial by ordeal would be held. The test was simple: each suspect must swallow an emetic. The first one who vomited would be considered guilty and punished. The twins took the emetic, and held it down. One of the others threw up immediately, was declared guilty, and summarily punished. However, an hour later the real thief was caught with the peacock tail feathers in his possession.

It was the twins' only bout with the law in a merchandising career which continued to prosper.

Meanwhile, in Bangkok, a new monarch had ascended the throne of Siam. King Rama II had been succeeded by thirty-seven-year-old King Rama III. Unlike his predecessor, the new ruler was a militarist, not an artist. He set his armies on a course of conquest, expanding his empire in the Malay Peninsula to the south, invading the Lao territory in the north, and subduing part of Cambodia. When not at war, the king's diversions were limited. He presented food to the monks who came to beg each morning. He enjoyed feeding his pet tortoise. A devout Buddhist, he gave much time to prayer and to denouncing Protestant missionaries (who had failed to gain a single convert in eighteen years). He held a one-hour audience every morning and a three-hour audience every night. He inspected new ships or the casting of artillery guns. He played with his children. He fought the growing opium trade. Under his supervision, nine new temples were erected and a ninety-foot-long reclining Buddha, made of brick and mortar and coated with gold, was built. Somewhat of a prude, he hated the ballet and sought further recreation in marvels and the bizarre.

King Rama III had been on the throne little more than a year when he heard of the wondrous curiosity in the village of Meklong. There were, he was told by travelers, two youthful merchants known as the Chinese Twins who were joined together by a band of flesh. The king was intrigued. He summoned the twins to appear before him and his royal court at the palace in Bangkok.

To understand the reaction of Chang and Eng, two fourteen-year-old peasant boys, to this summons from King Rama III, one must understand the exalted position of the nation's monarch in 1825.

The summons from the king was, as a nineteenth-century pamphlet reports,

. . . an event which nearly overwhelmed them with astonishment and awe, as the veneration attached to the person of the king of Siam, by his subjects, is, perhaps, without parallel in any other land. It is believed that his body is the vehicle of a soul in a highly advanced state of migration towards a final state of beatitude, and that the very fact of his being king is complete evidence of extraordinary piety in former conditions of existence. No one dares pronounce his name, nor is it ever mentioned in writing, or even known, except by a very few of his principal courtiers. It would be the height of presumption to inquire after his health, for however sick and wretched he may be, he must always be supposed to be free from all bodily infirmities. When he is obliged to call upon the services of his physician, it is not for a moment allowed that he can be in the need of any medicine, or that his system can, by any possibility, have become deranged, but his physic is offered him with the assurance that it is an exquisitely palatable and agreeable preparation, the swallowing of whch cannot fail to afford him unspeakable satisfaction and delight; whereupon his majesty bolts it down, and tries to look as if he liked it.

No heir to the throne is appointed during the lifetime of the king, for to imagine his death is not only in its legal, but in its popular acceptation, high treason.

In rank, there is no comparison between the sovereign and the most exalted of his officers or courtiers; and the idiom of the language itself takes care to mark the immeasurable distance which exists between them. If he wishes to compliment a young prince, or nobleman, he addresses him as "Illustrious Dog," or "Noble Rat," terms of condescension, which are received with the utmost thankfulness and gratitude. . . . No wonder that the youths felt some trepidation at the idea of facing such a personage. If the highest princes were set down as rats, where in the whole range of the animal creation could a creature be found humble enough to furnish them with an appelation?

Thrilled and trembling, Chang and Eng were prepared for their meeting with the king of Siam.

While they were to be briefed on the formalities and protocol after they arrived in the palace, their mother did her best to get them ready for the royal audience. She shopped for new clothes for each of them, and modified the jackets so that they could accommodate the twins' ligament. She learned what she could of what they might expect, and lectured them on behavior and the sights that would meet their eyes. As the time for departure neared, she combed their long hair and braided it into Chinese queues.

At last, officials of the palace arrived in Meklong to escort Chang and Eng to Bangkok. It was agreed that their mother and sister could accompany them. But something else also accompanied them. The twins insisted upon taking along a cargo of duck eggs, preserved so that they could be eaten two to three years later. These they wanted their mother to sell or trade in Bangkok, and thereby acquire a large stock of new goods that they might sell at a profit upon their return to Meklong.

With the palace officials, Chang and Eng and their sister, mother, and cargo traveled in a large junk up the river sixty miles to the capital of Bangkok.

Approaching the city, after passing rice fields and herds of buffalo, they moved between crowded rows of houseboats and floating shops, largely owned by Chinese. Soon the small, nondescript boats gave way to fleets of huge Siamese vessels and enormous Chinese junks that had just arrived from China.

Then the twins had their first view of Bangkok. What they saw was what was seen and described by a visiting British ambassador:

Numerous temples of Buddha, with tall spires attached to them, frequently glittering with gilding, were conspicuous among the mean huts and hovels of the natives, throughout which were interspersed a profusion of palms, ordinary fruit-trees, and the sa-

cred fig. On each side of the river there was a row of
floating habitations, resting on rafts of bamboos,
moored to the shore. These appeared the neatest and
best description of dwellings; they were occupied by
good Chinese shops. Close to these aquatic habitations
were anchored the largest description of native vessels,
among which were many junks of great size, just arrived from China. The face of the river presented a
busy scene, from the number of boats and canoes of
every size and description which were passing to and
fro . . . we were not aware that there are few or no
roads at Bang-kok, and that the river and canals form
the common highways, not only for goods but for
passengers. . . . Many of the boats were shops containing earthernware, *blachang* (a foetrid condiment . . .
composed of bruised shrimps and other smaller fish),
dried fish, and fresh pork. Venders of these several
commodities were hawking and crying them. . . .
Among those who plied on the river, there was a large
proportion of women and of the priests of Buddha;
the latter readily distinguished by their shaved and
bare heads, and their yellow vestments.

At this point, the twins and palace officials were
met by a boat carrying two representatives of the
king. They were presented with a gift—consisting of
fruit and tea—and guided to a special landing a few
hundred yards away. Once on shore, the party was
received by an important officer of the court, who
hurried them toward an isolated residence outside the
palace wall, explaining that "no one was allowed to
see them until his majesty had satisfied his royal curiosity."

Chang and Eng were told that they would have
to spend the night in seclusion, that not until the
following morning would the king receive them.
Meanwhile, they were given thorough instructions in
court procedure—how many obeisances to make to
the throne, how deeply to bow, how to address the
monarch, and how to answer any questions he might
put to them. In a state of anxiety and exhaustion,
they sank to their knees and practiced bowing their

heads to the floor, stretching their ligament as far as possible in attempting to bow in unison.

They spent a fretful, partially sleepless night. At last it was day, and at eight thirty in the morning they were dressed and immaculate and ready.

The court officer appeared. He led them to a twelve-oared barge—the oarsmen attired in scarlet uniforms—and they were rowed along the foot of the surrounding wall to the outer gate of the palace. There, they got into a net hammock suspended from poles, which was lifted by two men. Going through the entrance, they were carried across a vast open courtyard until they reached an inner wall and second gate "guarded by soldiery in singularly fantastic costume." Beyond it, they traversed a long, handsome avenue, lined on either side with sheds housing powerful cannons. Then, to their right was the Hall of Justice, and to their left a broad expanse where a dozen mammoth elephants were being exercised by their keepers.

Now they had reached the third and last gate. As they descended from their litter, the twins were ordered to remove their shoes. They did so, and passed through the gate to find before them three buildings—the spired Royal Palace with its tin roof, a magnificent Buddhist temple, and the sprawling Audience Hall. They were informed that the king was in the Audience Hall, surrounded by numerous courtiers, sitting in judgment on various legal cases. The king was disposing of the final case, and almost ready to receive them.

They followed the court official inside, and were momentarily dazzled by what met their eyes. The Audience Hall was a vast and towering room, eighty by forty feet in size, each wall and the ceiling painted in bright vermilion, decorated with cornices of shining gold. Two rows of giant wooden columns led from the entry door across the long expanse of the room to the throne, elevated fifteen feet above the ground. The throne was covered with golden plates, and over the throne was a canopy formed by seventeen gold umbrellas. The throne area was surrounded on three sides by a sheer yellow curtain with gold decorations.

And seated on the throne, bareheaded, in his loose gown of gold, was pudgy King Rama III of Siam.

The court officer escorting the twins whispered to them. Dumbly they nodded and instantly dropped to the floor, kneeling close together. As instructed, they raised their hands to their foreheads, and in unison bent their heads down lower and lower until their foreheads touched the floor. Then they repeated the entire act again and again, nine times in all. Finally, they stood up, and at a signal from their escort, they went forward, advancing toward the throne until they reached the feet of the king. They dropped to their knees a second time, and nine times more they bowed their heads to the ground. The last time, in undertones, they formally addressed the king: "Exalted Lord, Sovereign of many Princes, let the Lord of Lives tread upon his slave's head, who lies here prostrate, receiving the dust of the golden feet upon the summit of his head . . ."

A contemporary account reported what followed: "His majesty seemed highly pleased with their appearance, and, through one of his courtiers, addressed to them a vast number of questions relating to themselves, their family, their occupations and their sensations, all of which were answered in a satisfactory manner."

The questions asked, the answers given, the king made an almost imperceptible nod to someone nearby.

Suddenly, there was a deafening clash of gongs. At once, the multitude of courtiers emitted in chorus a mighty shout and fell to their knees, heads bowed, prostrating themselves. As the sounds of the gongs reverberated throughout the room, the yellow curtain surrounding three sides of the throne was hastily closed, hiding the monarch from view.

The unexpected noise and activity frightened the

twins. They recoiled and hugged each other protectively. The room was still. The royal audience was over.

But their day in fairyland had just begun. The assembled courtiers, now scrambling to their feet, soon crowded in on Chang and Eng. Until their king had seen the prodigies from Meklong, the courtiers had had to hold their curiosity in check. But once the king was gone, every person in the hall wanted a closer look at these human marvels. They pressed in on the boys from every side, examining the connecting ligament, asking endless questions that the twins tried their best to answer.

At last, the twins were rescued by the court officer assigned to them. It was the king's wish, he told them, that they visit his wives in the Royal Palace, and then they were to be permitted to tour the Temple of the Emerald Buddha—or Temple of Gautama, as it was sometimes called.

First, there was the Royal Palace and His Majesty's harem of seven hundred wives—actually thirty-five wives (who gave him fifty-one children) and the rest concubines. Timidly, the twins entered the king's harem. According to a contemporary account:

"They were taken into a large hall of the principal palace, where every possible inquiry that female curiosity of 700 woman power could devise, was made of them, many of which were not remarkable for their delicacy. They received valuable presents from several of these ladies, and then were allowed to examine the curiosities of the place, until the king's pleasure concerning them should be made known."

Outdoors once more, they were eager to see the sacred white elephants, which were shielded from public view. They were refused permission to do this. However, they were shown through the king's stable of stud horses—actually ponies—and shown two or three horses from the Chinese province of Yunau, all of which they enjoyed.

Finally, they arrived at an enclosure. Upon entering it they saw the Temple of Gautama, as well as several smaller temples. They walked under a covered passageway, its walls hung with paintings depicting the adventures of Rama, until they reached the Temple of Gautama, a plastered brick building. Inside the temple, the woodwork was oddly and elaborately carved, and throughout there were statues of mythical creatures—strange birds and serpents and demons. The twins came upon the altar on which rested a number of gold Buddhas, as well as the translucent two-thousand-year-old Emerald Buddha, sparkling with gems from India.

It was breathtaking, dizzying in its splendor, and when the twins tottered outside they were speechless. The court officer was waiting for them, laden with colorfully wrapped parcels. He told them that the king had given them permission to leave for home, and they were to take with them some personal gifts presented by His Majesty in honor of their visit.

Reunited with their mother and sister, regaling them with the wonders they had seen, the twins returned immediately by boat to their village of Meklong.

The neighbors turned out in hordes to greet them as heroes. They had seen the king. From local curiosities they had been transformed into personages of note.

For the first time they had an opportunity to become financially secure.

Chang and Eng had longed to expand their business of raising and selling ducks and duck eggs. Both the ducks and their eggs were considered delicacies in the area, and selling them netted a considerable profit. But an investment in more ducks required a fair amount of capital. Now, at last, the twins could raise the necessary money. They had returned to Meklong with the expensive gifts given to them by the king of Siam and by several of his wives, as well as the money their mother had obtained by disposing of duck eggs in Bangkok. Without a second thought, the twins sold their royal presents to local merchants for cash. With this windfall, they enlarged their flock of ducks.

On the shore, near their houseboat, the twins had built a fenced enclosure, and inside it was a pond where they kept the ducks. Twice a week, in a small boat, they sailed or rowed down to the Gulf of Siam, and there they caught shellfish to feed and fatten their birds. The precious duck eggs came readily. Using an ancient formula to preserve the eggs, the twins converted them into a much desired product. To preserve the eggs, the twins made a soft mixture of clay and salt, and dipped the eggs into this mixture. Then the eggs were covered with dry ashes for a short period. After that they were cleaned, and in this embalmed state they remained fresh and delicious for two to three years. In a single year, the twins sold 12,000 eggs, as well as the older ducks, at a profit, and their family prospered.

Not all the aging ducks, however, went to the market. From their earliest childhood the twins had kept and trained pets. There had been a pet mouse, followed by a sparrowlike bird, and inevitably there would be a duck. This duck, more friendly and intelligent than the others, they named Chee-kou. They trained her to hop on one leg, lie down and quack for food, and walk a slack balancing wire. When word of this duck got about the province, a wealthy lady decided that she wanted Chee-kou, and she made the twins an offer they could not resist. But a week after the lady took the duck, the bird died, and for months thereafter the twins were filled with guilt.

The twins were busy and happy. The idea of leaving Siam had never tempted them. They had never thought it possible, let alone desirable. The possibility came about quite by accident.

Actually, the accident—a chance meeting with a foreigner, a Westerner—had taken place in 1824, when they were thirteen, a year before they were received by the king of Siam.

Foreigners were rare in the cities of Siam. There were the Chinese, of course. But from the West, there had arrived only a handful of Dutch and Portuguese traders, who came and went. In fact, the only Western nation to have a consulate in Siam was Portugal.

One day a British merchant disembarked in Bangkok. He was Robert Hunter, a Scot, the first British trader to enter and take up residence in Siam. Hunter came from a long line of merchants. His ancestors had become wealthy by exporting tobacco from the Virginia Colony in the New World to France, where Jean Nicot, a minister under King Francis II, had popularized "American powder" and whose name had inspired the word "nicotine." Forced to leave Virginia after the Revolutionary War, Hunter's ancestors had returned to Glasgow, where they manufactured glass and later linen. Hunter had inherited the family interest in trade. Eventually, he had made Singapore his base, where he was part-owner of four ships and represented Hunter-Watt and Company. He carried on trade with many foreign countries, made a small fortune, and finally expanded his activities to include Siam.

Robert Hunter was enchanted by Siam, and apparently the Siamese nobility were charmed by him. At first he lived in a houseboat. Later, when permitted to do so, he bought a house in Bangkok, resumed his export business, and rented a warehouse across from the capital city. A latter-day relative has characterized him as interested in money and power, a man of quick temper and some arrogance, both attributes hidden beneath his dour Scots reserve. He was also characterized as shrewd, hard-headed, and persuasive. He made contacts in the Royal Palace, and eventually was able to form a partnership with the government in trading.

Hunter was also a man of boundless curiosity and enjoyed roaming the country, not only to collect goods and artifacts but for the pleasure he got from seeing new sights.

It was one of these side trips that brought Robert Hunter to the village of Meklong in 1824. Late of an afternoon, while crossing the river by boat, his attention was caught by an astonishing sight in the distance. He saw what he first took to be "a strange animal," one with two heads, four arms, four legs, swimming in the river. As he watched, the creature suddenly emerged from the water and clambered into a waiting boat. Drawing closer, Hunter observed the "strange animal" begin to row the boat toward the shore, and then he realized what he was seeing was actually a pair of scrawny boys, naked from the hips up, each tied to the other by a band at their breast-bones.

Hunter followed the boys, and when they went ashore, he came after them. Thus did Robert Hunter meet Chang and Eng.

Standing there on the bank of the river, the Scottish trader asked the twins numerous questions. He learned that they lived with their mother, brother, and sister in a nearby houseboat. He learned that they, too, were merchants, engaged in selling duck eggs. He inquired whether he might see them again, and they agreed. Before leaving, he pressed a small sum of money into the hand of one twin as a token of friendship.

Shortly after, Robert Hunter came calling on Chang and Eng at their houseboat, met Nok, met their brother and sister, held conversations with the family, shared food with them. This first visit was followed by many others. By the time the twins were received by King Rama III, Hunter had become a fast family friend.

Clearly, Hunter was not seeing Chang and Eng, two simple country boys, because he was entranced by their repartee or their personalities. Plainly, he had a business enterprise in mind. He saw the Chinese Twins as a spectacular export.

From the moment the idea of taking Chang and Eng to the West and selling them to the public as curiosities had entered Hunter's head, he was aware that there were three obstacles to overcome.

The first obstacle was Chang and Eng themselves. They were provincial youths—the farthest they had ever been from their native village was sixty miles. They loved their homeland, thought it the center of the world, and believed that the world that lay beyond Siam was dull and inferior. According to a nineteenth-century pamphlet, Chang and Eng, like almost all Siamese, had "but a poor opinion of 'outside barbarians.' They have heard of the Africans, whom they term 'pepperheads'; of the 'Markan' or Americans, and of the 'Angrit' or English, all of whom they believe to be inhabitants of extremely small and insignificant islands, situated in some unknown seas, which nobody has ever considered it worthwhile to discover."

One can be sure that Robert Hunter set out to correct the impression Chang and Eng had of the West, and to reeducate them about the lands known as the United States and England. No doubt he wooed them with tales of kings and presidents who rivaled their own monarch, of cities of stone buildings and brick pavements and gaslights and horse carriages and coaches that made Bangkok seem backward, of steamships that could easily outdistance their best sailing vessels and junks. No doubt Hunter dazzled them with tales of a race of remarkable beings who populated the vast lands of the West. No doubt he enthralled them with tales of riches and luxuries and lovely women.

And no doubt Chang and Eng reacted first with excitement—and then disbelief that such countries, people, inventions, pleasures could truly exist outside their Siam.

Yet the twins must have given Hunter sufficient promise of their cooperation to encourage him to proceed further. Hunter's next step was to attempt to convince Nok of the desirability of allowing her two fourteen-year-olds to travel abroad. No record exists of her initial response. It may not have been entirely favorable, but it could not have been totally negative, for in 1825, shortly after the twins' audience with Rama III, Hunter approached the king. All of the monarch's subjects were his personal possessions, and none could leave Siam without his specific permission. Hunter sought this permission through his business connections in the palace, intermediaries who spoke to the king on his behalf. In short order, Hunter had the king's reply. Permission for the twins to leave the country for the West was refused.

As a matter of fact, the king already had a trip in mind for Chang and Eng. But it was a journey to another place, and for another purpose.

King Rama III had been making plans to send a diplomatic mission, or embassy, as it was then called, to neighboring Cochin China. The purpose of the mission was to have the Siamese ambassador negotiate with the king of Cochin China on a revision of the laws regulating commerce between the two nations.

When King Rama III undertook the selection of the members of his diplomatic mission, he decided that the Chinese Twins must accompany the party. He felt the joined twins would demonstrate a remarkable Siamese product, as well as provide an amusement for a royal neighbor. Whether the king got the idea of sending the twins along with his mission because of their recent visit to his court, or whether he was suddenly reminded of them by Robert Hunter's request to take them to the West, is not known. What is known is that the king notified Chang and Eng that he wanted them to accompany his mission to Cochin China in the near future, and when the time came he would send for them and bring them to Bangkok, the departure point for the journey.

In 1827, when they were sixteen, Chang and Eng received the royal summons from Bangkok. They left for the capital almost immediately, and arrived just before the Siamese mission was to sail. They were taken aboard a huge five-hundred-ton, Siamese-built junk, its frame constructed of marbao wood, its decks made of teakwood. They watched the wooden anchor being lifted, saw the great square sails billowing, observed the ninety-man crew take their places, and before being led to their cramped quarters below deck they felt the junk moving and could see Bangkok receding from view.

They would always remember the voyage as uncomfortable but thrilling. They sailed down into the Gulf of Siam, made several lengthy stops at ports along the Cambodian coast, and after six weeks at sea they reached the Cochin China promontory called Vung Tau (later Cap St. Jacques under the French occupation). From there, the junk headed up the deep Saigon River, until it dropped anchor at a landing just below the city of Saigon.

Waiting to transport them to their residence were fourteen elephants sent by the governor of the district of Kamboja. Chang and Eng were hoisted onto the back of one elephant—a sight difficult to imagine —and then they were on their way to the public building, resembling a town hall, where they would temporarily stay.

Outside their residence an unruly crowd had gathered to view the Siamese strangers. According to a contemporary source: "When Chang and Eng descended from the back of their elephant, a simultaneous shout arose from all present, and a desperate rush was made in order to get a closer view, but a liberal application of the rattan over the head, face, and shoulders of the mob by the officials in attendance, had the effect of rendering them more moderate in their demonstrations. The news of the arrival of the twins soon circulated through the city, and to prevent further annoyance, a guard of a hundred soldiers was sent, who, during the rest of their stay, were enabled to keep the crowd at a respectful distance."

Meanwhile, King Rama III's appointed ambassador and head of the mission—described as "a nobleman of excellent judgment, well acquainted with trade and commerce, and a first rate drinker"—sent his letter from the king of Siam to the governor so that it could be forwarded to the king of Cochin China, who had his court in the ancient capital city of Hué. It was understood by the Siamese ambassador that the mission could not proceed further without the express invitation of the Chinese king.

While awaiting the royal permission from Hué, the

members of the Siamese mission were hospitably received and constantly entertained, and Chang and Eng
accompanied the ambassador to every event. The very
first evening in Saigon, some of the city's leading
mandarins, among them several judges on the highest
courts, came calling, and they sat down to indulge in
a lengthy drinking bout with their Siamese visitors.
The mandarins drank themselves into a stupor, and at
evening's end were carried away by their servants.
The Siamese ambassador indicated to the twins that
he was pleased, "as getting intoxicated on a first visit
was considered a flattering mark of confidence and
esteem."

In the days that followed, the twins, surrounded
by their military bodyguard, were taken on numerous tours of Saigon. Although they were particularly
fascinated by Saigon's main bazaar, a wide and handsome street lined with shops selling the best Chinese
silks and porcelain, one of the high spots of their enforced wait was an invitation to meet with the district
governor at his official residence. Along with the
other members of the Siamese mission, the twins
boarded elephants and, attended by a guard of honor,
went to call on the governor.

A half hour was taken up with protocol, each member of the Siamese party, Chang and Eng included,
prostrating himself and touching the floor with his
brow four times.

Two days later, the mission members were invited
to be spectators at an elephant and tiger fight. They
were escorted into the Saigon fort and seated just as
the governor arrived with a retinue of a thousand
soldiers in gold uniforms and eighty elephants. Upon
their entry into the fort, one of the elephants broke
rank and had to be chased and caught. Immediately,
the keeper of the rebellious animal was forced to his
knees and beheaded for failing to control the animal.

Chang and Eng, as animal lovers, could not have
enjoyed the elephant and tiger fight. It was a mis-
match, a one-sided cruelty. The tiger, much feared
and hated in Cochin China, had been reduced to the

role of a helpless victim since its claws had been extracted and its mouth sewn shut. It was also tied to a stake by a forty-foot rope. Fifty elephants, behemoths all, were lined up facing the tiger. One by one the elephants were urged to attack the tiger. The first half dozen bucked and reared, and then backed off in fright. Their keepers were quickly brought before the governor and were flogged with bamboo at least a hundred times or until they fell unconscious. Meanwhile, a bolder elephant had advanced on the tiger, impaled the cat on his tusks, and thrown him as far as the rope would allow. The elephant repeated this a number of times until finally the tiger lay dead.

If the twins wanted to escape witnessing the violent spectacle, they were unable to do so. The climax of the entertainment was a mock battle—a line of elephants ranged against a barricade of tree branches behind which a company of soldiers waited with rockets and muskets. At a signal, the elephants charged and, as they did, the soldiers set the barricade ablaze and began to launch their rockets and discharge their muskets. A few elephants halted, but the rest trampled across the flaming barricade, forcing the soldiers into a swift retreat, until the keepers brought the rampant elephants under control.

At the end of three weeks, a message came to Saigon from the Royal Palace in Hué that the visitors could embark for Touran, a port on the seacoast, to await further instructions. With relief, Chang and Eng boarded the junk, and soon were on their way. The junk dropped anchor in the harbor three miles from the village of Touran. The ambassador and his aides went ashore a number of times, but Chang and Eng went only once, attracting too many people to attempt it again.

According to a contemporary pamphlet:

In a few days a mandarin arrived from Hué, with four galleys of forty oars each, for the purpose of taking the party to the capital. . . . These galleys were warboats belonging to the king, and were magnificent affairs. Each one was nearly one hundred feet in length, narrow and sharp, but very strongly built, and rigged with two lug sails. . . . Their crew consisted of forty rowers, besides the commander and officers, all attired in rich and showy uniforms. The rowers were admirably drilled, plying incessantly, and in perfect unison, to the music of a monotonous song from one of the officers, accompanied by the beating of two pieces of bamboo. . . .

In less than twenty-four hours, they arrived at the mouth of the river Hué, and were received with a salute from the fort, which appeared to be garrisoned by a strong force; a few hours afterwards, they were opposite the city. Here they were received by a mandarin of high rank, and conducted to a house prepared for their reception. No sooner were they fairly inside of this, however, than all the entrances were barricaded, the building surrounded by soldiers, and the Siamese told to consider themselves prisoners. This was the usual custom of the country, in relation to ambassadors, and was intended to prevent the chance of any misunderstanding with the populace, who are very jealous of foreigners. . . .

While awaiting an audience from the king, they paid a visit to the mandarin of elephants, whom they found in great affliction, having recently lost seventeen of his children from the measles. This bereaved parent had previously buried thirteen, and only forty-two were now left him. As the party had been expected, great preparations had been made for their reception, and a table was spread for them containing seventy-six different dishes, among which, rats served up in five different ways, alligator steaks, and stewed cat, formed prominent features.

The climax of the mission was fast approaching. According to the same contemporary pamphlet:

The innumerable preliminaries to an audience being finally concluded, the embassy waited upon His Majesty, who after taking a good look at the twins, gravely remarked that he had several people similarly united in his dominions—an unqualified falsehood, of course, and quite characteristic of the vanity and utter disregard of truth, prevalent among the Cochin Chinese of all ranks. . . . A great variety of presents were exchanged among the parties concerned in the negotiations, and a letter, accompanied with numerous costly gifts, was intrusted to the embassy for the king of Siam. The day following the audience, a grand entertainment was given the members of the mission, by a high mandarin of the military order, and on the third day the party started upon their return home, traveling by nearly the same route as that by which they came. Great honors were shown them wherever they stopped, from the fact of their having been admitted into the presence of the king, an act of condescension very rarely bestowed on foreigners.

Upon their arrival at Bangkok, the twins were again brought before their own king, and on their dismission were liberally compensated for their time and trouble, although the journey had been nothing but a pleasure excursion to them. They immediately returned to Meklong, where they found their duck business constantly improving.

One consequence of their first excursion to a foreign land, as would soon become apparent, was that their native village of Meklong had suddenly become too provincial and confining for them. Their one desire was to travel again, to travel more and more extensively. They remembered their friend, the Scottish merchant Robert Hunter, and his glowing tales of faraway Great Britain and America, and now the twins tended to believe those of Hunter's accounts they had formerly held in disbelief.

They wanted to see Robert Hunter again, but Hunter was in Bangkok, attending to his multiple business enterprises. They could not know that one of Hunter's business enterprises would involve their own futures deeply.

For in Bangkok, Robert Hunter, through a chance reunion with a onetime business associate and old friend, had revived his interest in Chang and Eng as a potentially successful commercial export. The friend who had awakened these speculations in Hunter was a thirty-seven-year-old American trader named Abel Coffin, the master of the sturdy Nantucket sailing ship *Sachem*, which he had more and more frequently been bringing to Bangkok on business.

Of Captain Coffin, there was much to be said in his favor. He was a loving husband and father who communicated regularly with his wife, Susan, and his two children, Susan, six, and Abel, eight, all of whom had remained at home in East Boston, Massachusetts. But despite this virtue, and the fact that he was a God-fearing man—sincerely reminding his children, "I wish you both to remember in everything you are accountable beings, that God can always see you"—Captain Coffin saw himself as beyond accountability in his own business transactions. He was a shrewd Yankee trader, and not above shamelessly exploiting a product or person to turn a fast dollar.

In fact, at the time of his reunion with Hunter in Bangkok in late 1828 or early 1829, Coffin had just acquired a number of crates of firearms at an auction in Calcutta, and had come around from India to Siam to sell them at a substantial profit. By selling these arms, Captain Coffin was indeed catering to the war-like propensities of King Rama III. The king needed arms to implement his expansionist dreams and to subjugate restless vassal states. At the time of Captain Coffin's arrival in Siam, the king required guns to put down a revolt being led by the ruler of the vassal state of Wiang-chan in Laos. The rebel was Chao Anu, prince of Laos, who was attempting not only to free his country but to invade Siam itself. After annihilating a small Siamese garrison, Anu met the king of Siam's main forces in pitched battle. King Rama III's forces won the day. Prince Anu was driven to flight, but while in hiding he was betrayed by a son-in-law and turned over as a prisoner to the Siamese. Anu was brought to Bangkok on January 15, 1829, and installed in an iron cage by King Rama III.

Apparently, Captain Coffin enjoyed good relations with King Rama III. A short time after Prince Anu had been caged, the king invited Coffin to have a look at how traitors were treated in Siam.

A year later, Captain Coffin was to recall the experience in detail for a pamphleteer who printed the story:

". . . during the residence of Capt. Coffin in Bangkok, in 1829, he was ordered by His Majesty to witness the punishment preparing for the prince of Laos, who had revolted from his allegiance and was subsequently taken prisoner. When Capt. Coffin saw him, he and thirteen of his family were confined in an iron cage, loaded with heavy chains. From thence he was to be taken to the place of execution, and there hung by a hook to be inserted under his chin; he was afterwards to be seated on sharp pikes five inches long; then to be placed in boiling oil, and finally pounded to pumice in an immense mortar. All these cruelties would doubtless have been consummated, had not the prince escaped their horrible infliction, by poisoning himself the day before the sentence was to have been carried into execution."

When Hunter and Captain Coffin were reunited in Bangkok, the Scottish merchant could not have been unaware of Coffin's close connection with the king. Although Hunter himself had tried but failed to obtain permission for Chang and Eng to leave the country, he must have realized that with Coffin's assistance he might have a second and better chance.

Hunter told Captain Coffin of his discovery of the incredible Chinese Twins in the village of Meklong. Instantly, Coffin's business sense was piqued. Hunter suggested a partnership in the venture. If Coffin could get permission from the king to show the twins in America and Great Britain, he would share the profits with Coffin on a fifty-fifty basis. Captain Coffin said that he wanted to see the twins. If they lived up to expectations, he would seek a travel permit for them from the king.

Together, Hunter and Coffin went down to Meklong, and Captain Coffin was introduced to the twins. He studied their binding ligament, watched them

walk, row a boat, swim in tandem. He was entranced.
He felt that the twins could secure the partners a fortune if they were exhibited in Boston, in New York,
in London. The captain was ready to proceed. Again,
the three steps had to be taken.

First, Hunter and Coffin consulted with the twins.
This time the boys were enthusiastic, ready to leave
at once on a journey to the fabulous Western
world. Next, their mother had to be convinced. Hunter introduced Captain Coffin to Nok, and presented
their proposition to her. They would like to take the
twins to America and Great Britain, to display them
to the world with great dignity. The twins would be
absent no more than two and a half years, at which
time they would attain their majority of twenty-one
years and be returned to their family in Siam.

The proposition frightened Nok, and she had many
objections. Despite their close acquaintance with the
river, the Siamese villagers were not used to the open
sea and to long sea voyages. Further, Nok feared that
as exhibits her twin sons would be treated unfeelingly,
inhumanely, and would suffer. Finally, at seventeen,
Chang and Eng were the family breadwinners, and
she could not survive without their help.

Smoothly, Hunter and Captain Coffin met Nok's
objections one by one. The sea voyage was not to be
feared. Captain Coffin had spent years traveling between America and Southeast Asia in complete safety.
The security and welfare of the twins, the manner
in which they would be presented and handled—surely Coffin here invoked his relationship with his own
children—could be guaranteed. As to losing her
breadwinners, Nok would receive more than adequate
compensation. She would be left a large sum of money. Hunter and Coffin would later tell the press that
they gave the twins' mother what was a princely
sum for that day, $3,000 cash, for her approval. Three
years later, Chang and Eng—who often wrote as one,
in the first person singular—protested in a letter meant
for Mrs. Coffin, "Are you more over aware that $500
—(Five Hundred Dollars) is the amount paid to our

Mother (from first to last?)" In the same letter the twins remarked that together they were paid a total of $10 a month salary and expenses, and only after two years of exhibits were they raised to $50 a month.

Whether the sum Nok received from Hunter and Captain Coffin was $3,000 or $500 to release her two sons, it was still to her a magnificent sum that would support the remaining members of the family for some time. Reassured by this offer, and the sincere promise of the Scot and the Yankee to care for Chang and Eng, Nok gave her approval of the trip.

For the partners, that left one final obstacle—King Rama III. Hunter and Captain Coffin returned to Bangkok elated, and it was Coffin who contacted the king. According to an account of the negotiations written a year later, Coffin's arguments to His Majesty were psychologically persuasive:

"An appeal to national vanity, finally proved successful, and Chang and Eng were allowed to depart, in order that the world might behold that the favored empire of Siam could alone produce, of all the nations of the earth, such a living wonder as the famous united brothers. The king always retained an interest in their welfare, and frequently enquired of Americans who visited Bangkok, subsequent to their departure, respecting their health, and the manner in which they were treated."

There were other versions to explain the Yankee seafarer's successful negotiations with the king. But most likely it was the king's appreciation of Coffin's firearms and Coffin's appreciation of the king's ego that made the negotiation a favorable one for the two Western partners.

King Rama III forthwith gave his permission in writing for Chang and Eng to leave Siam.

On March 31, 1829, Chang and Eng, accompanied by the most portable of their worldly belongings, by a caged pet python, by a neighbor and friend—a boy named Teiu who would travel with them as a companion—and by their mother Nok, arrived in Bangkok and immediately boarded Captain Coffin's sailing ship, the *Sachem*. The partners, Hunter and Coffin—"the concern," as the twins would call them later—were waiting on deck to welcome them. After their mother saw that they would be comfortable, she bade each of her joined twins a tearful farewell. With that she left the ship.

Chang and Eng were now alone, yet together, about to sail in the morning for a distant port known as Boston in a land known as the United States of America.

They were sailing for Boston, but they could not know that they were also sailing into legend.

2
CHAPTER
2

Go West, Young Men

On Wednesday, April 1, 1829, the 387-ton American sailing ship *Sachem*, with Captain Abel Coffin in command, left Bangkok, moved slowly down the river, entered the Gulf of Siam, and started on its voyage halfway around the world to Boston.

In all, the trip would take 138 days—more than four and a half months.

The *Sachem* was a vessel equal to the voyage. It had been built nineteen years earlier by Thatcher Magoun, who had had his own shipyard in Medford, Massachusetts, from the time he was twenty-seven and who had the reputation of producing some of the most durable and best-equipped ships in America. The *Sachem*, 109 feet long, almost 29 feet wide, with two decks and three masts, was no exception. Its previous owners had sent it to Russia before it was taken over by John Bryant, a Bostonian, and William Sturgis, the tough, austere-living son of a Cape Cod shipmaster and a shipmaster himself (he had once fought off sixteen pirate junks in Macao Road outside Hong Kong). Bryant and Sturgis had purchased the *Sach-*

em for their merchant fleet, and had several times sent it around Cape Horn to California to deal in the hides trade. Recently, the owners had taken on Abel Coffin as the ship's master and sent him to the East Indies. Now Coffin was bringing the *Sachem* home.

No ship's log exists detailing the *Sachem*'s difficult and tedious journey from Bangkok to Boston. But based on a number of ports where Captain Coffin laid over for provisioning or trade and the letters he sent from those ports to his family in East Boston (the letters went on swifter ships having fewer stopovers), on knowledge of Coffin's earlier trips to the East Indies and Southeast Asia, and on the general trade routes used by Yankee vessels in those years, a fair guess may be made at the route that the *Sachem* followed.

It seems likely that the voyage took the ship from Siam to Singapore, then south to Batavia, then north to Anjier, then on a southwesterly course across the Indian Ocean to the island of Mauritius. From there, on to Table Bay or Captetown, South Africa; then along the African coast to the island of St. Helena, well out in the Atlantic Ocean; onward to thirty-four-square-mile, volcanic Ascension Island; and across the Atlantic to Boston, after a stopover in the Bermudas.

Likely the *Sachem* dropped anchor the first time off Singapore, because Robert Hunter had business interests in that port, then continued down to Batavia with a stop in Java, since Coffin would have found it advantageous to acquire a cargo of exotic East Indian goods to sell at a profit in Boston.

After that, Coffin would not have tarried, but would have tried to escape the wet season—the summer monsoon which, toward the end of April, blew southwest across the Indian Ocean to India. Following a brief stop at the island of Mauritius, the *Sachem* would have sailed to Capetown to take on provisions—fresh meat, vegetables, fruit, plus a supply of water. Next, the *Sachem* no doubt swung out 1,200 miles west into the South Atlantic toward the island of St. Helena, already renowned as the place of Napoleon

Bonaparte's six-year exile and the site of his death eight years before Coffin's arrival. Coffin would have stopped here to purchase meat, vegetables, sweet potatoes.

News of the strangest cargo Captain Coffin had ever carried reached the outside world as the result of a letter Coffin wrote to his wife and children while on board the "*Ship Sachem at Sea*." This he no doubt dispatched from St. Helena. In it Captain Coffin told his wife: "Susan I have two Chinese Boys 17 years old grown together they enjoy extraordinary health I hope these will prove profitable as a curiousity."

In the same letter Captain Coffin touched on a business aspect of his "curiousity": "Mr. Hunter is passenger with me & is an excellent companion he owns half the Chinese Boys."

Robert Hunter did not complete the trip to Boston. At some point, probably in the Bermudas, he left the *Sachem* to board another ship heading for England.

While Captain Coffin mentioned the twins—and invoked the Lord to protect his children—in his correspondence, he made no references to the voyage itself. However, many similar voyages by similar ships in that period have been recorded, and the sights the twins saw must have been the same.

The twins must have had their first exposure to Western ways in Capetown. To Bruno Tavernier, a sea historian, ". . . the old Dutch town, where water ran in the streets, seemed a paradise of coolness after so many days of heat and danger." And in its markets, he had found "all the fruits of Europe and the tropics, as well as an excellent local wine."

Soon, there would have been another surprise for the twins. As Tavernier reported it: "One morning, a silhouette appeared on the horizon—Ascension Island. A boat full of soldiers came out. . . . They deposited on board several enormous turtles, which served to make excellent soup, and took a few casks of spirits in exchange."

In the Atlantic, the twins may have experienced at

least one storm. But mostly the water was calm, and Chang and Eng, who adjusted readily to life at sea, were fired with the natural exuberance of seventeen-year-olds and the promise of a new life. They roamed freely, exploring the decks of the *Sachem* as energetically as any normal teen-agers. They were fascinated by everything they saw on the ship, and quickly made friends with the crew. In fact, the Yankee sailors adopted the twins and did everything possible to amuse and entertain them.

As the voyage progressed, the twins fell in love with the *Sachem*. According to a pamphlet, *The Siamese Twin Brothers*, published in 1830: "When on board the ship, they would often observe that they hoped at some future time to command a vessel of their own, and when any necessary orders were given, would frequently repeat them over in the order, and in the tone of voice in which they had heard them delivered."

According to this same pamphlet: "It is remarkable that, during [their] months on shipboard, on their voyage to America . . . they never for a moment experienced sea sickness, on the contrary, when others who had often been at sea, were obliged to remain below in their cabins, these boys were constantly upon deck, from morning till night, and would frequently go aloft for their own amusement, even in rough weather, without experiencing the least inconvenience."

The twins were ill only twice during the entire trip. On one occasion, they ate too much rich food (they were not yet accustomed to Western diet) and got stomachaches, but they had recovered by the next day. Another time, one twin had a toothache for three days. This annoyed the other, who complained that "he had not slept all night so much as that," marking off half of the nail of his forefinger. While the toothache lasted, they were both given a little brandy and water to help them sleep, and the difficulty soon passed.

Captain Coffin was interested in learning how closely their systems were related because of the joining ligament, so he tried a simple experiment. Sneaking into their bedroom at night, he would touch one twin, and every time he did this, both awakened simultaneously.

Once, Captain Coffin let a sailor tie a rope around the twins' connecting band and then give the rope a sharp tug. Neither twin reported feeling any discomfort, let alone pain.

Throughout the voyage, whenever he was free, Captain Coffin kept the twins under observation. He was the first to note, as he would later tell the press, that although they were twins and joined together, they were different personalities. Chang was mentally quicker, brighter, but more often irritable. Eng was reposeful, quieter, and more retiring, but had wider intellectual interests.

For most of their 138-day voyage, the boys were lively and even-tempered. From the crew members, they began to take lessons in English. By the time the voyage was over, they were able to understand the language fairly well and to carry on simple conversations in broken English, as well as to do a limited amount of reading. They also learned to play checkers with the crew, and became so proficient at it that they were soon able to beat the men who had taught them. In a short time, they were challenging anyone who was willing to oppose them, each in turn playing an entire game. When they matched themselves against each other, which they did infrequently, one would correct the other if he made a bad move.

The synchronicity of their physical movements amazed everyone on board. If Chang on impulse turned or walked to the left, Eng also went left. It was not as if Eng was pulled along, but as if his mind had anticipated Chang's motion. They instinctively moved together in the same direction, and were never seen walking out of step.

One shipboard incident in particular displayed their remarkable coordination. They were cavorting on deck, running at full speed while being chased by a crew member, when suddenly they came to an open hatchway. Had they hesitated for an instant, had one plunged ahead and the other halted, they would have fallen into the hole and been killed—but instead, automatically and with perfect grace, they both took to the air, leaped over the open hatch in unison, and landed safely on the other side.

They were often seen climbing the ship's masts, ascending higher and higher in tandem, a dangerous and scary feat for one boy, let alone two who were bound together.

They agreed on almost everything—where to go, what to do, what to eat, when to sleep—although they did not speak to each other very often. The only serious argument they had while on the ship was when one wanted to take a cold bath, and the other demurred, saying that the night was too chilly. Their disagreement became so intense that Captain Coffin intervened, discussed it with them at length, and finally the proposed bath was abandoned. When one imagines a life in which no daily function, no matter how small, can be fulfilled unless it is agreed to by another human being, one can appreciate how extraordinary it was that the twins performed as well as they did and with so little overt conflict.

For the twins, one distressing incident did occur on the trip, about the time they neared Boston. They had brought along their crated python, not only as a pet but because they felt that the reptile might make an exotic exhibit in the West. The python had taken the sea voyage well. But two hundred miles outside Boston, apparently due to rough weather, the box that confined the reptile broke open and the python escaped. When a thorough search of the ship did not produce the python, it was assumed that it had slithered overboard and been drowned.

The crossing of the Atlantic Ocean was almost completed, the New World before them, yet the twins showed not a moment's apprehension. Far behind them were the bobbing houseboats of Meklong, the familiar temples of the Golden Supreme, the awesome world of King Rama III, as well as the warm safety of their mother and kin and friends. But their unique human condition had prepared them for anything drastically new or different.

Apparently once, if not many times, they reflected on the change that was confronting them, and years later they discussed it with their Boswell, Judge Graves, who put to paper some of their youthful feelings and emotions. They had left their homes, as Judge Graves would write,

> ... to go upon an untried venture among strange people, wearing strange faces and speaking a strange language. To them all was strange indeed. The staunch ship, powerfully framed yet so skillfully proportioned to cut swiftly through the water, yielding to the slightest touch of the helm or change of sail was so different from the unwieldy, gaudily painted Chinese junks which they had been accustomed to see, the stalwart sailors with ruddy cheeks and heavy beard so unlike the low swarthy beardless men that they had hitherto associated with all impressed them with new and peculiar emotions. They began to think that perhaps after all the people of their nation was not so vastly superior to all others as they imagined. They did not dispond however, and young as they were their varied experience in real life had taught them to adapt themselves to circumstances and to endeavor in some way or other to improve every opportunity.

On Sunday, August 16, 1829, the *Sachem*, with Chang and Eng at the rail, entered Boston harbor and docked among the square-riggers at the Long Wharf, opposite the India Wharf. Its cargo, according to an announcement in the Boston *Daily Advertiser*, contained "sugar, sapan wood, gamboge [a gum resin from trees that could be used medicinally as a cathartic or by painters as a yellow pigment], buffalo horns, leopard skins, and tin."

Shortly after the *Sachem* docked, Chang and Eng each set foot in Boston, still a year away from the 200th anniversary of its founding, and on the soil of the United States of America, still a young nation only fifty-three years in existence. The twins had arrived at an exciting time in the new nation's history. The Democratic party had been established the year before, the first Democratic candidate for President, Andrew Jackson, had been elected, and five months earlier he had been sworn in and had celebrated with the most unruly, raucous inauguration party the nation had yet known.

There were twelve million people in the United States, and most of them hungered for diversion. Many were attracted to a theater in New York's Bowery where an upside-down acrobat, Peters the Antipodean, walked on the ceiling, and lifted ten coach wheels and sixteen men from the stage below. Everyone, it seemed, was trying to see Johann Nepomuk Maelzel, an Austrian, with his panharmonicon (a one-man orchestra), his talking dolls, his robot chess player called the Turk (a machine that had defeated Napoleon in a match, and was not a machine at all but a chess expert hidden in a wooden chest).

America's twelve million could not know that the team that would become the most popular and best-known entertainment of the era had just descended a gangplank and entered Boston.

The following day there appeared in the Boston *Patriot* the first newspaper article ever to be printed in the United States about the new phenomenon from Siam. Coffin and Hunter could have little imagined at the time the countless columns of newsprint their discovery would spawn in the days and weeks and decades to come. Coffin had arranged for the reporter from the *Patriot* to have a brief glimpse of the twins on the *Sachem* the day of their arrival. The reporter wrote:

Lusus Naturae [sport of nature]—The Sachem, arrived at this port yesterday, has on board two Siamese youths, males, eighteen years of age, their bodies connected from their birth. They appear to be in good health, and apparently contented with their confined situation. We have seen and examined this strange freak of nature. It is one of the greatest living curiosities we ever saw. The two boys are about five feet in height, of well-proportioned frames, strong and active, good-natured, and of pleasant countenances, and with-al intelligent and sensible—exhibiting the appearance of two well-made Siamese youths, with the exception that by a substance apparently bony or cartilaginous, about seven inches in circumference and four in length, pro-ceeding from the umbilical region of each, they are firmly united together. They have a good appetite, ap-pear lively, and run about the deck and cabin of the ship with the facility that any two healthy lads would do, with their arms over each other's shoulders, this being the position in which they move about. They will probably be exhibited to the public when proper arrangements have been made. They will be objects of great curiosity, particularly to the medical faculty. Their unnatural union is not more of a curiosity than the vigorous health they enjoy, and their apparent en-tire contentedness with their condition. One of the boys is named Chang, the other named Eng; together they are called Chang-Eng.

Before these "objects of great curiosity" could be shown "to the medical faculty" and before "proper arrangements" could be made to show them to a titil-lated public, Chang and Eng were given a chance to acclimatize themselves to their new surroundings and to have a brief look at their first American city. Their excursions about Boston were made in an enclosed horse-drawn carriage and were of short duration, since Coffin did not want the public to view for nothing what it would soon be asked to pay to see.

At a later date, they confided their earliest impres-sion of Boston to Judge Graves, who noted:

"They were . . . muchly surprised to see such great houses built of so heavy and solid materials as brick and stone, and lighted through such spacious win-dows closed with glass, a substance unknown to them in their native country. Nor were they less astonished at the handsome carriages, fine horses and great omni-buses in which people traveled instead of in boats as they had been accustomed to do. They also admired the neatly draped ladies whose complexions were so fair, and wondered at the customs of the men who were actually walking around in public without their cues."

At the time that Chang and Eng arrived there, Boston was at once a stately and a rowdy city with a population of 61,000, a growing number of these being Irish pauper immigrants, whom the native Yankee Puritans resented and often physically attacked. The city mayor elected in that year was the redoubtable Harrison Gray Otis, a former lawyer and U.S. Senator, with a grand house at 45 Beacon Street, overlooking the Boston Common. In his entry, at the foot of a staircase, Otis kept a ten-gallon bowl filled with punch as an oasis for parched visitors en route to his drawing room.

As Chang and Eng were driven over the cobblestone streets of the city, they were dazzled by the sights. There was the vast rolling pasture—a onetime parade ground, now a park known as the Boston Common—where a few cows still roamed and grazed. There was the magnificent three-story Faneuil Hall, given to the city by a French Huguenot merchant. Known as "the cradle of liberty," it was an assembly hall devoted to free speech where Daniel Webster often orated. There was the partially built Tremont Hotel, which in two months would open its 170 bedrooms and eight toilets (the first ever known in America in a public building) to become America's largest hotel. Charles Dickens would stay here on his first visit to the United States. There was the Old North Church (Second Unitarian Church), in Hanover Street, where Ralph Waldo Emerson held the pulpit. There was the Old Drury Theatre, where a few years earlier the great English actor Edmund Kean had offended a portion of the audience and had been bombarded from the stage under a shower of vegetables and stones. There was Massachusetts General Hospital, a granite edifice whose star surgeon was Dr. John Collins Warren, who was lobbying the state legislature to permit unclaimed bodies of paupers to be used for dissection. This act he believed would discourage body-snatching. There were newspaper print shops, and newspapers carrying front-page advertisements for wines, flour, rum, sugar, molasses, tobacco, wool, cotton, leather, tinware, whale oil, Calcutta silks. There were the public coaches, leaving on the hour from Washington Street and fanning out across the other Eastern states with their passengers. There were taverns and inns—at least a half dozen well-known ones—alive with gaiety, especially at night when the twins made their way past the dim oil lamps to their hostelry.

It was bewildering, it was exciting, and it was very far from Meklong.

In less than a week Chang and Eng ceased visiting the sights of Boston and prepared to become a local sight themselves. The first to view them were two eminent physicians. One was Dr. Joseph Skey, a graduate of Edinburgh University and Deputy Inspector General of Hospitals for the British Army. In 1823, Dr. Skey had been serving with the British forces in Barbados, British West Indies, where he devoted much of his spare time to geology. When he had a leave, he liked to spend it in Boston, which he found more convenient than returning to London, and presumably just as pleasant.

Dr. Skey, apparently on leave in Boston, learned of the arrival of Chang and Eng. Fascinated, he applied to Captain Coffin for permission to conduct a few simple experiments on the twins, to learn something about their physiology and motor responses. What he did was repeat the experiment that Coffin had performed on shipboard, that of waking one boy and observing what effect this had on the other. Dr. Skey undertook this test several times. Entering the twins' room at midnight, three nights in a row, Dr. Skey touched one twin and discovered he had roused them both. Sitting up sleepily, they wanted to know why they had been disturbed.

After these precursory experiments, Chang and Eng received their first real medical examination. This was at the skilled hands of Dr. John Collins Warren, professor of anatomy and surgery at Harvard Medical School, the man that the twins had heard about when they saw Massachusetts General Hospital. Dr. Warren was to be remembered for his removal of a neck tumor in 1846, since it was the first time a reputable doctor had used ether on a patient during surgery. This was a major breakthrough for anesthesia at a time when the word "surgery" was synonymous with both agonizing pain and possible death from septicemia.

Dr. Warren's appearance must certainly have been as striking as his reputation, for he was described as "tall, and painfully thin," with "bright piercing eyes under shaggy brows." He no doubt fascinated Chang and Eng as much as they fascinated him.

Dr. Warren found them cheerful and intelligent, and characterized them as "readily acknowledging any civility." He observed that their pulses, heart beats, and respiration were exactly alike, and that they shared the same "habits and tastes." In his paper, "An Account of the Siamese Twin Brothers, United Together from Their Birth," he wrote:

> My attention was called to the Siamese boys by a highly respectable gentleman [William Sturgis, one of the owners of the *Sachem*], who wished me to examine them, in order to ascertain if there was any thing indecorous or fallacious in their appearance. On examination, I found that the medium of their connexion was more complicated than I had expected, and that they exhibited other phenomena worthy to justify a statement of their condition. . . .
>
> The substance by which they are connected is a mass two inches long at its upper edge, and about five at the lower. Its breadth from above downwards may be four inches; and its thickness in a horizontal direction two inches. Of course, it is not a rounded cord, but thicker in the perpendicular, than in the horizontal direction. At its lower edge is perceived a single umbilicus, through which passed a single umbilical cord, to nourish both children in the fetal state. Placing my hand on this substance, which I will denominate the

cord, I was surprised to find it extremely hard. . . .

When I first visited the boys, I expected to see them pull on this cord in different directions, as their attention was attracted by different objects. I soon perceived that this did not happen. The slightest impulse of one to move in any direction is immediately followed by the other, so that they would appear to be influenced by the same wish. This harmony in their movements is not the result of a volition excited at the same moment; it is a habit, formed by necessity.

Dr. Warren noted that they never consulted each other on their movements, in fact rarely spoke to each other, but preferred to chat with their Siamese companion Teiu. Continuing his report, Dr. Warren stated:

Those who have resided with them say, that the alvine and urinary evacuations take place at about the same intervals in both, though not at the same time. . . . The pulsations of the hearts of both coincide exactly, under ordinary circumstances. I counted seventy-three pulsations in a minute while they were sitting, counting first in one boy, then in the other. . . . One of them stooped suddenly to look at my watch, his pulse became much quicker than that of the other; but after he had returned to his former posture, in about a quarter of a minute his pulse was precisely like that of the other boy. This happened repeatedly.

As for the ligament connecting them, Dr. Warren reported that it was not especially sensitive to touch. He concluded that the band was made up mostly of cartilage, with an insignificant number of connecting vessels, lymphatics, and small nerves. However, he stated that there was possibly a continuous peritoneal cavity within the ligament, which might make surgical separation dangerous. More important, he felt that the twins were not psychologically prepared for such an operation, and that until they were, any attempt to separate them would be improper. Only, he said, if one were to die before the other should they be cut apart immediately.

This first opinion concerning their separation from the lips of an eminent surgeon, apparently did not depress the twins. At eighteen, accustomed to their condition, enjoying constant attention, embarked upon a new and exciting life, they probably never thought of being cut apart.

Of the uniqueness of their personalities, Dr. Warren made the first recorded observation, saying: "The perceptions of the one are more acute than those of the other; and there is a corresponding coincidence in moral qualities. He who appears most intelligent is somewhat irritable in temper, while the disposition of the other is extremely mild." The "irritable" one, of course, was Chang, and in later years he would more and more frequently be thus contrasted with his mild-mannered brother.

Toward the end of his paper, Dr. Warren reflected once more on their individuality:

> Among the curious questions which have arisen in regard to these individuals, one has been made as to the moral identity of the two persons. There is no reason to doubt that the intellects of the two are as perfectly distinct as those of any two individuals who might be accidentally confined together. Whether similarity of education or identity of position, as to external objects, have inspired them with any extraordinary sameness of mental action, I am unable to say; any farther, at least, than that they seem to agree in their habits and tastes.

There was a final remark made by Dr. Warren—a prediction, really—that would be remembered by followers of the twins, for it would prove to be so very wrong: "Their health is at present good, but it is probable that the change of their simple habits of living for the luxuries they now obtain, together with the confinement their situation necessarily involves, will bring their lives to a close within a few years."

As news of the twins' arrival in Boston spread throughout the city, there were many who suspected them of being fakes—twins perhaps, but not really joined as one. The general mood changed and interest quickened, however, when Captain Coffin saw to it that Dr. Warren's observations appeared in the press. Before and after the physician's diagnosis was publicized, a constant flow of newspaper stories helped kindle public interest.

It was about this time that Captain Coffin found someone who might assist him in the promotion and management of the twins, as well as handle them while he was out of the country. The person Coffin retained was an energetic, amusing young man named James Webster Hale, a native of Boston. Hale was twenty-eight, ten years older than the twins, married and a father. Although his only known profession was that of notary, he was now ready to work for Coffin and Hunter. Assigned the job of looking after the welfare of the twins—he was their first business agent—Hale became absorbed by Chang and Eng. He was to write the first biographical pamphlet about them, one that would be sold at the exhibits he arranged, and he maintained contact with the twins as long as they lived.

The second week in Boston, Hale and Coffin rented a tent large enough to hold several thousand people and, to fill it, they launched a huge publicity campaign featuring a blizzard of provocative posters. Unfortunately, they left the wording on the first posters up to the printer, a man of insensitivity who initially billed the twins as THE MONSTER. Appalled, the twins' sponsors quickly changed the billing to read THE SIAMESE DOUBLE BOYS.

Lured by the publicity, crowds poured into the tent. Spectators paid a fifty-cent entrance fee. The profits were satisfying, and Captain Coffin was delighted that his exhibit was turning out to be an even better investment than anything he had imagined in Siam.

The exhibit proved equally satisfying to the public. However, some spectators were confused or bewildered by the spectacle. One old gentleman who came to see Chang and Eng inquired as to their age. When he was told that they were eighteen years old, he innocently asked whether they were *both* eighteen. Another spectator, overhearing him, replied that one twin was two years older than his brother, and the questioner went away quite content with his answer.

This sort of absurdity followed the twins for the rest of their lives, and taking an attitude of amusement, they developed a number of witty replies to such inane inquiries. People who came to view them found them unfailingly charming and gracious, with impeccable manners.

For their last appearance in Boston, Chang and Eng were moved from their tent to an exhibition room in the Exchange Coffee House. Advertisements were placed, reminding the public that the twins would soon be leaving town. The Boston *Daily Courier* announced on September 1:

GREAT NATURAL CURIOSITY
Last week of the Exhibition of the
SIAMESE DOUBLE BOYS

At the suggestion of many of the first families in the city, the forenoons of Thursday, Friday and Saturday next, will be devoted exclusively to the reception of Ladies, from 9 to 1; they will be exhibited until then, and on the afternoons of those days as heretofore, and on Saturday noon next will *positively* leave the city.

On the twins' last day in Boston, the *Daily Courier* printed a long piece about them:

All the town goes to see the Siamese twins, and people are set wondering, as well they may be, at this fantastical trick which dame Nature has taken it into her head to play for the special purpose of confounding the wits of us poor mortals. That these two pretty lads should be condemned all their lifetime to be as it were an eternal sticking plaster to one another, and live in a manner alone in the community without the benefits of individuality or the prerogatives of single gentlemen, is a circumstance odd enough to set us pondering. But passing over matters of this sort which might afford topics for edifying and fruitful speculation, the most curious view of the subject is that in which it offers itself to the learned masters of metaphysics and theology, not to mention divers other scientific departments. It is not difficult to perceive that simple as these young fellows are, they cannot fail to suggest some knotty questions . . .

The article then explored the "knotty questions" posed by the joined brothers. First, "profound theologians" were asked what were the religious implications if one twin remained a disciple "of the great Buddha" and the other twin "should be converted to Christianity"? Would both souls be saved since one twin was a Christian, or were both lost to Christ since one twin was a "heathen"? Next, "learned men of the law" were asked a three-part question: "Would ye indict two men as an individual? Dare ye send Chang and his brother to jail when only Chang shall happen to break the peace? Or, if Chang and Eng should fall out together, tell us we beseech ye, could Chang have his action for being assaulted by his other half, that is by himself?" Finally, "acute metaphysicians" were asked, "Can ye tell us in this case how the witchcraft of logic can turn darkness into light? how Chang and Eng can settle between themselves the great question in philosophy of what's what and who's who?"

As the twins' Boston stay neared its end, James Hale had been busy booking them in three other Eastern cities. With their profitable three weeks in Boston behind them, the twins packed their belongings, climbed into an enclosed horse-drawn carriage, and headed for the port of Providence, Rhode Island.

It was during their successful week's stay in Providence that Chang and Eng began to develop an act, probably for their own amusement as well as for the benefit of their audiences. In Boston, they had merely presented themselves and their exposed binding ligament, and had answered any questions put to them. In Providence, with a polished act, they became as much an entertainment as a curiosity. The high point of their performance consisted of a series of quick somersaults performed in perfect coordination, followed by a few back flips. Then, if the audience was a good one, the twins would invite volunteers to challenge them in a game of checkers. Upon occasion, they would lift and carry the heaviest member of the audience around the room. Once, they carried a man who weighed 280 pounds up and down a long hall, much to the delight of the applauding spectators.

The twins were able to act in unison because they were almost the same height. Eng was 5 feet 3½ inches tall, while Chang was an inch shorter. Chang eventually wore shoes with lifts to make up for the slight difference, so that Eng would not be pulling any extra weight.

By the time Chang and Eng left Providence on the ship *Chancellor Livingston*, bound for the climactic stop of their first American tour, New York City, their reputation had begun to grow. Hale, as their advance man, had preceded them to New York, where he briefed newspaper editors on their anticipated arrival. He also papered the big city with posters and handbills bearing a likeness of the twins. When Chang and Eng arrived in New York on September 18, 1829, the inhabitants of America's leading metropolis were expecting them and clamoring for a view of this Asian oddity.

Although New York was a city of horse carriages and pedestrians—the first horse-drawn streetcars were still a few years away—and although its substantial brownstone and granite buildings had not yet been supplanted by towering structures, the metropolis was nevertheless overwhelming to any newcomer—a bustling, active community.

Neither Boston nor Providence had prepared Chang and Eng for the grandeur and excitement of New York. They toured Broadway, gawking at the Franklin House hotel and the two-story depot for the stage line to Albany. On Broadway, too, they saw Bogert's popular bakery and Putnam's bookshop. They inspected the Cortlandt Street Ferry House, stared at the squat two-story marble city hall crowned by a cupola, enjoyed the buildings of the shipping companies and marine insurance underwriters filling the Hanover Square business center.

Most of all, the twins appreciated the diversions of the city, from the Park Theater on Chatham Street, where John Howard Payne's song "Home, Sweet Home" had been introduced six years earlier to an audience seated in boxes and on board benches, to Windust's richly decorated tavern that was the gathering place for celebrities before the advent of Delmonico's.

Three years before the arrival of the twins, the aristocratic diarist Philip Hone had been elected mayor of New York, and in his journal he recorded the diversions of his beloved city. In the months and weeks before the appearance of Chang and Eng, Hone set down some of his typical activities in his diary: He went to the shipyard to watch the launching of the packet *Erie;* he attended the arrival of the first steam locomotive seen in the city, one built by the well-known George Stephenson; he received the son of Marshal Ney, who brought a letter of introduction from Lafayette; he celebrated in the rain the fifty-third Fourth of July and noted that it was "ushered in by the usual accompaniment of pistols, firecrackers, and fireballs, and in despite of the Temperance Society, the Park is surrounded with booths, where everything drinkable is to be had but water." Philip Hone would not record seeing Chang and Eng on their visit this time, but he would do so later.

While public masked balls were declared an outrage and outlawed, people of the city still found their pleasure in theaters, restaurants, taverns, coffee houses. But even more was wanted. New Yorkers craved and demanded a greater variety of entertainment. When Modeste Malhoit, the 619-pound Canadian giant, was unveiled, the crowds congregated in droves. This demand for the bizarre, the innovative, the unusual, was insatiable. All social classes were one in their desire for new entertainment—for the poorer citizens, a mere fifty cents opened the door to an escape from poverty, monotony, the autumn's chill, and for the middle and wealthier classes, a paltry entry fee provided a fresh sensation. New York was ready for the United Brothers from Siam.

Large advertisements, beginning in the New York *Evening Post*, heralded the advent of Chang and Eng: "WONDERFUL NATURAL CURIOSITY—THE SIAMESE TWIN BROTHERS will be exhibited at the Grand Saloon, Masonic Hall, every day (Sunday excepted) from 9 till 2 in the morning, and from 6 to 9 in the evening."

Newspapers were generous in giving space to the twins. On September 21, the *Evening Post* reported:

"The Siamese boys.—These united twin children are now exhibited in this city, at the Masonic Hall, Broadway. They present a spectacle of great interest, alloyed, however, by those feelings of commiseration which human deformity must ever occasion. They seem not only contented with their condition of forced companionship, but, so far as we may judge from the display of their fraternal feelings during the short time that we were present with them, quite as happy as children of their age usually are. . . . From the opinion we have heard expressed we see no reason to doubt that the Siamese children might be disjoined; and if they can without suffering permanent injury, humanity requires that it should be done."

The following day, September 22, the New York *Courier and Enquirer* carried an open letter written by Dr. Felix Pasclair, "Special correspondent of the medical society of Paris" in New York, to "Monsieur Newquart, D.M.P., ex-President and Secretary General of the Medical Society of Paris; Dept. of the Sane [Seine], etc.," containing a lengthy account of Chang and Eng. The letter read in part:

One hundred and twenty-eight years have elapsed since the occurrence of the formation of a double human being; as recorded by the celebrated Buffon. It was that of the girl Judith and Helene, born in Hungary, united back to back with an only alvine organ. They lived 21 years; the first died from a severe attack of fever, and the other immediately followed her showing no specific symptom of disease!

The rarity of preceding similar cases in Europe or elsewhere, has induced me to communicate the recent occurrence of two male children now offered to our observation in the city of New York who are firmly joined at the epigastric region. They are from the kingdom of Siam. . . .

Among the subjects of natural curiosity which are derived from the animated creation . . . none could excite more really painful feelings of pity than the contemplation of these ill-fated fellow creatures. We are however much relieved by hearing that they were not abandoned by their parents—that an American navigator had received them in trust from their mother, to be returned under contract with such a stipulated fund as to be sufficient for their maintenance and future comfort; also to have them as far as possible instructed in our language. They have in their company another countryman, a youth, the son of a rich merchant in Bangkock, placed by his father under the care of Capt. A. Coffin for the special purpose of receiving the best American education. The other Siamese, Master Tien [Teiu], is a remarkably handsome lad, has a much darker complexion, has no Chinese features about him, and already begins to speak English.

This constant publicity had its effect. During their three-week stay in New York, the performances of Chang and Eng were almost always attended by overflow audiences.

After a week, Chang and Eng had begun to tire of hotel living and their lack of privacy. Until this time, they had permitted Hale and Coffin to arrange for their room and board. Now, suddenly, they wished to be independent and on their own, and they determined to find their own lodgings.

For an entire day, pushing past gaping fellow pedestrians, they wandered the streets of New York in search of accommodations. Together, in step, they traversed the spacious avenues shaded by weeping wil-

lows, moved through the winding, curving streets of
the older sections of town. Everywhere they saw
buildings in various stages of construction. There
were constant fires in New York, and the beautiful
wooden and brick buildings were always being replaced. They entered residential sections, where the
handsome, multicolored houses ranged from one
story to five—an incredible vision after the recent
floating huts of Siam.

The search for living quarters was more difficult
than they had anticipated. Not every landlady would
accept such strange tenants. After a series of disap-
pointments, they approached a large house on John
Street, where the proprietress was pleasant and
proved willing to rent to them. They were shown an
attractive room on the first floor, and they were about
to take it when they heard the shuffling sound of
footsteps over their heads. At once, they became distraught. Puzzled, the landlady reassured them that the
sound was merely another tenant walking on the second floor. But the twins remained upset. The ground
floor no longer pleased them. They wanted something
higher up, preferably at the top of the house.

Confused, the landlady explained that the only thing
available upstairs was the attic. She was quite sure
they would not want that, since it was dark and uncomfortable. Nevertheless, the twins requested to see
the attic, and when they were led up to it, they instantly announced that they would take it. The landlady was thoroughly mystified, but she pressed them
no further.

At the outset, Chang and Eng proved to be perfect
tenants, quiet and retiring, and they voiced no complaints about their cramped attic quarters. But after a
few weeks of trudging up and down three flights of
stairs—which were not wide enough for the two of
them to walk side by side—the twins approached their
landlady with a request to move downstairs. Unable
to contain her curiosity any longer, the landlady
asked why they had chosen the attic in the first place.
The twins finally explained the reason for their

choice. In Siam, they said, it was believed that a severe misfortune would befall a person who allowed someone else to walk over his head. It meant bad luck for the twins if they had anyone situated above them. But the strenuous daily trip up and down three flights of stairs had done much to dissolve their superstitious fear. They were now ready to live with people over their heads—and from that day on, they did.

Meanwhile, their successful exhibits in New York continued. Although some spectators made unfeeling comments about their abnormality, the twins were rarely bothered. In fact, far from being self-conscious about their own physical condition, they were sympathetic and concerned for others whom they felt had greater problems.

In New York, when a man with one eye attended one of their performances, they insisted that he be refunded half his admission fee because he could see only half of what the rest of the audience saw. This perhaps was more an indication of their wry sense of humor than of their humanitarianism. But soon after, they observed a cripple in the audience, a man who had lost his hands and feet. They were immediately sympathetic. They gave him a present, saying that since they had four hands and he had none, it was their duty and their pleasure to assist him.

If the twins' physical appearance continued to be a source of fascination, their behavior also drew attention. Visitors who questioned them were constantly astonished at the harmony that existed between the two. They continued to walk, talk, dress, and eat as one, with flawless coordination. What one disliked eating, the other also rejected. When one felt tired, so did the other. Since they were not often observed speaking to each other, yet acted in accord, visitors believed that they were in telepathic communication. The twins admitted that they did not enjoy playing checkers against one another, explaining that it was no more fun than playing the right hand against the left.

In less than a week, the twins' presence in New

York came to the attention of two prominent physicians—Dr. Samuel Latham Mitchell, then vice-president of Rutgers Medical College, and his colleague Dr. William Anderson. A contemporary London pamphlet praised the pair highly, saying: "Dr. Anderson was the pupil of Sir Astley Cooper [of London, perhaps the most famous surgeon in England], and enjoys high reputation in America. Dr. Mitchell is also well known throughout the whole civilized world as a philosopher of the most profound research." Intrigued by what they heard of the twins, Dr. Mitchell and Dr. Anderson volunteered to give them their third medical examination since reaching the United States.

The twins were agreeable, and the examination was undertaken. Dr. Mitchell and Dr. Anderson then compiled their observations in a medical paper written for members of their profession. They had some definite thoughts about the ligament that joined the twins:

"Into the canal of this almost cylindrical band, there is a protrusion of the viscus from the abdomen of its respective boy, upon every effort of coughing or other exercise; and these protrusions, from their particular hardness and size, more at some times than others, we might suppose to be made up of the abdominal viscera, as intestine, liver, stomach, or spleen, as each should happen in the various positions of their bodies, to be presented to the openings, since we believe that parts of every abdominal or pelvic viscus, excepting the kidneys, have been found from time to time to enter into the composition of hernial tumors."

In other words, if the connecting band were cut and the peritoneal membrane that lines the cavity of the human abdomen were ruptured, this would expose the intestines, liver, stomach, and spleen, thus subjecting these vital organs to possible infection.

Speaking directly to this point, the physicians gave their opinions on surgery: "A question has arisen, which has been discussed with some warmth, whether they could be separated with safety. We think they could not. . . . If such an operation could be practicable, for the liberation of these boys, then it might be deemed advisable, other permissions cooperating . . ."

In a personal letter to Captain Coffin, after minutely reporting on their examination of the binding ligament that held Chang and Eng together, Dr. Mitchell and Dr. Anderson employed layman's language (as best they could) to recommend strongly that the twins be left united.

New York, Sept. 24

To Captain Coffin

Dear Sir,—In accordance with your request, we have the pleasure to communicate the observations made at our visit this day to the Siamese youths. . . .

There can be no doubt that if these boys were separated by the knife, and this band cut across at any part, a large opening would be made into the belly of each, that would expose them to enormous hernial protrusions and inflammations that would certainly prove fatal. We have understood the mother to have noted a very curious fact, worthy the mention of accoucheurs, that, when they were born, the head of one was covered or encased by the lower extremities of the other, and thus they made the easiest possible entrance into the world.

They are so satisfied with their condition, that nothing renders them so unhappy as the fear of a separation by any surgical operation: the very mention of it causes immediate weeping. Indeed, there is a good reason for this uneasiness; for, as stated above, according to our judgment, there would be the most extreme hazard in any such attempt, and even after being cut asunder, they would experience much diminution of enjoyment. But it has been urged by many that they ought to be disconnected. We think such an opinion is incorrect. It cannot, consistent with our principles and usages, be done without their consent. To this they are totally opposed; and as they are under the protection of a kind and benevolent gentleman, we know you will take good care of them, and, if they live, return them to their homes again. As they are so alert and vigorous, we really coincide that "in ten seconds they can lay a stout ordinary man on his back."

We are, dear Sir, your most obedient servants.

SAMUEL L. MITCHELL
WILLIAM ANDERSON

Captain Abel Coffin lost no time in instructing Hale to turn the letter from the two physicians over to the press, which published it widely in the New York area, and later throughout the United States and Great Britain.

Next, Coffin and Hale took their charges to Philadelphia for a week of performances. On October 9, the *Aurora and Pennsylvania Gazette* told its readers: "We had the pleasure, yesterday, of viewing the Siamese boys, and were much gratified to find that their intimate union is attended with but little bodily embarrassment, and does not in the least interfere with their happiness. . . . They are well worth the inspection of the curious."

The curious came in droves. According to one account, Chang and Eng's exhibition grossed $1,000 during their short appearance in Philadelphia.

Once again, Captain Coffin depended upon the medical profession to certify and help sell his product. In Philadelphia, he invited the city's leading doctors, many from Jefferson Medical College, to examine Chang and Eng. One of these, described by a newspaper as "a distinguished Surgeon of this city," wrote a two-column account of the twins which appeared in the October 24 edition of the *Aurora and Pennsylvania Gazette*. The surgeon, who signed himself E.B., began by crediting Captain Coffin for the twins' present state of good health:

When obtained by their present proprietor, they bore marks of habitual exposure and hardship, without an adequate supply of wholesome nutriment. . . . They were emaciated, and their health apparently so frail, as to render it a matter of serious question whether they would be capable of enduring the fatigues of such a voyage as was contemplated for them.

Capt. C however found that a proper attention to their food, and a kind watchfulness over their wants, soon improved their health and vigour; and whilst on ship board, they entirely recovered . . .

The surgeon went on to describe the twins:

Their voices are disagreeable, coarse, and unmusical—apparently under the influence of their age of puberty. They are not observed to converse with each other often. By many this circumstance has been ascribed to an indifference to each other, supposed to arise from a feeling that they mutually interfered with each other's independence and comfort. This is not the case—it is simply they have no information to communicate to each other. Each being under precisely the same circumstances, and having the same opportunities of becoming familiar with such events as are usually the subjects of ordinary conversation. Talking to each other therefore would be like an individual talking to himself.

As to the possibility of separating the twins, the surgeon was of two minds—it might be done safely, yet he would not be willing to do it. He explained:

My own impression as well as that of several distinguished surgeons with whom I have conversed, is, that it could be accomplished by means not more hazardous in their consequences than many to which persons often voluntarily submit, with a view to relief of some disease only remotely endangering life. . . . The separation I think may be considered practicable, though not unattended with danger. If it were, who would urge it where there is such perfect union of feeling and concert of action; whilst they are healthy and active; happy and gay; and withal quite contented with their lot. At present I would be unwilling to disunite them, even if it could be accomplished without pain and without danger.

The question of the separation of the twins, in America at least, had been resolved for the time being. The two would remain one. But this question was to continue to be the incessant theme of Chang-

Eng's lives. Their weeping at the mere mention of separation during their youth would, years later, turn into weeping at the pronouncement of doctor after doctor that separation "would be attended with the most dangerous consequences."

However, at this stage any talk of separating the twins was mere talk, and possibly fodder contrived for publicity. The fact was, at eighteen, Chang and Eng did not want to be separated. And the fact was, no matter what their public utterances to the contrary, neither Robert Hunter nor Captain Abel Coffin wanted the twins separated. In England, Hunter at one point remarked that the connecting band was becoming more cartilaginous as time went on—a condition which, if it continued, would make the possibility of separation more feasible. But he added that "a dissolution of the partnership is not likely to be attempted so long as union is so profitable to the firm." Unfeeling as that remark may have been, Hunter was right.

It was to greater profits that the two entrepreneurs now turned their full attention. The United Brothers had been in the United States a brief two months and had proved to be a promising box-office draw. Hunter, who had been spreading the news about them in London, believed that the twins would be an even bigger draw in the British Isles. He convinced Captain Coffin of this, and they determined to bring their common investment to London as soon as possible. Coffin, after consulting with their booking agent, young James Hale, saw another advantage in this transatlantic trip. The British press was far more hospitable to exotic prodigies than any other press on earth. The attention that the twins might receive in London and throughout the British Isles, the fame that would attend them if they had a great success, would ensure an even greater success in the countless smaller cities of the United States, where a foreign build-up counted for much.

With his thoughts on a well-planned series of future exhibits in every nook and cranny of the Eastern,

Southern, and Midwestern parts of the United States, and on the steady profits that might accrue therefrom, Captain Coffin set his sights on England.

He told Chang and Eng that they were through with New York for the time. They were to prepare for London.

For their part, the twins were ready for anything that might provide them with more adventure—and more fame.

3
CHAPTER
3

To the Sceptered Isle

In New York, on October 16, 1829, the day before embarking for England, Captain Abel Coffin received a letter from a brokerage house confirming a special investment he had just arranged to have made for him in Chang and Eng.

By now, Captain Coffin was fully aware of the value his charges commanded in the marketplace, and he was determined to protect his commodity, not only in life but in death. To do this, he had signed a note payable to Peter Remsen and Company for $613.78. Of this, $339.50 was for the purchase of "70 Sovereigns," the British gold coins calculated at $4.85 per sovereign, in order to have money on hand for immediate expenses once the twins landed in England. Of the remaining sum, $199.09 was for three insurance policies that Captain Coffin had taken out on the lives of the twins, and $75.19 was for materials to aid in the preservation of their bodies in the event of their deaths.

This letter read, in part: "Paid Premium of Insurance on $3333. p Ship Robert Edwards from New

York to London with the privilege of landing in any part of the Coast of England—on the Bodies of the 'Double Siamese Boys' alive or dead. The assured warrant that in case of death on board the Ship the bodies shall be carried to the port of destination. The dangers for which the Insured are liable only excepted value at Ten Thousand Dollars—on one third of the valuation." The insurance policy of $10,000 on the twins was so high that three companies—American Insurance Company, Union Insurance Company, and Ocean Insurance Company—had joined together to underwrite the potential loss.

The letter also listed a sum of $63.68 owed by Captain Coffin for "1 Cask Molasses Rum 100 Galls," and a sum of $11.51 for twelve pounds—in three bottles and one box—of "Corrosive Sublimate." This odd cargo, like Coffin's stipulation in the policies that the twins' bodies should be carried to the ship's destination in case of their deaths on board, instead of being buried at sea, was one more contingency to preserve their corpses. Should the twins expire on shipboard, Coffin wanted the molasses rum and the corrosive sublimate handy to embalm their bodies. For Coffin knew that if the twins were an asset alive, they also had cash value in death, either by publicly displaying their united corpses or by selling the preserved remains to some eager medical college for autopsy purposes.

On October 17, 1829, Captain Coffin, insurance policies in order, his wife Susan, and James Hale, with Chang and Eng and their Siamese companion Teiu in tow, arrived by carriage at New York's Old Slip harbor, an area surrounded by the remnants of New Amsterdam, rundown Dutch houses, and the busy Franklin Market. With their baggage, the party ascended the gangplank to board the sailing ship *Robert Edwards*, commanded by Captain Samuel Sherburne. Hours later they were on their way to England.

The crossing to England took twenty-seven days.

The passage was neither a happy nor a comfortable one for Chang and Eng. While the Coffins and Ha had first-class cabins aboard the *Robert Edwards*, Chang and Eng found themselves traveling steerage. While the other members of their party were being served sumptuous meals in the ship's dining room, the twins existed day after day on a monotonous diet of salt beef and potatoes which they shared with the crew.

Upset and bewildered by this treatment, the twins complained bitterly to Coffin. He temporized, saying that the dining room was too crowded for them to eat with the other passengers. As to their quarters, Coffin insisted that since he had purchased first-class tickets for them, Captain Sherburne was the culprit. The twins then sought out Captain Sherburne and protested their lot. The captain, puzzled but sympathetic, moved the twins to better quarters, but their new accommodations were still considerably inferior to those of the Coffins and Hale, and they resented it.

It was not until almost three years later, when they were on tour in Auburn, New York, and had finally become disenchanted with Coffin, that they had a surprise reunion with Captain Sherburne and the mystery of their bad treatment on the voyage to England was dispelled. In a bitter personal letter written to Captain William Davis, Jr., a seaman friend of Coffin's, Chang and Eng—writing as usual in the first person singular, as if both of them were one person—recalled vividly the misery of that 1829 crossing to England:

When Captn. Sherburne came into my room yesterday, he appeared very glad to see me, shook me cordially by the hand, & his manner was friendly in the extreme. I, of course, received his civilities in a becoming manner but still I could not but recollect how badly (as I *was made* to think) he treated me on that passage to England, & how different to what I had a right to expect. To you, it may be necessary to explain this—and I must therefore acquaint you, that on my passage with Captn. Sherburne in the Robert Edward to London I had frequent occasion to complain to Captain Coffin of having very rough food & being treated altogether in a different manner to that in which the rest of the cabin passengers were treated; to these statements Captn. C. replied to me that the reason I did not dine with the rest of the passengers & get the same food was that the table was too crowded—Captn. Coffin's words to us were "Oh! never mind, Chang Eng—the table is very crowded & we shall soon get to England"—Afterwards I asked Captn. Coffin the question—whether or not he had paid the full *cabin* passage for me? he told me that he had paid the same rate of passage as had been paid for the other cabin passengers. I confess it surprised me to learn that the *full cabin passage* had been paid for me & yet that I was set down day after day to eat salt beef and potatoes with the mate; at the same time that I saw the *other cabin* passengers feeding on fresh meat & other luxuries furnished in a packet ship, to all which I *naturally* imagined myself as much entitled as any of the other passengers—but I was a little surprised that Captn. C never mentioned the subject to Captn. S so as to have the matter set right. . . .

If Capt. Coffin had told me that he could not afford or even that he did not choose to pay more than the passage money paid for servants I might not have had any cause to complain but—"*If Captn. Sherburne's statement be true*" (& the truth is easily come at), then a most pitiful & contemptible piece of deception was played off on me—a deception the more contemptible, & the more pitiful from my being at that time ignorant of English & unable to make any complaint except through the medium of the Siamese language. . . . This is the unfair manner in which I was allowed to abuse Captn. Sherburne on account of the meagre fare which he furnished to us for *a fully cabin passage money!!!!* Moreover Captn. Coffin invariably bore me out in what I said on this subject & he himself often said to those who asked me how I liked Capt S "Oh! Captn. Sherburne did not treat the boys well at all." *Whereas* under the circumstances Captn. Sherburne's conduct was most kind towards us & if it were not for his kindness I fear we should have been but badly off. . . .

Now, then, Captn. D—look how this matter stands —Capt C had realized a large sum by my exhibition in New York & Philadelphia, and yet we find that he *screwed a hard bargain* for our passage to England, *in the steerage* of the ship & having us under the denomination of *his servants*—all for the paltry savings of $100 and yet wishing to keep us in good temper & wishing moreover to make us believe that he spared no expence for our comfort, he *tells us* that the fault is Captn. Sherburne's and lays all the blame on him—whereas (according to Mr. Sherburne's statement) the reverse is the fact. . . .

Naturally a good deal surprised at the manner in which I was treated & it has ever since been a mystery to me but *"It is a Mystery No Longer."* Finding Captn. Sherburne treat me so civilly I thought I would ask him the question & accordingly asked him whether or not the full cabin passage had been paid for me . . . never did I see a man more surprised. He explained to me the whole affair & his story & Captn. Coffin's are so very different that a lie—a gross lie—lies between the two parties. However Captn Sherburne has given me a written memorandum concerning the affair of which we shall here insert a copy & also a copy of a letter written by Captn. Sherburne to John Griswold the Agent of the Robert Edward at New York which letter we shall deliver personally to Mr. Griswold as soon as we go to New York.

Chang and Eng enclosed a copy of both the memorandum and the letter from Captain Sherburne to Griswold. In these Cherburne stated that Coffin had paid a total of $450 to transport his entire party to England—$300 for himself, his wife, and Hale, plus an additional $150 for Chang, Eng, and their Siamese friend Teiu, "as servants at half price."

In his memorandum, Captain Sherburne had written:

Mr. Griswold told me & Captn. Coffin also told me that the boys would sleep *anywhere* in the *steerage.* And could make *any shift*—therefore when I put them in the cabin & to sleep in a state room & let them mess with the mate, I thought I had done a great deal more than the agreement entitled them to expect. Had I made the agreement, I would not have taken them less than others—all of which paid $130 to be found in wine, porter & liquors and $115 each without wine, porter & liquors with the exception of Genl. Murray who took his passage in. Cog. pretending not be able to pay more than $100 and a woman passenger —Neither of which were to be found in liquors of any kind—Captn. Coffin never complained to me that he was dissatisfied; on the contrary I expected his gratitude yet he talked to others as I was afterwards told—This I am not astonished at on reflection as I have always remarked that all cheap passengers are always the most discontented and endeavour to make disturbances with the other passengers. . . . I can only say that I have carried a great many passengers & have never met any but what I made friends with except Captain Coffin and his accomplished Lady; and the ex-Genl. Murray this latter gentleman was put out because I would not include wine, liquors & etc I am not certain that they were entitled to them from the price he paid —I should think not.

Incidentally, in closing their letter written to Captain Davis in 1832, the twins signed it "Chang Eng, Siamese Twins." While Phineas T. Barnum has been given the credit for coining the term "The Siamese Twins" in 1853, it is evident here that Chang and Eng coined the name themselves twenty-one years earlier.

But in 1829, the twins did not understand why they had been confined in inferior quarters or why they had had to share second-rate food with a member of the crew during their twenty-seven-day passage to England. They knew only that for the first time they were unhappy under the guardianship of Captain Coffin, and that—for the first time since they had left Siam—they were feeling exploited and demeaned.

But soon England was sighted, and the twins were to have other things on their minds. Before proceeding to London, the *Robert Edwards* docked at Dartmouth, in Devonshire, to disembark several passengers who lived in that area. This done, the ship sailed out of the harbor on November 13 and headed for Southampton. What normally would have been a short trip suddenly became a five-day nightmare. In the English Channel, the ship ran into terrible gales. Buffeted by heavy storms, the ship was able to make little progress —in fact it was forced to take shelter in small coves several times. Damage to the *Robert Edwards* was severe, including the loss of cables and anchors.

At last, on the foggy Thursday morning of November 19, the ship sluggishly reached the port of Southampton. Exhausted as they were, the twins found that their spirits revived when they were on land once more. With the others of their party, they entered a hired carriage for the trip to the North and South American Coffeehouses in London, nearly one hundred miles distant, where Coffin had rooms reserved.

Since their discoverer, Robert Hunter, had been delayed, he was not on hand to meet the twins when they arrived at their destination, but he had arranged for two correspondents from *The News* of London to be there to meet them.

According to the first correspondent:

These extraordinary and interesting youths are now at the North and South American Coffeehouse, where they arrived late on Thursday night from New York. As soon as their arrival was made known, the house was crowded with persons anxious to see them; but the boys being fatigued from the journey, no person, except the writer and one or two others, were permitted to visit them. People would be apt to imagine that there would be something unpleasant in the exhibition of two human beings joined together, but such is not the case. On the contrary, they must excite the most pleasurable sensations in all those who are capable in taking delight in beholding a perfect picture of innocence and happiness—for such is the appearance the two lads present. Each of their bodies is well formed, and complete in all its parts. The hands and feet, in particular, are beautifully symmetrical. Nor would any one on looking at them imagine, whether walking, standing, or sitting, that they were any thing more than two affectionate and happy brothers, with their arms round each other's necks. Not that they are always so seen, but such is their general habit.

The second *News* correspondent said of the twins:

When they arrived at the North and South American Coffeehouse, from Southampton, they complained of cold. One partook of fowl and cold beef for his supper, and the other of roast beef, and they both enjoyed their repast with as much pleasure and *goût* as the most experienced gourmands; they are particularly partial to coffee, drink a great quantity of water, but will not touch spirits or malt liquors of any kind.

The next day, Chang and Eng were reunited with Robert Hunter. *The News* had a correspondent on hand to record the meeting: "Mr. Robert Hunter, who first discovered them fishing on the banks of the Siam River, visited them on Friday morning. The delight of the boys when he came into the room was unbounded."

The afternoon of their second day in London was overcast and gloomy. The correspondent noted the twins' reaction to this:

"They express much disappointment at London; they say it is all night, and insisted upon going to bed about the middle of the day. On reaching their bedroom the chambermaid tapped their heads, and told them they should be her sweethearts, at which they laughed, and in a playful and boyish manner they at one and the same time kissed each side of her cheek. On being jocularly told of this, they said it was Mary that wanted to have them for a sweetheart, not they that wanted to have Mary."

Of the fifteen months the twins were to spend in the British Isles, seven months would be devoted to London. It was an exciting town. *The News* speculated: "It is expected that they will be first presented to his Majesty, and afterwards exhibited to the public." While the twins did meet members of the royal family, there is no evidence that they ever had an audience with the king. The reason for this omission was probably King George IV's declining health. The handsome king, now in his sixty-seventh year, had led a dissipated and lecherous life, leaving behind him a trail of mistresses, marrying and discarding Caroline of Brunswick, drinking constantly and heavily, and suffering consequent unpopularity among his subjects. At the time Chang and Eng were supposed to see him, George IV was beset by gout, dropsy, chest inflammation, liver problems, and asthma. He comforted himself with steady doses of brandy. On June 26, 1830, when the twins had been in England barely seven months, George died.

The successor to the throne, King William IV, noted for having fought against the Colonies in the American Revolutionary War and for having sired ten illegitimate children, was probably too preoccupied with his duties to receive Chang and Eng. The new king proved no better than the old. Upon William IV's accession to the throne, Lord Greville privately noted in his journal:

"Never was elevation like that of William IV. His life has, hitherto, passed in obscurity and neglect, in miserable poverty, surrounded by a numerous progeny of bastards, without consideration or friends, and he was ridiculous for his grotesque ways and little meddling curiosity. Nobody ever invited them into their house, or thought it necessary to honour him with any mark of attention or respect; and so he went on for about forty years, till Canning brought him into notice by making him Lord High Admiral. . . . In that post he distinguished himself by making absurd speeches, by a morbid official activity, and by a general wildness which was thought to indicate incipient insanity."

For the Siamese Twins, London would hold greater attractions than Buckingham Palace. During their lengthy stay, Chang and Eng would enjoy the sights of the Covent Garden Theatre and Haymarket Theatre, the Baker Street Bazaar, Grosvenor Square and Grub Street, Pall Mall, the Chapter Coffeehouse, Billingsgate, the public baths, Vauxhall Gardens, Willis's

Room, where were held the exclusive Almack's Balls, and Surgeons' Hall.

It was a literary London, where Chang and Eng would acquire their abiding taste for English literature. It was a London where Charles Lamb, after thirty-three years in India House, was writing in the British Museum; where Charles Dickens, having learned shorthand, was working as a journalist; where Elizabeth Barrett Browning, suffering an injured spine, was convalescing in Wimpole Street; where Thomas Babington Macaulay, after paying off his father's debts, was toiling as commissioner of bankruptcy; where William Hazlitt, living in Soho, was publishing an unsuccessful four-volume life of Napoleon Bonaparte.

Shortly, Chang and Eng, the Siamese Twins, would be almost as well known as the literary luminaries, and would themselves become one of the more popular sights of London.

To introduce the twins to London, Robert Hunter pulled off a publicity coup. Aware that during their first exhibits in America, the twins had been called a fraud by some people, that they had been called freaks and monsters not fit to be seen by ladies, but that they had been regarded with fascination by the medical profession, Hunter had all the ingredients he needed for his public relations stunt. He reasoned that if the most eminent physicians of London were invited to a preview of Chang and Eng, they would not be able to resist the temptation. Further, if the doctors were given the opportunity to examine the twins and were asked for their opinions, they would readily offer their reactions. In this way the physicians would give Chang and Eng their seal of approval, guarantee that they were not frauds but authentic united brothers, and reassure the public that the twins were acceptable for one and all to see. The press would succumb at once. The publicity value would be incalculable.

Hunter lost no time putting his planned event in motion. Invitations were delivered to the leading medical men in London, as well as to some politicians and members of the nobility and editors of the largest newspapers, inviting them to attend a preview exhibition of the Siamese Twins, during which the twins might be examined and questioned. This private levee would be held in Piccadilly at Egyptian Hall, one of London's most imposing showcases for entertainment (the façade of which resembled the ancient Temple of Tentyra), on Tuesday, November 24, 1829. Acceptances poured in, and the stage was set for the debut in England of "the greatest novelty of the age."

From the moment the doors of Egyptian Hall were opened and the distinguished guests arrived, the event was a resounding success. The roll call of medical greats who attended was astonishing. Dr. Leigh Thomas, president of the Royal College of Surgeons, was there, as was Sir Astley Paston Cooper, a former professor at the Royal College of Surgeons who had gained renown as the first surgeon to tie the abdominal aorta for aneurysm. Dr. Joshua Brooks, a foremost anatomist who possessed his own medical museum, was there, as was Sir Anthony Carlisle, among the most highly reputed of English physicians. Dozens more of the medical fraternity streamed in, followed by prominent political figures.

Acting as gracious hosts, greeting each guest, were Robert Hunter, Captain Coffin, and James Hale. Hale and the "concern" took each guest and introduced him to Chang and Eng, and later mingled with the visitors and answered their questions about the background, habits, and personalities of the Siamese Twins.

After Sir Astley Cooper had studied the ligament that bound the twins, someone asked him if it was operable. "Can they be separated?" Sir Astley shrugged and answered, "I should not like to try." Then he added, "But why separate them? The boys seem perfectly happy as they are." With a smile, Sir Astley turned to Captain Coffin and said, "Depend on it, those boys will fetch a vast deal more money whilst they are together than when they are separate." He stared off in the crowd at the twins. "This is certainly a most curious phenomenon."

Apparently, the thoughtful and cordial behavior of the hosts toward their visitors, as well as toward their united charges, made a favorable impression upon the medical men. As spokesman for all the physicians in attendance, Dr. George Buckley Bolton, of the Medical and Chirurgical Society, told his colleagues at the Royal College of Surgeons in an address four months later:

"I cannot here deny myself the pleasure of stating the kindness which has at all times been evinced towards these youths by Captain Coffin, Mr. Hunter and Mr. Hale: The unwearied anxiety manifested by these gentlemen for their welfare and happiness, and the liberal manner in which they have uniformly afforded the means of investigating so curious an object of philosophical inquiry, entitle them equally to the thanks of the philanthropist and the lover of science."

Before the preview exhibition was over, twenty-four of the physicians present had agreed to put their names to a document attesting to the authenticity, as well as the presentability, of the Siamese Twins. This document stated:

"CHANG AND ENG—Two youths born in the kingdom of Siam, whose bodies are, by a wonderful caprice of nature, united together as one . . . were submitted to the examination of the most eminent professors of Surgery and Medicine in the Metropolis, as well as some other gentlemen of scientific and literary pursuits, in order that through their report—if favorable —the public may be assured that the projected exhibition of these remarkable and interesting youths is in no respect deceptive; and further, that there is nothing whatever offensive to delicacy in the exhibition."

To this the twenty-four doctors, led by Dr. Leigh Thomas and the prestigious Sir Astley Paston Cooper, appended their names and sanctioned making the signed document public.

But the physicians were not the only ones in Egyptian Hall to voice their approval of the exhibit. The press were there also, looking, listening, and lending a cooperative hand to the Hunter and Coffin enterprise. The reporter for *The Examiner* of London filed a lengthy story, which read, in part:

We were on Tuesday favoured with a private view of the twin boys from Siam, whose extraordinary union has so greatly excited the public curiosity in America, from whence they reached London on Thursday week. When we entered the Egyptian Hall, they were sitting quietly by the fire, surrounded by a number of spectators, chiefly medical men. They soon however rose, walked about each with one arm around the neck of the other, and leapt from a stool upon the stage at the end of the room with great ease. They reel a little in their walk, but otherwise it is not remarkable. . . .

Various anecdotes are related of them. . . . On Monday, they saw several funerals pass the street. When they learnt that so many of the gentlemen who were examining them on Tuesday were healers of the sick, they expressed their surprise that so many deaths should take place! They speak a word or two of English only, and these relations are of course obtained from the interpreters. They rarely, we understand, speak to each other; but they are said to resent mutually an insult offered to one, and to feel alike grateful for a benefit conferred on either. A visitor, on Tuesday, put into the hand of one a couple of nonpareils [chocolate cookies covered with sugar]: The youth said in English, "Thank'ee," and immediately gave one of them to his brother.

After recounting the story of the twins' lives in Siam, their trip to America, their examinations by Drs. Warren, Mitchell, and Anderson, the reporter for the *Examiner* sensitively perceived the tragedy inherent in the lot of Chang and Eng, and waxed melancholy about their future:

. . . it is a mournful sight, to behold two fellow-creatures thus fated to endure all the common evils of life, while they must necessarily be debarred from the enjoyment of many of its chief delights. The link which unites them is more durable than that of the marriage tie—no separation can take place, legal or illegal—no Act of Parliament can divorce them, nor can all the power of Doctors' Commons give them a release even from bed and board. Taken, poor fellows, from their native land, from a mother's care, from the healthful occupation of fishing, in which they chiefly spent their time, they are doomed to pass their lives in a species of slavery, to be dragged about to all parts of the world, exposed to the painful vicissitudes of climate, and to the annoyances and dangers of which such a course of existence is necessarily fruitful. These surely are melancholy circumstances. It is said, indeed, that they are cheerful and happy, and that they are in the hands of intelligent and respectable people; which seems to be the fact. Their protectors certainly have a direct interest in the promotion of their health. When we saw them on Tuesday, though they occasionally smiled, they seemed to move with reluctance, and we discovered nothing of playfulness or merriment in their actions. They evidently longed for a release from the exhibition; for asking the time, and being shewn a watch, their attendant said that they complained of its being "too slow."

Whatever the reactions of Hunter and Coffin to the foregoing, the entrepreneurs must have been more than pleased by the concluding line in the reporter's story. The doctors were, said the *Examiner* man, "highly gratified with the exhibition, which will perhaps be the most attractive of any that has been opened to the public in the sight-loving metropolis."

A reporter for *The Times* of London found himself fascinated by the continual repetition of evidence that Chang and Eng were one, not two, since he himself had the feeling that they were two very different and distinct people. True, they did everything as one person. When riding through town in a coach, they looked out the same window together, not opposite windows. But the reporter felt that this was easily explained by the fact that they had been bound together (as if by a "metallic hinge") for eighteen years, obliged to exercise, eat, go to bed at the same time, and therefore always forced to act in harmony.

Actually, several of the doctors present did agree with *The Times* reporter that Chang and Eng, though joined, were independent of one another. An incident that occurred during the private exhibit that convinced these doctors that the twins were two separate persons. Chang and Eng had started together toward a unique glass door in Egyptian Hall to examine it. As they neared the door, Captain Coffin called out, "Chang." Immediately, noted one observer, Chang "turned in obedience to the call, whilst his brother went forward to gratify his curiosity by peeping through the door." Another observer, a physician, having seen this, said to his circle of friends, "Now I am satisfied that these boys cannot be governed by one will, for you perceive that the inclination of one boy was to return in obedience to the summons which he had heard, but he is drawn away in the opposite direction by the other, in the eagerness of his curiosity. These boys cannot, therefore, be governed by one impulse."

Another reporter who was in Egyptian Hall, representing *The Mercury*, was fascinated by the fact that the twins shared a common navel located in the center of their connecting band and by the fact that they moved across the room with "the ease and grace of a couple skillfully waltzing."

No sooner had all this publicity resulting from the private showing at Egyptian Hall commenced than the newspapers and periodicals of London and the provinces were inundated with letters, poems, cartoons, and articles on the Siamese Twins.

A typical exchange of opinion concerning the twins was published in *The Times* of London, the first on December 2 and the response on December 4, 1829. The first letter read:

To the Editor of The Times

Sir,—That they might be separated without danger is, I think, evident, as far as regards the operation, and the effect it might have on the nervous system, so as to endanger their lives, would not be in the least hazardous. We may refine upon refinement until we lose ourselves. It might perhaps render them happier in having it in their power to be at a distance, than to be compelled as they now are to be without the possibility of being apart. . . . The appellation of monsters I was sorry to hear applied to these interesting youths; it is a harsh word, and should not be used. The term monster is applicable to those preternatural births only that are analogous to animals, or more properly speaking, to a beast.

In making the above remarks it cannot be supposed I am an advocate for their being separated, though how far it might be advantageous to their happiness, after a sufficient sum has been saved to ensure their independency, I shall leave to their friends to determine.

I am, Sir, your obedient servant,

MEDICUS.

Two days later, a reply was printed in the Letters to the Editor section of *The Times*:

Sir,—After having visited the Siamese youths on the first day of their exhibition, and having there met some of the first physicians and surgeons of the day, I have been anxiously expecting a scientific account of their union, and of the possibility of their separation; but all I can collect from what has been advanced on the subject, is the mere fact of their being united, and that "perhaps they might be separated" . . . The one signed "Medicus," in your paper of this morning, must have been written without much consideration. Much stress has been laid on their having but one navel. Now this fact alone, in my opinion, decides what might or might not be done, and proves or disproves every thing that is interesting on this subject. There is but little doubt (if there is but one navel) that there was a double placenta, with one cord and two sets of vessels—one set emerging to one child, and one to the other. Should this have been the fact, it proves them to be two distinct individuals, in no way differing from twins without a union. Should there have been but one placenta and one set of vessels, entering the umbilicus, it then proves, on the contrary, that they are inseparable . . .

                 M.R.

Even as letters to the editor bombarded the press on the future of Chang and Eng, the poets of England were inspired to create loftier sentiments. Typically, a bit of doggerel about the twins published first in the *Sunday Times* of London and then in the *Berkshire Chronicle* on December 5, went:

> My yellow friends! and are you come,
>   As some have done before,
> To show the sign of "Two to one,"
>   And hang it o'er your door?
>
> How do you mean your debts to pay?
>   Will one discharge the other's?
> Or shall you work by subterfuge,
>   And say, "Ah, that's my brother's"?
>
> For well we know if one by chance
>   To Fleet or Bench is sent,
> The other would an action bring
>   For *false imprisonment.*
>
> Have you the consciences to sit,
>   And when your eating's done,
> Rise up and "pay the piper," but
>   Pay only as for one?

A second reader with a lyrical bent wrote in the *Literary Gazette:*

> If in the page of Holy Writ we find
> That man should not divide what God had joined,
> O why, with nicest skill, should science dare
> To separate this Heaven-united pair?
> United by a more than legal band,
> A wonder wrought by the Creator's hand!

Meanwhile, a steady stream of articles about Chang and Eng was beginning to find its way into various

English periodicals. Public interest in every facet of the twins' lives had to be sated, and no detail was too small to be overlooked. The *Universal Pampheleteer*, a popular magazine which in its previous issue had featured the "Life of Vidocq, the French Police Spy," gave over its entire twenty-seventh number to "A Full History of the Siamese United Twins: with Their Likeness." The magazine began with some biographical facts on Chang and Eng, and then went on to describe them:

> They are dressed in a short loose green jacket and trousers, the custom of their country, which is very convenient and allows the utmost freedom of motion, but does not show the form of the boys to advantage. . . .
>
> With their arms twined round each other, as they bend down or move about, they look like a group of statuary. . . .
>
> Without being in the least disgusting or unpleasant, like almost all monstrosities, these youths are certainly one of the most extraordinary freaks of nature that has ever been witnessed.

Because Chang and Eng found the foggy London weather disagreeable—they contracted colds soon after their arrival, and coughed constantly—Hunter and Coffin decided they must have their own doctor, someone who would be readily available. After making inquiries, they selected a noted London physician, Dr. George Buckley Bolton, to attend the twins regularly. From the time he first examined them, two days after their private debut at Egyptian Hall, until they left London, Dr. Bolton was their personal, and only, medical consultant. As such, he came to know the twins better than any member of his profession since their arrival in the West.

After four months attending them, Dr. Bolton was called upon by his colleagues to give a definitive report on their condition. In lucid language, Dr. Bolton wrote his paper, "On the United Siamese Twins," and on April 1, 1830, he read it to assembled members of the Royal College of Surgeons in London.

Following a brief biography of the twins, Dr. Bolton described their physiques to his fellows:

These youths are both of the same height, namely, five feet two inches; and their united weight is one hundred and eighty pounds. They are much shorter, and appear less advanced in puberty, than youths of this country at the age of eighteen years. . . .

The left eye of Chang is weaker than the right; but this is reversed in the case of Eng. so that each sees best with the eye nearest his brother. Their bodies are much paler now than they were on their first arrival in England. Their genital organs are, like all their other external parts, regularly formed; but the youths are naturally modest, and evince a strong repugnance to any close investigation on this subject.

Next, Dr. Bolton discussed their "band of union," which he found surprisingly strong:

In the month of February last one of them fell out of bed while asleep, and hung by the band for some time, and when both awoke, they alike stated, that they had experienced no pain in the band from this accident. Mr. Hale, their constant attendant, has lifted one of them from the ground, allowing the other to hang by the band with his feet raised from the floor; yet the whole weight of one of the boys thus suspended did not occasion pain to either, or even excite their displeasure. The circumstance of the small degree of sensibility possessed by the band, tends to corroborate the opinion I entertain of the possibility of effecting a separation of the twins by a surgical operation.

As a result of their "extraordinary intimacy," Dr. Bolton said, "they have each the power to bend their bodies in all directions, and turn their heels over their shoulders. They also often playfully tumble head over heels while on their bed, without occasioning the slightest pain or inconvenience in the band."

Dr. Bolton then resumed his medical diagnosis:

The tongue of Eng is at all times whiter than that of Chang, and his digestion is more easily deranged by unsuitable diet. I have never heard that Chang has passed a single day without alimentary discharges, but the contrary has often occurred to Eng. In general they both obey the calls of nature at the same time, and this happens even when these result from the operation of medicines.

It having occurred to me, that the odour given by asparagus to the urine would be a test of the extent of the circulation of the blood through both the twins, on the 22nd of March I gave that vegetable to Chang with his dinner, not allowing any to be given to his brother. On examining their urine four hours after this meal, that of Chang had distinctly the peculiar asparagus smell, but the urine of his brother was not influenced by it. The next day this experiment was reversed, and therefore with reversed results. These trials sufficiently prove a fact which was otherwise apparent—that the sanguineous communication between the united twins is very limited. . . .

They always take their meals together, objecting to being seen while thus engaged. Neither will eat or drink what the other dislikes, though they occasionally take different sorts of food at the same time, such as meat or fish. When the appetite of one is satiated, the other is also satisfied. In their habits they are very cleanly and delicate, and mutually assist each other in dressing. They are exceedingly affectionate and docile, and grateful for every kindness shown them. It is not often they converse with each other, although their dispositions and tempers agree, and their tastes and opinions are similar. Sometimes they engage in distinct conversations with different persons at the same time, upon totally dissimilar subjects. Both are very fond of music, and are equally interested in dramatic performances.

Dr. Bolton confessed that from time to time he had attempted an impromptu experiment on the twins. "On my tickling one of them, the other told me to desist, though he stated that he did not feel the touch, and it was quite clear that he could not see me tickle his brother."

Dr. Bolton also admitted that he had allowed some

of his colleagues to undertake simple experiments with the twins. The most notable of the outside physicians to experiment on Chang and Eng was Dr. Peter Mark Roget. The twins could not know at the time that the fame of this remarkable and versatile medical man would match their own and endure for as long. Dr. Roget, who was secretary of the Royal Society for two decades, laid the groundwork for the invention of the modern slide rule and of motion pictures. Eventually, he turned from physiology to philology, and in 1852 he published the most popular book of synonyms in history, one that listed ideas along with the groups of words that expressed them. Roget's *Thesaurus of English Words and Phrases* was destined to go through twenty-eight editions before his death, and has remained a standard reference work.

Roget had an abiding interest in bizarre experiments, both on himself and on others. Thirty-one years earlier, he had visited the Pneumatic Institution at Clifton, near Bristol, and joined the eccentric Dr. Thomas Beddoes, and his assistant Humphry Davy, in experimenting on himself with nitrous oxide—laughing gas—as an anesthetic as well as a substance producing a high.

It was this Dr. Roget who had come calling on Chang and Eng in London to determine whether they were really two or one. Dr. Roget supervised an experiment in which an aide placed a silver teaspoon on Eng's tongue and a disc of zinc on Chang's tongue to learn their reactions. When the metals were brought into contact, both brothers cried out, "Sour, sour!" Nevertheless, Dr. Roget urged that the experiment be continued, reversing the metals, this time placing the zinc on Eng's tongue and the teaspoon on Chang's tongue. Again both twins protested the sour taste.

Dr. Bolton explained the significance of Roget's finding. "These experiments prove that the galvanic influence passes from one individual to the other, through the band which connects their bodies, and thus establishes a galvanic circuit with the metals when these are brought into contact."

The paper that Dr. Bolton read to the Royal College of Surgeons was printed by Richard Taylor in Fleet Street and widely circulated throughout London in 1830. Now, it seemed, everyone was talking about Chang and Eng, and their every observed activity or overheard remark was converted into a fashionable anecdote.

For example, on the darkest and foggiest of days outdoors, they would go to their fireplace, "take a deadened coal from the grate, and, holding it up, call it the London sun." And when they witnessed their first snowfall in London, they were bewildered and asked "whether the ground was strewed with Sugar or Salt."

On one occasion, a religious visitor tried to proselytize them. "Do you know where you would go if you were to die?" the visitor inquired. Chang and Eng pointed their fingers upward. "Yes, yes, up dere," they said. To make certain they understood him, the visitor rephrased his question. "Do you know where I should go, if I were to die?" The twins nodded and pointed their fingers downward. "Yes, yes, down dere," they replied.

Many of the stories that made the rounds concerned their talent for mimicry. An effort was made to teach them to read, write, and speak English more readily. Sir Anthony Carlisle, the renowned physician, took a hand in this. One day, he brought a set of blank cards and, one at a time, printed the letters of the alphabet on them. He printed a large "A" on the first card, pointed at it, and said, "A A A." The twins imitated him, and burst into laughter. Ignoring them, he printed a "B," pronounced it, then a "C" and did the same, then a "D." The boys became impatient and restless. Exasperated, Sir Anthony exclaimed, "Pshaw, pshaw, attend to me!" Finally Sir Anthony gave Chang a blank card and told him to make an "A" on it. Because Chang held the pencil awkwardly while preparing to print the letter, Sir Anthony leaned over to position it properly in his hand. Chang quickly withdrew both pencil and hand, and sternly—mocking the physician's voice—exclaimed, "Pshaw, pshaw, attend to me!"

Apparently, the twins were making progress in learning English, for on March 6, 1830, Mrs. Coffin, who also needed some grammar lessons, wrote to her children in Boston that Chang and Eng "have learnt to speake very good English they can Converse very well." And on July 3, Captain Coffin told his children in a letter that "the Boys Chang & Eng are quite well and are very good they wish to be remembered to you they can speak English quite well."

In her letters, Mrs. Coffin provided another piece of information. Chang and Eng were not getting along with Teiu, their traveling companion from Siam, and he was being sent back to Meklong. As Mrs. Coffin informed her children in her March 6 letter, the twins "are made very much of by all that see them though the boys do not like here as they did in Boston thay say Boston the best Teiu has been a very bad boy indeed i am sorry to say it of him Mr Hunter is to send him home the boys wont spake to him they say they cant he is such a bad boy."

As the talk of the twins' sharpness and wit, their education, their break with Teiu, continued in London, there took place an incident that caused a sensation in all circles. Chang and Eng had never been shy with the opposite sex. They were very attracted by beautiful young women, and plainly there were some young women attracted by them. There was one woman in particular, and she created the sensation.

Dr. Bolton had earlier speculated on their possible involvement with a woman. "They are at present very much attached to each other," he had written, "but judging from what is now become a very common subject of discourse between them, it is not an unreasonable conjecture, that some female attachment, at a future period, may occur to destroy their harmony, and induce a mutual and paramount wish to be separated." While this conjecture proved to be true in the future, their "harmony" was not affected by their one "female attachment" in the present.

Her full name is not known to history. Her first name was Sophia. She was young and beautiful, and was a member of London society. She met the united twins and, as a pamphlet of the period reported, "by some unaccountable caprice, fell violently in love with both." Sophia pursued the twins, wrote poetry to them, and published her verse. She loved them as one, not either one separately—perhaps the perversity of it had some sexual appeal to her—but she realized the problem. As she wrote in one verse:

> How happy could I be with either,
> Were the other dear charmer away.

Despite this avowal, Sophia was willing to take both of them together in holy wedlock. She finally sought an opinion on the possibilities of such a marriage, but was firmly told that Chang and Eng were two, not one. If she married both at once she would be committing bigamy, and would be liable to arrest and a jail sentence.

The unhappy Sophia abandoned her pursuit of the twins. Later, it was said, she married someone who was one, having won "the hand and heart of a commercial gent of promising prospects and unexceptionable whiskers." More than twenty years after, a reporter who visited the twins noted: "Chang and Eng frequently refer to this episode in their eventful life, in a manner which seems to indicate that no deep impression was produced by the fair one's flattering preference, upon their deuce of hearts, notwithstanding that the lady was considered extremely popular."

Needless to say, this romantic interlude, as much as the pronouncements of the doctors and the press, helped excite public interest in Chang and Eng.

They were first shown to the paying public early in December 1830. Hale plastered London with playbills announcing their appearances, and he inserted advertisements in the major London newspapers. The advertisement on the front page of *John Bull* ("For God, the King, and the People!"), appearing below announcements of available subscriptions to concerts of the Philharmonic Society and a diorama exhibit of the interior of St. Peter's Church in Rome painted by Mr. Bouton, read:

SIAMESE YOUTHS.—These interesting Youths, whose appearance has created such intense curiosity with the Public at large, as well as among Scientific persons, may be visited daily between the hours of 12 and 4, at the EGYPTIAN HALL, PICCADILLY.—Admission a Half-a-Crown.

In their figure, countenance, manners and movements, there is nothing that can offend the delicacies of the most fastidious female—Vide Atlas, Nov. 29, 1829.

They were an instant hit. People came daily, by the hundreds, to view them. Once inside Egyptian Hall, the public could purchase a sixteen-page pamphlet written by Hale, *An Historical and Descriptive Account of the Siamese Twin Brothers from Actual Observations*. Two thousand copies of the pamphlet, at one shilling each, were sold in 1830. Arriving at the exhibition room, paying visitors could gaze upon the twins, question them, and then view their act. To their usual performance of acrobatics and weight lifting, Chang and Eng had added the difficult game of battledore and shuttlecock, which was popular in England but had originally been played in Eastern countries, among them Siam. Chang and Eng would each take a miniature racket, called a battledore, and hit a small cork ball with feathers on one side of it, called a shuttlecock, back and forth without letting it fall to the ground. Since the twins were held only four or five inches apart, the contest demanded incredible agility, and the audiences applauded this.

More than 100,000 persons saw the Siamese Twins in London, with another 200,000 paying to view them in the provinces later.

Among the celebrated persons who came to see the twins, the first and foremost was Queen Adelaide of England, the German wife of King William IV. After that a succession of royal personages trooped into Egyptian Hall to speak to Chang and Eng and enjoy their antics. There was Prince Esterhazy—known as Prince Pál Antal—who was the Austrian ambassador to England; there were, also, the Duchess of Berrí, the Duchess of Angoulême, and numerous other bluebloods. But the most famous personage to view the twins was the Duke of Wellington, who had crushed Napoleon at Waterloo fourteen years before and had recently been Prime Minister of England. The Iron Duke's visit to the twins inspired a burst of poetry in the press. One quatrain from a disgruntled reader suggested the duke might have better things to do:

> THE DUKE OF WELLINGTON AND THE SIAMESE
> Thou Waterloo Hero! though Minister Prime!
>   Whose only delight is the Nation to please;
> Tis surprising to me that your Grace should have
>   time
> A visit to pay to the young Siamese.

Later, another celebrated person, King Charles X of France, overthrown by a revolution in Paris and forced to abdicate and flee to England, visited the twins when they were on exhibition in Liverpool. Hale reported the twins' pun made when the former king "on leaving them, made them a present of a piece of gold; after he was gone, they observed that they supposed that the reason why he gave them gold, was because he had no crown."

For four hours each day during their seven months in London, Chang and Eng showed themselves and performed their act at Egyptian Hall. In the evenings, they usually relaxed in their quarters with new-made friends, whom they regaled "by relating some of the strange observations they [had] heard during the day, and in remarks upon those they [had] seen at the exhibition rooms."

Sometimes, however, there was something special to do for amusement in the evening. On Sunday, January 10, 1830, the newspaper *John Bull* carried an advertisement:

THEATRE ROYAL, DRURY-LANE.
—ON TUESDAY NEXT.

THE SIAMESE YOUTHS (who have Lord Chester-field's Box, an excellent opportunity for the Audience to see them).—Private Boxes in every part of the House. Admissions for the Season.

CHARLES WRIGHT, Haymarket

There were three shows being staged that eventful night at the Theatre Royal in Drury Lane. One was an opera, *Artaxerxes*, another a farce called *Citizen*, and the third a pantomime. But the attendance of Chang and Eng was the main attraction, and a reporter from the London *Mercury* was on hand to see their reaction and the reactions of members of the audience who had "flocked to behold the double wonder of the day."

Just before the curtain rose on the opera, Chang and Eng made their appearance in Lord Chesterfield's box. Observed the *Mercury* reporter:

A round of applause and generous welcome saluted the strangers, who seemed rather abashed, but came forward to the front of the box (next the stage, and in line with the dress boxes), and bowed modest thanks. Their appearance excited a momentary surprise, with an apparent disbelief that they were united, till the involuntary impulses of the one seemed to constrain the involuntary motions of the other. They looked like two boys, and were dressed in black jackets and trowsers. Their union could not be ascertained from the boxes; but might be inferred from the constant similarity and obsequiousness of their motions. The opera of *Artaxerxes* proceeded, and the audience were occasionally diverted from the actors on the stage to the mute but more attractive actors in the stage-box, who seemed to regard the passing scene with a mixture of curiosity and interest which betrayed great intelligence. At one time the audience seemed to doubt that the Siamese boys were really united; and at another that doubt was dissipated by the abrupt motions of the one boy suddenly exciting corresponding actions in the other. They gazed alternatingly at the actors, the audience, and occasionally when something odd or particular touched their fancy, communicated their delight or surprise to their friends near them in the boxes.

When the first act of the Opera was over, a loud huzza, and calls of "the Siamese Boys" attracted their attention, and they came forward at the instance of their friends, and bowed to the audience. It was remarked as singular how well timed and harmonious their motions were, as if springing from one common impulse. They had scarcely sat down when they observed some ladies over-head stretching out their fair necks from the boxes above to get a better view of the "strangers," when the twin on the right, who seemed the moving hero, and more active of the two, stretched forward his head, and looking up to the boxes, laughed and nodded to the fair ladies above, who half recoiled with shame and joy from such especial notice.

At the end of the evening, the reporter noted, the twins "rose, and bowing modestly in the applauses of the audience, they withdrew, highly delighted with the treat."

But mostly, such treats were rare. Their time was devoted to performing, and then, exhausted, to resting. As winter went and spring came, and the weather grew warmer, the partners in the "concern"—Hunter and Coffin—decided to try something new.

Hale was put to work, and in a few weeks there were posters everywhere in London inviting the public to share a river cruise with Chang and Eng. The public was promised an opportunity to enjoy the companionship of the twins during the steamer excursion. The poster announced: "They will each be happy to take a partner in a game of whist."

Also, either because of scheduling difficulties or to stimulate business, Hunter and Coffin moved the Siamese Twins out of Egyptian Hall and booked them into several other London auditoriums and theaters.

At one point, the twins did their act at Lewis' Great Sale Room, a huge hall rented out for exhibitions of every kind. Another time, they headed an all-star show at the Surrey Theatre. In his advertisements for the twins' debut at the Surrey, the manager boasted that he had "prevailed upon Captain Coffin to permit The Siamese Youths to appear on the stage IN THEIR NATIVE COSTUME!"

While normally they had little competition in London, the twins' appearance at the Surrey Theatre put them up against two of the major attractions of the day. After they had done their number, they were followed on stage by fifty-six-year-old Robert William Elliston. Not only was Elliston the manager of the Surrey—he loved promoting shows, and made and lost several fortunes as an impresario—but he was one of the leading Shakespearean actors of the period, ranked second only to the great Garrick according to Leigh Hunt. "Whenever Elliston walked, sat, or stood still," said Lamb, "there was the theatre." He specialized in doing Hamlet, Romeo, and Falstaff, and undoubtedly performed excerpts from some of those roles the evening he appeared with the twins.

The other star performer to follow Chang and Eng was an Irish child prodigy, the twelve-year-old Master Burke, who also rendered Shakespearean excerpts, doing Shylock and Richard III, as well as a musical number in which he played "God Save the King" on a violin with one string.

During the passage of winter, Chang and Eng's London successes had been publicized throughout the British Isles. Eager new audiences outside the city awaited their appearance. After they had made several forays into the hinterlands, Hunter and Coffin decided that spring was the right time to take their attraction on a major road tour.

For the twins, this was to be their first experience with brief one-night and one-week stands, a grinding journey of stops and starts filled with seemingly endless jolting coach rides over rutted country roads, with strange and ever-changing scenery, with a variety of wayside and city lodgings, and with a multitude of peering fresh faces.

Between this extended trip and their later jaunts outside London, the twins covered 2,500 miles in England, Scotland, and Ireland.

Now, in horse-drawn public stagecoaches, accompanied by Robert Hunter and Captain Coffin, Chang and Eng set out on the road. Hale had preceded them by some days, renting exhibition halls and living accommodations, and papering the villages and cities along the route with posters extolling the wonder of the "Siamese Youths, United Brothers" who had been such a sensation in London.

After successes in Bath, Windsor, Reading, Oxford, Birmingham, and Liverpool, Chang and Eng boarded a ship and continued on to Scotland. The first stop was Glasgow, where the twins enjoyed a happy social diversion. Before they left London, Robert Hunter had reminded them that they must see his family, who lived in Glasgow and would be expecting them. Susan Coffin wrote to her children, after returning to Liverpool with the twins on September 27:

"As your dear Mother has got to Liverpool i feel as if i was much nearer to you than when i was in Scotland an Ireland. . . . i thinke my dear A and Susan would like to know if their Mother had a pleasant time while i was in Scotland i had indeed your Mother found Mr. Hunters Family very nice people they scold me for not bringing my dear children i told them the next time I came to Scotland i would. . . . Chang Eng says i must send thier love to all the Newbury Port folks and want to know if I thinks Elisabeth B [a family friend] is as fat as ever say you must tell her when they come to America again they can talk English to her and if thier is such a gang about the house they will help her put them out doors and flog them."

The sight of the twins in Glasgow stirred one person who had met them, a Miss Janet Hunter, very likely a relative of Robert Hunter, to engage in poetic rhapsodies. Two of several verses which found their way into print read:

> Ye strange phenomena of nature,
>   Your like auld Scotia ne'er did see,
> The same in visage, shape and stature,
>   In mind (they say) you too agree.
>
> Ye dear and close connected brithers,
>   Sent to the warl' thegither knit,
> Your bond o' union beats a' ithers,
>   We ere have seen or herd o' yet.

Following their exhibitions in Glasgow, the twins went on to Edinburgh, a rough but hospitable city in which mob violence simmered but was contained by the civil police, a city in which only two noblemen maintained residences (the rest had country places), a hard-drinking city of taverns and inns where whiskey and port and claret flowed freely, a city where concerts and theaters provided routine entertainment. Chang and Eng were something new, and Hale went to the limit of his advertising budget to promote their appearance.

Seventy-two hours after the twins had opened in the Waterloo Rooms, their exhibition hall in Edinburgh, the Edinburgh *Evening Courant* was able to report that the twins "have attracted very great crowds both of ladies and gentlemen." A writer for *The Scotsman* of Edinburgh visited Chang and Eng, and then spoke philosophically about their condition in his article of July 31:

". . . these two beings are destined to pass through life united in an indissoluble tie, subjected to the same influences, exposed to the same dangers, partakers in the same pleasures, and actors in the same scenes. Whatever the one *wills* to do, the other must also will; whatever injures the one, must in its ultimate consequences injure the other also; and whenever the one happens to be gay and inclined for sport, the other must be ready to respond to his feelings; or misery to both would be the inevitable result. To love his brother as himself, is, in short, the only condition on which the existence of either can be tolerable, and it is very gratifying to perceive, that accordingly they do live on the best terms, and seem as happy as being so circumstanced can possibly be . . ."

After the twins had received this attention in Edinburgh, and had made two brief side visits to Perth and Dundee, Captain Coffin and Robert Hunter brought them back to Glasgow. There they all boarded a ship to cross the Irish Sea for a well-publicized engagement in Dublin.

During the twins' exhibition in Dublin, the *Irish Paper* devoted two lengthy articles to them. The readers were told that the twins had fully adapted themselves to the English way of life: "Were their mother with them, they say they would have no particular desire to revisit Siam. They often declare she would be astonished to see how much like little kings they now live; and that, if they return home, they must have an English cook and an English house to reside in."

Irish readers were then treated to a graphic account of their nocturnal habits: "While sleeping they are not confined to any particular position, but rest on either side, as may best suit their convenience, generally, however, with their faces toward each other. They usually sleep from nine to eleven hours each night, and quite soundly. When they feel restless and desire to change their posture, the one must roll entirely over the other, and they have frequently been observed to do this without either waking or being apparently disturbed by the change."

After Dublin, Chang and Eng performed in several other Irish cities, including Belfast. They enjoyed bantering with their Irish visitors. In Belfast, the city's mayor, or sovereign, came to see them. Hale introduced the sovereign to them.

Chang eyed the high official and said to him, "You are not a sovereign. You are only nineteen shillings."

Hale said quickly, "He is the sovereign of this place, and you will offend him by your remarks."

"Did he not pay a shilling at the door?" Eng asked.

Hale laughed. "Yes, but he may be displeased by your freedom."

"Tell him not to be vexed," said Chang hastily. "We will give him two shillings, and make a *guinea* of him."

After three weeks in Ireland, Coffin and the twins took a ship back to Liverpool. Now they resumed their short stands. They exhibited in Manchester, Leeds (where the local press said they "excited the greatest astonishment"), York, and Sheffield, and then returned to Birmingham.

On December 28, 1830, Chang and Eng were happily back in wintry London.

Susan Coffin wrote to her children: "I now inform you that your dear Father an Mother is back in London we have been on the move 8 months all over the kingdom and when we go from here it is uncertain your papa wish to go to France but he is not decied what to do yet. . . . Chang Eng send their love to you all say next Spring they hope to see you all in America . . . my dear Abel must tell the Doctor of that it will please him Chang Eng has gaind 30 pounds of flesh since they came to England."

Posted at the same time as Mrs. Coffin's letter was a note from Captain Coffin to his children. "I am going to the East Indies," he wrote them, "and expect to be gone about one year. Your Dear Mother & Chang, Eng I hope will be in New York in two & halfe months I hope you will try and comfort your Mother and by your good behavior compensate in part for my absence for I am going to get something to pay for your education, for which I only ask your good behaviour and attention to your studies . . ."

At this time, too, Chang and Eng were forced to bid farewell to their discoverer, Robert Hunter, who informed them he was leaving for Singapore to resume work with his import firm. Before parting from the twins, Hunter told them that after catching up with his work in Singapore, he would go on to Bangkok, and he promised to visit their family. Moved,

Chang and Eng gave Hunter messages and gifts for their mother, sister, and brother in Meklong.

After Hunter left, Captain Coffin lingered on briefly. Before departing for the East Indies, he made the decision that he would like to exhibit Chang and Eng across the Channel in France. He contacted a twin enthusiast in Paris, Étienne Geoffroy Saint-Hilaire, creator of a branch of science known as teratology, the study of monstrosities. Geoffroy Saint-Hilaire believed it would be instructive to have the united brothers shown to the French public. In all haste, Geoffroy Saint-Hilaire applied to the French police for an entry visa and permit for them. He did not have to wait long for a reply. The French police promptly and categorically turned down the application. Indignant at the refusal, Geoffroy Saint-Hilaire reported to Captain Coffin that his "monsters," as the police had characterized the twins, would not be allowed into France. Such an exhibit, the officials had said, might "deprave" the minds of children, and through "maternal impressions" might also be harmful to pregnant women who attended such a showing since it could deform their unborn children.

The rejection by the French police, based on an old superstition that had no basis in fact, made Captain Coffin alter his plans for the twins. He decided to have Hale arrange a few more special exhibits in London, and then take the twins back to the United States two months earlier than planned.

Leaving Mrs. Coffin and Hale in charge of Chang and Eng, Captain Coffin embarked on the *Hellen Mar* to resume his trading business in the East Indies. Off Deal, England, on January 8, 1831, he wrote a letter to his wife: ". . . be kind to Chang Eng but you must not let them have to much their own head it is necessary to have them mind you I feel convinced Mr Hale will do everything you wish as to his capability & honesty I have had sufficient proof to be easy on those points.

"Give my respects to Mr Hale and my love to Chang Eng tell them although they might think I was hard with them I think their own good sence will convince them that I have never done anything but what is for their good that I hope they will be kind to you and that you will be as happy as possible . . ."

The hint in this letter that Captain Coffin might have been "hard" on Chang and Eng, and that they resented it, was never fully explained. Coffin may have been referring to any number of things—that the twins were annoyed with him because he had brought them to England in steerage, or that he was miserly about giving them extra money, or that he had pushed them almost beyond their endurance during the British tour, or that he was too strict a disciplinarian. Whatever Chang and Eng felt about Captain Coffin would soon be intensified by their attitude toward Mrs. Coffin, who was now serving as their guardian and employer.

During their last weeks in England, they were compliant and went through their performances without protest. The final exhibit of Chang and Eng on this English tour was held at Lewis' Great Sale Room early in January 1831. Their farewell poster read:

POSITIVELY LEAVE
FOR AMERICA ON WEDNESDAY
January 12th.
SIAMESE YOUTHS
UNITED BROTHERS
In consequence of the detention
of the Vessel in which they embark for
America they will remain Until
Wednesday January 12th at
15 POULTRY
Hours of exhibitions from eleven to four
Admission One Shilling Each
Historical Books with full length Portraits
Sixpence each

In the week that followed, on the very eve of their departure from England, Chang and Eng had a serious falling-out with Mrs. Coffin over a trifle—what they called "a piece of blue cloth"—which they felt involved their honor.

Even eighteen months later, Chang and Eng would recall every detail of the incident that occurred that last week in England. Reviving the incident for a friend of Mrs. Coffin's, they wrote, in first person singular as usual:

When I was at Leeds a gentleman at Leeds sent me a piece of beautiful blue cloth to make me two suits of clothes. This piece of cloth I intended to lay aside & keep to take home with me (as it was no concern of mine providing my own clothes then) but Captn C *persuaded* me in Birmingham to have two suits of clothes made out of it, telling me that when I go home he would give me as good a piece of cloth. The two suits were made & there remained about 2½ or 3 yards of the cloth. When we returned to London we took up our quarters at Mr. Kipling's in the Poultry & I received so much civility from Mr. & Mrs. Kipling that I became quite attached to them; before I left London for Portsmouth to take passage for the United States I gave her (Mrs. Kipling) the piece of cloth which remained (for working as I had been for the benefit of others it was no pleasure nor profit to me to find my own clothes). At Portsmouth I told Mrs. Coffin that I had given the cloth to Mrs. Kipling—at which Mrs. Coffin was considerably vexed; saying that Captn. Coffin set a great store by that piece of cloth & would be angry when he came home & found that I had given it away;—To this I replied, that the piece of cloth was too much for one suit of clothes & not enough for two & that it was as well for me to give to one for whom I entertained so high a respect as I did for Mrs. Kipling; for much as she was disliked by others I had every cause to respect her—The course pursued by Mrs. Coffin with regard to this piece of cloth (which you will please to recollect was *mine* & *not* hers) was such as few *could believe*. She made Mr. Hale sit down and write a letter to James Everett [a friend of the Coffins' in London] asking him to call on Mrs. Kipling & get back the piece of cloth. Mrs. Kipling however, knowing me to be incapable of such crooked conduct as to give a thing *one* day & ask it back the *next*, told James Everett that if I (Chang-Eng) wanted the piece of cloth she would willingly give it up but not otherwise. When Mrs. Coffin asked Mr. Hale to write to Jas. Everett about this cloth—she cautioned Mr. Hale not to let C-E know anything about it—for that, if they knew it, they would be very angry. Mr. Hale said—then why do you write if C E will be angry? To this Mrs. Coffin made no reply except to repeat her request that he would write the letter—which was accordingly done. It was fortunate for me that I had in this case to do with such a clever straightforward woman as Mrs. Kipling for she saw thro' the matter directly & suspected that the application for the cloth was made without my authority & she consequently refused to give it up; otherwise I should have felt quite provoked at being thought so mean & pitiful as to give a thing one day & ask it back the next.

I have no doubt in my own mind that if Mrs. C had got it back from Mrs. Kipling she would have kept it for her own purposes—as she would have been ashamed to let me know that she had got it back. We can judge pretty well of persons conduct in matters of importance by the manner in which they behave in trifles—and I could not then nor can I now forget or forgive the mean, pitiful paltry *trick attempted to be played on me in this matter.*

Thus, brimming with anger at their new mentor, Chang and Eng, who had come to Portsmouth from London, boarded the vessel *Cambria* under Captain Moore the latter part of January to sail to the United States. After almost fourteen months in the British Isles—they had arrived well known, and had left famous—they were on the Atlantic and headed for the place they now called "home."

They landed in New York City on March 4, 1831. They may have had an idea, but could not know for certain, what momentous times lay ahead for them. They knew that in America they would once more be on the road. They did not know it would be freedom's road.

4
CHAPTER
4

America the Beautiful

There was to be no rest for Chang and Eng. No sooner had they arrived in the United States—after fourteen tiring months of exhibits in England, Scotland, and Ireland—than they were put right to work again.

The person who put them right to work was Mrs. Susan Coffin, wife of Captain Abel Coffin.

A change in the management of the Siamese Twins had occurred before or upon their return to the United States. Robert Hunter had decided to give up his partnership in the twins. He had sold out his half-interest to Captain Coffin. And Coffin, eager to resume pursuing his own commercial enterprises in the East Indies, had delegated control of Chang and Eng to his wife Susan and to a seafaring friend, Captain William Davis, Jr., who was to serve as Mrs. Coffin's assistant.

Having retained James Hale as the twins' business agent, Mrs. Coffin hastened back to Boston for a reunion with her two children. She had ordered Hale to keep in touch with her through Captain Davis, who made his home in Newburyport, Massachusetts. As for Hale, he was unhappy about the arrangement. He did not like the pressure he was under. He had been apart from his wife Almira and his children for a long time, and he wanted an interlude with his family. This he was not given. Furthermore, Hale, who had tolerated Mrs. Coffin until now, was angry because she had been rude to his wife. Nevertheless, he realized that until he could find something better, there was a job to be done, and he set out to do it.

Chang and Eng launched their first thorough American tour when they opened in New York City on March 15, 1831. There were contradictory reports about the success of their second appearance. According to an 1853 pamphlet, the twins were once again a hit attraction. Their recent success in the British Isles had "served greatly to stimulate the curiosity of the New York public." The author went on to say that "their levees were now more densely thronged than ever. An absurd story that their union had been discovered to be a deception, which obtained some credence about this time, only served to increase their receipts, as those who were inclined to believe it, were sure to visit them, and confirm or dispel their doubts by occular demonstration."

However, another version of the twins' success during their opening two weeks in New York was given by James Hale in a letter to Mrs. Coffin dated March 31, 1831: "The weather has been very stormy here, since you left *at times* so that the walking is bad—We have not had *forty ladies* since we opened—they you know are our best customers, if we can get them —Our receipts have averaged but $20 per day—and two nights at the Theatre paid $50 per night amounting in all—15 days to 424 dollars. . . . I expect to go to Philadelphia on Sunday next and try it there, and feel afraid on coming back we shall have to come down to 25 cents to make money—"

While worried about the admission price to see the Siamese Twins, Hale was more concerned about his own family. He apologized for having had to leave the twins for a day to visit his wife and two children in Boston, but his children were ailing and he was anxious about them. Then he told Mrs. Coffin: "Chang Eng are well and desire to be remembered to you—they wish if you know any one going to Phila to send them the 'Book about playing Chess'—their '4 blade penknife, in a morocco case,' and 'a Bible'—Their shirts answer very well—we have had Caroline and Josephine [daughters of a friend] here to overhaul Chang Eng's clothes . . ."

In a few days, Chang and Eng left for Philadelphia and the beginning of their virtually nonstop eight years on the road.

Until then, Chang and Eng had had only a brief glimpse of one corner of the United States. After they had first landed in Boston in 1829, they had exhibited in four American cities. Now, on the new tour, they would cover almost every hamlet, village, and city where entertainment was feasible, in fourteen out of twenty states in the nation. They would be almost continually on the move for eight years, crisscrossing the East, Midwest, and South, as well as venturing into Canada and traveling down to Cuba.

At the start, they traveled by regular stagecoach, occasionally by boat or train, but soon Mrs. Coffin realized that public conveyances gave too many members of the potential paying audiences a free sight of the twins. To rectify this, she invested in a private enclosed buggy for the boys, a wagon for their baggage, and three horses, and hired an extra man named Tom Dwyer to travel with them and assist them when Hale moved ahead of the caravan to arrange and promote bookings.

For Hale and the Siamese Twins, the time on the road was often a lonely time, and the only way they could keep in touch with their employers and friends was by correspondence. Their personal letters give an unretouched portrait of Chang and Eng as they were in their youth, revealing their moods and personal problems. They also present a down-to-earth picture of show business in America as it existed in the early 1830s, as well as a candid picture of life in the back roads of the nation in that period of history. In addition to the letters, there is also a daily expense book that the twins' manager kept for them from 1832 through 1839. How they spent their money day by day often gives valuable insights into their habits and personalities.

These hectic years, mostly passed in the backwaters of the adolescent United States, were catalytic years for Chang and Eng. In that time they became mature, independent, sophisticated, and their conversion from Siamese boys to American men was completed.

Their tour began with the showing in New York City. There, the indefatigable diarist Philip Hone paid to see them and noted in the opening of the fourth volume of his journal: "MARCH 15.—Went this morning to see the Siamese boys, who returned last week from England . . . their dispositions and their very thoughts are alike; when one is sick the other partakes of his illness, and the stroke of death will, no doubt, lay them both in the same grave; and yet their bodies, heads, and limbs are all perfect and distinct. They speak English tolerably well, and appear fond of talking."

Now the twins' travels were under way with their second visit to Philadelphia. Mrs. Susan Coffin came down from Boston to join them there. Chang and Eng were exhibited in a city theater, and they slept at night in a drafty back room of the Masonic Hall where Hale had set up two beds, one for the twins and one for himself. Food was purchased and brought in from a boardinghouse located at the rear of the Masonic Hall. Business was good, but not as good as it had been in Philadelphia a year and a half earlier. As Hale wrote to Captain Davis' sister on April 12:

"Chang Eng are quite well, excepting for the last two or three days they have had a small touch of their old complaint, the bellyache but that I hope will soon go off.—

"I have been two nights to the principal Theater

with them, & the night is to be announced for their benefit—I get one half the receipts of tonight.—We have done very well here, but do not come up to the week we were here before."

During the next five months, traveling through New England, then in the South, and then in New England again, Chang and Eng started to show signs of irritation toward their audiences. Mrs. Coffin commuted from Boston to wherever they were on exhibit to give advice and check the gate receipts and alternatingly flirt with Hale or berate him or attack his wife. Also, the natural tensions caused by constant travel, endless performances, and strange boardinghouses were having their effects on the twins. Furthermore, the twins were becoming less and less amused by spectators who failed to regard them as human beings. In the recent past, they had been good-natured about the insensitive inquiries and remarks made by audiences. But gradually their humor soured, and their tempers surfaced.

The fact that trouble was brewing should have been evident when Chang and Eng exhibited in Exeter, Massachusetts. There, a local physician, viewing them, wondered aloud if the twins were "identical or separate." The physician told Chang that he would like to stick a pin in his left shoulder to see what effect it would have on Eng. "If you stick a pin in me," snapped Chang, "my brother Eng might knock you down."

Soon enough, the twins *were* knocking people down. During a showing in Athens, Alabama, they were seated on a platform before an audience when a doctor emerged from the audience and approached them. He asked if he might examine their connecting band. The twins were aghast at the request. While they had often allowed their ligament to be examined by physicians or reporters in private, the idea of permitting such an examination in public appalled them. Curtly, they told the doctor he could not touch the band.

Infuriated by the rebuff, the doctor loudly accused

them of being a fraud. He then turned to the audience and shouted that the united twins were really two separate people and that everyone present was being cheated. The twins reacted instantly, both hitting the doctor with their fists. The doctor toppled to the floor. At once, everyone in the hall was on his feet, some spectators siding with the doctor, others with the twins. People rushed forward to attack both the twins, others to attack the doctor, while still others fought among themselves. Not only fists flew, but chairs and stools were thrown, and one spectator doused the twins with a pot of water. Chang and Eng desperately tried to escape the riot but failed, and they might have been seriously injured had not the police arrived. After a brief confusion, the police released the offending doctor, but arrested Chang and Eng for assault. They were fined $350 before being discharged. They also made note of an added expense: "Judge Posey for inserting C.H.'s statement of the Athens affray in Florence Gazette $2."

On another visit to Philadelphia, the fact that the twins were genuinely united saved them from a fine or jail. A spectator, shaking hands with Chang, squeezed his hand painfully hard. Immediately, Chang punched him, knocking him off his feet. The man rose, summoned the law, and the twins were hauled before a magistrate on a charge of assault and battery. The magistrate, after studying the twins' connecting band, addressed the complainant. The judge agreed that Chang could be jailed for assault, but added that if Eng were also jailed it would amount to false arrest and the complainant himself would have to be prosecuted. Needless to say, the injured party dropped his charges.

Around this time, Chang and Eng, accompanied by Hale, took a vacation in Lynnfield, Massachusetts. The twins were edgy—from overwork, from constant feuding with Mrs. Coffin—and they wanted to find some isolation and peace. Instead, they found trouble. A headline and story in the Salem *Mercury* told what happened:

ARREST OF THE SIAM YOUTHS

Chang and Eng, the Siamese Twins, were arrested on a warrant from a magistrate for a breach of the peace at Lynnfield, on Monday last, and bound over to be of good behaviour and to keep the peace, in the sum of two hundred dollars. They have for a few days past been rusticating for recreation, and staying at the Lynnfield-hotel, so as to enjoy the sports of fishing on the pond and shooting in the woods. The neighbouring inhabitants have had a very eager curiosity to catch a glimpse of their movements while on their excursions, and have sometimes been rather troublesomely obtrusive to the Siamese, whose object was seclusion. Last Saturday afternoon [when] they were in the fields, shooting, each with his fowling piece, a considerable number, fifteen or twenty idle persons, followed to observe their motions, and some of the men or boys were probably obtrusive and impertinent. Two persons from Stoneham, Colonel Elbridge Gerry and Mr. Prescott, went towards them in the field, after they had been harrassed and irritated considerably by others;—the attendant of the Siamese [Hale] requested these persons to keep off, and by way of bravado threatened that, if they did not, the Siamese would fire at them. The Colonel opened his waistcoat and dared them or him to fire, but they did not—The Colonel then indiscreetly accused them or him of telling a lie—The attendant spoke to the Siamese about the charge of lying—they exclaimed "He accuse us of lying!" and one of them struck the Colonel with the butt of his gun; the Colonel snatched up a heavy stone and threw it at the Siamese, hit him on the head, broke through his leather cap, and made the blood flow; the Siamese then wheeled and fired by platoon at the Colonel, who was horribly frightened, as most other people would have been, though it turned out afterwards that their pieces were charged only with powder. The noise and smoke were just as great as if they had been loaded with ball. The Siamese went immediately into the Hotel and loaded with ball—the Colonel and Mr. Prescott learning this were greatly alarmed, and endeavoured to keep out of the way.

Mr. Prescott fled to the barn, and secreted himself in a hay-mow. The Colonel went to Danvers and lodged a complaint against the Siamese and their attendant, a young Englishman, for breach of the peace. An officer went to arrest them, but by the interposition of a gentleman, who happened to be at the Hotel a truce was concluded. On Monday, however, Prescott made complaint to Mr. Justice Savage of this town, and they were taken before him and bound over.

There was no escape from staring faces, and after paying their $200 fine the twins went back to work.

Meanwhile, James Hale was having his own problems. He liked Chang and Eng, and despite the pressures of handling them and the difficulties they were getting into, he got along well with them. They were not his main problem. Hale's main problem—in fact, most of his difficulties—came from his employer, Mrs. Susan Coffin. Hale resented the insulting manner in which Mrs. Coffin had frequently spoken of his wife. And he suspected that Mrs. Coffin accompanied him on some of the travels to make his wife jealous. Finally, he was angered by Mrs. Coffin's charges that he was neglecting Chang and Eng.

By September 1831, having had his fill of Mrs. Coffin and ready to quit if her harassment continued, Hale, arriving in Portland, Maine, from Boston, sat down to address a letter to Captain Davis:

Now after [I have] said all that I can about business, I am obliged to enter upon a topic which no doubt will cause you as unpleasant feelings to read as it does me to write upon, but as I feel that my duty requires it, I shall say what I wish, expecting it will be communicated through you to Mrs. Coffin.

I will not say a word upon which I consider to be an outrage upon hospitality, respecting Mrs. C's treatment of my wife after I left N.P. [Newburyport] let her own heart answer to herself, but I do most sincerely reprobate her conduct in laying before her, what she certainly had no right to do to a wife what Mrs. Coffin was pleased to call my errors.

She informed her, and that too when ill, that I was not half the man I was when in England, that I could not attend to *her* business and to my family also, and that Chang Eng were most shamefully neglected while in Boston, because she (Mrs. H) took up much of my time—that she was at liberty to turn me away at any moment, and that if things did not go on strait, I very well knew the consequences—with many other remarks of the like nature. Now, Capt Davis, supposing all that she said to be perfectly true, which by the bye I do not allow, but allowing it for a moment, what right has she to tamper with the feelings of my wife in that way, or rather why so *insult* her, and under her own roof too? If she has fault to find, let her do it to me, but no, to me everything is always smooth, and I have frequently heard that she has said that I was a very good man to conduct the business, and I have *more* frequently heard of her telling that she could turn me away at any moment, and that probably I never should get so good a situation again. If a "good man," why tell the consequences of behaving ill? It is damned hard, after completely ruining my constitution for her husband's interests, when I am doing in the United States *alone* that which in England was performed by Capt. Coffin, myself, and generally another, it is hard to hear these insinuations and to have my own wife insulted too by them. That Mrs C has insulted her before me more than twenty times, is a fact, and I like a fool took no notice, because I did not wish to quarrel with the wife of my employer. But it must be so no longer, if she considers me worthy the confidence placed in me by Capt. Coffin, then let me manage my own business in my own way, without any interference, and when I have surplus funds it will always be written, but I have seen these things done so frequently that I cannot suppose they will now cease —therefore, as I agreed with Capt. Coffin to give a week's notice before leaving, *I now do it*, and request that some one may be sent to examine & settle my accounts and take the charge off my hands, of which I assure you I am most heartily tired. Should it be wished for me to remain, I will still endeavor to do as heretofore and use my undiminished energies for the concern and in that case I shall be most happy to write to and hear from *you*, but as I cannot be at peace with Mrs. Coffin I must from this time decline any further intercourse with her, either personally or by letter.

When in N. Port I took an opportunity of doing what I thought my duty, to Mrs. Coffin, alone—I told her of many reports in circulation which I thought injurious to her character and to mine too that it was thought strange that she should wish to be travelling about the country with me, meeting me at various places &etc. Now altho' these stories are very foolish, still I should hardly think she would wish to brave public opinion but she says she cares not a cent for the opinion of the world, she shall go when and where she likes. Now this is very *independent* but is it the course a prudent woman would pursue who wishes to sustain an honourable situation in society? Mrs. C probably thinking to harass Mrs. Hale with it told her she believed she *should* go to Portland while we were there altho' much was said against it, and declared her determination to go where she chose with me. Was this treating Mrs. H kindly or was it endeavoring to excite in her the worst of all feeling, jealousy? I think you will be able to judge —I strongly advised Mrs. C *not* to come to Portland, as Chang Eng had often said they did not wish her or any other woman to be with them and I thought it better to silence idle tales at once by her not coming at present, but without effect, she should do as she pleased in spite of any body. I will now say to you friend D. that when Mrs. C. comes to Portland, I quit it with pleasure. I do not wish to be thought to threaten, because I had rather quit than not—but I wish to have it most distinctly understood that I am no longer to be led by the nose by her. I will stay if it is wished, and I shall if I stay endeavor still to exert myself for the interest of Capt Coffin, for whom I shall ever cherish the highest regard, for to me he was always a friend—but we owe each other nothing, *he* has been a friend to me, *I* have done my duty to him—therefore the a/c is balanced, and I should always hope to be on friendly terms with *him* but I *will not* be ill-treated any longer by his wife.

Hale and the twins remained in Portland for ten days. The day before leaving to exhibit Chang and Eng in Dover, New Hampshire, Hale wrote a letter to a friend, Charles Harris, who lived in a boarding-house in Newburgh, New York. Hale had apparently struck up a friendship with Harris, an Irishman, while touring with the twins in England. When Harris came to the United States to seek his fortune, the friend-ship resumed. The two men corresponded regularly during the time Hale was on the road with the twins. Evidently, Harris had written Hale in Portland that he was down on his luck, doing poorly, and therefore planning to return to England. Now, in an effort to dissuade his friend from returning "across the Pond," and worried about Harris' bad fortune and shortage of funds, Hale was writing to offer him a $100 loan. In the letter Hale expanded on his own future plans, which he had already confided to Harris.

First, Hale brought his friend up to date on his relationship with his employer. "I have been so dis-gusted lately with the improper conduct of Mrs. Coffin, and so offended with her for her insulting treatment of Mrs. Hale, that I have written a very severe letter to her, and have cut all connexion with her either personally or by letter—I gave her either that alternative or promised to quit—So I have no more trouble with the old hag."

Hale then confided that he was going to quit work-ing for Mrs. Coffin within seven months and take over as proprietor of an inn or tavern he had just purchased in Lynnfield, Massachusetts. He was going to become a "Boniface," he told Harris, "and set up my staff in mine own habitation, and *locate* as 'mine host' of Lynnfield . . . in May next to hang out the bloody flag near the battle ground in Lynnfield 'fam'd for deeds of arms'—and I think for a device shall have the valiant Colonel in battle array with the Sammeneses." Since Harris was "a *liquorish* fellow," Hale invited him to enjoy "board and liquors" as his guest for a year, or longer if he wished. Apparently, Chang and Eng also knew and liked Harris, for in concluding his letter Hale wrote, "C. Eng desire their love and thank you for your kind remembrance of them—they say 'its no use to say much to the feller, as I expect to see him soon in N. York.' "

Hale moved the twins on to Dover, where business was not good, then on to Boston. Hale's real purpose in returning to Boston was to have a confrontation with Captain Davis, to whom he wrote: "I do not feel that I can consistently travel much longer, my health is suffering so much. There is no mistake about this I assure you and I should feel very sorry to leave them if you could not get anyone who would answer the purpose as well as myself. However no doubt we could make everything right when I see you—and I hope that while I am with them I shall not give cause for any more grumbling."

It may be inferred from the ensuing correspondence that the meeting in Boston between James Hale and Captain Davis was crucial. Despite his affection for Chang and Eng, Hale could endure the tour no longer. He was tired of the rain and sleet, tired of the perpetual movement, and tired of the ever-hovering presence of Susan Coffin. In Boston, either Hale quit on the spot or gave notice that he intended to quit shortly thereafter. Certainly by October 1831, Hale's professional relationship with Chang and Eng had ended for the time being, although he would surface again later.

A successor to Hale was needed immediately to manage the twins. Hale knew someone who needed a job, who would be as competent as he himself at his work. Undoubtedly, it was Hale who recommended that his confidant, Charles Harris, become the new manager of Chang and Eng.

Harris came from Newburgh, New York, either to New York City or Boston to have an interview with Susan Coffin. The interview went well, for immediately after it a contract was signed between the two parties. The contract began:

"It is mutually agreed between A. C. Coffin on the one part and Charles Harris on the other part that the said Abel Coffin doth agree with the said C. Harris, that he is to take charge of the Siamese Youths on the following conditions that the said Mr. C affording to pay the said Charles Harris the sum of Fifty Dollars per month, for the time he is employed in the services of attending the youths . . ."

There is no evidence that the changeover in management troubled Chang and Eng in any way. They had become used to James Hale, dependent on him, and they cared about him, but they had known Charles Harris socially and liked him also. Harris, born in Ireland, was thirty years old when he took over the twins. Although trained as an accountant, Harris listed himself as a doctor in a passport obtained in 1835. In fact, the twins always addressed him and referred to him as "Doctor."

With a fond farewell, Hale left to rejoin his Almira and their two children, and the twins set off with Charles Harris to resume their tour.

A prolific letter writer, Harris bombarded Captain Davis with communiqués for Mrs. Coffin, detailing the troupe's progress. More carefully than Hale, he recounted summaries of their travels, their business, the needs and activities of Chang and Eng. By November 20, 1831, Harris and the twins were in Pawtucket, Rhode Island, where he started a letter which he concluded a week later in Norwich, Connecticut:

I wrote to you that our success in Providence was very doubtful. I am sorry to say that my forboding on the subject were but too fully realized—for our receipts did not pay our expenses—If we had not advertised that we would remain there until Thursday 17th I really think Chang-Eng would have been pleased to clear out the second day—but having reckoned on a good business—we thought it better to fix a certain time to stay in the Place & so have time to settle our arrangements for other places—And having fixed on a Certain number of days to stop it would have made us appear ridiculous to have left before that number of days had expired—On Friday morning we left Providence & got to Woonsocket Village for breakfast. We stopped there until the morning & did a very satisfactory business having a good deal of company and a very moderate bill.

We left Woonsocket Village this Morning & got to the Inn here [Pawtucket, Rhode Island] about 11 o'clock—we hope to do a good good business here on Monday & Tuesday & on Wednesday morning we shall start for Centreville a Village about 10 miles south of Providence...

A week later, Harris was writing:

I shall . . . now give you an account of our proceedings since we reached Pawtucket. We continued there on Monday & Tuesday & did a very good business—On Wednesday morning we rode thro' Providence to a small Village which is eleven miles south of it—where we continued until Friday morning—when we left for this City [Norwich].—

At Centreville I expected to have done a good business—but in this was much disappointed, which arose from the very uncomfortable state of the Weather —as it blew a keen frosty wind all the Time, and the population is scattered in Villages, some as near as one mile & others as far as four miles distant from Centreville. . . . A good business might be done in Summer—but under the circumstances in which we are placed I thought we were lucky in getting as much as paid our bill—On Friday we left Centreville & reached this City at 8 o'clock on the same evening; having travelled 39 miles in 12 Hours—We rested our Horses twice on the road & dined at Plainfield—but the evening was dark and we found it very uncomfortable during the last two hours of our ride. . . . We shall remain here until Wednesday morning & then start for New London where we intend to remain until Sunday morning on which day we hope to travel some distance on the way to New Haven—but I don't think we shall do any business after we leave New London until we reach the Village of Bridgeport in Connecticut which is about 16 Miles from New Haven & nearer New York—After we leave Bridgeport I am unable to tell you where we shall be found—but we calculate on making a short pause at Newark in New Jersey. . . .

I am glad you think that we have got on well—since I have been with Chang-Eng—I have the satisfaction to say that we are all anxious to do a good business & if we do not succeed—I don't think it will be the fault of any of the party—I am happy to find that Mrs. Coffin is pleased with our progress & our doings; Our balance up to last Evening was $222—but of this $112 will be due on the 1st of December for the pay of our *Squadron* . . .

With business out of the way, Harris went into personal matters. He sent regards to the twins' regular physician in Newburyport, Dr. John Brickett, and then added for the doctor and the others:

"At present I have nothing to say that would interest him. We are all well except Mr. Dwier [Tom Dwyer, the troupe's extra man] who has a slight cold—In consequence of the Severity of the Weather—I have purchased two comfortable Buffalo Robes & 2 warm fur caps for Chang-Eng—I am having a suit of blue clothes made for them in this City they are to cost $41—The blue cloth which they chose is a good color of a most excellent texture—They made as good a bargain with the tradesman as they could & I hope they will take good care of them when they get their new Clothes."

As in most of his letters, Harris passed on the good wishes of Chang and Eng to the many friends they had made in Newburyport. And he reminded Mrs. Coffin to send Chang and Eng "Seven of their new Cotton shirts & four pair of their thick, *long* woollen stockings."

There was one more friend the twins had on their minds. As they had left pets behind in Siam, they also had left pets in Newburyport, and one was a favorite rabbit named Tom. Wrote Harris: "Chang-Eng wish to know how their little pet 'Tom' is—they wish to know if he has as yet got a wife—as the weather gets cold."

When the party reached Bridgeport, Connecticut, nine days later, the winter was fully upon them. In Norwich, despite "the very extreme severity of the Weather," they did a fairly good business. In New London, the snow fell heavily and the thermometer dropped close to freezing, and they did "poor business—but we took enough to pay our bills & to give us a small remnant to carry with us." After crossing the Connecticut River, they covered thirty-eight miles between early morning and sunset before reaching Guilford. "We had our horses prepared for the snow before we left New London—and although a good deal of snow had fallen, yet the road was tolerably good for Wheel carriages." The next day they headed for New Haven, there rested their horses overnight, and went on into Bridgeport. Harris reported:

"Chang-Eng bear the cold much better than I expected—in travelling they continue to keep themselves tolerably warm by putting on the extra jacket & an extra pair of stockings—but they suffer more from cold when in bed, in consequence of which I procure them a bed room with a fire whenever it is possible to get it."

To this, Chang and Eng wished a postscript added:

"Chang Eng desire their love to all—& say 'the further South we go the more snow we see'—they wish to know if the weather is severe 'down East'—as in that case they strongly recommend the use of *buffalo robes*.—They are quite in a fright at our business being so bad—as they are afraid if this very severe weather lasts we may starve!!!! and that would be a very sad business. . . . C & E's *love* to their rabbit—they wish to know if he bears this severe weather well—& whether he has a companion to keep him warm."

After a brief stand in Rye, New York, the small caravan passed through New York City and halted in Newark, New Jersey. The first day in Newark "we took almost sixty dollars—which considering the miserable cold of the weather I could not help thinking tolerably well . . ."

After three days in Newark, they went on to Morristown, New Jersey, where a letter awaited them. Since the letter, addressed to Harris, was from the twins' physician Dr. Brickett, and not Captain Davis, Harris was surprised.

Dr. Brickett stated that Mrs. Coffin had received no word for weeks concerning the twins' whereabouts or the business they were doing—none of Harris' three recent letters had yet reached Captain Davis—and Mrs. Coffin was upset with Harris. Therefore, Dr. Brickett was writing on Mrs. Coffin's behalf:

> In conversation with Mrs. Coffin this afternoon she expressed a desire to learn your present *location* & future destination and success thus far in your pursuit. I informed her that I had heretofore solicited a continuance of correspondence with you & hoped, e're long, to get a letter from you & as considerable time had already elapsed, I am induced, feeling as I *truly* do, a deep solicitude for the interest of my *very* worthy and *absent* friend *Captn. Abel Coffin, t*o violate etiquette, so far, as to write to you again, without being able to acknowledge an answer to my last. . . .
>
> In conformity with your agreement with Mrs. Coffin, be assured, Sir, it will be highly gratifying to her to hear from you by return mail, wherever this may find you, advising her, the minutia of your *proceedings*, Prospects etcetera.

Now it was Charles Harris' turn to be upset. In his contract with Mrs. Coffin, he had agreed to keep in touch with her regularly through letters written to her intermediary, Captain Davis. Even though his last three letters had not yet arrived in Newburyport, Harris had written them to Davis to fulfill his part of their contract. Here, suddenly, in breach of their contract, Mrs. Coffin was asking him to make reports to a second party, Dr. Brickett.

For the first time, Harris was irritated by Mrs. Coffin. He immediately dashed off a letter to Captain Davis—not Dr. Brickett—protesting that he had written regularly, that he would continue to report to Davis as previously agreed, that it would be "unpleasant to me as well as unsatisfactory" to "extend the correspondence on business beyond one person," and that he was "in the dark" about what Mrs. Coffin meant "in the message concerning the *minutia* of our proceedings &c." He then repeated details of the recent business Chang and Eng had done, went into the bad weather once more, and stated that shortly they would be on their way for exhibits in Reading, Bethlehem, and Harrisburg, Pennsylvania.

Arriving in Bethlehem three days before Christmas, Chang and Eng had something on their minds that they wished to discuss directly with Susan Coffin. They decided to write her—or rather to dictate a letter for Harris to put to paper. Apparently, their arrangement with Mrs. Coffin had been for them to pay for the maintenance of their horses and conveyances out of a two-dollar expense allowance she gave them weekly. This was what was on their minds, and as usual they dictated their joint letter to her in the first person singular:

> I begin to find the expence attending our horse and chaise much more than I expected, when I made the arrangement with you at Boston—in consequence of which I shall in the end find myself out of pocket by the present plan—I am quite sure it is not your wish that I should lose any thing by the agreement entered into with me & I should like therefore to come to some new arrangement.
>
> I think if you would increase the allowance to 3 dollars per week it would about keep me square, otherwise I am sure I shall be a loser as the chaise will certainly want a new pair of wheels & new lining throughout in course of the spring—which will come to a very large sum. You may be able to form an idea of the amount paid for trifling articles when I tell you that since I saw you I have laid out for

sundry articles for my horse & chaise more than nine dollars & very little to shew for it.

If you think 3 dollars a week more than you would like to give I can leave my Gig & Horse where he will be boarded cheap & well taken care of & we can then travel by the Stage, as we have done heretofore, or in any other manner which you would consider more advisable.

The request by Chang and Eng for a raise to three dollars a week in their travel allowance—or else to board their horse and chaise and use public stage-coaches—soon became a matter of contention. Captain Davis' reply quoted Mrs. Coffin as saying, "about the chaise CE can do as they please." Since this ambiguous reply neither granted them a raise nor agreed to let them abandon their horse and chaise, Chang and Eng were upset. Harris was equally upset, believing it would be a mistake to board or sell the horse and chaise rather than receive money for their upkeep. He argued the point with Mrs. Coffin through Captain Davis:

I shall endeavour to do as well as I can as respects the Horse & Waggon, but I would be very unwilling to make a sacrifice in the sale of them. I confess for my own part shall regret our leaving off our present plan of travelling—it has very many advantages & one of the most striking advantages is that it is a *decided saving of expence;* in addition to this it enables us to travel when we like & likewise to stop at pleasure—The annoyance endured by Chang-Eng in travelling in public conveyances is likewise completely done away with—I read to them your letter & I am sorry to say that they are very deeply mortified at Mrs. Coffin's answer to their letter; in fact they do not know what to say or do about it & they are much hurt at Mrs. Coffin for not saying either "Yes" or "No" to their proposal—as it stands, they say Mrs. Coffin's reply means nothing—They say that at present they have no opportunity of either selling their horse & gig or of leaving their horse where he would be well taken care of so for the present they will travel in their gig, paying their horses board, and also tolls &c. & expect me to pay them for 2 seats in the stage from place to place—I wish you would let me know what you think of this plan—as I feel rather awkwardly situated in the affair—an awkwardness arising from my being the medium of communication between Mrs. Coffin & Chang-Eng on this subject which seems to annoy them so much.

Eight days later, still not having resolved the issue, Harris wrote another letter to Captain Davis pursuing the subject further:

... you say (in speaking of Mrs. Coffin's wishes) *"and about the chaise CE can do as they please."* Now considering the letter which they had written to Mrs. Coffin & that this letter was written to Mrs. C—in the most discreet manner—they thought the short answer sent by Mrs. Coffin was intended (as they expressed it) to place them in an awkward place, and that it was like taking a bird, clipping off his wings & then holding it up on one's hand & saying "Now you may fly if you wish." (This latter sentence is in their own words.)

After stating that he would now have to cancel the twins' twenty-five-cents-a-day allowance and use the money to buy three seats for the two of them on stagecoaches, Harris went on to make another plea for an extra allowance to keep up the private chaise and horse:

It seems to me that no great loss could accrue to the concern if C & E's request were complied with *"until Captain C's return"*—I have mentioned above that Chang-Eng thought Mrs. C wished to place them "in an awkward place"—what is meant by this expression is that she sent them this answer (which *they* consider so unsatisfactory) at a time when they had no opportunity of leaving their horse & gig where they were sure of its being taken care of & taking into consideration the extravagantly high price of horse food in this part of the country. . . .

The above being a subject dictated entirely by Chang-Eng they wish me to make a separation or division in this letter & have asked to sign their name to it—to this I can offer no objection.

CHANG ENG.

While in later correspondence there exist no further allusions to the disagreement, it is clear that Chang and Eng somehow won out and gained a raise in their expense allowance. They continued to travel with Harris in a repaired carriage drawn by their own horse, always followed by a horse and wagon driven by Tom Dwyer, their all-around man. Sometimes, to lighten the load for the carriage horse, Harris—and occasionally Chang and Eng—would travel ahead by train or stagecoach.

Sometimes, when Chang and Eng traveled by public transportation, they liked to take advantage of their condition and have fun with the authorities. On one widely publicized occasion, Chang and Eng, sharing a voluminous cape which hid their connecting ligament, bought a single ticket and boarded a train to Louisville. When the conductor came around to collect the passengers' tickets, he asked Eng for his ticket.

"I don't have a ticket," said Eng.

"Then you'll have to get right off the train," said the conductor.

"Very well," said Eng, rising to leave, with Chang rising to his feet beside him. The cape fell open to reveal their connecting band.

"But wait, *I* have a ticket," Chang announced, showing it, "and if you put me off, I'll sue the railroad."

The conductor stared wide-eyed at them, then quickly backed down. They completed the journey, but did buy a second ticket when the conductor recovered from his shock.

The twins had celebrated the coming of the New Year—1832, the year they would come of age—a few weeks earlier in Lancaster, Pennsylvania. They arrived there in a snowfall, having left Reamstown the day before, and, according to Harris, "we opened a room, but the villagers had never before been called on to pay more than 12½ cents for any show, or sight or exhibition & were therefore quite unwilling to pay 25 cents—we would of course take no less & in consequence we took no more than enough to pay our bill."

After Lancaster, the tour had ground on, with engagements scheduled almost daily despite the bitter cold and steady snowstorms. Cities came and went, without rest for the travelers. There was Harrisburg, where they did "a very satisfactory business." Then in early January they were in Carlisle, with Harris reporting, "The weather still continues wet & uncomfortable, & I much fear it will cut up our business very much here—for although the town is full of people rainy weather will interfere very much with their coming to see us.—In a few minutes I expect a physician in to prescribe for Eng—who has had a very bad pain in his side for a few days past—but he is so much worse today that when he breathes very freely it causes him a great deal of pain—Chang's pain has likewise given him a good deal of trouble lately—today they are both in miserable spirits."

Next they set out for Shippensburg, Pennsylvania, with Chambersburg their more important destination. Along the route there was a dangerous incident, which Harris immediately reported:

. . . although we reached the village that evening, very unexpected events occurred before we reached the place—After leaving Carlisle we got along very merrily & had completed 6 miles of the 21 when the Axle of the Gig snapped & down came one side flat on the ground.—Chang-Eng's horse, Charley, set off at full speed, but after running about 70 yards he stopped quietly from being spoken to by Chang-Eng. . . . On getting out of the gig we found that of all three the only one who had received any damage was Eng who was sitting next the wheel which came off, he had a slight blow on the side of the head from the falling wheel which caused a trifling swelling which has since disappeared. I think you will agree with me that we escaped well in the matter & have great cause to feel thankful for our escape.—An empty carriage passing accidentally at the time we got into it & led Charley behind leaving the gig & broken wheel in care of a cottager near to whose house the accident took place. . . . [We] got to Chambersburg before 6 o'clock—time enough to open there as we had advertised at 7 o'clock in the evening—but the news of our accident had travelled quicker than we had & so no one expected us until Friday morning when we opened our room & closed it on Saturday Night having taken at our doors more than 74 Dollars—we expected to have done better but must not complain.

In this letter written at Greencastle, Pennsylvania, Harris also addressed Captain Davis on a matter of the troupe's business. Near the entrance at each exhibit, a sixteen-page pamphlet prepared by James Hale, carrying a full-page lithograph of Chang and Eng, was always on sale. Now Harris discussed the necessity for a new edition:

I forgot to mention the subject of the pamphlets and on this subject I have many reasons to urge why it would be desirable to have a fresh supply printed— in the first place selling the pamphlets makes the two hours every morning & evening pass much more pleasantly than they would without them and did you know how heavily those 4 hours a day pass sometimes when we are unlucky enough to have a room full of dull stupid persons—you would not be surprised at my grasping at anything which gives a chance of breaking the monotony of such a company . . . I am certain you would agree to it, if you know how much the selling of those little books lightens the amount of foolish questions asked in the Exhibition Room.

After an appearance in Hagerstown, Maryland, the party made its way to Frederickstown. Once there, Harris found a letter waiting for him, written half to him and half to Chang and Eng, from his friend and predecessor, James Hale.

Hale wrote from Boston to give Harris some advice on the next leg of his tour, which included Baltimore and Washington, D.C. Also, having heard of Eng's recent pains in his side, Hale wrote that he was "sorry to observe by your last few words that old Eng was threatened with Chang's old complaint—I really hope it may not be the case, as the poor fellows suffered extremely from it in Phila—and moreover couldn't eat any *birds* or *broiled pigeons*—they'll understand this."

In the second half of his letter, Hale addressed Chang and Eng directly. They had written him from Bethlehem about a young lady they were romantically interested in, and Hale was responding:

"Now my old stick-in-the-mud, rapscallions, a few words for you.—Your last . . . was copied and sent 'down East' the day after I recd it—and as I have not heard a word from her since, I cannot tell whether it was recd—whether she is sick, or if the old folks have smelt the rat and put a stop to her writing—I cannot think the latter is the case, for a woman will *always* find means to do as they please, father & mother notwithstanding. Your last letter, from Carlisle was sent yesterday to her, and the moment I get any thing in return you may depend I will forward it to you. Don't be uneasy my dear fellows for I expect the former letter must have miscarried—and no doubt the last will be shortly answered." The letter was signed, "Believe me your friend Jas. W. Hale."

The twins' use of Hale as an intermediary in their wooing of this young lady is one of the rare written references to their continuing interest in the opposite sex. From the time Chang and Eng toured the British Isles, when they were eighteen and nineteen, they made no secret to those in their inner circle about the attraction young British and American women held for them. With strangers, or even good acquaintances, however, they were very circumspect about discussing their romantic inclinations. They sensed, instinctively, that the public might be at once titillated and appalled to know that the two of them who were one could fall in love with a single woman or enjoy sexual relations with a normal woman. To the public, the very thought of the joined brothers going to bed with a woman boggled the imagination. As a result, much of their romantic activity was never made public. But from certain remarks in their correspondence, it is clear that during their eight-year American tour they were often attracted by the women they met, fell in love frequently, and may even have had sexual intercourse with prostitutes.

In Frederickstown, Harris also received word from Captain Davis that Captain Abel Coffin had written his family from Batavia, Java, saying he expected to be home soon. Replying to this letter, Harris gave Davis a report on the recent business the twins had done:

"We opened a room in Greencastle & only took $15 —but the cause of this was evident to me on learning that there has been (& still continued when we left) a four days meeting [religious revival meeting] which was protracted to 10 days & as might be expected all the good folks were literally mad on the subject. Last Tuesday morning we left Greencastle & got into Hagar'stown *Md*. but here religion was all the fashion likewise & altho' in course of our evening & two whole days we received a few cents more than 80 dollars yet from the size of the town & other causes I expected to have done better but I fear religion stood much in our way."

Less than a week later the troupe was in Baltimore, and once again they ran afoul of bad weather. On January 27, 1832, Harris wrote Captain Davis:

"The cold is now more intense than any which we have felt before. The ink in my glass was frozen hard this morning & so severe was the cold in the Holliday Street Theatre last night that after an attempt to go through their parts the actors were obliged to give in and make an apology to the audience. . . . We are eating, drinking and sleeping *but not making any money* . . . but what can we expect? considering the weather."

During seven days in Baltimore, the exhibit of Chang and Eng was able to enrich the concern by $85.62½. Since Harris calculated that good business should earn them $280 in a week, by his standards Baltimore had been a disaster.

Entering the District of Columbia—the occupant of the White House was President Andrew Jackson, serving the fourth year of his first term—the travelers found that Washington was too crowded to accommodate them immediately. Every theater and exhibit hall was booked with other acts, and the hotels and inns were filled. As a result, the troupe was forced to open in nearby Georgetown. Again bad weather haunted them. In eight days, according to Harris, they took in only $109.73½.

Meanwhile, Harris had obtained a showroom in the Masonic Hall in Washington, D.C. He booked the twins in there for eight days, later explaining to Captain Davis:

"During the time we had the Masonic Hall in Washington open we continued to board in Georgetown & we saved a good deal by this arrangement—for having our own horse, gave us the opportunity of going & returning cheaply & moreover for some nights we had moonlight which gave us an advantage in returning after 9 o'clock in the evening. The distance from Roach's Tavern in Georgetown to the Masonic Hall is very little short of three miles—so that during this time we had good exercise."

The weather continued inclement, and few customers ventured out in the cold to see the Siamese Twins. During the eight days in Washington, the troupe members grossed only $170.25 for their efforts.

Now, moving into Virginia to continue their exhibitions, Chang and Eng suffered an incident in Norfolk that angered them deeply. As Harris related it to Captain Davis:

. . . a Medical man drew up a Memorandum concerning C & E for one of the Norfolk papers, which was a very well drawn up paper & calculated to do us much good—were it not for one sentence which stated that they (the Twins) were sold by their Mother to Mr. Hunter & Captain Coffin. On hearing this C E's rage knew no bounds & they made me go immediately to the Young Doctor who drew out the Memorandum & ask him how he came to state such a thing as that they had been bought of their Mother. The young man immediately stated that his information was obtained from a paper published by Dr. Warren of Boston in a Medical Book wh. was in every medical man's hands. I think that if Chang at that moment had Dr. Warren by the nose & if Eng had the person who gave the Doctor these particulars—the two noses would have been very much lengthened; at all events *they* would have tryed their best.

By late April, Chang and Eng were in Greensburg, Pennsylvania, where a letter dated "Boston April 25th" from James Hale was waiting for them. It was a significant letter, for it is the earliest letter extant to hint at a revolt Chang and Eng had been secretly planning. Hale's letter read, in part:

"Nothing from Capt. C. yet—Nor from Mrs. C. neither—she has not been in town lately, and I am told that she keeps pretty close—short of funds probably, ha?—I dare not put on paper all the scandal I hear—but it's pretty much after the old sort. . . . I expect it's almost time to be looking out for yourself (Chang Eng) now—May is near."

Almost time to be looking out for yourself. . . . May is near. Meaning that on May 11, 1832, Chang and Eng would be twenty-one years old. They would legally be of age, and for the first time would have the legal right to determine their own future. In secret, they had been plotting their future with both Harris and Hale, and now, above all else, they wanted a face-to-face meeting with Captain Abel Coffin.

The insistence of Chang and Eng to meet with Captain Coffin was so great that, from Greensburg on April 30, Harris felt it necessary to write a letter to Davis in which the second paragraph was bracketed in ink to indicate that it was to be treated as "private" and strictly between them:

"The same anxiety for Captain Coffin's speedy return continues & this rather increases than diminishes —a few days since they were anxious that I should write and tell you that they are anxious for either you or Mrs. Coffin to come on to them—but again they changed their minds & desired me to write, however *this* I write to you in confidence & shall ask you to consider it as 'private.' But I am anxious at the same time to let you know all these things that you may know exactly how we go on & as to their anxiety for the return of their friend Captn Coffin it is so frequently & particularly mentioned that I cannot account for it, but felt it to be right to let you know it —Please to consider what I enclose in brackets thus ( ) as 'private.' "

From this passage it is clear that Chang and Eng wanted an immediate confrontation with Captain Coffin about something important—were at one point eager to see Mrs. Coffin or Captain Davis instead, but then changed their minds about that. What is not clear is Harris' motive in writing the passage to Davis. Harris must have known why the twins wanted a personal meeting with Coffin, yet he was writing Davis that he could not "account" for their anxiety to have such a meeting. Perhaps he did not know specifically what the twins planned to discuss with Coffin about their future, or perhaps he did know and was worried about his own future.

In any case, the next four weeks proved to be among the most vital in the lives of the Siamese Twins.

Somewhere, between Pennsylvania and New York, they learned that they could not see Captain Abel Coffin in person. He was still abroad, and would not return to the United States for four more months.

The twins then said that it was urgent that Mrs. Coffin meet with them in Buffalo, New York. She later replied that she was unable to meet with them. Since Chang and Eng could not meet with either of the Coffins in person to tell what was on their minds, they decided to do so by mail.

On May 11, 1832, in Pittsburgh, they celebrated their twenty-first birthday by announcing that their relationship with the Coffins was at an end, that their contract had been fulfilled, that henceforth they would be free, and that on the evening of May 31 it was over and they would be on their own.

This fell like a bombshell on Mrs. Coffin. She reacted immediately by ordering Captain Davis to advise the twins that if they quit, they would be breaking their word to Captain Coffin. They were to be reminded that they had promised Captain Coffin that they would stay in her employ until he returned to the United States. She would not allow them to go back on their word. They were also to be reminded of how much she had done for their comfort, and how much she loved them.

When Chang and Eng checked into Mansion House in Buffalo, they found Davis' letter transmitting Mrs. Coffin's strongly worded message. A year or two before this, they might have trembled and complied with her wishes. But now they had come to adulthood, had seen and experienced much, and were not only grown but hardened.

They stood firm. They vented their deepest feelings about their employers of three years to Charles Harris. They made him sit down and write Captain Davis—and through him, Mrs. Coffin herself. Although Harris made some remarks of his own, most of his letter was devoted to Chang's or Eng's comments and rebuttal, as dictated to him, and indeed Chang and Eng affixed their own names to this letter.

The letter to Captain Davis in its entirety, dated from Buffalo on Tuesday, May 29, 1832, read as follows:

Dear Sir,

Your letter of the 22nd came to hand last evening & I must thank you for your promptitude in so quickly replying to mine from Pittsburgh. It was of great importance to me to know that my letter had been received & whether or not Mrs. C. could make it convenient to come on here—as without a letter from you I would have been not a little embarrassed as to the course which I had to pursue on Thursday evening—when *they* mean to close the concern.

I have read your letter over to Chang-Eng & they say that as to the "*promise*" made to Captain Coffin "*that they would stay under Mrs. Coffin until the return of Captn. to the U.S.*"—as to *this* they say there must be a great mistake some where as they must deny this altogether. When they last saw Captn. C.—they distinctly understood from him that he would in all human probability be home in January (1832)—but on this they stated their wish (in case of any accident to *him*) to have a memorandum under his hand as to the time they were to consider themselves under his control—he immediately stated that of course when they attained the age of 21— they were "Their Own Men"—to use the words of Captn. C on the occasion. Moreover they say January, February, March, April & May have all passed & the chance of seeing Captn. Coffin seems (they say) as far off as ever.

Suppose, they say, that Captn Coffin should prefer remaining altogether in Batavia or any other distant region—is it reasonable that they should wait from month to month & year to year until his return? In fact, they say, such an undefinable term as that of "till Captn C. returns" is quite absurd after 4 months having passed since the time fixed for his return. Under this view of the case they don't altogether consider it right in Mrs. C. to tax them with not "*keeping their word*" for according to that view of the case (say they) if Captn. Coffin should never return to the U.S.—they would to the end of their lives remain as they *now are*—As to Mrs. Coffin doing all she could for their comfort & loving them & liking them—they say, they have no doubt that the number of thousand of hard shining dollars which they have enabled her to spend have made her like them—but let Mrs. C. look into her own heart & they feel confident she will discover that the great loving & liking was not for their own sakes—but for the sake of the said Dollars. If there is any doubt in her mind on this subject they say, she has only to retrace in her mind the cruel manner in which they were forced to go into a crowded room when they were more fit to be in an hospital. If they wanted to give a few instances they would remind her of New York (their first visit) & likewise London & Bath—they say to Mrs. C. —let her look over these things in her own mind (they hope she has not forgotten them), & after this let her make up her mind as to her loving & liking them—In fact, they say, the less she says about loving & liking—the better.

Chang-Eng desire me to tell *you* that it is very unpleasant to them to be unable to write all this to Mrs. Coffin themselves—which they would much prefer—but on finding Mrs. C. bring a charge agt. them of not keeping *their word*—they cannot avoid letting her know all which they have stated before. They desire me to say that their great anxiety has been to close the business in peace, quietness & friendship & they are determined that nothing shall be done by them to prevent this from taking place—but after the fatigues & dangers by Sea & Land in Ships & Carriages —by Night & Day—which they have endured to make money for Captn C they consider it to be rather out of the way for her now to accuse them of breaking their word to Captn C. They say that you (Captn D) know little of their fatigues endured when in England—but they would merely look back (and ask you to do the same) to their first visit to Newbury Port when they expected to have a little rest—but even here (they say) the wish to make money was so great that instead of having any time to themselves a room was procured & visitors admitted just as it had been a few days before at Boston. Give Chang-Eng's best wishes to all friends they desire me [to] say it is very unpleasant for them to be obliged to get another person to write such a letter as this but there was no way of getting out of the difficulty—but to submit to the imputations contained in your letter. They have asked to affix their signature to it to stamp it as their deed, their sentiments & their feelings, concerning the transactions.

CHANG ENG
SIAMESE TWINS

Their bondage to the Coffins was over. They would be, forever after, for better or for worse, "Their Own Men."

5
CHAPTER
5

"Their Own Men"

"Since June 1st, 1832, we have ceased to be under any arrangement with Captain Coffin," Chang and Eng wrote at a later date to their discoverer, Robert Hunter, in London. "We had then attained the age of 21 and considered we had fulfilled to the letter and spirit all the engagements entered into between Captain C. and ourselves at Siam."

It is clear that Chang and Eng had no second thoughts about quitting the employ of Captain Coffin and going on to become "their own men."

According to the unpublished biography prepared by their friend Judge Jesse Graves—who had discussed every aspect of their lives with them—they felt that Coffin had been swindling them. Wrote Judge Graves:

Chang and Eng had for a long time been very greatly dissatisfied with the conduct of Captain Coffin who as they alleged received very large sums as the proceeds of the exhibitions and always refused to pay over anything to them saying he was to pay all over to their mother. They had agreed to remain with him until they became twenty-one, and that same strict and rigid compliance with all their promises and engagements which characterized them all through life induced them to remain with the man who they regarded as unfaithful, until their full term should be completed lest they should prove as faithless as he had been. But looking to the time when they would be released and free again they had been as industrious as possible prosecuting their studies until now they found themselves able to read and write very creditably and to understand so much of arithmetic as to enable them to keep their own accounts and to make their own calculations, and as they thought abundantly able to take care of themselves. They therefore left the employment of the captain as they styled him and sought to enforce their own claim and their mother's against him; but they never [were] able to effect any recovery. They always felt that he had acted in very bad faith.

In the years that followed, all biographers of Chang and Eng, in articles, pamphlets, books, flatly stated that the twins broke with Captain Coffin because he had defrauded them, robbing them of portions of their box-office receipts.

However, except for the fact that Captain Coffin owed the twins' mother a second payment of $500 for their services, which he never delivered to her, and except for the fact that Mrs. Coffin confiscated some of the twins' personal effects after they left the concern, there exists not a shred of evidence that Coffin swindled or defrauded them in any way.

Captain Coffin may have exploited the twins badly, he may have misused them and lied to them, but there remains no proof that he was a thief who appropriated money that rightfully belonged to them. Actually, Captain Coffin was far from the United States during Chang and Eng's tour undertaken for him in 1831 and 1832. Neither his wife Susan nor Coffin's friend Captain Davis, who spoke for her, directly handled the money the twins had earned. All income from the twins' exhibits was collected by their friends and managers—first James Hale, then Charles Harris, both of whom were trustworthy, and both of whom deducted and paid out the twins' salaries and expenses at the source, before sending the profits on to Mrs. Coffin.

Chang and Eng had not ended their relationship with Captain Coffin because they had been swindled. They ended it for numerous other reasons. They ended it because, from the time of their tour in England with Coffin and the time of their tour in the United States under Mrs. Coffin, they felt the Coffins were parsimonious regarding traveling expenses and allowances. They ended it because they felt that they had been and were being ill-rewarded—being paid only $10 a month abroad until March of 1831 and $50 a month when they returned to the United States from England—while their employers were profiting out of proportion from their earnings. They ended it because they felt that the Coffins treated them as second-class beings, and because they believed that they had been unfeelingly and ruthlessly overworked. They ended it because they resented being in bondage, ordered about, controlled and driven by fellow humans. They ended it because they believed that they had a legal right to do so, that their verbal contract expired on their twenty-first birthday. They ended it because they wanted to be independent and to reap the profits from their exhibits themselves, while it was still possible.

For these reasons, on June 1, 1832, in Buffalo, New York, they cut their ties with the past and set out as self-employed performers.

One of their first acts on their own was to retain the services of Charles Harris as their manager. They were aware that he knew his job, and they liked and respected him as a person. A month later, Harris himself confirmed this in a letter to Captain Davis:

"You ask in your letter to be informed 'who is to attend with C-Eng in their movements.' I have to acquaint you in reply that I continue with them for the present, how long I may remain in their company is uncertain; should anything occur to render it expedient or necessary for me to discontinue travelling with them I have no doubt that they would write to Mr. Hale & ask him to manage their business for them."

At no time did Harris find it "expedient or necessary" to leave them. He stayed with them as their faithful manager throughout the following eight years of their American and foreign tours.

The twins' next act was to return the carriage, wagon, and horses to Mrs. Coffin and cast about for replacements. After Captain Davis instructed Harris to sell the vehicles and equipment, Harris replied to Davis, "I of course looked about what I could do with the Horse, Waggon & other things belonging to Mrs. Coffin. After enquiring I had sufficient cause to come to the conclusion that the offer of $103 made by Chang-Eng was an eligible one, & I therefore closed with them & have got the money." With that, Harris mailed the $103 to Mrs. Coffin, and now the twins were in possession of their own horse and carriage and baggage wagon.

The twins' final act of business, before returning to the exhibition circuit, was to dismiss their handyman Tom Dwyer. He was dropped solely as a matter of economy. Harris informed Captain Davis of the move, stating, "Chang-Eng did not like to keep Tom any longer under the same arrangement as Mrs. Coffin made with him; for his board alone cost $1 a day in addition to his wages & they thought that they might get as well attended for $25 which was the monthly sum paid to the boy who traveled with them last summer & which sum of $25 p month included *every expence* except travelling & which was considered too dear then by them."

At last they were ready, and now that their earnings would be entirely their own, they were prepared to work even harder. Finishing with Buffalo on June 6, 1832, they toured almost every village and city in New York State, then spent the rest of the year covering New Jersey, Pennsylvania, Virginia, and Ohio.

Because Chang and Eng were in business for themselves, Charles Harris had begun to keep two daily record books for them. One was an account book of their earnings each month. The other, "An Account of Monies expended by Chang Eng," was a day-by-day listing of money they spent and what they spent it on.

To celebrate their new freedom on June 1, 1832, Chang and Eng had bought "500 Cegars" for $9," "A Horse named 'Bob'" for "$72.50." "A Pocket book" for "$1," and "Candles" for "14¢." Meticulously, thereafter, Harris had noted the twins' expenses: "Apples" for "65¢," "Washing" for $2.25," "Expences for boat hire at the [Niagara] Falls" for "$4.31¼," "Advertising in Niagara County Courier" for "$1," "Opodeldoc" (a liniment for horses) for "25¢," "Two suits of Thin Clothes" for "$13.50," "Mending Jackets" for "25¢," "A Trunk" (they bought numerous trunks for their traveling effects through the years) for "$10," and "Lemon Syrup" for "50¼ ¢."

One interesting notation for the last day of June was "Mr. Doty's Bill—Seneca Falls" for "12.75." Chang and Eng later knew a Dr. Edmund H. Doty as the result of their close friendship with three brothers, William, Bethuel, and Frederick Bunker, wine and tea merchants whose firm was Bunker & Company at 13 Maiden Lane in New York City. Because of this friendship, Chang and Eng allowed Bunker and Company to do much of their business and banking for them. One of the Bunkers had a daughter named Catherine, with whom Chang had fallen in love on the twins' first visit to New York City. When Chang drew up his earliest will, he named Catherine Bunker as his major heir. Catherine Bunker eventually married Dr. Edmund H. Doty. This apparently did not end Chang's affection for Catherine, which now included friendship with her husband. Doty was regarded as something of an entrepreneur, and in 1849 he signed the twins for a tour. It is possible that the "Mr. Doty" in Seneca Falls and Dr. Edmund H. Doty were one and the same.

For the remainder of 1832, the expense ledger continued to be a record of the costs of their tour as well as a kind of Rorschach test of their interests, habits, personalities. The expense book revealed that they bought "2 pairs of Suspenders," "Horse feed," "A pair of *lucky* Pistols," "Curry Comb & brush," "2 Black Silk Cravats," "A Rifle," "500 Havana Cigars," and "7 lbs of Spermaceti Candles" (needed for lighting hotel rooms and to go to the stables).

The expense book also revealed costs for altering shirts, buying an additional twenty-three pounds of candles, mending the twins' shoes and boots, buying two pairs of gloves, and finally hiring a replacement for Tom Dwyer, which was entered as "Thomas Crocker (including board & washing) $30."

In September, Chang and Eng were spending money on two mustard plasters for Chang, repairs for their wagon, cravat stiffeners, oil for harnesses, advertising in an Ithaca newspaper, toll charges, toothbrushes, quills. There were also entries for "Cutting hair of C.E." (while they still retained their Chinese queues, their hair in front was kept short) and "Catching the horse Bob," which cost "18¾ ¢."

With the coming of October there came also the costs of four custom-made flannel vests, a new inkstand, "Seidlitz Powders" for "37½ ¢," "2 suits of Claret Colored Clothes," one new buffalo robe, "$2.25," a bearskin (exchanged three days later for a second buffalo robe), "$3," and then there was an unusual bill paid for "Expences at Kenyon College $1.50." Apparently the experience at the Ohio campus was enjoyable, for to their expenses the twins added, "Book presented to Kenyon College (Moore's life of Byron) $4."

Although Chang and Eng were free and on their own the last six months of the year, they were not free of Captain Abel Coffin and Mrs. Coffin, or her surrogate, Captain Davis. Acrimonious exchanges over the falling apart of their relationship continued in their correspondence during June and July. Harris had had to wind up the financial accounts of the defunct concern. Chang and Eng, incited by Mrs. Coffin's efforts to woo them back, brought up past grievances and vented their anger over difficulties in recovering their personal effects.

Chang and Eng, as well as Harris, looked forward to seeing Captain Coffin in person as soon as possible after he returned to Boston from Java. While Harris merely wanted to have Coffin audit his bookkeeping, and so be done with him, Chang and Eng wanted to meet their former employer so that they could get all the festering grievances off their chests. For his part, Captain Coffin, unaware while at sea that the twins had broken with him, would certainly want to see them upon learning of their defection, everyone agreed. Coffin would want to meet with them, if only to make an effort to coax them back into the fold.

On July 27, writing from Madison Village, New York, Harris advised Captain Davis that "Chang-Eng fully expect . . . that Captn. Coffin is come home & have asked me to write to you again to let you know our intended movements." Harris included part of their itinerary for the next month, and reiterated, "I make no doubt that Captn. C is now returned & that we shall very soon see him."

During this time, beginning two weeks after they had quit the Coffins, Chang and Eng had carried on a furious exchange with Captain Davis. In their opening salvo on June 15, 1832, from Rochester, New York—having come of age—they had referred to themselves for the first time as two people:

"In the letter you say that as regards Capt. and Mrs. Coffin's treatment of us, you still continue of the same opinion—as to this we can only refer you to what we asked Mr. Harris to insert in his last letter to you respecting the cruel & severe manner in which we were treated when attacked by sickness, in being forced into a close hot & crowded room when we were more fit to be in bed; we shall leave you to judge whether such treatment as this was kind or not!!!"

At one point, Captain Davis had written the twins,

"For a certainty Captn Coffin will lose a large sum of money by the concern as it stands at present."

This had been a red flag to the twins. In a fury, weaving in and out of singular and plural reference to themselves, they answered:

To this our reply will be a question as to whether you are aware of how many thousand dollars have been received at the door of our exhibition room since we were first purchased of our Mother (as *some folks* have called it).

If you know the amount recd. we would beg to let you know that but a very small part of it has been spent on our account. Are you more over aware that $500—(Five Hundred Dollars) is the amount paid to our Mother (from first to last?) Perhaps you are not aware that from my first landing in Boston to my arrival in New York from England, there was only $10 p month allowed to me out of this I bought all the trifling little articles which I wanted from time to time.

Since my arrival in New York (in March 1831) I have had $50 per month. Put all these together & if you will compare it with the sums which we have been the means of collecting together you will find our share to be *very, very paltry* indeed. We would state one fact to you to shew you how *considerately* we have been treated. Capt. C. had a good offer made to him for our appearance on the stage of one of the London Theatre's & on accepting it he told us that in consideration of our standing in our room from 10 to 5 (7 hours) & having after this to go to the Theatre he promised us £12 sterling p. week. The engagement lasted 18 nights, which would have come to 36 pounds sterling. How much do you think we received? Only One Third—that is 12 pounds sterling—well, with that we bought a little gold watch & we often & often had the annoyance to hear Mrs. Coffin say to many persons "*See what a nice watch my husband has given to Chang-Eng?*" Whereas it was bought with money hard earned by wearying & continuous attendances at the Theatre night after night to fill her & her husband's pockets with money.

Later on the same day that they wrote the preceding letter, Chang and Eng were still brooding over Captain Davis' charge that Captain Coffin and the concern had lost money exhibiting them. Because they had more to say on the subject, the twins dictated a second letter three pages in length.

The twins told Davis that if the concern had lost money on them, it was because it had mismanaged its affairs. In their opinion, they said, the trip to the British Isles could have been done "at less than one third of the expence." First of all, Chang and Eng pointed out, Captain Coffin had had too great an entourage in London, and had spent too much on the *"persons & animals,"* and in the second place Mrs. Coffin had been brought along to save money and had instead proved a deadweight. Detailing a part of the expenses abroad, the twins wrote:

We shall begin with persons, Captn & Mrs. Coffin, Mr. Hale & myself—Teiu (the boy who accompanied me from Siam) one cook, one man servant, one chambermaid (Ann), one coachman, a boy to clean the horses, 4 or 5 men to carry boards, one doorkeeper, one cheque taker, a man employed every day to clean our room & in addition to all these, two living animals in the shape of horses. In addition to this long list—we can tell you (which most likely you were not aware of before) that when any of our clothes wanted repairing, a girl was hired to come into the house and do it at more or less expence. Altho' we heard with our own ears the speech made *often* & often "That Mrs. Coffins going to England would cause a great saving of money by her being able to do all the repairs to the clothes of those composing our party." The savings under this head must have been *very very great!!!!* I confess I may perhaps be blamed for stating these facts but I never should have entered into such particulars if it was not that the first stone has been thrown at me!!!!!!!

To this, Chang and Eng added a lesson in arithmetic:

> If a man receives $100 in one day & finds his ex-
> pences in the evening to be $101—we know very
> well that he is a loser by the day's work, still he
> may go on for a short time & fancy that he is making
> money & may remain of the opinion until he adds
> up both sides of his book, then he finds his mistake.
> We have stated all these "facts" to you—because we
> feel certain that this letter will let you into the
> knowledge of many things of which you were before
> ignorant, and of this we feel pretty sure because
> otherwise we think *you* would not have written in
> the harsh manner in which you have done.

Almost three weeks later, on the night of July 4, in
Auburn, New York, the twins had gone to bed but
had been too agitated to sleep. Fatigued as they were
—they had performed before 650 persons that day—
they had awakened Harris (who was sleeping in the
same room) after midnight and asked him to write a
letter for them to Captain Davis. The cause for their
agitation was an unexpected visit that evening from
Captain Samuel Sherburne, who had been master of
the ship *Robert Edwards* which had taken them to
England in 1829. During the evening, the twins had
learned for the first time that Captain Coffin had
bought them steerage tickets to England and had
listed them as common servants.

All of this ill-treatment Chang and Eng recounted
to Davis. Once again they aired their resentment at the
claim that the concern had lost money exhibiting
them, and once more they derided Mrs. Coffin's claim
that she and her husband had always been concerned
with the twins' comfort:

> I stated in a former letter that all this attention to
> my comfort was entirely to be placed to the account
> of my being the means of making money & of course
> I must be well fed, well clothed, & always live in the
> best houses—as in such I have always had the best
> success in business; but my situation now reminds

me of an Old Merchant Ship lying in the mud &
waiting to be sold for firewood or any other purpose.
Whilst this ship was young (If I may so speak of a
ship) & strong & seaworthy enough to bring home rich
freights to its owners, it was well kept, well painted,
well furnished, with masts, rigging, or sails when
requisite & in fact kept in high condition with a good
crew & an able commander:—But the lapse of time
having at length rendered her crazy, & weatherbeaten
& therefore unsafe any longer to be trusted with
valuable cargoes, she is condemned & left to crum-
ble to dust, unless there is old iron enough in her
timbers to make it worth while to break her up. It
is no use to take any more trouble about her—as all
source of income from her has ceased & all that now
remains is to sell her for whatever "*she will fetch.*"
The poor old ship reminds me of my situation—but,
thank God, all parts of the comparison are not presented in my situation; it is true I am no longer a
source of revenue to my "*owners*"—they can no longer reckon on the income arising from my exertions;
& *therefore* notwithstanding all I have been the means
of doing is worse than forgotten, yet in one particular I am more fortunate than the poor old un-
serviceable ship, for altho' "*I have been bought*" (as
has been said to many of me) yet "*I cannot be sold*";
I have, moreover, to be thankful for continued good
health & the prospect of still being able to do something for myself, notwithstanding the cold ingrati-
tude of those for whose benefit I have so long & so
laboriously toiled & endured hardships.

By July, Chang and Eng were eager to wipe the
slate clean of the Coffins. There had remained only
two pieces of unfinished business with the old concern. One was to hold the long-delayed meeting with
Captain Coffin. The other was to recover their personal belongings, which were still in the hands of
Mrs. Coffin. In early July, on behalf of the twins,
Harris wrote Davis from Auburn:

"Chang-Eng request me to say that they will be
much obliged to Mrs. Coffin if she will pack up all
their things & have them enclosed in a strong deal box

& addressed to them to the care of Elliott & Palmer 20 William St., New York. They are anxious to have this done *as soon as possible* as there are some of their things which they are in want of & when they go down to New York City they can select those things which they are in want of."

Chang and Eng had then waited a few weeks, hoping to hear that their personal belongings had been packed by Mrs. Coffin and sent on to New York. Instead, they received word that their effects had not been shipped. "The reason Mrs. Coffin has not sent the things as requested," Davis wrote them, "is the expectation of her husband home & then she did not know but Chang-Eng would come East [to New England] & would not want the things at New York."

Infuriated, the twins had Harris reply to Davis at once:

"As to Captn. Coffin's return that need not have anything to do with it. For in the first place even now I consider the time of his return quite uncertain & in the next place the season is so far advanced, that I shall not have time to go to the East. Eight months ago the subject of Captn. Coffin's return was mentioned in the same manner it is now, and if I had sent for my things in February, I supposed the same answer would have been sent & that I should have been kept waiting all this time for *'Capt. Coffin's return.'* This waiting for & expecting *'Captain Coffin's return'* is becoming an old story to us, as it is now a story of eight months standing—therefore we hope to hear no more of it & to save all parties trouble we hope the things have been sent before now."

In this letter to Davis, the twins also struck out at him, attacked him for the tone of his earlier letters, which they felt had been both unreasonable and insulting. Nor were they assuaged by the more conciliatory tone in Davis' last letter. By now they had lost all patience with him:

. . . you have stood up as long as you could for your friend Captain Coffin & tried to defend his conduct as long as you could, but when you find yourself beaten you endeavour to retreat—but, as it requires a very clever tailor to sew a tear in a new coat—so that the mark of the sewing may not be afterwards seen—so it requires some person more capable than you seem to be to defend such conduct as that of Captn. & Mrs. Coffin to me; but we know that sometimes a coat may be so badly torn that the trouble of sewing it up is more than it is worth—as when it is done everyone can *trace the seams*. In fact we will confess you have done as well as you could under the circumstances; but it is hard work to *"wash coal"*—so as to make it *appear white*. As to "Captain Coffin *making his own arrangements on his return home*" we are at a loss to suppose what this can mean as relates to us—but suppose his arrangements may be to return me to my mother at the end of 18 months from the day of my leaving Siam which was the 1st April 1829!!!!!! And taking me back to her himself!!!!! As to the first of these arrangements—returning me at the end of 18 months —I need hardly draw your attention to the state of the case—if I were to go home *immediately* it would be almost 48 months instead of 18 months from the time I left till the time of my return home, but if I remained quietly for *48 years* in the same situation of *servitude* in which I have been up to a very late period, the promise of sending me home would not have been once thought of—And at the end of that time I make no doubt there would be found persons ready to say (as now) that *"Captn. C would lose money by me."* This assertion shows a degree of *Impudence* which I was unprepared to expect—But this is a strange world!!!!!! As to Captain Coffin's promise of giving my mother $500 more (& which promise I was witness to) I very much fear that as *"Captn. C will be a loser by the concern as it now stands"!!!!* so my mother has a slim chance of seeing 500 cents much less Dollars; but I hope that without this she will be able to get on pretty well. When a man breaks his word in one particular it is rather difficult to rely on him for the keeping of his word in other matters.

Chang and Eng then went on to say that their traveling with the Coffins in England had provided "a very good insight into their Characters." The more the twins came to know the Coffins, the more they disliked them. Especially did the twins dislike Susan Coffin—because she discussed their "private affairs" with "everyone," because she constantly lied, because she "hated" any person who "liked" them. In fact, said the twins, "I fear I shall be driven to let my friends know the *real* state of the case between me & Captn & Mrs. Coffin. Indeed it will save me a good deal of trouble to have a short statement of my treatment by Captn & Mrs. Coffin *printed*, so as to satisfy the numerous enquiries made of me on the subject."

This letter proved to be the last letter that Chang and Eng wrote the Coffins through Captain Davis which has survived. In fact, it may have been the last letter to pass between the two warring camps. But for the twins, it was not the end of Captain Coffin in their lives.

Two months later, Harris received a hasty letter from James Hale, written from Boston: "Capt Coffin . . . leaves Boston tonight for the purpose of visiting you and Chang Eng." To this, Hale appended a note to "My friends Chang Eng" which told them: "I am glad Chowtapow [the twins' name for Coffin] has come back to see you, and I hope all difficulties may be made strait."

Hale added that he had met with Captain Coffin, and Coffin had accused him of inciting the twins to quit and go off on their own so that Hale could once more manage them. Hale told the twins, "Whatever he asks you about the advice I have given you, I hope you will tell him true. I am not afraid he shall know the truth. I have not had much time to talk to him since he came home, and I hope he will greet you more cordially than he did me, since he would not shake hands with me when we met. I felt very sorry for this, for as you *very well know*, I was always pleased to call him my friend."

Chang and Eng girded themselves for the meeting.

It had been almost two years since they had set eyes on Captain Coffin. Now, at last, he was on his way to see them.

It was in the first week of October in 1832 that Captain Coffin caught up with Chang and Eng in Bath, New York, and he met with them there at length.

Three letters written by three different persons relate what transpired at the meeting between the Siamese Twins and Captain Coffin and what finally happened between them.

The first report, from James Hale, elaborated upon his earlier meeting with Coffin in Boston, before he left to see the twins, and it gave some idea of what Coffin expected to discuss with the twins. Wrote Hale: "His whole tune then was to find out where Chang Eng were, and to get my opinion as to what kind of bargain he could make with them to go to France—in fact he was so sure of his prey that he actually made me an offer if I would go to Europe with them. I told him I didn't believe he would succeed . . ."

Before departing to find the twins, Captain Coffin had said to Hale, "Well, Mr. Hale, I hope I shall make it all right with Chang Eng, and on my return I will let you know immediately, and hope then to meet you as a friend."

The second report on the meeting, from Chang and Eng themselves, was contained in a letter they wrote on May 5, 1834, to Coffin's former partner, Robert Hunter, in London:

"In Sept. 1832 when Captain C. followed us to the western part of the state of New York he told us that the arrangement with the government was for *seven* years, and that 2½ years was mentioned to our mother in order to quiet her fears and prevent any obstacle from being in the way of our leaving home with him. However, this kind of double dealing was but badly calculated to induce us to remain with him any longer."

The third report on the meeting came from Captain Coffin, in a letter addressed to his wife: "I have at length found Chang Eng after a wild goose chase last night I arrived here I have travelled night & day. . . . We have had much talk they seem to feel themselfes quite free from me they seem glad to see me I shall settle as soon as possible & return home. . . . PS C & E are going to Ohio."

Chang and Eng were through with Captain Coffin, at last. But as it turned out, he was not quite through with them.

Hale's letter written on November 4 also related the aftermath:

> From various sources I have been able to collect the following *facts*. They *must* be true for they all emanated from Coffin!!!!???
>
> "That Coffin on finding you out, immediately went into your room, told Chang Eng that it was no use to undertake to show any airs, he was their master and would exercise his authority—he then overhauled all your trunks and not finding my letters believes they were smuggled away because my damn'd stuff wasn't proper for him to see—that he found Chang Eng indulging in all sorts of dissipation—whoring, gaming and drinking—that he urged the impropriety of their having connexion with women, and that Chang Eng said they had as good right to a woman as he had—upon which Coffin gave Chang Eng 'the damndest thrashing they ever had in their lives'— and that before he left them, they acknowledged he 'was perfectly right in beating them, as it was for their own good'!! That he found Harris a damned little rascal, and upon his interfering he gave him a thrashing, kicked him down stairs and out of the house. That he ordered them on to Cincinnati and that altho' he had reason to believe Hale was a cursed scoundrel, and had put Chang Eng up to a great deal, yet, that Harris was a cursed sight worse."

Captain Coffin's tale of how he had gone to Bath, New York, and accused the twins of intercourse with prostitutes, of gambling, of drinking, provoked Hale to declare "my belief that he is as great a liar as his wife." As for the gossip that Coffin had beat up the twins, Hale, who knew the strength of Chang and Eng, wrote them that he had told those who repeated the story, "It *cannot* have been so, for he (Coffin) is *yet alive*."

While Chang and Eng were finally free of Captain Coffin, their friend Hale in Boston was not. On November 13, 1832, Hale received a stiff note from Coffin, who stated that he was going abroad again and "before I leave I wish you to relinquish your right of the copyright of a book relating to the Siamese Youths in my favor. . . . I allso request every thing you have in your hands belonging to the Siamese Youths previous to there becoming of Age as you are knowing to their being under my protection previous to that time."

Concerning Coffin's demands, Hale informed the twins, "As I have not nor do not intend to answer his note, I suppose he will wait a day or two and then see if can't get me entangled in a lawsuit. If he does, by the gods, I'll write such a 'History of the Siamese Youths' and their *owner* Capt Abel Coffin, as shall make him curse the day he ever heard of Siam."

Now fully enraged by Coffin, Hale wrote him a long letter saying that he was aware of the "base and calumnious lies" Coffin had been circulating about the twins and himself, and that he "would immediately publish to the world a full account of every transaction in which you had been engaged since our first acquaintance."

Hale was able to counterattack after he learned that the Coffins had had a silent partner in their management of Chang and Eng, a man named Captain Daniel C. Beacon who owned one-eighth of all the profits made on the twins. While Bacon had received his share of the cash profits, he did not know that some of the profits had been skimmed off by Mrs. Coffin to buy personal effects and household belongings. Hale informed Bacon of this, and Coffin was immediately forced to settle with Bacon by giving him $800 more.

Captain Coffin's only response to Hale's letter and his own involvement with Bacon was to hire a Boston lawyer to sue Hale for the copyright of the original pamphlet on the twins. Hale sought a lawyer of his own, and was advised that while Coffin's suit was weak, it could entangle Hale in the law and cause him all kinds of difficulties, including an audit of the records he had kept while he had managed the twins. Reluctantly, Hale gave up. As he reported to Chang and Eng, "I had better swallow a little wrong than to have to pay too dearly for insisting upon my right."

The loss of the old pamphlet was not serious for either Hale or the Siamese Twins. It was outdated, and could easily be supplanted by a new biography of Chang and Eng. In fact, Hale set out to write the new biography at once, and on May 17, 1833, he reported the news of it to the twins:

"I have obtained the copy right of a new pamphlet which bears this Title 'An Account of the Siamese United Brothers, by themselves; United we Stand. Published for the exclusive benefit of the Twins, and sold by them only. Price 25¢.' . . . The new book will be entirely different from the other, and many things will be left out of mine. Your request that the public should know you 'are no longer slaves' will of course be attended to . . ."

On November 19, 1832, Captain Abel Coffin, master of a new vessel, the *Monsoon*, sailed out of Boston for Calcutta, India, and then Sumatra. In effect, he had also sailed completely out of the lives of Chang and Eng, as well as Hale and Harris.

In the late fall of 1837, while Chang and Eng were touring New York State, they were to hear of Captain Coffin for the last time. Weeks earlier the Nantucket *Inquirer* had carried a story about Coffin, which would be summarized in the seafaring records of the Nantucket Library as follows: "August 28, 1837: Captain Abel Coffin of Boston, died at the Island of St. Helena, aged 47:04. A descendant from Nantucket, he was Master of a vessel and died of a fever."

His heirs—his son Abel, his daughter Susan, and two

more children, all raised close to God—would do much to redeem the family name in the Siamese Twins' eyes. Years later, Judge Graves wrote the postscript on Captain Coffin and Chang and Eng: "Long after his death however they [the twins] were very kindly treated by his son and daughter living in or near the City of Boston."

But with the advent of 1833, the Siamese Twins were still touring Ohio. Hale wrote them that he was coming out to see them, and to help Harris in any way he could. Hale added, "Capt Davison sails tomorrow for Java. He has given me a very interesting account of his first interview with your mother which I will bring with me."

The twins were forever eager for reports of their mother Nok, in Meklong. Hale, whenever he could, picked up news for them. On April 4, 1834, he wrote them:

> I have seen Capt Davison, with whom Hunter came from Singapore. He says that Hunter had seen your mother, and that she was very anxious to see you even for a short time; but that when Hunter explained to her how well off you were, how well you were doing, and the difficulty [of] making a voyage to Siam, she was very well satisfied, and expressed great pleasure you were doing so well. She, your father [the twins' stepfather Sen], brother and sister were all well when Hunter left Siam, and were in want of nothing but to see you, which they hoped to do in a few years.
>
> Capt Davison informs me that Hunter has been in great favor with the King, who has made him a great Chowkoon, with a heavy title, but I am afraid without much profit. He also says that Hunter's losses by the great flood, by the rascality of his partners, and other cause have been very great, and that he is now quite poor. I am glad to hear however [that there now] is a prospect [of his] friends in England getting him up a voyage . . . which I hope will be profitable.

The twins wrote to Robert Hunter on May 5, 1834, in London:

We are very much obliged by the information which you have communicated to us respecting our mother. . . . We fear that the great rising of the waters in Siam were disasterous to you as well as to many others, but we hope to hear after some time that you are doing well, and that you are "very rich" instead of being as you say you now are, "very poor," but we supposed you mean that you are "very poor" in comparison to what you once were. We are fully determined to go back to Siam but cannot at present fix any time.

We have enjoyed good health since we saw you and are now completely acclimatised to America. We have nearly completed the tour of the United States, being now in the 19th state of the 24 which compose the Union.

In the year or more before this letter to Robert Hunter, the twins and Harris had continued their tour of the nation without pause. During 1833, they spent four months in and out of Ohio. Then, for the first time, they invaded the South, where they had never been seen, and their profits soared. In September they were in Kentucky, where they earned a fair $413. But in October, when they toured Tennessee and Alabama, their income jumped for the month to $1,105. In November and December they were in Mississippi, where their income for the two months reached $2,433.

During those months, Harris' expense ledger continued to tell the story of the twins' travels and tastes. The ledger listed "Hire of an ox team to draw us out of mud 25¢," "Soaling Eng's Monroe shoes 60¢," "Ferriage over Detroit River $1.50," "Purchase of 3 wild Ducks from Indian boys 50¢," "1000 Cigars from Mr. B $18" (these were bought wholesale, and sold retail along with the pamphlets at the exhibits), "A ring given to Caroline Scovill $1.50" (possibly a romantic gift, maybe only a friendly one), "Two suits of Clothes made at Canton $28," "Physic for Charley's (the Horse's) legs 10¢," "Violin $10," and "Cleaning Chang Eng's teeth $3."

The new year of 1834 found Chang and Eng in Baton Rouge, Louisiana. They spent that entire year exhibiting up and down the East Coast. In December 1834, the expense ledger bore two entries that signaled a new adventure. On December 18 there was a listing reading "Passport for J. W. Hale to Havana $2," and another on December 19 reading "Hale's passage to Havana $34."

Two years earlier, James Hale had urged Chang and Eng to try their luck in Cuba, and after that to visit Europe. Again in November 1833, he had written them, "I presume by the direction you are now taking, that you intend visiting Mobile and N. Orleans and perhaps to take a sail over to Havana in the winter . . ." However, the twins had rejected his notion and decided to continue touring in the United States at least another year. Learning of this, Hale was disappointed and again tried to get them to go to Havana. On April 4, 1834, he wrote them from Boston:

"Your resolution to remain in this country another year somewhat surprises me, but of course I cannot so well judge of the probability of success, as you can yourselves. . . . However desirable it may be to you to remain a year longer in this country, I fear your success in business will not be so great as you ought to have, owing in a very great degree to the pressure on the people; for I assure you at the North people look devilish hard at their quarter dollars before they part with them."

For the most, Hale proved to be right. In September 1834, working in New York City, Maryland, and Virginia, the twins grossed only $526 for the entire month. Shortly after that, they determined to heed Hale's advice. They set their sights on Cuba, then made up their minds that it would be best if Hale joined their company and went ahead to Havana to book them and advertise them while Harris continued to handle their affairs during their last weeks in the United States.

And so, in December 1834, Hale came down from

Boston to join the twins and Harris in Charleston, Virginia. After spending nine days with the twins, Hale set off for Cuba, while the twins went on to exhibit in Savannah, Georgia.

On January 14, 1835, the twins, accompanied by Harris, sailed for Cuba on the schooner *Evaristo*. Ten days later, the party arrived in Havana, where Hale was waiting to take them to a pension owned by a Mrs. West.

Hale had mounted an extensive advertising campaign for Chang and Eng in Havana. In advance of their arrival he had spent $12 for a sign announcing their opening and $15 on hand-bills in Spanish.

While there remains no record of how well Chang and Eng did in Havana during February, the income account Harris kept indicates the exhibit took in $914 in March and about $500 in April.

As for the twins' activities in Cuba, these were best mirrored in Harris' expense ledger.

Since the language of Cuba was Spanish, and the twins spoke only English and Siamese, some help was needed to answer spectators' questions at their exhibits. After a week in Havana, Harris noted in the ledger: "Paid to a sort of an Interpreter for 6 days $6." Two weeks later the "sort of an Interpreter" was disposed of, and a better and cheaper one hired for the remainder of the twins' stay: "Wm Gardner (interpreter) 2 weeks to the 14th Inst. $8.50."

After four weeks at Mrs. West's pension, the ledger carried the entry: "Expence of moving to Calle de Dragones $2.50." This was a place with rooms owned by "our friend Don Martin de Ferrety." To cut costs, Chang and Eng had decided to forgo restaurants, buy their own food, and cook their meals in Don Martin de Ferrety's lodgings.

The twins were inveterate sightseers, and when they were not working in the exhibition hall they were out in the city like any other tourists. They constantly traveled from their rooms to various sights in a volante, a two-wheeled covered carriage drawn by a horse on which the driver sat, which was the popular taxi of Cuba.

On April 2, $50 was spent on "Hale's passage to New York," and then on April 9, Harris and Chang and Eng paid $150 to take the steamship *Edward* to Philadelphia.

In the next three months the twins were showing in the Peale's Museums in New York City and Albany, and then they toured Vermont. In early July, they traveled north by steamship to visit Lower Canada for the first time. Their tour of Lower Canada was a financial success. Their gross income for July 1835 was $1,041.

They exhibited two more months in the United States, and then they prepared for an important new trip, one they had never taken before but one that promised glamour and excitement.

Nearly five years before, Captain Coffin had wanted to take Chang and Eng to France, but the French government had refused them a visa out of fear that the sight of such "monsters" would be harmful to children and pregnant women. Two years later, after they had broken with the concern, Coffin had sought a reconciliation with the twins and again had wanted to take them to France. By that time, the French government's attitude toward the Siamese Twins had changed. Undoubtedly, their continuing popularity in the United States, where their public appearances had neither frightened youngsters nor caused pregnant women to give birth to deformed babies, had assuaged the fears of the French. The twins' staunch advocate in France, Geoffroy Saint-Hilaire, let it be known that Chang and Eng would be admitted to France any time they wished to visit.

James Hale had long held that they should make a continental tour. Now, at last, in October 1835, Chang and Eng capitulated. They would tour the Continent, or at least part of it, with an itinerary of bookings that would include touching on England and six months in France, Belgium, and Holland.

In mid-October, the twins, accompanied by Charles Harris, boarded the ship *Resolution* in New York harbor, once again said good-bye to the United States, and sailed for England.

Chang and Eng were at sea on the *Resolution* four to five weeks. They arrived at Dover, on the English Channel, November 22, 1835.

The small boat that brought them from the *Resolution* to the shore entered the harbor at low tide. When they reached the pier, Chang and Eng were forced to climb up a twenty-inch-wide iron ladder to get to land, a mean feat even for one man. But, as usual, they scurried up the ladder with natural agility, to the delight of onlookers.

A British newspaper carried this account of their arrival: "On Sunday Chang-Eng the Siamese Twins, who were exhibiting in London five or six years ago, landed at Dover from the ship *Resolution*, from New York, on their way to Paris. They went to the Ship hotel, where they were viewed by the Earl and Countess of Warwick, the Earl of Scarborough, and other persons of consequence staying at the hotel. They have since appeared under the verandah, smoking their cigars, so that passers-by had an opportunity of seeing them. They are much improved in their general appearance and particularly in stature, since they were in England."

The twins had no intention of going to London. They planned only a brief stay at the Ship Inn before catching a boat that would take them from Dover to Calais, and thence they would go to Paris, their primary destination.

On November 24, Chang and Eng, with Harris, crossed the English Channel on the steamboat *Firefly*.

Once safely in Calais, and on French soil at last, they stopped over long enough to refresh themselves with a hearty dinner of mutton chops, cold fowl, and wine. Harris made arrangements for a horse and carriage to take them to Paris.

The following morning, their dollars converted into French francs, the trio set out for Paris. By night-fall, they had reached Abbeville, where they paused for supper, then rode on in the night to Beauvois, arriving there in time for breakfast. After having their carriage wheels greased, they continued on the road to Paris. Here and there along the way, Chang and Eng saw beggars, and tossed some of them a few sous. At one stop, the twins indulged themselves with pâté de veau and sponge cakes at a cost of 1 franc 14 sous. The next day, at an overnight stop, Chang and Eng had a haircut in preparation for their arrival in Paris.

Finally, on December 3, 1835, they were in Paris.

It was a Paris recovering from the costs of glory. Napoleon Bonaparte lay in his grave these past four-teen years. Only the year before, the Marquis de La-fayette, an international hero, had died. It was largely through Lafayette's sponsorship that France now had a moderate and dull king, whom the radicals had mis-read as a revolutionary and had supported. The king was sixty-two-year-old Louis Philippe. "Intelligent he might be," wrote historian René Sedillot, "but nobody could call him glamorous. He was an easy-going husband and a good father. His umbrella be-came a national joke, his pacific nature a lasting re-proach. When Belgium rose against the Dutch and wished to place itself under the wing of a French prince, Louis Philippe refused to accept the proposal for fear of offending the English. On two, on three occasions he chose retreat rather than defiance. He was obstinately wedded to peace. His subjects began to get bored. Of their great and glorious twenty years they remembered only the triumphs."

Three months before the Siamese Twins arrived in Paris, King Louis Philippe had introduced the Sep-tember Laws to curb the outspoken press. Every-where Chang and Eng went, they found Parisians seething at this censorship.

In the City of Light, the twins also found artistic ferment. The recent novels of Honoré de Balzac and Stendhal were in the bookstalls, along with Victor

Hugo's *The Hunchback of Notre Dame* and Alexis de Tocqueville's classic study, *History of Democracy in America*. In this Paris resided Frederic Chopin, 25, George Sand, 31, Alexandre Dumas *père*, 33, Hector Berlioz, 32, and Eugène Delacroix, 37.

Chang and Eng were quick to settle in Paris. Harris found rooms with a landlord named Bolot at eight francs a day, and hired a servant and an interpreter. The twins then bought three pounds of candles to illuminate their quarters in the evenings, and because the winter was cold they rented a dray to bring them firewood. Soon they discovered a favorite restaurant, Michele's, which they frequented daily. They also stocked their rooms with refreshments—"essence of anchovies," champagne, and ices ordered from Tortoni's. They could not resist the French shops, acquiring black silk for their hair, two new clay pipes, a set of chessmen and a board, and lavishly spent 370 francs with a tailor.

But business was not neglected. Paris was to feel the impact of the twins' presence. Harris arranged for the printing of 150 large placards and 1,000 handbills advertising the exhibit of the Siamese Twins, and these were distributed and posted throughout the capital. Nor did he stint on newspaper advertising. During December 1835 and January and February 1836 no week seemed to pass without sizable ads on the twins in *Galignani's Messenger* and other leading newspapers.

The basic advertisement, as carried in the *Constitutionel* of January 16, read: "The united Siamese Twins will receive visitors everyday from 1:00 to 4:00 at the Hôtel de l'Europe, rue Richelieu at 111 near the boulevard. The twins intend to stay in Paris only a short time. Price of entry 2 fr., 50 cent."

One newspaper, *La Quotidienne*, sent a particularly sensitive reporter to cover Chang and Eng's first performance. The reporter was impressed, and his graceful and sympathetic coverage gave the twins a splendid send-off in Paris:

The *monsters,* since we must call them by their name, are not monstrous at all. . . . One remembers that these twins born in that part of India situated between China and the Ganges, in the famous kingdom of Siam, in this country of *free men* were already offered to Paris; it has been five or six years since they were repulsed from France as monsters of Satan. All the protests of M. Geoffroy Saint-Hilaire could not move the police, who nevertheless welcomed the unfortunate Ritta-Christina [Sardinian female twins with only one pelvic organ and one pair of legs, brought surreptitiously into Paris and exhibited]. . . .

They are now twenty-five years old; and what I admire about them, is the intelligence with which they have profited from their position. It is the first time I have seen monsters or savages with enough spirit to conserve their independence, take care of their own affairs themselves, and not sell themselves as weird beasts to an avid master who profits from their dependence. How far superior are the Siamese brothers to the Osages and to the poor Charruas who came from so far away only to be worthlessly dragged down streets and shown in sideshows, and dying of hunger and misery beneath the French sun, without having ever demanded their liberty! The Siamese twins have never been sold, they belong to no one, they travel on their own expenses, in their own coach, with their own servants, and when they arrive in a big city, they depose their passport to the police, go to a good hotel, take a commodious and well-heated apartment; they move in and dine well, without waiting for someone to throw them a crust of bread after the exhibition. They hire an interpreter, and inform the public that they will receive them at certain hours. It is fitting that we cannot do better than these young monsters from the banks of the Ganges, in my opinion, of all the monsters, savages, Charruas, Bedouins, present and future, who come to seek their fortunes in Paris.

The Siamese twins are twenty-five years old; their height is about five feet tall, one of the two, Eng, is a

little smaller and less strong than the other; their skin
is olive, their eyes small and raised in the Chinese
way; their hair is of the most beautiful ebony black;
they wear it short in the front, but in back it forms
long braids which circle their heads like crowns.
Dressed in European clothes, they wear little open
vests, and the only visible part of their bodies is the
band which unites them; a little opening in the shirt
suffices to show this communal part which forms as a
hyphen-mark between the two brothers. . . .

When one is hungry, the other is hungry, when one
is tired, the other rests; they both like to eat well,
and in this, as in everything, they have the same
tastes; they are particularly fond of oysters and fish,
and they enjoy, so they say, delicious and big meals.
They have never put to the test, thank God, any desire to be married, and yet they are fond of children.
One of the two was stricken, in America, with an in-
termittent fever, and the other fell ill, that one also
felt the effects when blood was taken from his
brother's arms; what, finally, can I say to you? This
double man is, in all respects, but one and the same
man, and we are more burdened to find individual
facts by action of community between two beings so
ultimately united, and at the same time so complete,
each in his own.

When it comes to purely intellectual phenomena,
it is clearly evident that they are equally double and
independent, the one does not know the thoughts of
the other; thus one can read a novel while the other
studies history; but it is true that they don't like to do
different things at the same time; in general, they read
the same book together, as together they execute all
the actions of their life.

Despite their warm press reception, the public response to the twins' exhibits was disappointing. During their three months in Paris, their expenses were
higher than their income. Nevertheless, they loved
Paris and avidly took in the sights. They hired a coach
to go to the Bois de Boulogne, to the Jardin du Roi, to
the rue de l'Université. In a fiacre, they went to
Panthéon. They visited the Church of the Madelaine,

the royal mint, the palace and gardens of St. Cloud, and hired a coach to take them to a china manufactory in Sèvres. They paid two visits to the Jardin des Plantes, a museum of plant and animal anatomy and history, and were intrigued most of all by the giraffe. Throughout their stay, the twins were active socially. While it is not known whom the twins met in Paris, it is known that they visited the better houses and salons of the city, and they may well have rubbed elbows with the cream of Parisian society and culture.

While still in Paris, Harris made a cryptic note of an expense for the twins: "A frame for the portrait 8 francs." This likely referred to a five-by-seven-inch portrait of the twins—an "Ingreslike" miniature exquisitely detailed on a block of fine ivory—done by an unidentified French or Dutch artist. In the miniature, Chang and Eng may be seen as they were seen by Frenchmen in Paris. They wore black silk cravats, dark blue coats, and brown trousers.

The only blemish on the twins' stay in Paris occurred as the result of a tenuous partnership they formed with a fast-talking French promoter who had extravagant plans for their future. The promoter convinced the twins that they could be the stars of an enormous Siamese museum he planned to build, one replete with every imaginable type of Siamese artifact. In the museum there were to be models of Siam's major cities, temples, and public buildings. There were to be groups of wax figures representing the different classes of people engaged in their various occupations. There were to be stuffed Siamese animals and birds, as well as giant Buddhas. The promoter promised to import a full orchestra of Siamese musicians—eight gongs, five drums, and a flageolet—and a company of Siamese jugglers. Chang and Eng, of course, were to be the main attraction, and the whole package would be advertised as "Chang and Eng's Wonders of Siam."

The twins were favorably impressed by the idea, and first steps were taken toward executing the project. It soon became apparent, however, that the promoter was a little on the shady side. While he had pretended to have money, actually he had been using the twins in order to finance the whole scheme. When the twins realized the promoter's talk was bigger than his wallet, they broke with him and abandoned the project. The promoter later came to America, where he made a fortune with a patent medicine.

While in Paris, the twins attracted their usual complement of curious doctors. One French surgeon conducted a simple experiment on them. He applied strong pressure to the five-inch ligament that bound them together, in an effort to see how they would respond. They responded by fainting, although whether from pain or fright was not reported.

The British *Medical Gazette* printed the speculations of another French doctor: "M. Coste has visited these singular strangers, and raised rather a curious question about them; namely, at what epoch during uterine life their union took place? He has satisfied himself that it occurred during the last days of the first month of pregnancy!"

A second French physician who examined the twins was so impressed by their ability to speak English that he speculated in his report that they had probably forgotten their native Siamese, which was not true. The physician's report contained the standard medical information about the twins, but then gave way to a goulash of nonmedical philosophizing: "Plato said that in the origin of things, human beings were created in doubles, but of a different sex. As we see here, Nature has realized to a certain point the imagination of Greek philosophy: she has produced two beings, but she has produced them of the same sex; the young Siamese are two boys."

It was definitely time to leave Paris, if only to escape the doctors and their prose.

On March 1, 1835, Chang and Eng, accompanied by Harris, set out for the next stand, which was to be in Brussels. It took them eleven days to cross France into Belgium.

The Belgian metropolis was still suffering the after-effects of the liberal workers' revolution five years earlier. Following the defeat of Napoleon, the allied powers had forced Belgium and Holland to unite as one country under a Dutch king. The Belgians revolted in 1830, and gained an uneasy independence that was not made secure until nine years later. After Chang and Eng checked into the Hotel de Flandre in Brussels, they were eager to see the remnants of the revolution. They were escorted on a visit to the beautiful Palace of Orange, which the reigning prince and princess had occupied for two years before being driven from it. The twins found the royal rooms had been left untouched since the revolution—the princess's gloves and ink-stained pens were still lying upon a table in her boudoir.

Harris lost no time in getting down to business. He ran off 1,000 handbills and distributed them. He made the rounds of the leading Brussels newspapers and placed advertisements announcing the arrival for exhibition of the Siamese Twins. He also advertised for a Belgian interpreter, and then the twins were shown to the public for thirteen days.

After that, the twins traveled to Antwerp, a city still recovering from the fighting that had ensued in 1831 when the Dutch invaded the country. The Belgians, aided by a large French force, had driven them back. In the years since, the Dutch had withdrawn their major businesses from Belgium, and this had sorely affected the local economy. Chang and Eng found the city quiet and subdued.

The twins exhibited in Antwerp for about two weeks. Being insatiable sightseers, they found the time to visit Notre Dame Cathedral, where they enjoyed Rubens' *Descent from The Cross*, and then, difficult as it was, they climbed the five-hundred-foot staircase to the top of the spire for a look at the city below. The twins would always remember the Flemish paintings and old churches of Antwerp, but what they would remark on most often were the attractive women of the area, many of whom were of Spanish descent and wore the traditional mantilla.

On April 13, Chang and Eng left Antwerp in a carriage, on their way to Holland and an eleven-day engagement in Rotterdam. On this trip across the Belgian countryside, they encountered an unusual local tradition that they would never forget.

In Belgian towns at that time, young men, after serving their apprenticeship in the trade of their choice, were expected to take three-year traveling tours. The purpose was to educate them practically as to how their vocations were practiced in other parts of the country. By custom, the young men asked for money from anyone they met on the road —which was called "fighting" for a living, and consequently they were called "fighters."

As Chang and Eng rode through Belgium, one of these fighters stopped them and asked for a donation. The twins gave him a small sum, hardly believing that such a well-dressed and respectable-looking young man was serious in his request. The fighter thanked them for the donation, then observing that they were bound together, inquired if they were "the vast celebrity, the Brothers of Siam." Chang and Eng acknowledged that they were indeed none other than "the Brothers of Siam." Hearing this, the young man quickly reached into his pocket and pulled out a handful of silver coins, at least fifty times the amount that the twins had given him. He offered it to them in return for a closer look at their wondrous ligament. Amused, Chang and Eng stepped down from the coach and displayed themselves to their one-man audience—but would not accept the proffered money.

Proceeding by coach to the Dutch frontier, the twins ran into difficulties. The Dutch border guards would not let them enter the country, pointing out that they lacked a necessary signature on their visa. Unhappily, they were forced to turn around, make the long ride back to Brussels, obtain the necessary signature, and then return to the frontier, where they were finally passed into Holland.

Rotterdam was their first stop. They moved into the Hotel des Pays-Bas, sent out fifty-six articles of clothing to be washed and pressed, had their boots cleaned, and replenished their supply of cigars.

Their appearance in Rotterdam was well received. About this time, the twins had ceased to put on their acrobatic act, preferring simply to stand or sit while on exhibit. To judge by the turnout, the Dutch public was satisfied just to look at them and question them through their interpreter.

Next, Chang and Eng moved on to The Hague, where they were booked for a two-week stay at the Hotel de Maréchal. Their last stop on the European tour was Amsterdam, which they reached on May 15. They were on exhibition there for a month, and the public which attended their shows was enthusiastic. Their appearance in Amsterdam came to the attention of King William of Holland, and curious as any plebeian, the ruler summoned them to the royal palace for a visit.

In what remained of their spare time, Chang and Eng indulged themselves in their favorite pastime of shopping. Their expense record revealed the variety of their acquisitions during their four weeks in Amsterdam: "A pair of silk Gloves . . . Two Umbrellas . . . 2 Silk Stocks . . . Three pair of Trowsers of 'droll pattern' [undoubtedly Dutch pantaloons] . . . A pair of boots for Chang . . . 1300 Cegars . . . Wooden Shoes . . . 5 pair of Trowsers . . . 2 Velvet Vests."

They also acquired several canaries, which accompanied them home.

On June 15, 1836, Chang and Eng, with Harris, boarded the transatlantic brig *Francia* for their voyage back to the United States.

Following a smooth ocean crossing of almost eight weeks, the trio arrived in New York on August 7. Their first purchases in the United States were a new bird cage and a large quantity of birdseed for their imported pet canaries.

For the next three years, from their return to New York City in 1836 until 1839, Chang and Eng, accompanied by Harris, continued to tour steadily through the eastern and southern portions of the

United States. Tirelessly, almost daily, they exhibited in town after town, continued to take in money and save as much as they could while they faced ever-dwindling audiences (for so many had seen them before), working toward the day when they could finally be free of the routine of one-night stands and public displays. Their mutual secret desire was to change their means of livelihood and alter their way of life. Renowned on two continents, they were fast reaching a crucial point, a crossroads in their lives.

Always uppermost in their minds was the desire to go back to their native Siam, return to their home and family, far from the curious eyes of strangers. They had from time to time received news of their mother. They had learned that in 1833 she had remarried, and her second husband was a Chinese named Sen. No children had been produced by that marriage. More recently, an American naval officer, finding himself in Siam, had called upon Nok at her family's houseboat in Meklong, and was able to inform the twins that she was well.

The twins often spoke of going home and seeing their mother again one day. Yet they were not certain where their true home lay anymore—whether in Siam or in the United States.

The resolution would come soon, and it would occur in the place where they opened this last phase of their almost continuous eight-year tour. The place was Peale's New York Museum, under the proprietorship of Rubens Peale, son of the founder of America's foremost theatrical showcase before the advent of Phineas T. Barnum.

It was because of the twins' frequent appearances at Peale's Museum in New York—sometimes for a month at a time, sometimes for three months—that they were to encounter the person who would be responsible for changing their entire direction in the years that lay ahead.

Peale's Museum, first established in Philadelphia in 1786, had been the brainstorm of an eccentric naturalist and artist named Charles Willson Peale, who had painted the earliest known portrait of George Washington as well as fifty-nine other Washington portraits.

Peale's main interests had been painting—he had studied in London under Benjamin West—and natural history. His career had been interrupted by the Revolutionary War, during which he fought in the Battle of Trenton, and by three marriages. He found his true calling with the establishment of his museum in Philadelphia. There had been earlier museums, small collections mainly intended for scholars. Peale's Museum was the first designed for the general public. In the beginning, Peale's Museum was devoted to natural curiosities. The main feature was an exhibit of animals carved out of wood and covered with hide, depicted in their natural habitats. From this, the museum grew to include botany, mineralogy, and all the natural sciences, as well as life-sized figures of different human racial types. To this, Peale added a room for lectures and concerts. The enterprise was a commercial success, and several members of Peale's large and talented family continued in their father's footsteps.

Peale had twelve children, and named five of his seven sons after great Renaissance painters. Each of his seven sons chose a career drawn from some aspect of his father's life—Raphael and Rembrandt were painters; Rubens was a museum director; Linnaeus was an adventurer; Franklin was a mechanical engineer; and Titian and Titian the 2nd were both naturalists. Three of the sons were interested in expanding the museum idea.

While Titian managed the Philadelphia museum, it was Rembrandt Peale who attempted to establish a museum of fine arts in Baltimore, and Rubens who eventually bought it and made it popular. It was this same Rubens Peale who opened the most famous of the family showcases, Peale's New York Museum, on Broadway opposite City Hall, on October 26, 1825, four years before the Siamese Twins arrived in New York on their first visit.

Slowly over the years the various Peale's Museums changed their character, from staid showplaces of natural history and galleries of art to repositories of oddities, wonders, and freaks. The changes were necessary in order to appeal to a wider spectrum of public interest and to compete with a major Manhattan rival, Scudder's American Museum, later to become truly famous as Barnum's American Museum.

In the year of its opening, in 1825, Peale's New York Museum was already making concessions to popular taste by featuring Egyptian mummies, which created a sensation. By 1829, live Indians were introduced, and Peale's "showed them in all their hair-raising acts of tribal meaning." The Indians were followed by freaks, namely Deborah and Susan Tripp, the incredible fat children—Deborah, three years old, weighed 124 pounds, and Susan, five years and ten months old, weighed 205 pounds. The obese sisters, in turn, were followed by Nicholas the Ventriloquist and a troupe of "Trained Canary Birds" who "awakened amazement and delight, one by feigning death or standing on its head, the other by playing dominoes, 'with any of the company!' "

Peale's New York Museum was plainly ready for the Siamese Twins. In 1831, Rubens Peale had booked Chang and Eng into his lecture hall. According to a New York historian:

"The Siamese Twins and an Italian Band of Music were at Peale's . . . in December. The Wallace family of clever children began on December 19th; on New Year's Day, 1832, Gray's 'Fantocini,' from London, including an Indian juggler, performing with golden balls, Grimaldi, the clown, the Old Soldier, who disengages from his body the whole of his limbs. . . . The stuffed figure of a Bengal Tigress that killed a lion in the Tower of London was set up about this time . . ."

After that, whenever Chang and Eng were not on the road, they became regulars at one Peale's Museum or another. Between 1834 and 1837, they made over a dozen appearances at various Peale's Museums in New York City, Philadelphia, Albany, and Baltimore.

While Chang and Eng were on exhibition in Peale's New York Museum, there occurred the fateful meeting that would affect their entire future. At one of their showings, a member of the audience was a Southern physician visiting New York from his native North Carolina. The physician "was so impressed" by the twins—apparently not only by their oddity, but by their personalities and intelligence—that he determined to meet them on a personal basis. After their exhibit had concluded and they had left the stage, the physician asked an attendant if he might have the honor of meeting them. Permission was granted.

Finding Chang and Eng in their private dressing room, the physician introduced himself as Dr. James Calloway, of Wilkesboro, North Carolina. The young Dr. Calloway was well known in his own right. A grandnephew of the frontiersman Daniel Boone, Dr. Calloway had been elected to the North Carolina legislature at the age of twenty-three, had studied medicine at the University of Pennsylvania, and had then set up a medical practice in Wilkesboro, a practice that ranged over seven North Carolina counties. Later, he would become an officer in the Confederate Army and a stalwart of the Episcopal Church.

Now, attracted by Chang and Eng not as abnormalities of nature but as human beings, he sat in their dressing room in Peale's Museum and became deeply involved in a friendly conversation with them. According to Shepherd Monroe Dugger, who had met the twins and would publish a privately printed reminiscence of them in 1836, the talk between Dr. Calloway and the twins took a personal turn:

"In the conversation of that call, it was revealed that the Twins, being fond of sport, went on a hunting or fishing vacation twice a year.

"The Doctor told them that Wilkes County was replete with clear streams teeming with fine fishes; that the hills and mountains abounded in deer and wild-turkeys, with smaller game, as squirrels and pheasants galore. He invited them to come to Wilkesboro, on their next vacation, assuring them the abundant courtesies of the town and country. This was the beginning of a friendship between them and Dr. Calloway that ended with their death . . ."

After exhibiting in North Carolina in early 1839, Chang and Eng were ready for a long-deferred vacation, Dr. Calloway's vivid description of his corner of North Carolina, which they dimly remembered from having exhibited there, had made a lingering impression. The twins consulted with Harris and agreed to accept the physician's invitation, and together the three arranged to spend their free time in Wilkesboro.

Soon, the twins were on their way to Wilkesboro, little aware of the profound effect the visit would have on the rest of their lives.

6

CHAPTER
9

Love Conquers All

'Although North Carolina had been part of the United States for almost half a century when Chang and Eng settled there in 1839, it was still one of the most backward, underdeveloped, and primitive states in the Union.

Of the state's 236,000 people who had occupations, 217,000 were engaged in farming. Most of the farmers had relatively small plots, generally under 50 acres. There were 25,761 farmers in the state with farms from 11 to 50 acres in size, 2,050 with farms 10 acres or less, and only 311 persons who owned more than 1,000 acres.

The main produce of the farms was either cotton or tobacco. Some wheat and corn was grown. Many farms raised livestock. An important home industry was the distilling of liquor. The distillers turned out about a million gallons a year. The fields were largely manned, and the farms maintained, by black slaves. An efficient field worker brought $800 in the slave market. The Baptist Church in North Carolina, evok-

ing the curse of Canaan, was satisfied that slavery
had been sanctioned by the Bible.

The more prosperous planters attired themselves in
cutaway wool coats which they wore with white
silk or cotton stocks and high-waisted loose trousers
that were kept neat by footstraps. Poorer whites and
blacks wore cotton or woolen homespun. For rich
and poor alike, the favorite avocation was hunting. No
farmer was without his guns and dogs. Fishing the fertile streams also enjoyed great popularity.

In North Carolina in 1839, the densely populated
metropolis was unknown. Forward-looking citizens
bemoaned the fact. A committee reported to the
North Carolina legislature: "It is a singular circumstance, that North Carolina, with a wider sea coast
than any State in the Union, and the fifth in extent
of territory and in population, has less commerce and
fewer important towns than any of her Atlantic
sisters." The Industrial Revolution had not touched
North Carolina. A traveler from England, visiting the
state's major cities, found them filled with "quiet, old-
fashioned people, content with little, and not at all
disposed to trouble themselves with the mania of internal improvements."

Internal improvements were, indeed, lacking. Roads
between cities were poor, and the state's first railroad
was still a year away. Communications were sparse,
and the people were ill-informed. Only twenty-seven
newspapers existed in the entire state. The newspapers
were little more than political organs, highly partisan,
carrying hardly any objective national news and almost no local news. Furthermore, they were dreary
to the eye, devoid of informative headlines, the
stories often introduced with the legend "Important"
or "A Fact Worth Knowing."

Nor was there a school system funded by either
the state or local communities to educate the young.
There was but a handful of schools, and these had
been privately built by small groups of concerned
citizens. Medical services were a shambles. Dysentery was commonplace. Occasionally, a cholera epi-

demic decimated a section of the state. In this era before anesthesia, surgery patients were tied down to the operating table and given liquor or opium. When the well-to-do needed surgery, they did not trust the local physicians but hastened off to consult more advanced practitioners in Virginia or Pennsylvania or even New York.

There was some sense of order in the communities. To further this, the Cherokee Indian population had been forcibly removed from the state. The law was excessively harsh. For assaulting and maiming another person, the offender was punished by two hours in the pillory and thirty-nine lashes on his bare back. If the offender committed a second assault, the penalty was death without benefit of clergy. Teaching a slave to read or write, or selling the slave a book or pamphlet, was a crime carrying a penalty of $200.

In North Carolina in 1839, the staple fare for the poorer classes was fried ham, eggs, grits, red-eye gravy, and coffee. Among the upper classes, the women enjoyed snuff—they did not sniff it, but ate it. Married women had no rights—no right to sue, own property, make out a will. Dueling to defend one's honor with "smooth-bore pistols" still survived as a custom.

Yet for most visitors, this was an attractive place and way of life. One traveler, struck by the quiet of the countryside and the peacefulness of the villages, thought it was heaven, a relief from "the bustle, the speculation, and the embarrassment of the large Cities."

Chang and Eng, touring in Georgia, South Carolina, and North Carolina in late 1838 and early 1839, were among those travelers and visitors who instantly found North Carolina heaven.

Of course, they had been through the state before during their interminable tours and exhibitions. As recently as two years earlier, they had made an appearance in the town of Wilkesboro, located in Wilkes County, a wild, picturesque area not far from the Blue Ridge Mountains, where "For One Day only

THE UNITED BROTHERS, CHANG-ENG" received "Visitors at the TENT . . . ADMITTANCE 50 CENTS." But at that time, constantly on the move, constantly trying to please and make money, Wilkesboro had been just another hamlet, another blur on their itinerary where wide-eyed faces came to gather around them, to gawk and stare.

Now, arriving in this isolated, untamed northwestern corner of the state, without the pressure of being exhibited, coming instead as onlookers, Chang and Eng saw the area through new eyes. Certainly the two of them were curiosities, would forever startle and provoke amazement, yet somehow in this remote sector they had a feeling of acceptance. To a few they were freaks and Orientals, but to the majority they were welcome guests and human beings.

To the twins, in turn, the natives of Wilkesboro were a delight. They found the people private and unobtrusive, yet friendly and generous. They also felt that the natives were appreciative of the same virtues that they themselves held in high regard, namely industry and honesty. As for the landscape, with its mountains and valleys, forests and rivers, it offered them their first opportunity to enjoy peace, tranquillity, and ease, along with the promise of such sports as fishing and hunting deer, wild turkey, pheasants, squirrel.

In his unpublished manuscript, the twins' friend Judge Jesse Graves recounted their coming to Wilkesboro and the early days of their vacation:

Mr. Chang and Mr. Eng . . . having travelled over most of the United States and much of Europe and having been for eleven years constantly before the public began to grow weary of that way of life and to wish for some rest and retirement. In this frame of mind they arrived at the quaint village of Wilkesboro nestled down on the banks of the Yadkin River away up among the blue mountains traversing the western part of North Carolina. Captain Carmichael, a most agreeable, entertaining and accommodating host dispensed the comforts of his well supplied table most elegantly; and his excellent brandy purely distilled from the best apples in the world, was not without its charms to Dr. C. Harris who knew how to appreciate the luxury of the bowl. So, partly from their own inclination and partly at the instance of their old and long tried friend, the Doctor, it was determined they would spend an indefinite time in that retreat. Deer abounded in the neighboring mountains, foxes in the fields around the village, and perch in the clear streams of the valleys, and in the brooks on the mountains the beautiful speckled trout were found in great abundance.

Fishing had been a sport and a business in which Chang and Eng had delighted in early life; they had now become very expert in the use of fire arms, and had acquired a great fondness for hunting. Being now in a situation to engage in chasing stags and catching trout, they determined to remain at least until winter to enjoy the recreation which they had desired to find far away from the hurrying crowds.

Along with Harris, Chang and Eng rented rooms from Captain Carmichael, and now they extended their stay. Gradually, it had dawned on the twins that they did not want to leave Wilkes County. They did not want to return to Siam. They did not want to go back to touring the United States. Wilkes County was the closest thing they had found to a haven, and they wanted to make it their home.

There was, of course, the matter of a livelihood. Financially, they were comfortable but not wealthy. For some years before they had come to Wilkesboro, and in the years to follow, the press speculated that they were worth between $40,000 and $60,000, a fortune in those days. The figures, however, were grossly inaccurate. The income and expense records they so religiously kept revealed the truth about their net worth. The fact was that Chang and Eng had savings of $10,140 when they came to Wilkesboro. This was a large sum, but certainly not a sufficient amount to retire on. Furthermore, Chang and Eng were only twenty-eight years old, healthy, energetic, and im-

bued with the work ethic and the desire for absolute
security.

Total retirement was out of the question. But
what could be done to provide income?

There was one possibility that they had apparently
discussed privately. As children in Siam they had done
well as merchants. As adults in North Carolina they
might be merchants again.

Presently, Chang and Eng rented, stocked, and
opened a retail store in Wilkes County. On their
shelves and in containers they offered a wide variety
of goods for sale: women's dress patterns, linen
goods, feathers, turkeys, wheat, cotton cloth, beef,
pork, coffee, potatoes, bedcovers, oats, apples, brown
sugar, corn, salt, harness leather, mattress ticking. The
store remained open briefly. Then, because business
was bad due to a depression in the country, they abandoned their enterprise, but with little regret.

For at last, Chang and Eng knew what they wanted
to do. Now that they had set down roots in Wilkes
County, they wanted to live off the land, to become
gentleman farmers. Early on, they had bought property in the community of Trap Hill, first settled in
1775, and according to a local history "named Trap
Hill for hunter William Blackburn's railpen snare
which he frequently set on a nearby hill to catch wild
turkeys." The property, isolated and wild, was next
to Little Sandy Creek, near the Roaring River.

When Chang and Eng had purchased the land, they
were issued the first deed ever signed in that area.
The deed read: "October 17, 1839. From Caleb Martin
to the Siamese Twins, Chang & Eng. 100 acres plus 50
acres, for $300. Along little Sandy Creek." The twins
paid their $300 for the 150 acres with a bag of silver
coins.

In the next four years, the twins expanded their
property holdings, buying two additional parcels of
land, one 26½ acres, the other 37½ acres.

Once they had chosen Trap Hill, they set out to
build themselves a house. The wooden house that
eventually rose on a slope was two stories high, with a

spacious veranda on three sides of the ground floor. The interior was divided into four rooms, two rooms downstairs and two upstairs. The chimney, which served all four fireplaces, was huge, five feet wide. The staircase that led to the second story was extra wide, so that the twins could ascend side by side without difficulty. Because the twins wanted a view from every part of the house, as well as plenty of daylight inside, they designed most of their rooms with oversized windows. In one twelve-by-fourteen-foot room, there were six windows that reached from the floor almost to the ceiling. The kitchen was placed in a small building next to the house, and contained the largest fireplace in the area. Another separate building was partitioned as a dwelling for slaves, a storehouse, and a stable for horses.

In June 1840, when the Trap Hill house, as it came to be called, was ready for occupancy, Chang and Eng dispatched Charles Harris to New York City to buy furnishings. Harris spent $467 acquiring rugs, tumblers, forks, spoons, tea trays, candlesticks, and dozens of other congenial items. The heavier furnishings—the bed, the double-sized chairs, and the tables—the twins either purchased or had custom-made in Trap Hill or Wilkesboro.

But even as the Trap Hill house was undergoing construction, Chang and Eng were taking steps to legitimatize further their belonging, their Americanization. Just as their friend Harris had already done, the twins applied to the Superior Court of the state on October 12, 1839, "to become naturalized citizens of North Carolina and the United States of America." Their petition read:

Chang and Eng (commonly known as the Siamese twins) represent to this Honorable Court that they are natives of the kingdom of Siam, in Asia; that they arrived in Boston, Massachusettes, United States, on the 16th day of August, 1829. In October of that year they went to England and returned to the United States in March, 1831, and resided therein without leaving there until the fall of 1835, when they went to lower Canada, soon after they went to the continent of Europe and were absent about 12 months. After their return in 1836, they went to the province of lower Canada where they remained until October, 1836, when they returned to the United States and have continued therein without leaving there ever since; and since the 1st day of June, 1839, have continued within the State of North Carolina; they further represent that during their continuance within the United States they have behaved as men of good moral character; that they are attached to the principles of the Constitution of the United States and are well disposed to the good order and happiness of the same—and they here before this Honorable Court declare their intention to become citizens of the United States and to renounce their allegiance to the King of Siam and of every other State, King or Prince and Potentate, and they respectfully pray that this Honorable Court may receive their declaration, made before this Court with the view of becoming naturalized citizens of the United States and that a record thereof be made and such order or judgment in the premises as is by law required.

CHANG ENG

Sworn to before me, Oct. 1,
1839. J. Gwyn, Jr. C.S.C.

Shortly after, in the minutes of the Superior Court, there was set down the following entry: "Chang and Eng appeared in open court and took the oath of allegiance to the United States and to the State of North Carolina."

Still, something was missing. Chang and Eng were names appropriate for Siam, but for American citizens the names seemed foreign and incomplete. Real Americans had surnames. Chang and Eng had none.

An oft-told story survives to this day as to how the Siamese Twins finally acquired a surname.

According to the story, Chang and Eng visited the Naturalization Office in New York to sign some citizenship papers. They waited their turn in line, and when it came, the clerk at the desk looked up and asked for their names. "Chang and Eng," they replied together. The clerk was puzzled. Surely, they must each have another name. They shook their heads. No, neither had a last name. The clerk was dismayed. He told them that they could not become American citizens unless each had a Christian or given name and a surname. If they could find one, their application could then be completed.

The twins stood there, uncertain as to what to do. In the midst of their confusion, a gentleman who had been standing not many feet away suddenly came toward them. He introduced himself as Fred Bunker. He lived at 41 Warren Street in New York, and had seen the twins perform at Peale's Museum. He had also just overheard the clerk's protest. "Well," said Fred Bunker, "I'd consider it an honor if you two gentlemen would care to use my name. You are most welcome to 'Bunker,' if it would help you."

The twins were delighted. They thanked the man, turned back to the desk, and told the clerk their application should carry the names Chang Bunker and Eng Bunker.

Unfortunately, the story is untrue.

The twins did want a surname, but the way they got one was much more prosaic. Judge Jesse Graves told the true story—as it had been told to him by the twins—in his unpublished manuscript:

"Probably in the year 1832 they [Chang and Eng] formed the acquaintance of three gentlemen then living in the City of New York, Fred Bunker and William Bunker and Barthuel Bunker, residing at No. 41 Warren St. to whom they became very greatly attached and in whose families they spent some very happy times. So great was this friendship especially on the part of Chang for Miss Catharine M. Bunker, his particular favorite in the family of his friends, that he at one time in his life duly made his will bequeathing all his estate to the object on which his affections reposed, and for many years the testament was unrevoked—in truth it was never revoked until he loved again and not so much in vain. In honor of their friends, Chang and Eng assumed the name of Bunker in 1840."

Chang Bunker and Eng Bunker used their new surname frequently thereafter, although it was not until four years later that the Superior Court of Wilkes County made it legal.

Chang and Eng were no strangers to law courts during the early years of their residence in Trap Hill. Besides the more amiable occasions when they appeared in the Superior Court of Wilkes County to obtain their citizenship and adopt their new name, they were in the same court twice in 1842, once as plaintiffs and once as the accused. On the first occasion, a laborer named Thomas Gross was cited, according to the minutes, for taking "one pocket knife of the value of six pence of the proper goods and chattels of Chang & Eng the Siamese twins then and there being found personally did steal take and carry away against the peace and dignity of the State." On the other occasion, Chang and Eng, Charles Harris, and two friends were hauled into court for "an assault" upon John Bartley and three of his friends, whom they "did beat, wound and ill treat." Whether or not they were found guilty is not known. Despite their handicap, the twins were always ready to fight anyone who they felt was insulting them or invading their privacy.

During the period that Chang and Eng were deciding to stay in North Carolina, they changed their temporary quarters. With Harris, they moved from their rented rooms in Captain Carmichael's hostelry to rooms in a home owned by a local merchant and farmer named Robert Bauguess. This move, as it turned out, would alter Harris' life, as it would dramatically change the lives of Chang and Eng.

The thirty-eight-year-old Harris found that his landlord, Bauguess, had a daughter named Fannie, described by Judge Graves as "a beautiful daughter, a blushing bouncing, buxom mountain maiden, whose charms the doctor found more captivating than even the good cheer of the host at the village hotel." At once, Harris' heart went out to Fannie Bauguess. "The handsome and intelligent showman," wrote Judge Graves, "who had been adding annually to his capital for the past ten years, and now had a snug little competence, and on whom many a village beauty had smiled, actually loved, wooed and won and married the pure but unpolished girl whom he had met in her mountain home apparently so much by accident. At the marriage of the Doctor and Miss Bauguess according to the custom of the hospitable people of that section a great feast, a real marriage supper was made and all the friends for several miles around were invited to come and witness the ceremony and partake of the good things provided for the occasion."

Among those present to see their friend Charles Harris launched into matrimony were Chang and Eng. Also attending as guests were two of the most sought after and popular young women in the community. These young women were sisters—Sarah Yates, more often called Sally Ann or Sallie, who was eighteen, and Adelaide Yates, known as Addie, who was seventeen—both the daughters of David Yates, a prosperous farmer who had a handsome white house and cabins for his fifteen slaves on a hill overlooking the valley of Mulberry Creek and 1,200 acres of land six miles outside Wilkesboro.

The Siamese Twins had met David Yates some months earlier, but they had neither seen nor met his daughters. Toward the end of the Harrises' wedding feast, the twins were introduced to or introduced themselves to Sallie and Adelaide Yates, to whom they had been attracted. An account of their initial conversation has survived in a book privately published in 1936 in Burnsville, North Carolina, written by Shepherd Monroe Dugger, who as a young man had met the twins. Dugger's account reflects the

tone of the twins' conversation, which was frequently impudent and humorous.

According to Dugger, once the introduction had
been effected, "a lively conversation" ensued.

Eng addressed Sallie and Adelaide Yates. "My
brother wants to marry," he said cheerfully, "and if
any young lady here will have him, we will have a
wedding today."

"It is he who wants to marry," said Chang quickly,
pointing to his attached brother, "and he is putting it
off on me just to raise a conversation with you about
love. He'd marry at the drop of a hat, and drop it
himself, if he could get the ugliest girl in town to say
'yes.' "

"The reason I don't marry," said Eng, indicating
the ligament that bound them together, "is because
I'm fast to him."

"The reason I don't marry," added Chang, "is because I'm fast to him. Isn't it a pity that neither of
two brothers can marry, because he is fast to the
other?"

"Indeed it is," answered Sallie Yates solemnly. "Is
there no chance for you to be separated?"

"The doctors say not," said Eng, "and each of us
decided that we would rather look on pretty girls,
with a lean and hungry lovelook, and continue to
want a wife than to be in our graves."

Now Adelaide Yates spoke up. "What a pity that
you who love ladies so dearly can't marry, and that
two young ladies can't have such lovely husbands as
you would have been."

There was a lull in the conversation. There seemed
little more to be said.

"Good-bye," said the Yates sisters.

"Good-bye," said Chang.

Eng offered a promise. "Good-bye, my brother
will be back to see you some day."

"If I come back," said Chang quickly, "I will leave
him behind, because he always monopolizes the conversation of the girl I love best."

Eng was not through. "To show that I want to be

fair," he said lightly, "I will let him take the choice of you girls now, and if we get back, the other shall be no less a choice to me."

Chang made his choice. He pointed to Adelaide Yates.

On this, "they parted joking." Chang and Eng watched the Yates sisters make their farewells to Harris and his guests. Years later, Chang and Eng recollected the leavetaking for Judge Jesse Graves, who wrote it down:

"In the morning the guests all departed, each taking his way home. Chang observed that a rather handsome young fellow dashed up by the side of Miss Adelaide as she cantered off on the prancing bay; and Eng saw that a rather good looking young Methodist preacher, named Colson, rode more soberly along by the side of Miss Sally. If any emotion of interest stirred the breast of any of the parties at that time it is one of the unrevealed secrets."

But, according to the story as told by the twins' 1936 historian, an "emotion of interest" did stir both Chang and Eng. Once alone in their bedroom, Chang brought up the Yates sisters.

"We will keep in touch with those girls," he said, "for they think more of us than we are thought of by all else in America."

Eng was less certain. "Maybe you are mistaken. It was only an acquaintance, and they did not want to render things unpleasant by bluffing our familiarity."

"It was more than that," said Chang earnestly. "I felt the thrill of their sympathy deep down in my soul. Maybe they will marry us."

Eng, ever aware of their condition, refused even to entertain the thought. "Marrying with us is a forlorn hope," he said. "No modest girl is apt to marry, where the pleasures of her bridal bed would be exposed, as ours would have to be."

"Brother, you see it wrong," Chang persisted. "It is the refined—and those only—who can excuse whatever is necessary to become a mother. We are not responsible for our physical condition, and we should not have to die childless on that account. We will see again, the dear girls who talked so good to us today; and, through their love we may have children to carry our blood and image in the world, when we and their mothers have gone to the Glory Land."

But Eng remained cynical. "Brother," he said, "I never saw you so great a philosopher as you are now. Those girls inspired you, and when you go back to see them, don't fail to take me, and I will do my best in helping you win Adelaide, who sent that thrill to the bottom of your craw. I know you have sand enough in your gizzard to digest it."

In the years to come, Chang and Eng would learn a good deal about the Yates family.

David Yates was of Dutch and Irish stock, and a church-going Baptist. He was a busy and successful farmer and a county justice. He and his wife Nancy had six children, three of them older than Adelaide and Sallie. Chang and Eng would always feel comfortable with Nancy Yates because she, like they themselves, was "an object of curiosity." Nancy Yates was grotesquely fat. Wrote Judge Graves:

> This lady was about five feet seven inches in height and nearly nine feet in circumference. Her accurate weight was never ascertained for the reason that there were in that neighborhood no adequate means of weighing her. Several contrivances were resorted to ascertain her weight, but the nearest approach to success was by using two pairs of steel yards drawing together four hundred and fifty pounds which being firmly secured a sort of swinging platform was attached thereto. When this good woman stepped upon the platform both beams flew up; but the gentleman engaged in the enterprise estimated that her weight could not have been less than five hundred pounds. She was unquestionably the largest woman in this state, perhaps in America. Long after the time we have been speaking of, she died of obesity. When her coffin was taken from the undertakers it could not

be gotten into the house until an opening was made for it.

While Chang and Eng thought constantly of Mrs. Yates's two comely daughters and how they might see them again, they busied themselves settling into their new Trap Hill house. "Their place was situated eighteen or twenty miles Northwest of Wilkesboro, the County seat of Wilkes County in the midst of the most beautiful and picturesque scenery," wrote Judge Graves:

> Their business transactions were chiefly with the merchants of that village; and during their building operations and subsequent merchandising, they made very frequent trips thither.
>
> The road over which they passed led close by the residence of David Yates, Esq., that stood six miles from the village upon the high hill overlooking the rich valley of Mulberry Creek. The large house painted white with its surroundings of kitchen and garden and "cabbins" were unusual marks of wealth and pride in that remote section and gave the place a rather aristocratic aspect. It had then a much more inviting appearance than it has now. It was then a place of nice quiet entertainment where the host was kind and the hostess "a host within herself." . . .
>
> It was not so very strange then that Chang and Eng should visit one [who] like themselves [was] out of the ordinary course of nature. So in their frequent visits to and from town, Chang and Eng fell into the habit of stopping at Esq. Yates for dinner, or in the evening to stay all night and chat with the old gentleman and the old lady. As their acquaintance became a little more familiar, they often devoted much of their time to the young ladies whom they entertained most agreeably with accounts of their adventures, and the amusing scenes they had witnessed—interspersed with very soft sweet sounds on their flutes—melody very greatly admired by the girls who had never heard such instruments before. Chang and Eng [had known] the young ladies

nearly five years and had become very much in love with them. They had not made any very marked demonstration and could not well form any opinion of the feelings of the young ladies for them.

It was difficult for Chang and Eng to think of anything except their love for Sallie and Adelaide Yates, but they tried. They concentrated on clearing their acres of stones, rubble, and brush, then plowed and planted their crops. They populated the farm with animals, not only horses, but livestock like cows and pigs.

The twins wanted to be accepted by their fellows as more than a curiosity, and when the North Carolina legislature passed a resolution making them honorary citizens of the state, they were proud. They settled into the community, later even acquiring a family doctor in the person of their old friend Dr. Calloway.

According to Kay Hunter in her book *Duet for a Lifetime*, on November 15, 1842, Chang and Eng wrote of their situation to their discoverer, Robert Hunter, who was once more back in London: "We have bought some land in this country, and raise our own corn and hogs—we enjoy ourselves pretty well, but have not as yet got married. But we are making love pretty fast, and if we get a couple of nice wives we will be sure to let you know about it. We weigh 220 lbs. (together) and are pretty stout fellows at that!!!!"

In the same letter, Chang and Eng went on to say that they lived near the Blue Ridge Mountains, twenty-five miles from the Virginia border and 180 miles from the nearest railroad. "So we are quite removed from the march of intellect," they wrote.

To keep up with the march of intellect, Chang and Eng continued to see their former manager and close friend, Charles Harris, and his young wife Fannie, who had recently given birth to the first of several children, a boy who was named Joseph. The Harrises had a house not far from the twins', located in a valley between the Blue Ridge Mountains and a pile of granite known as Rock Mountain. Harris had resumed his original profession, that of accountant.

To Harris, alone, the twins were able to pour out their hearts. They told him of their love for the Yates sisters and their secret desire to get married. Harris had misgivings, which he imparted to confidants like James Hale in Boston. To Harris, the idea of the twins, bound together by a five-inch ligament, unable to act except in tandem, actually marrying two normal young woman seemed too bizarre, and an invitation to disaster.

No doubt, Chang and Eng harbored the same thoughts. But their dual passion for Sallie and Adelaide Yates, and their determination to live like ordinary human beings and enjoy the connubial bliss less worthy men enjoyed, overcame all inhibitions and obstructions.

So far, Chang and Eng had not let the Yates sisters know their true feelings. At last, they decided to do so. Judge Graves recorded what followed:

They finally determined to know the worst, and began to show marked signs of interest as could not be misunderstood. They were not repulsed entirely, although Miss Sally Ann gave Eng very little encouragement. The next visit they found Miss Sally Ann away from home. It was certainly a very unfavorable sign for Mr. Eng. Chang however felt encouraged to hope for success and declared his passion with as much correctness as any other lover ever did, and although it was rather an embarrassing situation for Miss Adelaide, she with a woman's tact gave him to understand that his love was reciprocated.

Eng was in a sad dilemma. He was fearful some rival, perhaps the young parson, had already won the affections for which he was pining. As he was necessarily a confidant of his brother and Miss Adelaide, he determined to confide in her and ask her to deliver some friendly messages to her sister, Interested herself in the success of his suit, she was not unwilling to bear the messages, and if necessary to add a few words in commendation of him that sent them. Sally began to think rather more favorably of the matter, but still she gave but slight encouragement.

Indeed, Eng's sad dilemma was not his alone. Both Chang and Adelaide Yates were involved as well, and all three had equally as much at stake. It was not enough for Chang to have loved and won, with the possibility of soon possessing a mate. It was illogical for one of two joined twins to be married and the other to remain a loner and bachelor. It had to be four of them together, or none of them. And so, for the three who conspired in pursuit of the reluctant Sallie, it had to be one for all, and all for one.

In fact, a Bunker family tradition has it that while Adelaide was truly in love with Chang, Sallie was either not in love with Eng or not disposed to let herself fall in love with him. This would explain her brief obstinance. Perhaps the thought of forever being married to two men instead of one, of spending a married lifetime without a moment's privacy with a husband, of sharing meals and conversations and going to bed as a threesome, not a twosome, cooled any ardor she might otherwise have felt.

And so while Adelaide and Chang grew closer, Sallie continued to be friendly but still impersonal and somewhat withdrawn. Judge Graves wrote:

> While matters stood in this condition, the idea occurred to Eng that if he could find the opportunity for further and more earnest conversation than he had hitherto had, he might present his love in such a manner that his beloved would relent. In order to afford a favorable chance for the interview, and also to show their new neighbors that generous hospitality which they really felt and for which they were always distinguished, they determined to celebrate their removal into their new house by a social entertainment given to their friends and neighbors, to which Miss Sally Ann and Miss Adelaide were to be especially invited.

The gathering was to be both a "quilting" and "a house warming." Preparations on an adequate scale were duly made. Pigs and lambs and "the fatted calf" were slain to make ready for the feast. On the appointed evening the guests all came and among them Miss Sally Ann and Miss Adelaide. The quilting was soon done, and the supper over, the young folks betook themselves to the various amusements in which they enjoyed until a late hour. The next day Miss Sally did not leave for home until she had heard the earnest vows of her lover, nor did he cease to plead, with that persuasive eloquence sincere passion inspires, until success was attained. The maidens were both won . . .

Until then, the serious pursuit of the Yates sisters by Chang and Eng had been a secret, known only to the four of them. With the exception of Harris, no one in Wilkes County—the parents Nancy and David Yates, least of all—could imagine such a match or take the possibility of a double marriage seriously.

But sooner or later, the four of them knew the matter would have to be brought out in the open, and so they decided to do it at once. Chang and Eng and the sisters chose to announce their courtship by displaying themselves together publicly. One afternoon, the four of them rode into Wilkesboro.

Those who saw them were shocked. Word of the brazen spectacle spread from one native of Wilkes County to another. Soon the news of the match was everywhere. Or almost everywhere. The girls' parents still had no inkling of what was going on.

However, the citizens of Wilkesboro assumed that David Yates not only knew of the grotesque match, but that he had sanctioned it. Angry and righteous neighbors, appalled at the thought of two of their fairest maidens pairing up with freaks, gathered together, hotly discussed the matter, and determined to protest.

According to biographer Kay Hunter, several groups advanced on the Yates house and threw rocks, breaking the front windows. When the bewildered Yates emerged, the protesters berated him for allowing his daughters to play it fancy free with the Siamese Twins.

They warned him that if he did not break up the unholy alliance and discipline his daughters, they would burn his crops.

No doubt David Yates, stunned by the news, informed his wife what was happening, and together they must have sought out their errant daughters. But Adelaide and Sallie were ready for their parents, and they quickly proclaimed their feelings for Chang and Eng.

"The father and mother were both indignant at the idea of such a union," wrote Judge Graves, "and forbade their daughters any further communication with their lovers. Their objection to these gentlemen did not arise from any want of character or social position, for in point of morality, probity, strict integrity, they sustained a spotless reputation, but it had its origin in an ineradicable prejudice against their race and nationality."

Incredibly, then, if the twins, speaking through Judge Graves, were to be believed, the objections to them as suitors came not from the fact that they were physically bound together—anomalies of nature—but from the fact that they were yellow-skinned and Orientals.

"The sisters considered this repugnance to their union as most unreasonable," said Judge Graves, "and concluded 'there are always crises in love.' The brothers were informed of the difficulty, and they hastened over to see their friends about the matter; but the stern parents would not listen or relent."

Chang and Eng then prevailed upon Parson Colby Sparks, one of the two local ministers, who was sympathetic to their desires and also had some influence on David Yates, to intercede on their behalf. Parson Sparks went to Yates and found him "inexorable upon that subject." Still refusing to give up hope, the twins approached the Methodist circuit preacher, the Reverend James L. Davis, and pleaded with him to speak to David Yates. Like the clergyman who had preceded him, the Reverend Davis was also firmly rebuffed.

Since they were banned from the Yates residence,

where their loved ones were being kept virtual prisoners, Chang and Eng retreated to their Trap Hill house to brood on the injustice of the human condition. Nature, while being fair to almost everyone else, had played a cruel trick on them. After all their travels, they had thought that they had finally found a place on earth where they might be treated as normal beings. After all their dreams, they had finally found two women who were willing to help them live and feel as most other men lived and felt. Now, once more, they were being reminded that they were aberrations of nature, could not belong, did not belong to anyone but themselves.

Then, in this dark hour, a ray of hope came to the twins.

A note arrived from Adelaide and Sallie. The note asked for a secret meeting on a certain date at a designated place where they would not be seen.

Chang and Eng were elated. They had not reckoned on the determination, aggressiveness, and independence of the Yates sisters. In a few days, the secret meeting was held. In the weeks to follow there were more clandestine meetings between the couples. This exciting revival of their courtship led to their ultimate decision—they would get married without permission.

What had motivated Adelaide and Sallie to fly in the face of convention and each marry two men? The sisters never spoke for themselves. But many others, in the years to follow, spoke for them. There were some who said that the sisters were revolting against the strictness of their parents and the puritanical community standards. There were others who said that they wanted the attention that might be derived from marrying a famous pair. There were still others who whispered that the sisters sought the thrill of sexual perversion. But most people at the time believed—which descendants of the family to this day deny—that Adelaide and Sallie were marrying for money, marrying Chang and Eng because they were among the wealthiest men in the county. Even Judge

Graves took this into consideration. "It has been charged by some that these ladies were actuated by mercenary motives—a charge most unfounded in fact . . ." Nobody, it might be said, mentioned the fact that they were marrying because they were in love.

However, no sooner had the decision been made to marry than Chang and Eng, privately, between them, had second thoughts. The public and parental objections to the marriage, they deeply believed, were based not only on racial prejudice but on the repellent idea that each sister would have to live with two men at once. There was only one solution. They would risk being surgically separated, so that if the operation succeeded they could meet their brides-to-be as two separate men.

From the moment that they had entered Western civilization over a decade before, from the seemingly endless procession of renowned doctors who had examined them in Boston, Philadelphia, New York, London, Paris, they had been warned that they could not be cut apart successfully. A few physicians, a very few, had thought that one, possibly even both, might survive such an operation, although even these medical men had felt that the odds against them were considerable. And, indeed, in earlier days, the twins had not wanted to undergo the risk. They certainly had seen no reason to invite the possibility of premature death. But now, for the first time, there was a reason.

According to the story told by biographer Kay Hunter, Chang and Eng left Trap Hill and headed north for Philadelphia. There, at the College of Surgeons, were the physicians who had examined them before, physicians they personally respected. Now, they met with these doctors and requested that an effort be made to separate them. The doctors once more told them that the surgery was too dangerous to undertake. Chang and Eng explained that they had found two sisters they wanted to marry and that their only hope for acceptable and successful marriages was separation. If they were willing to chance the surgery, the doctors should be willing to gamble, too. The doctors had no argument against this. Since the twins knew they most likely would not survive surgery, yet were willing to submit themselves to it on the outside chance that it might succeed, the doctors agreed to go ahead. A date was set.

Chang and Eng returned to Trap Hill. They took up their life as before, farming their acres, hunting and fishing, resuming their secret meetings, and making plans for marriage with Adelaide and Sallie.

The date for the surgery rapidly approached. Again, making some excuse, Chang and Eng left Trap Hill and traveled to Philadelphia. At the College of Surgeons, the doctors examined them one last time. The operation would take place the following day. On the following day, as the twins were being made ready, Adelaide and Sallie burst in upon them.

The distraught sisters had learned of their plan, possibly from Charles Harris, in whom the twins may have confided. The sisters knew the risk of surgery and would not allow it. Chang and Eng argued with them, tried to reason with them, tried to persuade them to go along. Adelaide and Sallie would not have it. The sisters begged them to give up the idea. They became hysterical and wept, assuring and reassuring the twins that they loved them as they were, and that the four of them could find happiness without the necessity of risking death. At last, deeply moved by Adelaide's and Sallie's concern and love, Chang and Eng complied with their wishes. They canceled the surgery, and the foursome left Philadelphia and returned to Wilkes County.

What remained was the marriage, how to achieve it in defiance of the wishes of Nancy and David Yates. Once more, Adelaide and Sallie appealed to their parents and pleaded for their consent. But Nancy and David Yates would not yield.

Adelaide and Sallie went back to the twins. Their parents were obdurate, they said. The four of them conferred until they reached a unanimous agreement. They would take matters into their own hands.

An elopement was agreed upon [wrote Judge Graves]. Of course it was to have been kept profoundly secret. The plan agreed upon was this: For a time the matter was to be apparently dropped until the ensuing county court week when Esquire Yates, who was one of the county Justices, would go to Wilkesboro to assist in holding the court, when the parties at an appointed hour should meet at a "Covenant Meeting House" which stands on the hill near the South Fork of Roaring River, and there, their old friend Colby Sparks, the Baptist pastor, was to be waiting ready to perform the ceremony, easy to be done before there could be any danger from pursuit. They understood pretty well there could then be no pursuit, for the irate father could not know of their flight in some time, and the mother who weighed five hundred pounds could not follow over such roads as lay between the Yates homestead and "Covenant Meeting House."

The elopement was never consummated. The parents having ascertained that the daughters intended to marry, and that they would not be dissuaded from their purpose, allowed them to be married at home . . .

Despite the grumblings and snickers of a minority in the community, plans went ahead for an immediate wedding.

The first formality the twins had to attend to was to obtain the marriage licenses. The licenses were issued, and Eng's read:

STATE OF NORTH CAROLINA,
Wilkes County.

To any regular minister of the Gospel having the care of souls, of whatever denomination, or to any Justice of the Peace, for said county:

You are hereby licensed and authorised, to solemnise the rites of matrimony between Eng Bunker and Sarah Yates, and join them together as man and wife.

Witness Wm. M. Mastin, Clerk of the County

Court, at office in Wilkesboro, the 10th day of April, A.D. 1843, and in the 67th of our independence.

WM. M. MASTIN, C.C.C.

On the same date, Chang received an identical license to wed Adelaide Yates.

The next formality, undertaken three days later, was fulfilling the legal requirement for a marriage bond.

In that period—and in fact until 1868—North Carolina had an "Act Concerning Marriages" that required the posting of a marriage bond before a couple could be legally married. The marriage bond was a guarantee that there was no legal obstacle to the proposed marriage. For example, bigamy was illegal. If either Adelaide or Sallie was committing bigamy (which they were not) by marrying joined brothers, the marriage bond of $1,000—guaranteed by a volunteer bondsman and the grooms—would be forfeited. Again, if it was later learned that a free white had married a person of Indian, Negro, mustee, or mulatto blood down to the third generation, the marriage would be illegal and the marriage bond forfeited. As it happened, Chang and Eng were Chinese, and North Carolina had never passed legislation against Orientals.

Jesse Yates, Adelaide and Sallie's brother, was the volunteer bondsman, and his guarantee of the $1,000 marriage bonds was shared by the twins. There were two identical marriage bonds, one for Chang and one for Eng. Chang's marriage bond read:

CHANG:: ADELADE
STATE OF NORTH CAROLINA
Wilkes County

Know all men by these presents that we Chang one of the Siamese Twins and Jesse Yeats [*sic*] are held and firmly bound unto the state of North Carolina in the sum of one thousand Dollars, current money, to be paid to the said state of North Carolina for the payment whereof, well and truly to be made and done we bind ourselves our Heirs executors and administrators jointly and severally, firmly by these presents sealed with our seal and dated this 13th day of April A.D. 1843.

The condition of the above obligation is such, that the above bounden Chang one of the Siamese Twins has made application for a license for marriage to be celebrated between him and Adelade Yates of the County aforesaid now in case it should not hereafter appear that there is any lawful cause or impediment to obstruct said marriage, then the above obligation is to be void otherwise to remain in full force and virtue.

> CHANG
> JESSE YATES.

The same day that the marriage bonds were secured, April 13, 1843, the wedding—actually two weddings—took place.

David Yates had sufficiently capitulated to his daughters' wishes to allow the wedding ceremonies to be staged in his living room. Judge Graves noted that the Reverend Colby Sparks, parson of the local Baptist Church, officiated at the unions. However, his memory was contradicted by the official record of the event:

To all whom it may concern

This is to certify that I have this day solemnised the rites of matrimony between Eng Bunker and Sarah Yates, of Wilkes Co., N.C.

> JAMES L. DAVIS
> MINISTER OF THE GOSPEL

In the presence of
David Yates, Thos. Yates,
C. H. Jones, and others.

The marriages were performed before a small gathering of family and friends. First, Eng and Sallie were married. Then, Chang and Adelaide were married.

The improbable had become a reality. There followed, said Judge Graves, "a most elegant supper." After that, wrote Dugger, everyone celebrated with "the biggest dance of all." There would have been the Virginia reel, with Chang and Eng dancing as a single partner. Next, the guests no doubt joined in a modified cotillion, which always "set the Twins flying round with the ladies, in the blissful delirium of the dance.

At last, the celebration was over, and the four of them headed for the Trap Hill house to start their honeymoon and their domestic life together. In the sleeping chamber of the Trap Hill house, reported Judge Graves, there waited "a very wide bed" built specially to accommodate all four of them.

"Marriage Extraordinary," the *Carolina Watchman* announced in a rare display of headlines. "In Wilkes county . . . Chang and Eng, the celebrated Siamese Twins, to two young Ladies, the daughters of David Yates of that county. May the connection be as happy as it will be close!"

CHAPTER 7

Three's Company, Four's a Crowd

Having given their hearts and hands to the Siamese brothers, Adelaide and Sallie Bunker were soon settled in happily with their new husbands. Their neighbors at Trap Hill welcomed them warmly, accepting the marriages as a fact of life and bearing no prejudice toward the bizarre household.

In the beginning, and for nine years thereafter, the foursome lived together under one roof. The honeymoon house, a simple, sturdy dwelling set back from the main road, was furnished plainly and neatly with oak and hickory furniture. The one bedroom contained the specially built bed, large enough to accommodate four occupants. While it is possible that another room in the house was also converted into a bedroom, to serve alternatingly three of the four Bunkers, it is more likely that conjugal duties were carried on with all four people in the same bed at the same time.

So devoted were the twins to these conjugal duties that in two years the Bunkers had produced four children.

Within three or four weeks after they were married, Eng and Sallie conceived their first child. Nine months later, on February 10, 1844, Sallie was delivered of the first Bunker child, a girl, named Katherine Marcellus, after the twins' early friend Miss Catharine Bunker of New York.

Also about four weeks after the marriage, Chang's Adelaide became pregnant. Nine months later, on February 16, only six days after Eng and Sallie had had their child, Chang and Adelaide became the parents of Josephine Virginia.

Learning of this in New York, James Hale was impressed and wrote back to Harris: "Your twin-children story creates a good deal of astonishment with those to whom I have told it. That was pretty close work—within 6 days of each other!"

But that was only the beginning of procreation at the Bunkers'.

On March 31, 1845, Sallie gave birth again, this time to another daughter, Julia Ann.

And on April 8, just eight days after her sister's delivery, Adelaide bore Chang a son, Christopher Wren.

It is clear from the almost constant childbearing that occurred that the four Bunkers led active sex lives from the start. The questions about this aspect of their marital life, in their own time and the years after, never stopped. People would ask one another, "Just how did they do it?" And, "Wasn't it inhibiting or embarrassing for the twin and his wife who were making love to have the other twin inches away?"

There exists little actual information as to the twins' sexual practices, and any answers to the persisting questions must therefore be largely speculative. Dr. Worth B. Daniels, of Washington, D.C., who undertook a study of Chang and Eng and announced his findings to the American Clinical and Climatological Association in 1962, made a statement on the twins' sex lives that was representative of the general attitude of propriety toward them: "It is not the purpose of this paper to enter into speculation upon the conjugal arrangements of Chang, Eng, Adelaide, and Sarah Ann. Possibly some imaginative member of The Climatological can report on his conjectures as to this at a later date."

It was observed, after their deaths, that the twins' genitals were normal. The only unusual thing about them, also observed in an autopsy report published many years later, was that the pubic hair of each of them was half black and half gray, being divided vertically.

As to the practical accomplishment of the act of love, Chang and Eng's connecting band limited the number of possible positions available to them.

The ligament held them five and one-half inches apart. There was enough flexibility in the ligament, however, to enable them to pull eight inches apart. Normally, when standing they were side by side and their adjacent shoulders overlapped. Yet a writer who knew them stated that "the flexibility of the cartilage is so great, that they can readily turn those shoulders outwards (which are close together), when they walk." After their deaths, physicians noted, "When the bodies were laid upon a table Chang's left side and Eng's right side were drawn somewhat toward one another. This was most marked in Chang, and gave a greater inclination of his trunk toward his brother's."

Physically, the twins could not maneuver very far apart. They were bound tightly when lying down, too close for either to achieve any real degree of independent performance or privacy. In sexual intercourse, only the obvious missionary position—with the man on top—could have worked well. Yet it could not have worked too well. The anatomical restriction was always there. If Eng mounted Sallie, then Chang could not be far behind—indeed, he would be dangling seven or eight inches to one side. Moreover, it meant Chang had to be curled against Sallie, partially covering her body throughout. The same condition would have occurred when Chang made love to Adelaide. Eng would have been drawn against or partially across Adelaide.

Another likely position of copulation that may have been employed was that of the woman mounting the man. Whether the straitlaced prudery of the period would have allowed such lovemaking by Sallie and Adelaide will probably never be known. In the later years of the marriage, such a position was unlikely because Sallie and Adelaide tended to a corpulence which would have made the act extremely difficult. Other possible positions, and the difficulty they presented, can only be left to one's imagination.

As to the possibility of both couples making love simultaneously, it was quite possible with both women on top, but quite improbable with both men on top, because their mates beneath would have had to be lying one partially across the side of the other's body, evoking images of an incredible orgy of flesh.

To the ever-titillating question of how much inhibition and embarrassment was created by the necessity of three persons being in bed at one time, an answer was once offered. It was the physician who attended Chang and Eng after their deaths, Dr. William H. Pancoast of Philadelphia, who asked this question of either Sallie or Adelaide, and received an answer:

"The twins . . . had become so accustomed to their curious relation as to act and live under certain regulations of their own as one individual. We were told in North Carolina that they had agreed that each should in turn control the action of the other. Thus Eng would for one week [actually for three days] be complete master . . . and Chang would submit his will and desires completely to those of Eng, and vice versa. Though it seems most immoral and shocking that the two should occupy the same marital couch with the wife of one, yet so thorough was this understanding of alternate mastery, that, as I was told by one of the widows, there had never been any improper relations between the wives and the brothers."

This "alternate mastery" referred to the alleged ability of one twin to become mindless, to "blank out," as it were, thus allowing his joined brother to enjoy his wife in what might be termed at least mental privacy. Presumably the method of "alternate mastery" disposed of all inhibitions and embarrassment when the twins lived together in a single residence, just as it did in later years when they had two separate homes.

While this kind of mentally controlled separation may be difficult to imagine, necessity demanded the invention of a workable method of some kind, and other Siamese twins have remarked on possessing the same ability. Violet and Daisy Hilton, a renowned pair of Siamese twins who were born in 1908 and who were joined at the hips, were eloquent on the subject.

Said Violet: "When Don came to see my sister, he just stood there gazing at her. A big thrill ran through both of us. At that time I had not yet learned how to will myself to be immune to my sister's emotions. Later on each of us acquired the ability to blank out the other in romantic moments.

"This was our first real-life romance, and it intoxicated both of us. I was as anxious for Daisy to experience her first kiss as she was herself. Then Don held out his arms to her. She moved closer—and he kissed her on the forehead!

"Our first kiss was a little disappointing to both of us. Don was of the old world and he didn't believe a man should kiss his ladylove except on the forehead, until they were engaged."

In later years, after having developed their own form of "alternate mastery," Violet remarked:

"Sometimes I quit paying attention, and didn't know what was going on. Sometimes I read and sometimes I just took a nap. Even before that, we had learned how not to know what the other was doing unless it was our business to know it."

While the girls seemed to be satisfied with their "blank out" abilities, it was not so easy for their mates.

Daisy was married once, but her husband moved out after ten days, saying, "Daisy is a lovely girl, but I guess I just am not the type of fellow that should marry a Siamese twin. . . . As far as being a bridegroom under such conditions is concerned, I suppose I am what you might call a hermit."

Fortunately for Chang and Eng, their wives, Sallie and Adelaide, expressed no such sentiments. The twins' old friend James Hale expressed his own doubts about the arrangement in a May 12, 1843, letter to Charles Harris: "Do write me as soon as you can for I am *very* anxious to know how they got into such a stupid scrape. If they only wanted *skin*, I think they might have managed to get it for *less* than for life. Depend upon it—the result will be, a desire to attempt a surgical operation upon themselves."

If two's company and three's a crowd, then four might be called a convention. It quickly became obvious that while the Trap Hill house was large enough for the comfort of two attached brothers, it just was not large enough for two married couples and their growing family of children. The search was on for a bigger house, and finally, in the summer of 1845, the twins went to look at a farm for sale in Surry County, near the village of Mount Airy, which they immediately purchased and occupied.

Shortly after their move, the twins sought a new doctor in the immediate vicinity to look after children, wives, and themselves. They sought one physician, and found two. They found the Hollingsworth brothers, both well known in the community. Dr. Joseph Hollingsworth and his brother, Dr. William Hollingsworth, owned houses and counseling rooms side by side on Main Street in Mount Airy. Dr. William Hollingsworth, born in Mount Airy, a graduate of Jefferson, Medical College in Philadelphia, was in his early thirties when he first met Chang and Eng. The twins called their physicians Dr. Joe and Dr. Billy, and were not only patients but lifelong friends.

Besides devoting their time to the producing and raising of offspring, Chang and Eng pursued their lives as farmers with great vigor. They put into effect methods and techniques that are known today as "scientific farming." They read widely on agriculture, and used the most modern methods available.

Again they cleared the brush and stones from endless acres, fertilized their land, and nourished it by
ditching, deep plowing, and turning under clover
and peas. They brought in the best new farm imple-
ments, introducing several of these into Surry
County. Their innovations enticed landowners from
along the Yadkin River to pay inspection visits to the
twins' booming farm.

Chang and Eng were among the first farmers in the
state to produce "bright" or "bright leaf" tobacco,
which was especially prized for use in cigarettes.
They owned a tobacco press, which their slaves used
to manufacture chewing tobacco. The twins were
very fond of smoking clay pipes and chewing tobacco, and it was observed that whenever one put a
fresh quid of tobacco in his mouth, the other did the
same.

The Bunkers' farm provided for almost all of the
family dietary needs. They raised milk cows, cattle,
sheep, pigs, and fowl, and they grew wheat, rye,
Indian corn, oats, peas, beans, and both Irish and
sweet potatoes. They made butter, obtained fruit from
their orchards, and kept bees for honey and beeswax.

In addition to being skilled farmers, the twins were
considered to be excellent carpenters, especially so
when they built themselves a larger house on their
Mount Airy farm.

It was said that Chang and Eng were the first to
chop wood by the method that is known today as
the "double chop." This involves two men, the first
man hitting the tree trunk with his ax slanted in one
direction, and the second wielding an ax slanted in
the opposite direction. By this method, the tree can
be cut right through without either man having to
shift the direction of his ax. Of course, for Chang
and Eng, this was the easiest and most natural way
to attack the task; it became widely adopted as a fast
and efficient means of chopping wood.

Chang and Eng donated some of their land as a site
for the White Plains Baptist Church, which they
helped to build. They cut and hauled the logs, con-

structed the roof, and installed a special two-seater pew for themselves. The building was small, plain, and sturdy.

All of this participation in the church's construction was probably done more out of goodwill and community fellowship than out of religious devotion. Adelaide and Sarah were avid churchgoers, but while Chang and Eng attended services fairly regularly, they were not nearly so devout as their wives.

No one knows exactly what the twins' religious beliefs were, but they seem to have embodied a personal blend of Buddhist and Christian fundamentals. Judge Graves speculated on this:

> When we consider the circumstances of their childhood and youth it will not seem strange if Chang and Eng with all their clear conceptions of the doctrines of orthodox Christianity were yet unable to remove entirely from their minds some faint influences of the early training of the mother before the household image, and of the instructions of the priest in the temple of the "Golden Supreme." Notwithstanding there may have lingered some tinge of the superstitions of their native land, some shadowy dreams of transmigrating spirits, yet they were firmly impressed with the reality of all the great essential truths of the Christian system of theology. They believed in the One Supreme God, in Christ the intercessor, the atonement for all men, in the Bible as the word of God, in the punishment of the evil and the reward of the good. . . . They were not faultless. Who is except the blameless one? They did not love their enemies, they did not bless those that cursed them, but they hated an enemy with an honest hatred, returned blow for blow, but were ready to forgive and quick to repair a wrong.

The twins were avid readers of the newspapers, and took a lively interest in local elections. They were staunch Southerners, before and after the Civil War. When traveling in the Northern states, they had to take pains to control their Southern indignation re-

garding the Fugitive Slave Law, and controversial
South versus North questions in general.

As to their actual political affiliations, Chang and
Eng were described as "zealous followers of Henry
Clay and the Whig party." Henry Clay—a handsome,
charming Kentucky lawyer who became Speaker of
the House of Representatives, Secretary of State, a
U.S. Senator, and leader of the Whig party—was beloved by his fanatic followers, including Chang and
Eng. Clay, known as the Great Pacificator or Great
Compromiser, believed in nationalism and a unified
United States free of sectionalism. Northern manufacturers liked him because he advocated a protective
tariff, and Southern landowners liked him because he
was easy on slavery. He was a colorful man who
fought duels, drank Kentucky whiskey, enjoyed
high-stake card games and horse racing. He once said,
"I had rather be right than be President." Yet he
wanted to be President, and ran twice, against Andrew Jackson and James K. Polk, and lost both times,
to Chang and Eng's dismay.

The Whigs were popular in North Carolina, and
their membership generally consisted of the "better
elements" of society. Since it was unusual for immigrants to become Whigs, the twins' support of the
party indicated their strong desire to identify with
the majority of native Americans. Chang and Eng
were often heard to say that they much preferred the
democratic system of government in America to the
monarchy of their native Siam.

There was one element of the Whig party that the
twins disliked—they were "greatly displeased at the
illiberal views which the 'know nothing' element
in their party evinced." After the Whig party dis-
solved in 1852, this element was referred to as the
Know-Nothing party, a secret society and political
group which was anti-Catholic and anti-foreigner,
and wanted to bar naturalized citizens from public
office. Its leaders told members that when they were
questioned about the workings of their organization,
they should simply answer, "I know nothing." Chang

A
FAMILY ALBUM

Photographs and drawings of
Eng and Chang, the original Siamese
twins, their wives and children.

An idealized drawing of Eng and Chang
at the age of 18 on their first visit to England
in 1829. Their five-inch connecting band
and common navel are plainly visible.

DRAWING BY H. BERTHOUD.

Left: An oil portrait of Captain Abel Coffin, a
Nantucket seaman and trader, who brought Chang and Eng
from Siam to the United States in 1829. He arranged
the Twins' first tours, until they quit him when
they reached the age of 21. PHOTOGRAPH BY WALTER KEMPTHORNE.

Right: An oil portrait of Robert Hunter, a Scots
merchant who traded in Siam. In 1824, he first saw the
13-year-old Siamese Twins, and five years later,
in partnership with Captain Abel Coffin, he brought
them to Boston. PHOTOGRAPH BY WALTER KEMPTHORNE.

The *Sachem*, the 397-ton American sailing ship
under the command of Captain Abel Coffin that carried
Chang and Eng from Bangkok to Boston in 1829.

A copy of a lithograph of the Siamese Twins
in 1839, when they were 28 years old. Chang is holding
the pamphlet sold at their exhibitions, and behind
him can be seen their chessboard. LITHOGRAPH BY HOFFY.
(The original artist mistakenly reversed the Twins.)

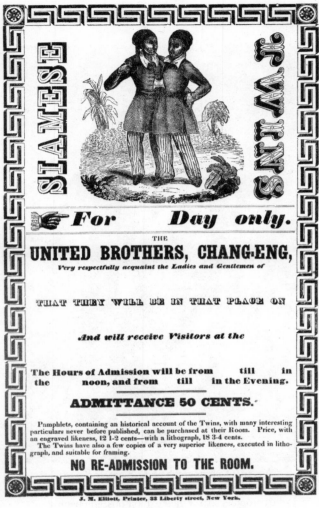

The standard advertising poster for the Siamese
Twins' appearances in the United States. These were
printed in quantity in 1830, leaving the city,
date of appearance, exhibition hall, and hours blank,
to be filled in when the bookings were made.

Two typical pages of an income account book
Chang and Eng kept during their appearances in the
United States and Europe between 1833 and 1839.

An oil portrait of Dr. James Calloway,
a renowned North Carolina physician, who
met the Siamese Twins and persuaded
them to move to Wilkesboro, North Carolina,
where they became gentlemen farmers.

Top: Eng's original house in Mount Airy,
North Carolina. It burned to the ground in 1956.

Middle: Chang's house in Mount Airy,
North Carolina, as it looked in earlier years.

Bottom: Chang and Eng's bedroom and bed
in Eng's house, as they appeared in 1952.

Left: Chang and Eng's double-sized chair with an extra supporting piece down the middle of the seat.

Below: An early photograph of the Siamese Twins after their marriages, when they had become fathers. Each is with his first-born child—Eng (left) with daughter Kate, and Chang with daughter Josephine, both born in 1844.

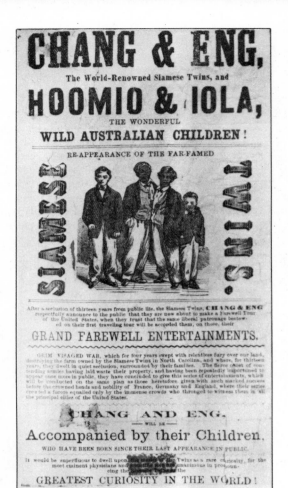

An advertising poster announcing the comeback appearance of Eng and Chang in New York City in 1866, and the photograph (probably taken in the fall of 1865) that was used for the poster. The Twins undertook the tour at the age of 55 in an attempt to recoup the money they had just lost in the Civil War. Eng is shown with his 15-year-old, Patrick Henry, and Chang has his arm around his 8-year-old, Albert.

Mathew Brady, who had photographed Abraham
Lincoln, took this Bunker family group in his elegant
New York studio, probably in the spring of 1865.
Chang (right) is seated next to his wife, Adelaide, with
his son Albert before him; and Eng is with his
wife, Sallie, and son, Patrick Henry.

Above: Eng and Chang posing with their wives and 18 of their 21 children, probably taken in early 1865 when the Twins were 54 years old. On the far right, holding a child, is Grace Gates (shown below when she was much older), the slave given to Eng and Sallie as a wedding present when they married in 1843. Known as Aunt Grace by both Bunker families, she cared for all the Bunker children and was fondly remembered for her huge feet; she is said to have died in 1921 at the age of 121.

Opposite, Far Right: The great American showman Phineas T. Barnum. He did not discover the Siamese Twins and managed them only twice, for brief periods in 1860 and 1868. Barnum and the Twins disliked each other intensely.

Eng's wife, Sarah Ann Yates Bunker, known as Sallie,
with daughter Rosella Virginia, about 1870.

Above: Chang's oldest son,
Christopher, who fought for the
Confederacy in the Civil War;
he died in 1932.

Below: Eng's daughter Kate (left) and
Chang's daughter Nannie. Photograph taken
in 1868, before they accompanied their
fathers on a tour of the British Isles: Both
died of tuberculosis by the age of 27.

Right: Chang's wife, Adelaide, in her later years as a widow. She died in 1917 at the age of 94.

Below: Eng's youngest offspring, Robert Bunker, the last surviving child of the Siamese Twins. He died at 85 in 1951. Here he is seen in Eng's Mount Airy house beside the bed in which the Siamese Twins died.

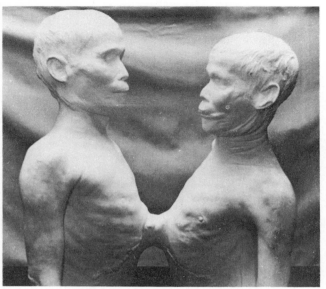

Above: After the Siamese
Twins died in 1874, their
bodies were removed
to the Mütter Museum in
Philadelphia, where an
autopsy was performed by
doctors of the College
of Physicians. Then these
plaster casts were made
of their corpses (Eng is on
the left). Incision marks
made during the autopsy
are clearly visible.

Left: Dr. Joseph
Hollingsworth, of Mount
Airy, North Carolina,
who treated the Siamese
Twins until their deaths
and persuaded their widows
to permit the autopsy.

The double headstone over the final resting place of the Siamese Twins in the cemetery behind the old Baptist church, White Plains, North Carolina. The engraving indicates that the Twins and both their wives are buried here, but in fact, Eng's wife, Sarah (Sallie), was buried on Eng's farm. PHOTOGRAPH BY WALTER KEMPTHORNE.

and Eng, as foreigners and naturalized citizens, felt threatened by the so-called Know-Nothing party and fervently opposed it.

Despite the fact that Chang and Eng's opinions on most political matters coincided, there were rare instances when they disagreed. On at least one occasion, in 1847, Chang voted for one local congressional candidate, and Eng for his opponent. It was never revealed which twin voted for the more conservative candidate, and which for the more liberal.

Chang and Eng, like their affluent Southern neighbors, owned slaves. In North Carolina, it was the custom to own "house slaves" and "field slaves." The field slaves' daily life consisted of rising before dawn, feeding the animals, then rushing to the fields before sunrise. Depending upon the season, the laborers would work the fields, plant or harvest the crops, cut down trees, build fences, and engage in numerous similar activities.

After working from dawn to sunset, the field slaves would then care for the livestock, put away tools, and cook their own meals before the master's horn sounded bedtime. During cotton-picking season, work lasted until nine at night; and on the sugar plantations, slaves worked eighteen hours a day during harvest season.

For the house slaves, the physical labor was somewhat less demanding. However, they had to suffer the constant surveillance of their white masters, who had the legal right to beat them at the slightest hint of "insolence," as well as for actual mistakes. While some masters were kind to their slaves, others were brutal to the extreme. Women were raped, and children were frequently beaten. Flogging was common practice. Even worse was the psychological torture the slaves were forced to undergo—mates and children could be abruptly separated from their families and sold to new masters.

Many slaves rebelled and ran away, and some escaped to freedom, though many more did not, and these were subjected to severe punishment upon re-

capture. Others became the docile "Sambo" stereo-
type, passive and nonresistant.

The slaves, when not hard at work for their masters,
spent time cultivating a community of their own.
They preserved the essential elements of their African
religion in their voodoo ceremonies. Some attended
church at the insistence of their masters, and what
they drew from exposure to Christian beliefs was
expressed in highly emotional form, singing, dancing,
and shouting, the roots of later black revival meetings.

Much of the slaves' free time was spent making music on homemade instruments or getting drunk on
corn whiskey, in an attempt to cope with the degra-
dation of their position.

Surviving documents reveal that Chang and Eng paid
as high as $450 for two female slaves, Mary and Nicey,
who were only 5½ and 7½ years old at the time of
purchase. This was a great deal of money, considering
that female slaves were probably less useful than male
slaves, and that the girls were so young. Other expen-
ditures that the twins made were $600 for a 17-
year-old boy named Briant, $500 for a 16-year-old
female named Emilia, $470 for a 23-year-old female
named Lyde, $425 for a 40-year-old male named
Berry, and $217 for a 7-year-old boy named Charles.

As the twins prospered, they were able to afford
more and more slaves. By 1860, they owned a total of
twenty-eight slaves, Eng owning six males, two of
whom were mulatto, and ten females. Chang owned
four black males, six black females, and two mulatto
females.

Besides sharing one ancient female slave, Chang and
Eng each had an older female slave, forty and thirty-
five years old respectively. With one exception,
neither owned any males older than twenty-three.
This may have been coincidence, or it may have been
a matter of deliberate choice, because older males
would be the most likely perpetrators of a rebellion.

The slaves' living quarters were crude, roughly built
one-room cabins. Not only were the dwellings cold

and uncomfortable, they were usually overcrowded as well. Chang and Eng had an average of seven slaves living in each of their four cabins.

The black "mammy" was a deeply important figure in slave culture. More often than not, she was more influential in the raising of the white children than their own mothers. She nursed them, rocked them to sleep, told them bedtime stories, punished them and loved them.

The Eng Bunkers received as a wedding present the venerable Grace Gates—known as Aunt Grace—a buxom woman who managed both twins' large broods. She once posed in a family picture taken of the Bunkers, holding a little boy on her lap. Aunt Grace was known for wearing oversized men's shoes, because she had such unusually large feet. She could chew tobacco and smoke a pipe at the same time, and it is claimed that she lived to be 121 years old.

In the South, it was common practice to allow the black and white children to play freely together, and this must certainly have been the case in the Bunker household. Not until age ten or so did the social relationship change from playmates to master/slave, as the young blacks were treated more and more harshly by the white adults. When black children were fathered by their white masters, some of these were lucky enough to become "favorites."

The Siamese Twins were rumored to be hard on their slaves, sometimes whipping them. J. E. Johnson, editor of the Mount Airy *News*, whose mother had shared teaching duties with Chang's daughter Nannie in their own private school, recounted something of the twins' relationship with their slaves:

> On one occasion a negro desiring to see them on business appeared at their front door. It was the custom in those days for negro men to apply at the back door of a Southern man's home. When the Twins saw the negro standing in the front door they instantly made for him with a malignant air and that negro lost no time in taking himself away. After that he knew his place.

Another story that is current is one they tell about a bad negro and illustrates the spirit of the Twins in their dealings with their neighbors. They owned many negroes and one developed into a desperado and was considered dangerous. In those times occasionally a negro would refuse to obey his master and run away. He usually was a pest, for the hand of every man was against him. There was no law to protect such slaves and it was considered the proper thing to do to kill him on sight. This bad negro, the property of Chang, was reported one night to be in the negro cabins of a slave owner near Mount Airy. The citizen went with his gun to investigate and the negro ran from the cabin and as he ran the citizen fired his gun intending to shoot him in the legs. But as luck would have it he aimed too high and killed the negro.

There was no law to punish him for his deed; but he saw a big bill facing him in the way of pay for the value of the dead slave. At once he went to the home of the Twins hoping to make the best settlement possible. Imagine his surprise when the Twins refused to accept a cent and expressed their satisfaction that the negro was out of the way.

The twins themselves were fond of telling this story: One time, when they were traveling in Virginia with a neighbor, they were urged by some gamblers to join in a game of cards. They did not engage in gambling games, and so they refused. However, they agreed to back the neighbor, who was "handy with cards." The neighbor won royally, and the gamblers, in their desperation, bet "a negro." The twins won him, and then sold him back to the unlucky gamblers for $600.

Slaves were usually forbidden to leave their cabins to visit other slaves on neighboring farms. Nevertheless, they frequently managed to sneak out for after-hours parties. Chang's daughter Nannie had a favorite little dog, who barked whenever a slave tried to slip away at night. While Chang and Eng were in New York City, one of the slaves killed the watchdog, so upsetting Nannie that she sent off a tearful letter to her father reporting the pet's demise. Upon receiving the letter, the twins decided to consult a spiritualist who claimed to see the past and the future. Many people had heard stories from blacks about the powers of fortune-tellers and conjurers, and some had come to believe them. The twins, carrying with them the remnants of their early Eastern culture in which oracles were more highly accepted than in the West, were willing subjects.

The twins asked the fourtune-teller the name of their mother, and to their surprise received the correct answer, Nok. Then they asked who had killed Nannie's dog, and they were given a man's name, the very name of one of their own slaves back home. When Chang and Eng returned to North Carolina, they confronted the black man and accused him of killing the dog. The frightened slave confessed, and got, as Johnson put it, "what in those times was supposed to be coming to him."

For their part, the Bunkers' slaves must have found it odd to have Oriental masters, not to mention masters who were anatomically joined together. A reporter from the *Southerner*, a Richmond, Virginia, publication, could not help remarking on "the unusualness of the twins with their slant eyes giving orders to their black slaves." Then, the reporter went on:

> The twins frequently took their slaves out with them on early morning possum-hunting expeditions, and this was one of their favorite recreations.
>
> They attended the local shooting matches, where a turkey or beef was the reward for the best marksman, and Chang and Eng acquired reputations as crackshots with rifles or pistols. It was the object of much curious speculation on the neighbor's part how two men tied together could be so adept, often more adept than a single man.
>
> The farmers in Surry County were frequently plagued by wolves, who wreaked havoc among their livestock. There existed one particularly notorious wolf, christened "Bob-Tail," because he had lost part

of his tail in a trap. This wolf did not merely limit his dinings to sheep and cattle, but was believed to have eaten a negro baby who wandered into the woods. Bob-Tail made trouble for three years, and no one was able to trap him, until one night when Chang and Eng were awoken by noises coming from among their livestock. They ran out, taking with them a gun and a slave carrying a lantern. It was Bob-Tail, and the wolf breathed his last at the twins' hands. This coup gave Chang and Eng considerable prestige in the community, especially as no more negro babies were ever known to be stolen or eaten.

The twins were also skilled at horsebreaking, the taming of wild horses for domestic use.

A Surry County neighbor owned a beautiful black colt, whom no one could handle. Several people tried to tame him and were injured in the process, so no others dared to go near him. One day the twins saw him, and they asked the owner his price. They were told that they could have the colt for almost nothing, provided they could catch him and take him away. To the owner's great amazement, Chang and Eng approached the horse, made "a few mysterious manipulations," then walked away, with the horse following submissively behind them. After owning him for a couple of weeks and working him in harness daily, they sold the now gentle creature back to the original owner at a handsome profit. No one discovered what their secret was for taming horses, but it always worked.

Besides hunting, fishing, and shooting, Chang and Eng enjoyed other recreations. For one thing, they were great music lovers. They both played the flute well, having serenaded their wives with this instrument during courtship.

They were fond of reading poetry, especially Eng, who often read aloud to Chang, or to his whole family. Alexander Pope, the English poet and translator of Homer, was their favorite author. Curiously, one of Pope's poems celebrated the visit to London of the

Hungarian twins, Helen and Judith, who were joined at their backs and shared a single pair of legs. The twins also appreciated the works of Shakespeare, Lord Byron, and John Fleetwood's *Life of Christ*. Eng was so partial to Pope's poems that he read all of them ten times over.

"They never spent a day in the schoolroom for the purpose of study, yet they were educated and intelligent men," a future son-in-law, Zacharias Haynes, would say of them. "They could read and write very well, and transact all of their business with facility. Their wisdom did not consist of Greek and Latin . . . but in practical common sense."

The twins continued to enjoy checkers, having learned to play the game at seventeen while on shipboard coming from Siam to America. Their skill at chess was renowned, but, as with checkers, they never enjoyed playing against each other.

One point of contention between the brothers was Eng's penchant for late-night poker games. One of Eng's sons, Patrick Bunker, recalled:

"Father loved poker and he would often sit up all night and play. Uncle Chang never played and it took a good deal of persuasion to get him to stay up so long. I remember that once father won two Negro boys at a poker game. Father was a great checker player, too, and many a game I played with him. He would sit up all night to play with a good checker player and that irked Uncle Chang."

There was, in their later years, a great deal of controversy about whether or not these differences led to ill will between the twins. However, too many stories of arguments between them have survived to allow any doubt that it was gradually becoming more and more difficult for the brothers to coexist peacefully. Indeed, on occasion, they actually resorted to physical violence during their disputes.

While they were building the roof of the White Plains Baptist Church, they got into such a heated argument that they fell to the ground. According to legend, this fight was provoked when Eng's hammer accidentally (or not accidentally) hit one of Chang's fingers.

In an earlier dispute, in 1845, they were so angry that they came to blows—over what, was never known, but the sight of them fistfighting at such close range must have been extraordinary. They were very much ashamed of the brawl afterward and tried to keep the incident hushed up, but the news of it traveled fast. A grand juror in the next county heard about the incident and reported it to County Attorney Lee Reeves, who "sent a bill for an affray against them," whereupon they were hauled into court for disturbing the peace. The presiding judge was Jesse Graves, the man who was to become their close friend. Observing that their wrath had dissipated, Judge Graves fined them a nominal fee and closed the case.

There were several reasons for the slowly growing discontent between the twins. After all the public exhibition and travel, they had now settled down into a regular routine that was free of the pressures and demands of their early years. While this contributed to the twins' happiness, there was also time for the many conflicts of domestic life to creep in. As their families expanded, they yearned for separation, and each became an albatross around the other's neck. Furthermore, it was said, their wives were quarreling.

As they grew older, their personality differences hardened and were accentuated. The most serious point of contention between them was undoubtedly Chang's increasing fondness for whiskey. While Eng took his liquor in moderation, Chang drank to excess. Unhappily, Chang did not hold his liquor well. His more fiery temperament was often excited by imbibing, and he sometimes got out of control.

Dr. William H. Pancoast reported one such incident: "Thus Chang would become intoxicated in spite of his brother, and much to his inconvenience; would break things in his own house, and, upon one occasion, threw a featherbed into the fire, and made himself otherwise disagreeable, in spite of the remonstrances of his brother."

When Chang drank, Eng did not get drunk, contrary to what many people thought. However, Eng sometimes voiced his displeasure over the difficulties he suffered being attached to a disagreeable, violent, drunken man.

For all their differences, however, it may safely be said that Chang and Eng probably quarreled less than most of the legally attached couples whom they counted among their friends.

It was at this time that the twins shared two common losses.

They had remained in touch from afar with Robert Hunter, continually interested in his ups and downs. After his financial reverses due to a Siamese flood, Hunter made a comeback and in recent years had been prospering. The British government had a trade treaty with Siam, and Hunter, who was close to King Rama III and enjoyed what amounted to a business partnership with the ruler, had a virtual monopoly on foreign importing and exporting. He had received permission to build a spacious dwelling on the riverbank outside Bangkok, and there he lived comfortably and entertained extensively. He enjoyed his cognac every morning (supposedly as a measure against cholera), ran his business affairs in the afternoon, and evenings played host to old friends like Marsinello de Rosa, the longtime Portuguese consul and Siamese scholar. Often, Hunter relaxed by playing games with visiting British and American seamen and travelers. As one foreign visitor recalled, "Occasionally we amused ourselves at Mr. Hunter's by playing *Lagrace*, and we were once or twice guilty of a game at ring-taw, the marbles being our own manufacture out of sealing-wax."

Then something went wrong, and Hunter's commercial monopoly was threatened. According to a biography of King Rama III, "When the Siamese nobles began to trade on their own, Hunter became their competitor instead of their middleman. Thus the obstacles placed in the way of foreign trade at this time also affected Hunter, cutting into his profits and prompting him to act rashly." Despite the fact that the king had issued an edict against the importing of opium, Hunter, to bolster his diminishing income, began to bring large quantities of opium into Siam and sell it to the Chinese. He was found out, and severely reprimanded by the king. Next, Hunter imported a British steamer, which the Siamese government had ordered. The government officials refused to buy it because "they were dissatisfied with its condition and the price Hunter set on it." In a fury, Hunter insulted the officials. If that was not enough, Hunter appealed to the British Governor General of India, telling him that the Siamese had broken their treaty and demanding that he send warships to Siam. The Governor General felt that there was not enough reason to intervene.

Finally, King Rama III had had enough of Hunter. In December 1844, the king expelled him from Siam. Hunter had no place to go, except home. He returned to his native Scotland, and after languishing there for four years, he died in 1848.

All of this Chang and Eng learned that same year, and together they mourned the passing of the man who had made their present lives possible.

Less than a year later, the twins suffered their second and even greater loss.

Charles Harris, the self-styled doctor, their onetime manager, had always been a stabilizing influence in their lives, and they had great affection for him. Harris and his wife Fannie had produced four children, while he struggled to support them as the Trap Hill postmaster and by working for St. Paul's Episcopal Church in Wilkesboro. Then, Harris contracted tuberculosis. In two months, his decline was rapid, and on July 5, 1849, he died.

With their old travel companion and friend of so many years gone, Chang and Eng were drawn ever closer to their own families.

As time passed, the Bunker families continued to

grow with remarkable consistency. After the appearance of the third child in each family, the previous pattern of Adelaide and Sallie giving birth almost simultaneously was altered. Instead, with only one exception, the Bunkers were having one child each year, but by alternate wives.

After Katherine Marcellus and Julia Ann, Eng and Sallie had nine more children. In order of birth, they were: Stephen Decatur, James Montgomery, Patrick Henry, Rosalyn Etta, William Oliver, Frederick Marshall, Rosella Virginia, Georgianna Columbia, and Robert Edmond.

This gave Eng and Sallie a total of eleven children—six boys and five girls.

Chang and Adelaide had a total of ten children—three boys and seven girls. In order of birth, they were: Josephine Virginia, Christopher Wren, Nancy Adelaide, Susan Marianna, Victoria, Louise Emeline (who was a deaf mute), Albert Lemuel, Jesse Lafayette (also a deaf mute), Margaret Elizabeth, and Hattie Irene.

It is possible that the alternate childbirths were coincidental, but there is a likelihood that they were planned. If this was the case, it may have been a decision made in order to simplify the running of the household: while one wife was carrying a child or recovering from a birth, the other wife could take over the household affairs for both families. Judge Graves observed that, after the first few children, Adelaide and Sallie began to show signs of "hereditary obesity"—each of them weighed 250 pounds or more—although they never attained their mother's massive proportions.

As the younger Bunkers grew up, the question of educating them arose. There was a school in Mount Airy at the time. Chang and Eng were eager to see their children educated, particularly their daughters. Adelaide was adamant in her desire for this, while Sallie did not particularly care.

In 1852, the Bunkers bought the C. W. Lewis house in the village of Mount Airy. Adelaide moved into it

with those children who were old enough to begin
school, while Sallie remained at the farm. Chang and
Eng divided their time between the two places.

Later, the Bunkers built and shared a schoolhouse
with the Greenwoods, who were their next-door
neighbors on the farm. James Greenwood was a good
friend, but the twins and Greenwood maintained a
certain formality with one another: the twins always
addressed him as "Mr. Greenwood," and he always
addressed either twin as "Mr. Bunker."

The Greenwoods and the Bunkers built their one-
room log cabin—austerely furnished with table, chairs,
and a stove—on the boundary line of the two farms,
and hired a young man as the first teacher. Any of the
local children were welcome to attend classes. Eventually, James Greenwood's daughter Emma and
Chang's daughter Nannie taught the younger children.

Through the years, the twins continued to remain
objects of curiosity to an inquisitive public. They
cordially received the numerous visitors who came
from all over the country to see them. A good number of reporters called upon the Bunkers, and several
of the more important biographical pieces concerning
them were written at this time.

In 1847, a reporter from the Raleigh, North Carolina, *Biblical Recorder* went to pay the twins a visit,
and not finding them at home, interviewed one of
the wives, not specifying which:

> In company with my friend, William M. Nance,
> Esq., I called to see the Siamese twins, Chang and
> Eng, residing one and a half miles from Mount Airy,
> on a valuable farm which they have lately purchased,
> and removed to from the county of Wilkes. To my
> great disappointment they were not at home, being
> absent on a visit to their plantation in Wilkes. The
> wife of one of them was at home, and four of their
> children, all of whom favor them much in appear-
> ance. . . . The Mrs. Bunker whom we found at home
> appeared to be a good-looking, intelligent woman,
> with a fresh, open countenance, apparently about

twenty-five years of age. There appeared to be a number of servants about the premises, of different ages and sexes. Their home is small, but they are making arrangements to build a new and commodious one. The wife of one of them, and two of their children, were at Wilkes. They live alternately at each place, and will so continue until they build a new house, or sell their plantation in Wilkes, which they design to do.

They take pleasure in farming, have a fine crop, are quite plain and economical in their dress and manner of living, are fond of hunting, and with their wives and little ones, apparently quite happy and contented.

A typical account of the twins at home was given by the reporter from the *Southerner*, of Richmond, Virginia. In early 1850 the newspaper sent a representative to get a firsthand view of the Bunker farm life. The journalist sent back an account of his findings:

When we got off the stage at Mt. Airy we were told by the townspeople that the Twins were moody, sulky people and often refused to see anyone who called on them.

After a few glasses of ale and a meal at the Blue Ridge Inn in Mt. Airy we felt more in place in calling on the Twins. It was an extremely warm day and the driver gave the horses plenty of time, in addition to taking the long way around. After having arrived we drove up into the shade of a large cottonwood tree. Everything seemed quiet except a colored boy doing some metal work in a shop nearby. There was a large male peafowl strutting across the yard. Then the twins appeared in the doorway dressed in rough cotton. Each had a quid of tobacco in his mouth, each was barefooted. They stood in the doorway a minute or so, then waved good naturedly. They approached our carriage and asked how they could serve us. We told them the nature of our business, that we were representing the *Southerner*. They bade us come inside.

They led us into the living room which contained a bed and other necessities. We found them to be extremely interested in farming as well as moderate conversationalists, often speaking in unbroken English. One would talk awhile then the other would take over and talk for a few minutes. A colored boy was instructed to bring in some fresh cider, which we really enjoyed. The conversation went on for quite sometime. Often they would introduce new topics. These two men are perhaps the world's greatest travelers and are known world wide, and perhaps have already faced more people than most folks would in 100 years. They are still a bit conscious of stares from strangers. But now it was getting later in the afternoon and we bade them a fond adieu after stealing another look at our hosts. We explained that we had to get back to Mt. Airy and make lodging preparations. That we would return tomorrow for a look at their crop, etc. They asked us to stay and sup with them, of which we thanked them most kindly . . .

Most of the stories published about Chang and Eng in this period treated them sympathetically, although there were a few exceptions. One notable exception, a newspaper article that appeared in the Greensboro *Patriot* in 1852 and purported to give an unblemished picture of them, proved to be the most scandalous piece ever written about the brothers. The author signed himself merely "D.," which was undoubtedly prudent, for had he not remained anonymous he might have suffered physical violence at the hands of Chang and Eng.

This infamous article began with deceptively mild and standard paragraphs about the twins' homes and families, but by the third paragraph the author's dagger was unsheathed:

Messrs. Eng and Chang are alike remarkable for their industry and belligerent dispositions. They are strict and thorough going business men, and woe to the unfortunate wight who dares to insult them.

Formerly they resided in Wilkes County, but in consequence of the numerous actions for assault and battery brought against them in the county, they removed into the adjoining one, shortly after which they were fined fifteen dollars and costs, at Rockford, the county seat, for splitting a board into splinters over the head of a man who insulted them.

As regards the supposed sympathy existing between them, it may be stated that their most intimate acquaintances deem them to be entirely independent of everything of the kind, and give us instances to sustain their opinion—that not long since they attended an auction sale of hogs, and bid against each other till they ran up the prices altogether above the market rates—also, that on one occasion Mr. Eng or Chang was taken ill and took to his bed, where he lay complaining for some time, although his brother scolded him severely all the while for detaining him in bed when he ought to have been attending to the business of their plantation.

On another occasion, as they were passing up the road, a gentleman inquired of them where they were going—whereupon Mr. Chang replied, "I am going over the Blue Ridge in the stage," and, at the same instant, Mr. Eng, looking over his shoulder, replied with an arch smile, "I am going back home to look after our wives and children." When questioned about their mother some time since by an acquaintance, they stated that they had formerly received letters from her, but latterly they had heard no tidings of her, and even if they were to receive letters from her, written in the Siamese language, they would not be able to read them, as they had forgotten their mother tongue.

When they chop or fight, they do so double-handed; and in driving a horse or chastising their negroes, both of them use the lash without mercy.

A gentleman who purchased a black man a short time ago from them, informed the writer that he was "the worse whipped negro he ever saw." They are inveterate smokers and chewers of tobacco—each chewing his own quid and smoking his own pipe. It has been remarked, however, in support of the sympathy supposed to prevail throughout their systems, that, as a general rule, when one takes a fresh quid, the other does the same, notwithstanding they do not always expectorate the same quantity of saliva or spit at the same instant. It is also generally admitted that there is a marked difference in the systems and temperaments of the gentlemen, and still they almost invariably draw the same inferences from topics submitted to their consideration, and arrive at similar conclusions. Mr. Eng not unfrequently gives serious offence to Mr. Chang, by jesting him about his having one more child than he has, whereby he claims to be the better man of the two. When shooting (a sport they are very fond of), one sights or takes aim and the other (it is said) pulls the trigger. Now if this be true, it would go far to prove the doctrine of supposed sympathy existing between the brothers, but it is questioned by most of their neighbors.

Whether these accusations were true or false may never be known, but Chang and Eng were enraged by the gratuitous attack. They responded by writing a letter to the editor of the Greensboro *Patriot*, dated October 30, 1852. In this letter they defended Chang's manhood, their treatment of their slaves, and their standing in the community:

Messrs. Editors: We have noticed in your paper of the 16th a communication signed D, a portion of which we ask permission to answer, as it immediately interests us. It is true that we live in this place surrounded by our wives and children, and that one of us is blessed with more of these "little responsibilities" than the other, but that it is or was ever unpleasant for either of us, needs no denial in this community.

That portion of said communication which assigns the cause of our leaving Wilkes County and becoming citizens of Surry, is unqualifiedly false, as is also that portion which represents us as having been indicted and fined in this county for splitting a board into splinters over the head of some "one insulting us." We have never appeared on the State docket in any county but one (and that in Wilkes County, and were fined sixpence and cost). We have had no difficulty of that kind with any man, woman or child

in Surry County; and have endeavored to live soberly, honestly, and in peace with all the good citizens
of this country.

The portion of said piece relating to the inhuman
manner in which we had chastized a negro man
which we afterwards sold, is a sheer fabrication and
infamous falsehood. We have never sold to any man a
negro as described, except to Mr. Thos. F. Prather,
who denies the truth of said accusation, or of ever
having told any person that which the author of said
communication says he heard. We are well aware that
to some who have not seen us, we are to some extent
an object of curiosity, but that we were to be the
objects of such vile and infamous misrepresenta-
tion, we could not before believe.

It is a well known fact that for some 18 months
or 2 years after we moved to Surry, we spent at least
one third of our time, if not one half, in Wilkes
County, and indeed, we are very frequently there
now, and receive from the citizens of that County
nothing but the kindest treatment.

We are partners in business and consequently are
not often guilty of the folly of bidding against each
other for any species of property.

Finally, in conclusion, we would like to say to your
correspondent, that hereafter when he wishes to
parade the character of private citizens before the
public in newspaper columns, that his communications should at least have some semblance of truth.
Who he is we do not know, and if his communication is anything like a fair index to his character, we
wish no further acquaintance.

CHANG & ENG BUNKER

Chang and Eng had their letter endorsed by thirteen local citizens and friends, to authenticate their
denial and preserve their dignity:

The undersigned citizens of Surry County, do
certify that we have been acquainted with the Siamese
Twins since they became citizens of our county, and
some of us for a much longer period, and we take

pleasure in bearing our testimony to their good character, peaceable demeanor and strict integrity, in all their intercourse and business in this country.

We further say we have examined the foregoing letter from them, repelling a portion of a communication signed D., in *The Greensboro Patriot*, and that the statements in said letter *are* substantially correct.

Among the thirteen signatures to the postscript were Chang and Eng's close friends Robert S. Gilmer, S. Graves, Elisha Banner, and T. F. Prather, the purchaser of the slave.

A more objective article on Chang and Eng appeared a year later. In 1853, the *American Phrenological Journal*—which had already published a piece about the twins in 1835—published a second analysis of them. The study of phrenology, created by the German anatomist Franz Joseph Gall in 1800, was a means of deducing a subject's mental attributes and personality by examining the contours and bumps of his head. Gall believed that different mental abilities were seated in different parts of the brain, and that the extent of each ability could be judged by the shape and feel of the skull in a specified area. Phrenology had achieved widespread popularity in the twins' lifetime, although interest in it would decline later.

Chang and Eng allowed their heads to be studied by a phrenologist. The examiner's findings led to the following article, in which capitalized words (such as "Destructiveness" or "Benevolence") referred to the parts of the twins' heads where those traits were believed to reside:

Eighteen years ago, we examined the heads of these world-renowned twins, and have just reexamined them. The only perceptible difference is, that one is a little larger than the other. The head of the largest one is a quarter of an inch larger than that of the other, and his individual organs correspondingly fuller; but otherwise, we could not detect the slightest difference. Their characteristics are so perfectly alike, that many have maintained that they were but one being. We usually find the heads and characters of twins very nearly alike, yet never before have we seen any two heads, even of twins, that began to correspond on every single point as perfectly as these do. This complete correspondence, considered in connection with their perfect similarity of character, corroborates as far as one marked fact can do, the truth of our science.

The shape of their heads is very peculiar. Nothing like it is ever found in the Caucasian head. We have never before seen, even in our women, as high, long and full a moral lobe, along with as narrow a head at the ears, as those of these twins. Combativeness is well developed, yet of Destructiveness and Secretiveness they have almost none. Their Benevolence is of the very largest order; while Veneration is much larger than we almost ever find it in our own race. Their immense Benevolence and almost nominal Destructiveness corresponds with their national characteristic of being so very tender of the lives of animals; to kill which, they consider a heinous sin: while their very large Veneration corresponds with their nation's extreme devotion to their religion.

Firmness is large, and the lower or Will part of Self-esteem is also large, while the upper part or Dignity is small; and Approbativeness and Cautiousness very large. As large Adhesiveness as theirs we never find in Caucasian men, and rarely as large Parental Love or Inhabitiveness. Judging from this, they must be a most affectionate and domestic people. Amativeness is full, but not over-grown, while Continuity is full. Appetite is large, but Acquisitiveness only moderate; and we suspect they lack this element in character.

Of Hope, they have scarcely the least, and this, as far as we can judge, is a national characteristic. Conscientiousness is also small, and Spirituality almost wanting.

Their intellectual lobes are well developed as a whole, yet while the reflectives are large, the perceptives are deficient, except that Form is quite large. But Individuality, Color, and Weight are the smallest we ever find. Mirth and Ideality are also only moderate—other national characteristics. Imitation is very large, and Time very small, while Language is fully developed, but Eventuality rather weak.

While the fame of the Siamese Twins was being spread through newspapers, magazines, and pamphlets, their story was not the exclusive property of journalists. Soon, playwrights and novelists would use them in their creations.

The playwright who had the most success with a stage piece based on their lives was Gilbert Abbott à Beckett, an English writer, barrister, and judge, who was a friend of William Makepeace Thackeray and Charles Dickens. At the time Chang and Eng were raising their families, à Beckett was a writer of humourous pieces for the new *Punch* magazine. Before he died of typhus fever in France in 1856, he had also written and produced stage plays. One of his biggest hits, based entirely on Chang and Eng, was a play entitled *The Siamese Twins,* a romantic farce that had its debut in London and later became equally popular in New York City.

The play revolved around the scheme of its protagonist, a man named Vivid, who hoped to marry a pretty young thing for her money. The young lady was the ward of an eminent surgeon named Forceps. Vivid's plan was to disguise two of his friends, Dennis and Simon, as the Siamese Twins, whom he called Ching and Wang, and to impress the eminent surgeon by separating them.

Novelists, also, were aware of Chang and Eng, and numerous works of this time carried references to the twins. For example, Herman Melville in his 1857 novel *The Confidence Man: His Masquerade* wrote a passage in which one character leaned against another with "an air of trustful fraternity with which, when standing, the less strong of the Siamese twins habitually leans against the other."

But the most enduring writing about Chang and Eng in their lifetime was to come from the pen of Samuel L. Clemens, who, as Mark Twain, was to become the author of *The Adventures of Tom Sawyer*, *The Adventures of Huckleberry Finn*, and *A Connecticut Yankee in King Arthur's Court*. Mark Twain was born six years after Chang and Eng came to the United States. In 1857, while the twins were still in Mount Airy, Twain was serving as an apprentice riverboat pilot on the Mississippi. After two weeks in the Confederate Army as a second lieutenant, he went to work as the city editor of the Virginia City, Nevada, *Enterprise*. In 1865, he published his short story "The Celebrated Jumping Frog of Calaveras County" in the New York *Saturday Press* and became famous almost overnight. Three years later, Twain seized upon Chang and Eng as a subject. Always attracted by the bizarre and the unusual, he found Chang and Eng's unique situation perfect material for his extraordinary sense of humor.

In 1868, when Chang and Eng were once again touring, Mark Twain wrote an essay entitled "The Siamese Twins." The essay began with an account of the twins' childhood:

> They nearly always played together; and, so accustomed was their mother to this peculiarity, that, whenever both of them chanced to be lost, she usually only hunted for one of them—satisfied that when she found one she would find his brother somewhere in the immediate neighborhood.

Next, readers were treated to a delightful description of the twins' personal habits:

> The Twins always go to bed at the same time; but Chang usually gets up about an hour before his brother. By an understanding between themselves, Chang does all the indoor work and Eng runs all the errands. This is because Eng likes to go out; Chang's habits are sedentary. However, Chang always goes along. Eng is a Baptist, but Chang is a Roman Catholic; still, to please his brother, Chang consented to be baptized at the same time that Eng was, on condition that it should not "count." During the war they

were strong partizans, and both fought gallantly all through the great struggle—Eng on the Union side and Chang on the Confederate. They took each other as prisoners at Seven Oaks, but the proofs of capture were so evenly balanced in favor of each, that a general army court had to be assembled to determine which one was properly the captor, and which the captive. The jury was unable to agree for a long time; but the vexed question was finally decided by agreeing to consider them both prisoners, and then exchanging them.

The following was an imaginative reverie by Twain on the courting of Adelaide and Sallie:

The ancient habit of going always together had its drawbacks when they reached man's estate, and entered upon the luxury of courting. Both fell in love with the same girl. Each tried to steal clandestine interviews with her, but at the critical moment the other would always turn up. By and by Eng saw, with distraction, that Chang had won the girl's affections; and, from that day forth, he had to bear with the agony of being a witness to all their dainty billing and cooing. But with a magnanimity that did him infinite credit, he succumbed to his fate, and gave countenance and encouragement to a state of things that bade fair to sunder his generous heart-strings. He sat from seven every evening until two in the morning, listening to the fond foolishness of the two lovers, and to the concussion of hundreds of squandered kisses—for the privilege of sharing only one of which he would have given his right hand. But he sat patiently, and waited, and gaped, and yawned, and stretched, and longed for two o'clock to come. And he took long walks with the lovers on moonlight evenings—sometimes traversing ten miles, notwithstanding he was usually suffering from rheumatism. He is an inveterate smoker; but he could not smoke on these occasions, because the young lady was painfully sensitive to the smell of tobacco. Eng cordially wanted them married, and done with it; but although Chang often asked the momentous question, the young lady could not gather sufficient courage to answer it while Eng was by. However, on one occasion, after having walked some sixteen miles, and sat up till nearly daylight, Eng dropped asleep, from sheer exhaustion, and then the question was asked and answered. The lovers were married. All acquainted with the circumstance applauded the noble brother-in-law. His unwavering faithfulness was the theme of every tongue. He had stayed with them all through their long and arduous courtship; and when at last they were married, he lifted his hands above their heads, and said with impressive unction, "Bless ye, my children, I will never desert thee!" and he kept his word. Fidelity like this is all too rare in this cold world.

By and by Eng fell in love with his sister-in-law's sister, and married her, and since that day they have all lived together, night and day, in an exceeding sociability which is touching and beautiful to behold, and is a scathing rebuke to our boasted civilization. . . .

Having forgotten to mention it sooner, I will remark in conclusion, that the ages of the Siamese Twins are respectively fifty-one and fifty-three years.

Twenty-two years later, in 1891, Twain drew again on his fascination with the freakish, and began to write a novel that was published in 1894 as *The Tragedy of Pudd'nhead Wilson*. He created in the story a pair of Italian twins named Angelo and Luigi, who had two heads and two pairs of arms, but only one pair of legs.

Although still inspired by the memory of Chang and Eng, Twain based his fictional twins largely on another real-life pair, Giovanni and Giacomo Tocci, born in 1875 in Turin. The Toccis were one body below the sixth rib, two bodies above. Each brother had control over one of the legs. Because they were unable to coordinate their movements, they were never able to walk. The brothers exhibited themselves for some years, but despite money and fame they were exceedingly morose about their condition.

Twain took their tragedy, overlaid it with his

knowledge of Chang and Eng, and turned it into a witty comedy. While Luigi was olive-skinned and dark-haired, Angelo was blue-eyed and blond. Luigi liked to drink and cavort, thus getting his brother drunk in the process. Angelo was president of the Teetotalers Union, and very religious.

Twain solved the problem of his twins each not having a pair of legs in a most unusual way. For one week one of the twins possessed complete control of the two legs, and the next week the other twin took over. This alternation was an act of God, and occurred with unerring regularity. According to Luigi: "So exactly to the instant does the change come, that during our stay in many of the great cities of the world, the public clocks were regulated by it; and as hundreds of thousands of private clocks and watches were set and corrected in accordance with the public clocks, we really furnished the standard time for the entire city."

At the climax of the story, the twins were accused of being "a pair of scissors." At this insult, they kicked their accuser, and were brought to trial for assault. The poor judge was unable to ascertain which twin was the guilty party. A lawyer named Pudd'nhead Wilson defended the twins, who were freed because it was decided it would be impossible to punish the one without punishing the other.

One of the more interesting passages in the book revealed Twain's musings on the subject of *lusus naturae:*

At times, in his seasons of deepest depressions, Angelo almost wished that he and his brother might become segregated from each other and be separate individuals, like other men. But of course as soon as his mind cleared and these diseased imaginings passed away, he shuddered at the repulsive thought, and earnestly prayed that it might visit him no more. To be separate, as other men are! How awkward it would seem; how unendurable. What would he do with his hands, his arms? How would his legs feel? How odd, how strange and grotesque every action, attitude, movement, gesture would be. To sleep by himself, eat by himself, walk by himself—how lonely, how unspeakably lonely! No, no, any fate but that. In every way and from every point, the idea was revolting.

This was of course natural; to have felt otherwise would have been unnatural. He had known no life but a combined one; he had been familiar with it from his birth; he was not able to conceive of any other as being agreeable, or even bearable. To him, in the privacy of his secret thoughts, all other men were monsters, deformities: and during three-fourths of his life their aspect had filled him with what promised to be an unconquerable aversion. But at eighteen his eye began to take note of female beauty; and little by little, undefined longings grew up in his heart, under whose softening influences the old stubborn aversion gradually diminished, and finally disappeared. Men were still monstrosities to him, still deformities, and in his sober moments he had no desire to be like them, but their strange and unsocial and uncanny construction was no longer offensive to him.

Twain eventually decided that his novel was really two books in one, so he performed a "Siamese twin" operation on his own work. As he put it, "I dug out the farce and left the tragedy." The "farce" part retained the book's original title, *Those Extraordinary Twins*, and the rest became the well-known *Tragedy of Pudd'nhead Wilson*.

Chang and Eng's continuing fame inspired more than prose. A countless number of sentimental odes were written in their honor. Occasionally, the poems were amusing. One of these, one of the earliest and longest, was composed by Edward Bulwer-Lytton, the popular English novelist who had gained fame with *The Last Days of Pompeii*, among other books. In 1831, when he was twenty-eight and Chang and Eng were at the peak of their success in Great Britain, Bulwer-Lytton published a book, *The Siamese Twins*.

In one typical verse, in which Eng had committed a public disturbance and been brought into court with Chang, Bulwer-Lytton had Eng defend himself before the magistrate:

> I made the row, sir, I alone
> While Chang was gazing in the sky, sir;
> He press'd me greatly to come on,
> But—*such* a girl was in my eye, sir!
> And so not deeming it could hurt
> You, or your laws, I stopped to flirt;
> And tho' my weakness you may blame, sir,
> Perhaps you might have done the same, sir.

Eng continued his plea to the magistrate, and then concluded:

> But one word more;—in this affair
> If I have sinned, my sin not knowing,
> Such penance I consent to bear
> As you may deem it worth bestowing;
> But *he*—my brother—no offence
> Committed; you must let *him* hence!
> Take me to prison, if you please,
> But first this gentleman release;
> And while to jail the guilty sending,
> Take heed, nor touch the unoffending!

Another poem was one written in 1902 by William Linn Keese entitled "The Siamese Twins, A Chapter of Biography." These are a few select verses from the poem:

I.

> 'Tis common to speak of things in pairs:
> A pair of eyes or a pair of stairs;
> With a pair of trousers for the sake of rhyme;
> A pair of gloves, and a pair of shoes,
> The hands and feet to match if you choose;
> A pair of scissors; a pair of bellows;
> A pair of capital jolly fellows;
> A pair of pigeons, a pair of wings—
> And pairs of numerous other things;

But the pair with which my lay begins
    Is that singular dual,
      Original plural,
Known round the world as the Siamese Twins.

II

From far Siam came my heroes hight,
(The land where the elephant bleaches white),
Whence Siamese; and if ease they ever
Enjoyed, it must have been there, for never,
When in this country they cast their lots,
Did they heed the teachings of Doctor Watts.
Their names were respectively Eng and Chang,
Their surname Bunker, which has a twang
Of that Island, you know, just off Cape Cod,
Nantucket yclept; and it's rather odd
That a name so calmly unsentimental
Should be borne by a native Oriental.
Conceive yourself saying *"Mr. Bunker!"*
To either festive Siamese younker—
Bunker, avaunt! thou hast no claim
To Chang and Eng's united fame . . .

VII.

What shall be said of this state of things,
Prolific of many imaginings?
Suppose, for a moment, Chang were ill,
And felt like remaining perfectly still,
And Eng felt splendidly *au contraire*,
And of all things wanted to take the air—
How would they fix it! Why, Eng, of course,
Must stick to his brother's side, perforce,
And hear him fret and murmur and groan,
And see pills and powders down him thrown—
Be dragged off finally, willy-nilly
To bed at an hour absurdly silly,
And lie there, trying to sleep in vain,
With thoughts that were certainly most profane.
Or suppose some fell, contagious thing,
Small-pox for instance, had captured Eng.
Unhappy Chang would be sure to catch it,
And then how inconceivably wretched
The situation—for brother and brother

Would then be *pitted* against each other!
Or, fancy that Eng was to church inclined,
And Chang preferred to stay behind—
Either Eng must relinquish his pious path,
Or Chang go with him in holy wrath!
      Ah, how hard the fate
      That makes one await
The whim of another without debate!

"The Siamese Twins," wrote one commentator, "were even better known than John L. Sullivan," who became the world champion heavyweight fighter, and "more widely noted than the President of the Republic."

Yet, in Mount Airy, North Carolina, oblivious of their ever-widening fame, Chang and Eng had remained in seclusion, concentrating their time on their wives, their children, their farms, and their sports. They had been in retirement from show business since 1839, out of the limelight and the public eye as performers for almost ten years.

Now, suddenly, in 1849, that would all change.

8
CHAPTER
8

The Gold Diggers

The Bunker families continued to grow. As more and more children arrived, the twins realized that the income from the farm would not provide for their eventual education.

There was one avenue open to Chang and Eng: once again to show themselves before the public as freaks, after ten years in retirement. It was a difficult decision, for the twins were known for being "great home-bodies," and undoubtedly they had dreamed that settling in North Carolina would free them forever from the rigors of public life.

In 1849, their old friend Dr. Edmund H. Doty approached the twins with an offer to exhibit them under his management. Doty wanted to show the twins with two of their daughters—Katherine and Josephine, each aged five—for eight months, with an option for four months more.

After much deliberation, the twins agreed, with these terms: that their salary would be $8,000 annually but would be paid monthly; that all expenses would be covered by Doty; that they would not travel at night except by steamboat or train; that they would have first-class accommodations; and that their working day would be only six hours long.

On April 25, 1849, Chang and Eng went to New York to renew their professional lives. The series of exhibitions proved to be unsuccessful. Perhaps Doty's management was poor, or perhaps the twins had already been overexposed in that area, or possibly the competition was too great—Tom Thumb, the famous midget, was all the rage in New York at that time. A letter from R. E. Martin, a friend of the twins, had forewarned them that "Gen. *Tom Thumb* is the Lion of the City at present." Perhaps the Siamese Twins, renowned though they were, were no longer unusual enough to usurp Tom Thumb's seat of popularity.

After a mere six-week stay in New York, the twins and their daughters returned to North Carolina with nothing to show for their trouble but an IOU from Doty (he paid them a third of the amount due some years later).

Despite their disappointment, the twins accepted another offer made them by a Mr. Howes. This time they were to be paid weekly. The new excursion was a lengthy one—twelve months, beginning in April 1853.

As before, two of the young Bunkers were brought along on the trip. Eng again took Katherine, his oldest child, but this time Chang took Christopher, his oldest son.

Following an appearance in Boston on April 11, the twins covered the Rhode Island Sound area and the Connecticut River Valley, making stops in Vermont, New Hampshire, and Massachusetts. Then they made an extensive tour of the coastal towns of New Hampshire and Maine as they headed for New Brunswick, Canada. They continued on to Nova Scotia, Canada, crossed Nova Scotia to reach the Atlantic Ocean side, then boarded a ship to return to the United States. Next, they exhibited in Connecticut; western Massachusetts; the Albany, New York, area; New

England's Green Mountains area; moved on to Quebec and upstate New York; and then backtracked to central New York, returning to New York City on November 20. They stayed in New York for some time, then resumed their travels to outlying villages.

In all, the twins visited 130 towns and cities.

The entourage generally sought towns that were approximately fifteen to twenty-five miles apart, which usually involved a day's journey by coach. In the twelve months of the tour, the group traveled a grand total of amost 4,700 miles. Chang and Eng were old traveling hands, of course, but for Christopher and Katherine it was a memorable adventure.

Wherever they went, the twins constantly hoped to find letters awaiting them that would report on their homes and families. Elisha Barnum, a friend of the Bunkers' in Mount Airy, wrote to tell the twins the news of the crops.

A second friend, Robert Gilmer, also wrote, having received a letter from Chang and Eng. He informed them that "Sarah [Eng's wife] was at my house and yesterday she says that they have got all the rye sowed and a good part of the crop of corn gathered and says that she thinks they will make corn aplenty to do them she says that Mr McKinney says they have the best crop that you have ever had on the place."

A rare letter exists from this trip, written by Chang and Eng themselves to their wives and children. Rare, because it is one of the handful of letters extant which was actually written by the twins rather than dictated by them to someone else. While it would appear that the average letter writer of the 1800's could not spell properly, the twins' spelling was particularly unusual. The letter, dated November 29, 1853, indicated that they were still being exhibited by their new manager, Mr. Howes:

Dear Wives & Children

We have received your of the 22—this day & glad to fine you all well—We got here last Sunday night week—Mr Howes say he want us to stay here till

news year. . . . Cathrine & Christ have had very bad
cold—but quet well now & fat—Great many our old
friends has come to see us they all say they would
like to see all our families together not only friends
but the visitor also We are glad Mr. Coud has call
on you—Please tell Mr. Gilmer we shall write to him
shortly you may tell him that if he can not get the
corm 25 cents per bushele not to buy at all. . . . We
and children want to Mr Hale last Sunday & took dinner their house Our house next Mr Bray—we wanted
rent out again just tell Mr Gilmer to have it rented
for the best term he can not less than $25—We
wanted you to tell Mr Gilmer if any money come to
us from Bound tell to put in Mr G Handerson of
Philad we shall call for it let us know—Our master
Mr. Howes take in last week not lest than $3000—
but his expence are very hie say from 2 to 225 dollars a day—Be side he has 5 or 6 defferend show—
they all bring in money—We think none bring so much
money as the Siamese Twins & their children

Good night 12 o'clock

at night

all well yours as ever
C & E B

Christ & Kate are sound sleep now—write soon

There was another letter, probably written by Eng
personally, from Baltimore on March 19, 1854—at the
very end of their long tour:

Dear Wives & Children

We are happy to enform you that Kate is getting
well fast—& also Chris—we want you to write to us
when you received this to Petterburgh Va be sure
to put Siamese Twins to it—

We have writen to you a few days ago telling you
bout Kate having the measles—thank god she is nearly
well—we have seen good many our old friends here—
We are long to be home the time past off very slow
with us we hope when we come to fine you all well—

in haste yours as ever
C & E BUNKER

When Chang and Eng returned to North Carolina from the tour, the home they returned to was no longer their common home. Before their departure, a change had taken place. While their financial pressures had temporarily eased, there had remained another pressure that continued to grow more and more nerve-racking. This was their worsening domestic situation. On the surface, it seemed to be simply an over-population problem. By the summer of 1852, Eng's Sallie had had her sixth child, and Chang's Adelaide her fifth. There were fifteen members in the house, besides the servants. The Chang and Eng families had become too large to be contained within the confines of their farmhouse. But there was more beneath the surface. Two wives under one roof were one too many. Adelaide and Sallie had to be together in the kitchen, at the dining table, in the parlor, and still share their husbands in the single oversized communal bed. With the lack of privacy, bickering and resentment intensified.

Another major difficulty, according to Zacharias Haynes, Chang's son-in-law, was that the two families of children had often been at odds: "The families lived together ten years after they were married, and of course the children could not at all times agree, and this was and would be the constant source of trouble, so long as the families remained together. . . . In truth, instances of two large families being brought up in the same house in perfect love, peace and harmony are very rare, and this is the true cause of the families being separated."

In 1852, an experimental separation had been instigated. Adelaide had taken a house in the town of Mount Airy, while Sallie remained on the farm. Then, after three years, Sallie had also moved her brood into a different house in Mount Airy. But, apparently, none of them were happy with the impermanence of their situation and their distance from the farm.

By 1857, the twins realized something drastic had to be done.

Surely, the four Bunkers had discussed their strange

togetherness many times, seeking a permanent solution that would admit more privacy and comfort. Now, in 1857, the four consulted over the matter, and at last a kind of solution was found based on their Mount Airy experiment. It was decided that each family should have a separate house, its own house on its own farm.

Immediately, a thorny question arose: How was their common property to be divided? While ill feeling between the brothers was not the cause for the move, the situation was still similar to a couple getting a divorce after being married for many years and owning everything in common. An arbitrator was necessary. To assure fair play, the twins called in three of their neighbors, men who were, according to Judge Graves, ". . . good, honest men in whom they could both confide, and men of sound judgement. . . . Owing to the situation, or rather the location of the real estate the land was not equally divided; but much the most valuable part was given to Chang; and in order to equalize the partition the deficiency in value was made up in slaves to Eng. Eng was never satisfied with the division but he determined to abide by it and did not complain."

Eng retained the original house they had built after moving from Trap Hill, and improved it, while the twins went to work building a house for Chang and his family, a mile away from Eng's house.

Along with the division of property, the Bunkers divided their time, and they devised a unique but sensible rule based on their practice in earlier years when Sallie lived in Trap Hill and Adelaide in Mount Airy: they decided they would spend three days at one brother's house, and then three days at the other's, alternating residences at the end of every third day. For three days Chang and Eng would dwell in Chang's house with his Adelaide and his children, leaving Sallie alone with her children in her house. Then Chang and Eng would board their carriage and drive over to Eng's house to spend three days with Sallie and Eng's children, leaving Adelaide and her family behind in her house.

The moment that Chang's house was ready, this arrangement was begun, and would be maintained without change for the rest of their lives. The routine of three days in each house never varied. It became a sacred and inflexible rule. No emergency, hardship, or even illness was considered cause for a break in the arrangement. On one occasion, a child of the twin at whose house they were staying unexpectedly died on the last day of their visit. But since that evening was the time set for the three-day move, move they did. The lone wife left behind tended to the funeral, as well as to her surviving children and the housekeeping chores.

Another aspect of the agreement was that each twin was to be absolute master in his own house. Whatever the host twin did, the joined brother had to agree to silently, without protest. In fact, the visiting twin was not even allowed to discuss his personal business with anyone while at his brother's home, but had to wait until the three days were up to handle his affairs.

When the pair moved into Chang's house, said a descendant of Dr. Hollingsworth, "Eng willed himself out of the picture, his desires suppressed, his opinions unexpressed, his judgment unspoken. He was a silent partner."

An old clipping from an unidentified local newspaper in another descendant's scrapbook described the twins' pact: "When Eng would enter the house of Chang, he would maintain steadfast silence until [the three days had] elapsed and he returned to his own house. It was as if he did not exist. He said nothing, did nothing save eat and sleep, saw nothing and was nothing. When the [time] was done Chang entered upon the role of self-effacement and went with Eng to the latter's house. In his active [time Eng] lived actively, and transacted all of his business. In his quiescent [time] he was as if he was not."

From available evidence, the arrangement worked well, and alleviated considerable conflict between the families.

However, by 1860, with two houses and farms to support instead of one, and with steadily expanding broods of children, Chang and Eng realized that their financial resources were slowly being depleted. Faced with the necessity of supplementing the income from their farms, they felt they had no choice but to return once more to show business.

They had covered the terrain of America's East, South, Midwest so extensively, and so often, that they were reluctant to go over the same ground again. They sought elsewhere for virgin territory, and were quickly aware that one promisingly lucrative area that had not seen them at all was America's Far West. Distant California had been much in the news —and on the twins' minds—in the previous twelve years. California had become news not long after the momentous morning of January 24, 1848, when James Marshall, a contractor and builder for his landlord, John Sutter, had discovered some flakes of gold in the shallows of a stream in Coloma, near what would become Sacramento, California. An excited Marshall had hastened to show the bright flakes to Sutter, who sent them down to San Francisco for scientific tests— and within a month the incredible California Gold Rush was under way.

The influx of gold-greedy miners from every corner of the world, all seeking overnight riches, was overwhelming to California's handful of old-time settlers. At the time of Marshall's discovery, California had had a population of 20,000 residents. A year later the population was five times as large. Four years after the discovery, there were 225,000 people in California. By 1860, the year the twins were contemplating a trip to California, the population had soared to 380,000. The population would have been much higher had it not been for the fact that California was difficult to reach—all modes of transportation were slow, tedious, hazardous, expensive.

In North Carolina, Chang and Eng reasoned that California's new affluence, plus its isolation and hunger for amusements, made it fair game for two of the most famous entertainers in the world. Chang and Eng decided to join the Gold Rush—not to mine the gold in the hills, but rather the gold in the miners' pockets.

But it was not money alone that attracted Chang and Eng to the Far West. They had another reason for going to California. They wanted to see their home again—their original home—one last time. They wanted to return to Siam, to Meklong, which they had not seen in thirty-one years, for a sentimental visit. The trip to California would bring them closer to their native Siam than they had been in all those absent years, and the journey from California to Siam would be a relatively pleasant and easy one.

In the time since they had become husbands and fathers, Chang and Eng had not been entirely uninformed about their mother Nok, their stepfather Sen, their brother Noy, and their sister, who was said to have become one of the wives of a polygamous Bangkok nobleman. Their main informant had been Robert Hunter, who erratically sent them messages about their family in Siam. However, in 1844, the twins had got a more detailed account of their family through a secondhand source, a friend who had received a letter from two Christian missionaries in Siam. The missionaries, the Reverend William Benel and his unnamed colleague, had visited Meklong and then written the following:

> Early in the afternoon we went in search of the mother of the Siamese twins, and were so happy as to find a man who conducted us directly to her house. On learning that we had brought intelligence respecting her absent children, whom she supposed to be dead, she gave us a hearty welcome. We assured her that they were living when we last heard from America and that they had recently married sisters in one of the Southern states. With this intelligence she was much gratified and expressed much affection for

them. . . . She is of lighter complexion than most Siamese women, and has every appearance of having once had great energy of character. It seems that both her husbands were China men and that she herself had a Chinese father, so that the twins are in no sense Siamese, except that they were born in Siam.

In this same period, a relative of the Yates family, Mrs. Roper-Feudge, who had been to Siam and known the twins' mother, was planning to visit Siam once more. She had approached the twins and offered to deliver any message from them to their family. Chang and Eng had consulted one another in their native tongue, and then Chang had spoken to Mrs. Roper-Feudge for both of them: "Tell our mother we will see her some day—as soon as we have enough money to make the trip."

But Chang and Eng had delayed their reunion with their mother too long a time. Eleven years earlier, in 1849, they had heard from another missionary in Siam, the Reverend Samuel R. House. His envelope contained two letters—one from himself, another from their brother Noy—reporting one piece of distressing news. The news was that the twins' beloved mother, Nok, had died the year before. The Reverend House's letter read:

BANGKOK KINGDOM OF SIAM. Jan 29, 1849
Messrs Chang and Eng.

This letter comes to you from a far off country —the country far away over the sea where you were born. It comes to you from one who though he has never seen you is your friend, and it will give you tidings of your aged mother whom I am sure you have not forgotten, tho' more than 20 years have gone by since you saw her last.

A month or two ago I was journeying with another missionary from Bang Kok to Petchaburn (Pripee) when we stopped at Meklong to see if any of your friends were still living there. Your older brother, Noy, the only one of the family left now, told us he wished to send a letter written in Siamese we would transmit into English and send it on to you. So on our return 5 or 6 days after he handed us the enclosed. Along with the translation I send the sounds of the Siamese words written down in English letters. Five years ago your mother heard from a missionary who called to see her that you were still living and they they you had bought a farm in . . . "Amerikan" and had married wives there and very glad was she to be told of this for she had long thought you dead. She herself breathed her last one year ago.

Your brother "Noy" gets his living like most of his neighbors at Meklong by raising ducks and fishing. How well off he is I can not say. His house, though not perhaps so poor as some around him, would still look very poor to you.

The Reverend House's translation accompanied Noy's letter, which was written with a blunt instrument in Siamese characters, on rough paper:

The second month, first day of the New moon (Siamese year) 1208 (A.D. 1848, Dec. 25). This letter the older brother, Noy, who is the elder brother, sends to Mr. In and Mr. Chun [Eng and Chang] because he thinks exceedingly much of his younger brothers. Moreover father Sen died in the year of the rabbit the 5th day of the full moon of the 1st month (Dec. 14, 1843), and mother Nok, the mother of Mr. In and Mr. Chun died on the year of the goat, first month, 6th day of full moon (Dec. 28, 1847) If Mr. In and Mr. Chun when they understand this letter saying that Noy, the elder brother sends a letter to Mr. In and Mr. Chun, and saying that Mother Nok the mother of Mr. In and Mr. Chun when the old lady was about to die directed Noy, the elder brother, saying "Should In and Chun think to return the favors of their father and mother let them . . . come back and do works of merit in reference to their deceased father and mother; then they may go back, their elder brother will not object. Moreover mother, when dying, thought exceedingly much of Mr. In and Mr. Chun, saying "they have been gone a long time, many years and I have not seen any letter sent, arrive at all. How are they? I do not know in the least. . . . If they can not come, they can let a letter be sent. If they would wish to let their elder brother know, then let Mr. In and Mr. Chun send something that will be a token by which the elder brother can know whether Mr. In and Mr. Chun are doing well or no. As for Noy, the older brother of Mr. In and Mr. Chun, he is already growing old and with great difficulty gets a living. He thinks of, he looks to, Mr. In and Mr. Chun with extreme interest. The older brother is left alone in the world and has no one to look to at all. He thinks of Mr. In and Mr. Chun very much indeed. This letter Noy, the elder brother, sends the 2nd month, first day of full moon. It is a token.

Chang and Eng were grief-stricken to receive word of their mother's death, and anxious to comply with her deathbed wish that they return to Siam and pay homage to their deceased mother and stepfather's memory. No doubt, too, the twins felt guilty after their older brother's letter pointed out their long neglect of him. They may have wanted to go to Siam at once, but no immediate opportunity presented itself. At the time, the twins were deeply involved with their own wives and offspring, with family support, and so the visit to their native land had had to be constantly postponed.

Now at last the right time had come for a trip to Siam. And the trip to California would provide a convenient departure point.

The journey to far-off California, the twins knew, was a long and arduous one, and they had to decide by what conveyances and by which route to make the trip. In 1860, there were four ways of reaching California. There was the traditional journey from New York by clipper ship around Cape Horn—circling all of South America—to San Francisco. It was the safest of the four routes—although eleven passenger ships had been lost in heavy seas and storms since the Gold Rush—but it was also the longest of the trips. The passage from New York to California around Cape Horn took about a hundred days. Then there was the land route from the Midwest to California. Just two years earlier, Butterfield's overland stagecoach had begun a regular run from Missouri to California, leaving for the West eight times a month. To take this land route meant that the twins would have to travel from North Carolina largely by canal boats and trains to Missouri, and there catch the Butterfield stage to California, traveling 2,800 miles, much of it through dangerous Indian country.

The other two routes combined sea and land travel, each in a complicated journey. The first of these meant traveling from New York to San Juan, Nicaragua. There were no docking facilities, and passengers had to be carried piggyback by natives from a small boat to the shore. After that, in intense heat, Nicaragua would be traversed on mules, horseback, in oxcarts, by schooner. The inconvenience and perils were many: no dining places, no hotel beds (only hammocks), exorbitant prices, swindlers and robbers, cholera. Once on the Pacific Ocean side, the twins would have had to await a ship to San Francisco. There was an alternate sea and land route that had become increasingly popular. By this route the twins would take a paddle-wheel steamer from New York to Aspinwell, Panama, then cross the Isthmus of Panama to Panama City, and there pick up a luxurious steamship to San Francisco. Only six years earlier, this route also had been hazardous, since the strip of Isthmus had to be crossed on foot, on mules, and in small boats, pushing through terrible jungles and malaria-ridden swamps. But in 1855, a railroad running from one side of the Isthmus to the other had been opened, and now the land journey could be made quickly and safely.

For Chang and Eng, the choice was simple—they would go to California by the Isthmus of Panama route.

However, a month before starting for California, Chang and Eng decided to give one more exhibit in New York. Although the twins had exhibited under the

auspices of a great many managers during their lifetime, the one they were about to work for was the
most extraordinary of all their sponsors. He was fifty-
year-old Phineas T. Barnum, the foremost American
showman, the legendary promoter of the bizarre and
the unusual. Contrary to popular belief, the twins
had little to do with Barnum in their long career, yet
tradition was forever to link them closely to the impresario who became known as the Prince of Humbug.

Phineas T. Barnum was born in Bethel, Connecticut,
in 1810. He was only nineteen years old when Chang
and Eng arrived in America in 1829. Barnum's first
profession was that of storekeeper, like his father before him. After that, Barnum went into the lottery
business, and then tried publishing his own newspaper, *The Herald of Freedom*, in Danbury.

Barnum, ambitious to the core, saw that he could
not realize his dreams of greatness and excitement in
ordinary endeavors. At last, in 1835, he found his true
calling. He became a showman. What set him on his
lifetime's course was a strange discovery. He was
brought face to face with President George Washington's Negro nurse, Joice Heth, 161 years of age.

A friend of Barnum's, Coley Bartram, had found this
marvel, and possessed proof of her age—a fading bill
of sale that had belonged to the Washingtons. Bartram took Barnum to visit the ancient governess on
display in Philadelphia, and this is what Barnum saw
as he recorded it later in his autobiography:

> She was lying upon a high lounge in the middle of
> the room. She was apparently in good health and
> spirits, but former disease or old age, perhaps both
> combined, had rendered her unable to change her
> position; in fact, although she could move one of her
> arms at will, her lower limbs were fixed in their po-
> sition, and could not be straightened. She was totally
> blind, and her eyes were so deeply sunken in their
> sockets that the eyeballs seemed to have disappeared
> altogether. She had no teeth, but possessed a head of

thick bushy gray hair. Her left arm lay across her breast, and she had no power to remove it. The fingers of her left hand were drawn so as nearly to close it and remained fixed and immovable. The nails upon that hand were about four inches in length, and extended above her wrist. The nails upon her large toes had also grown to the thickness of nearly a quarter of an inch.

Barnum decided that she could as easily be "a thousand years old as any other age." Bartram offered to sell her for $3,000, but Barnum's innate haggling ability brought the price down to $1,000.

Barnum's real career took off from there, and while the newspapers called Joice "an animated mummy" and "a loathesome old wench," the public could not get enough. Joice reminisced about "dear little George," sang hymns, and chatted with her audiences.

When Joice Heth died in 1836, a doctor examined her corpse and declared that she was certainly not over eighty years old. Barnum was scandalized, or at least he pretended to be. Whatever the truth of the matter was, Barnum began to acquire his reputation as a "humbug." This did not hinder the advancement of his career, however; perhaps the surge of publicity even helped it.

Barnum's greatest discovery did not come until many years later, when he chanced upon Charles S. Stratton, better known as General Tom Thumb. Barnum met Stratton, the son of a poor New England family, when the boy was five years old. Stratton was twenty-eight inches in height, and weighed a mere fifteen pounds. His feet were three inches long. Barnum recognized at once a salable oddity in the intelligent little fellow. After having arrived at a financial agreement with Stratton's parents, Barnum christened the boy "General Tom Thumb" for dramatic effect, and began to show him on exhibition.

In the United States and in Europe, Tom Thumb was a raging success. As well as being a box-office smash, he was a personal favorite of Queen Victoria and assorted European nobility. During the course of his long association with Barnum, Tom Thumb distinguished himself by leading an extravagant life. He enjoyed such luxuries as playing miniature billiards and sailing on his Lilliputian yacht. He eventually married Mercy Lavinia Warren Bump, who was thirty-two inches tall and weighed twenty-nine pounds.

The discovery and promotion of the world's most famous midget launched P. T. Barnum into true stardom. In later years, besides Chang and Eng, Barnum continued to have remarkable successes. Jenny Lind, dubbed "The Swedish Nightingale" because of her extraordinary voice, and Jumbo the giant elephant, twelve feet tall and weighing six and a half tons, were but two of his coups.

The place where Barnum displayed all his wonders was the American Museum, an imposing five-story marble building located at 218–222 Broadway, in New York City. The museum had originally been founded in 1780, and already housed a collection of oddities from around the world, largely donated by sea captains who had made exotic voyages. Barnum purchased the museum in 1842, filled it with unusual acts and exhibits, and made it the most famous showcase of its kind in American history. The museum remained an unparalleled success until June 1865, when it fell afoul of an arsonist and burned to the ground. This did not halt Barnum's career, however, and he went on from sensation to sensation. He lived to be sixty-two, spending much of his last years writing nine published versions of his autobiography.

Now, in October 1860, before leaving for California, Chang and Eng, accompanied by two of Eng's sons, twelve-year-old Montgomery and ten-year-old Patrick, arrived in New York to fulfill a short engagement at Barnum's American Museum, for which they were paid $100 a week. After several appearances, an advertisement in *The New York Times* announced they would be exhibited daily:

BARNUM'S AMERICAN MUSEUM
Under the personal supervision of . . .
P. T. BARNUM
EVERY DAY AND EVENING THIS WEEK
COMMENCING MONDAY, OCT. 15 1860
Last week but one of the
ONLY LIVING SIAMESE TWINS,
CHANG AND ENG,
WHO, WITH TWO OF THEIR CHILDREN

will be on exhibition Day and Evening, Those who
have ever seen these most wonderful and extraordinary human beings, know them to be the most interesting and curious of all objects, while those who
do not, need only to be told that they are TWO
LIVING MEN 49 YEARS OLD, SO INSEPARABLY UNITED
AT THE PIT OF THE STOMACH that what one feels the
other does . . .

Barnum was known worldwide and the Siamese
Twins were internationally famous when they met
and decided to work together, and therein lay part of
their problem. From the beginning, they did not get
along. Chang and Eng did not like Barnum, and he did
not like them.

Barnum resented the twins from the start. Some
say that it irritated him not to have discovered them
himself. Much of the affection Barnum felt for his
attractions came from finding them, developing them,
and making them famous. Chang and Eng were self-
made men, already household words, and they never
needed P. T. Barnum. Furthermore, Barnum considered
the twins too independent-minded, and sensed their
dislike for him and growing reluctance to be public
property.

As for Chang and Eng, they disapproved of Barnum
from the first, finding him to be tight-fisted and ex-
ploitive. They were not the only ones to accuse him
of such traits. Many years later, one of Eng's sons,
Patrick Bunker, remarked in an interview, ". . . they
never liked Barnum. He was too much of a Yankee,
and wanted too much for his share of the money,

and my father and uncle were close figurers themselves."

Nevertheless, the showman and the twins contracted to work together, because each side saw that
it could make profit out of the other.

It was while Chang and Eng were showing at Barnum's American Museum, on October 13, 1860, that
they received an important royal visitor. Albert Edward, the Prince of Wales, later King Edward VII of
England, had just begun an American tour. One of the
sights he wanted to see was Barnum's place. He was
driven there in a carriage. What followed was reported by *The New York Times:*

> The Museum was full of people. By causing the
> performance in the lecture-room to commence half
> an hour earlier than usual, Mr. Greenwood [Barnum's
> assistant manager] was enabled to clear the corridor
> somewhat, but as soon as the distinguished guests
> arrived, crowds began to pour in. The people, how-
> ever, kept at a respectful distance from the Prince,
> and he had ample opportunity to see everything. He
> availed himself of it to the fullest extent. He examined
> the "What is it?" [it was Zip, the Man Monkey, an
> African pinhead Barnum promoted as the missing link,
> actually a deformed, intelligent Negro named Wil-
> liam Jackson] with interest, and when Mr. Green-
> wood told the man in charge of the curiosity that he
> need not repeat its history, the Prince interposed
> and requested the man to tell him all about it. He
> heard him with attention, then proceeded through
> the building inspecting the Albino family, the twins
> from Siam . . .

The Prince of Wales was intrigued by the Siamese
Twins, and examined them closely. Leaving, the prince
asked for Mr. Barnum. He was told that Barnum
had not expected him and was at his home in Bridgeport. "Ah," said the prince, "we have missed the most
interesting feature of the establishment."

As the twins neared the end of their exhibit for
Barnum, there was some talk of their traveling on the
road with a Barnum carnival after their return from

California. This the twins would not consider. Later, when Barnum became a circus man, first with William Cou, then with James A. Bailey, the twins would have no part of working with him. They were proud of the fact that they had never in their lives participated in an American circus.

On November 12, 1860, having completed their engagement for Barnum, Chang and Eng, together with Eng's sons, boarded the paddle-wheel steamer *Northern Light* in New York harbor for the first portion of their journey, the sea voyage to Aspinwell, Panama.

Unlike many of the vessels on this run, the *Northern Light* was a splendid ship. It was made of oak, locust, and cedarwood and painted dark green, with a gold scroll decorating the prow. The ship was 260 feet long, 40 feet wide, and weighed 2,057 tons. It belched coal smoke from two funnels, and the coal it burned propelled the paddle-wheel on each side. It was also fitted with two masts for sails, to be used in an emergency. A feature of the ship was the vast dining saloon, located in the center of the main deck and extending from one side of the ship to the other, thereby providing plenty of light and ventilation.

What was most noteworthy about the *Northern Light* was that it was owned by sixty-six-year-old "Commodore" Cornelius Vanderbilt, a blustering, bewhiskered financial pirate whose earlier ships had a reputation as bad as his own. In 1838, steamers had come into use in the United States for passenger travel, cargo, and mail, and Vanderbilt saw their promise early. Quickly, he parlayed a single two-masted barge into a shipping company that owned one hundred steamers. Through price wars, bribery, and stock-market manipulations, Vanderbilt accumulated $100 million and became the richest man in America.

By 1858 a fierce competition existed between Vanderbilt's Atlantic and Pacific Steamship Company and the Pacific Mail. The rivalry between them was bitter, but in February 1860—eight months before the twins would leave New York on the Vanderbilt steamer—

an agreement was reached between the two warring companies. Vanderbilt's fleet would take complete control of the Atlantic traffic, and Pacific Mail's line would confine itself to the Pacific Ocean.

Vanderbilt was notorious for the poor pay and hard conditions he imposed on his captains. His crews were frequently inadequate for the overwhelming workload, and it was not uncommon for crew members to die of exhaustion during a voyage. While the vessels of the Pacific Mail had "a splendid reputation," the Vanderbilt ships were known as "floating pigsties."

Chang and Eng might have been aware of the conditions that could confront them. The *Northern Light* had been built to carry nine hundred passengers, but there were often more than a thousand persons aboard. As a result of the overcrowding, there were not enough benches in steerage for all the passengers to lie on at night, and many bribed the stewards to get even this meager space.

"This is on a par with all the rest of the Vanderbilt coterie's grasping conduct," wrote the *Panama Star Herald* the very year the twins boarded the Vanderbilt ship. "With them the 'almighty dollar' is not only the primary, but the only consideration, and the 'dear public' once within their clutches, have literally got to 'sweat it out' until the end of the voyage; and we really believe if one of their vessels were to sink with a full living cargo on board, the Company would only lament the loss of their ship, and never give a second thought to the sacrifice of life."

While this criticism was harsh, it was confirmed by many other writers. One, reporting a few years later on another Vanderbilt ship headed for Panama, wrote:

> Although it is very dark, you will observe that the benches around the ship's rail are filled with human beings. Some are stretched full length, others half reclining. You will see as you inspect these benches females in the close embrace of the sterner sex, their heads reclining in the most loving manner on the shoulders of their male protectors. You will naturally

enough suppose them to be husband and wife or sister and brother. They are in some cases, but more frequently are not, but only a couple whose acquaintance dates back to the ship's sailing, or probably a shorter time. . . . Around the mainmast is a dark mass composed of forty or fifty persons, of all ages and both sexes, heaped together en masse, and all apparently are sound asleep. . . . We . . . go down into the second cabin. . . . Directly at the foot of the steps, lying on her back, is an Irish woman weighing not less than two hundred and fifty pounds. She is almost without clothing, so great is the heat. Around her, like a litter of pigs, are five children, the eldest being five years of age. Every berth is filled. Women can be seen in this second cabin who have apparently lost all sense of decency, who at home would cover the legs of a piano, so particular were they in regard to anything appearing naked.

The same writer pointed out, "There are four water closets for the use of about three hundred people of the first and second cabin."

While these sordid conditions may have prevailed on the *Northern Light*, Chang and Eng and the children apparently did not suffer from them, since in their correspondence after they reached their final destination they offered no complaints. Perhaps this was because they were traveling first class, where accommodations were relatively luxurious.

After an eight-day voyage, the *Northern Light* arrived in Aspinwell (now Colón). A small steamer from the port met the ship and brought the passengers and baggage to the wharf. A short time later, Chang and Eng and Eng's offspring boarded a wood-burning train that would take them across the Isthmus to Panama City on the Pacific side.

The train was, of course, a relatively new innovation. With the coming of the Gold Rush, William H. Aspinwell, owner of the Pacific Mail line, who had made $4 million in shipping, decided that the forty-seven miles of Isthmus jungles and swamp land was too dangerous and too slow to cross on foot or by mule. In April 1849, Aspinwell formed the Panama Railroad Company, established the port that was named after him, and set out to build a railroad from the Atlantic side to the Pacific side of the Isthmus. Laborers were recruited from many nations, including 705 opium-addicted coolies from China. In the five years of construction, eight hundred workers died of numerous causes, most falling prey to cholera, yellow fever, and deadly reptiles. On January 28, 1855, the first train crossed the forty-seven miles between Aspinwell and Panama City—and the journey from New York to San Francisco was cut to one-fourth the time, since it was no longer necessary to sail around the Horn.

Now, on November 20, 1860, Chang and Eng and Eng's sons entered a passenger car of this train—there were fifty-six other passengers in the car—and in three hours and ten minutes they had traveled across the Isthmus to alight at Panama City on the other side.

Chang and Eng did not linger long in Panama City. A ship of the Pacific Mail line, the *Uncle Sam*, was waiting for them at the island of Flamenco, a dozen miles outside Panama City. The Bunker entourage joined other passengers on a small steamer that ferried them across the water to their San Francisco–bound ship.

The sea voyage from Panama City to San Francisco took sixteen days. The only description of the voyage —in fact, of the entire trip from New York—was provided by one of Eng's sons, who wrote about it to his brothers and sisters in North Carolina four days after his arrival in San Francisco:

"My dear brothers and Sisters we are all well and i hope these few lines will find you all the same We was twenty four days coming from New york to California Thier was about 6 six hundred pashingers on Bord of Ship We saw a plenty of whales I was sea sick a little We was eight days Coming from New-york to Aspenwall and we got on the cars and went to Panima And we got on the boat at Panima the Boats name was Unkle San We was sixteen Days Coming from Panima to California We was very much received that we do not receive any more leters We saw plenty of flying fish We have plenty of green corn and beens and pease we Saw a Plenty of Coaker nuts & coaker-nuts Trees we stoped at a litle place to get coal [the "little place" was Acapulco, where the ship stopped to take on coal] ..."

The *Uncle Sam* docked at the Folsom Street wharf in San Francisco on December 6, 1860. The first announcement of the twins' imminent arrival had appeared in print four days earlier in a front-page dispatch delivered to the *Alta California*, the ten-year-old San Francisco daily, by pony express. The dispatch carried the first-class passenger list of those who had left New York for San Francisco, and the twins were introduced to California's first city almost casually: "C A Eastman and family, Miss Thompson, Mrs J D Farwell, Miss E Elliot, Jas Findla and wife, Mrs C J Dempster, Rev J A Benton, Rich'd Hockman and wife, Col Perry, Mrs E Brown and family, H H Smith, J Sands and wife, Siamese Twins and children ..."

Now, at last, Chang and Eng were in fabled San Francisco, in a new metropolis that had never seen them, prepared to replenish their purses before continuing onward for a nostalgic reunion with their older brother in Siam.

The San Francisco the twins found, and would perform in for almost two weeks, had undergone a drastic transformation in the dozen years since the Gold Rush.

Before the discovery of gold, San Francisco had been a sleepy hamlet consisting of fifty adobe huts and a few hundred inhabitants. With the finding of gold, the hamlet burst into a hodgepodge of a city of 20,000 people. From the shorefront to the nearby hills rose wooden shanties, tents, lean-tos, brick buildings, and abandoned ships' hulls. In those early boom years San Francisco was a raucous, unruly, lawless community dominated, it seemed, by saloons, brothels, hotels, and warehouses.

But the passage of ten years had sobered San Francisco into a growing, prospering, relatively dignified metropolis. The city Chang and Eng saw in 1860 possessed 1,500 new fireproof commercial buildings made of stone and iron, restaurants that served baked hog's head and fricasseed oxtail and three-dollars-a-bottle sherry, a library of 3,000 volumes, 175 major manufacturers, horse-drawn streetcars, neat plank sidewalks, and a population of over 50,000. There were now three major sections to San Francisco. There was the city's main square, the Plaza, filled with merchandise booths and surrounded by hotels, medical buildings, law offices, and a public schoolhouse. There was staid and imposing Montgomery Street, known as the Wall Street of the West. And then there was the Barbary Coast, where the majority of the city's one hundred international houses of prostitution and many gambling halls were to be found. In the decade preceding the arrival of the Siamese Twins, there had been one thousand murders in the community. But four years earlier, the Vigilante Committee, with nine thousand disciplined volunteers, had taken the loose laws into its own hands, tried and hanged killers, deported other criminal elements, and brought about order and safety.

Isolated as it was from the rest of the nation, San Francisco was interested in a continuous supply of entertainment. Some of the entertainment was free. Here, in 1860, flourished forty-one-year-old Joshua Norton, a bankrupt merchant who had declared himself emperor of the United States, abolished Congress, banished the Republican and Democratic parties, issued fifty-cent bonds to finance himself, and strolled the streets attired in a general's cap, blue navy uniform, and Chinese umbrella. But most entertainment was paid for, and paid for well, and this was what had originally attracted Chang and Eng to the city. One showman dominated the city's entertainment. He was Tom Maguire, an uneducated New York hack driver turned impresario, who had made a success with his $200,000 Jenny Lind Theatre, had managed the Maguire Opera House, and now owned all of the city's important music halls.

The twins, who had moved into a boardinghouse on Washington Street, were enchanted by San Francisco, but their thoughts were never very far from their families in North Carolina. The twins had been in San Francisco no more than four days when Eng was moved to write a letter home:

Dear wife & children we wanted to know very much how are you coming on. we have not hear from you for 6-weeks. we got two letters from you since we left. i hope you has done hauld the corn from Mr. Whitlock befor now Tell Mary to take care of catle & pigs—i wanted to know very much how mill coming on—most likely we will be back in march —maybe not till may or june—you must tell Mary to have every thing carige on wright—i leave a truk in n york with Mr. Hale he send it home by way of Marmadow tell Mr. Gilmer if we have any thing to hauld from their to have our truk bring it on too— nothing in them but shoese & coat for Mary—We has not seen much gold yet but hope to get some befor long—i mut bring this close—Hope this will fine you all well & happy take good care of the five—write soon to this Place your has ever E

E BUNKER

No sooner had Eng posted this letter (via the nine-month-old pony express to St. Joseph, Missouri, at five dollars a half ounce) than he and Chang were ready to get down to business. "We has not seen much gold yet," he had written, "but hope to get some befor long." That very afternoon the twins began their quest for California gold. The *Alta California* for December 10, 1860, announced their opening performance in an advertisement:

THE ORIGINAL & WORLD-RENOWNED
SIAMESE TWINS,
Accompanied by Two of their Children
HAVE ARRIVED
And will Exhibit for a short time, only, at
PLATT'S NEW MUSIC HALL,
on and after

Monday . . . . . . December 10th, 1860.
DOORS OPEN DAILY, (Sundays Excepted,) from
2 to 5 P.M., and from 7 to 10 P.M.
ADMISSION 50 CENTS
Children under 9 years of age, half price.

On December 13, the *Alta California* publicized the twins with a bit of wordplay: "SIAMESE TWINS—Chang and Eng have already installed themselves in the good graces of the community. They are now fifty years of age. It is not true that Chang is two years older than Eng, as has been asserted—on the ground that Chang is fifty and Eng is fifty-*too*."

On December 15, the *Alta California* published a more extensive news story on the twins: "THE SIAMESE TWINS.—The interest in these wonders of nature continues unabated. One of the twins has seven children and the other eight. Two of the boys are with them. The mothers are both living in the Atlantic States. They will not visit Siam, as has been supposed, but after a short jaunt in the interior, will return to the Atlantic States."

This story was the first evidence that Chang and Eng had changed their minds about continuing to Siam after finishing their engagement in San Francisco. What had changed their minds, evidently, was the disquieting news, published daily in the San Francisco press, that the Southern states were preparing to secede from the Union and that a war between the North and South was inevitable. While the twins had been en route to San Francisco, a crucial presidential election campaign had been taking place. The much-feared Abraham Lincoln, Republican, had been pitted against Stephen A. Douglas, Northern Democrat, John C. Breckinridge, Southern Democrat, and John Bell of the Constitutional Union party.

The day after their arrival in San Francisco, Chang and Eng had their first serious intimations of trouble back home. The *Alta California* carried a front-page story, "Per Pony Express," from its "St. Louis Correspondence" that "up to 10 P.M., Nov. 8, returns of 90,000 votes showed Lincoln 2,000 ahead of

Douglas, and Breckinridge behind both." Another front-page account reflected the alarm of the South at the possibility of Lincoln's being elected President. "There is every reason to believe," began the story, "that the Democrats from the Southern States in Congress may attempt to defeat the inauguration of Lincoln, by refusing to declare the result, or to count the votes."

Six days later, the twins read a front-page report in the *Alta California* that alarmed them further: "South Carolina, it is believed, is determined to precipitate disunion, and will wait for no advice from any quarter."

Meanwhile, all about them in San Francisco, talk was in the air about the likelihood of a civil war. Among Americans in California at the time, there were 74,000 who favored the North and 29,000 who favored the South. There were also many Californians who did not want to become embroiled in a sectional dispute, who felt that California (in its tenth year of statehood) should withdraw from the Union and declare itself a neutral nation, the Pacific Republic. But those who were pro-Union, anti-slavery, anti-South were clearly in control.

Realizing that North Carolina might soon be involved in war, that their wives and children might be in danger, Chang and Eng made their decision not to proceed to Siam. Instead, they hastily determined to conclude their stay in San Francisco, make one side trip of exhibitions for whatever profit it could earn them, and then head for home.

On December 20, 1860, the twins and Eng's sons boarded a shallow paddle-wheel river steamer and sailed north up the Sacramento River toward the raucous new state capital. The year before the Gold Rush, there had been no Sacramento. There had been just a piece of potential real estate, at the fork of the Sacramento River and the American River, near Sutter's Mill. A year later, after the discovery of gold, a townsite had been laid out and a city of tents and wagons populated by 12,000 Argonauts had sprung up.

This was Sacramento, the river port which had become the capital of California.

Because Sacramento was isolated from the rest of the state, there was a persistent hunger for outside entertainers. In 1852, the flamboyant dancer Lola Montez, fresh from a series of European love affairs including one with King Ludwig I of Bavaria, had trekked into town to perform for some of its abundant gold. When the miners laughed at her dances, Lola had castigated her audience and walked off the stage. Other, less notorious performers, singers, and actors had followed after Lola and received heartier welcomes. Now, a Californian named William Pridham, employed by Chang and Eng as their advance agent, had booked them into Sacramento.

Their first two public appearances were reviewed in the Sacramento *Daily Union* on December 22:

"SIAMESE TWINS—The Siamese Twins held their levee at the Forrest Theater yesterday afternoon and evening, and were visited by a large number of citizens. They are introduced to the audience by their agent, who gives a brief sketch of their history, etc.; after which, they mingle with their visitors, conversing freely and pleasantly, in good English. They are accompanied by two sons—boys, of nine and twelve years old—bright and intelligent boys. They will receive visitors again today, at from two to five o'clock this afternoon, and from six to nine this evening. There will be no other opportunity for the present to see them."

After that, Chang and Eng left Sacramento for a month. Most likely, their agent booked them for a series of exhibitions in nearby gold-rich towns such as Marysville, Placerville, Reno, Stockton. Then they were on their way to Sacramento, where on January 25, 1861, they performed for one day.

A week later, the first week in February, Chang and Eng were once more in San Francisco for a single farewell exhibition before heading home. Their final advertisement appeared in the *Alta California* for February 7:

LAST CHANCE TO SEE!
The World-Renowned
UNITED SIAMESE TWINS!
THESE GREATEST OF LIVING WONDERS
will be on exhibition
at Platt's New Musical Hall on
SATURDAY AFTERNOON and EVENING,
February 9th.
POSITIVELY FOR ONE DAY ONLY!
As they sail for New York on the
steamer of the 11th instant.

On February 11, 1861, Chang and Eng, with Eng's sons Montgomery and Patrick, boarded the 2,864-ton wooden paddle-wheel steamer *Golden Age*, a veteran of the South Seas, for the journey that would take them back to Panama City. Then they would travel on to Aspinwell, to New York, and finally back to Mount Airy. As they moved up the two-mile-wide Golden Gate strait connecting the Bay with the Pacific Ocean and watched San Francisco fade from view, they could feel pleasure in the fact that their two-month foray into the Far West had been both fascinating and financially successful. But as they turned toward the open sea, they could feel only apprehension—for their own future and the future of their beloved country.

9
CHAPTER
6

Let Not Man Put Asunder

About the time that Chang and Eng set sail to return home from California, the United States cracked and began to come apart. South Carolina, which had threatened to leave the Union if a Republican were elected President, had seen Republican Abraham Lincoln win the presidency on November 6, 1860. On December 20, the Convention of the People of South Carolina had unanimously voted to secede from the Union. Other Southern states quickly followed. Then, in the first week of February, the Confederate States of America was formed. The terrible schism was under way.

After two ocean voyages totaling twenty-six days and the journey south from New York, the Siamese Twins were finally back in Mount Airy, North Carolina. They had most of March 1861 and the first week and a half in April to reacquaint themselves with their families and organize their business affairs before the last peace they would know for four years would come to an abrupt end.

On April 12, 1861, the army of the two-month-old Confederate States of America fired upon the federal garrison at Fort Sumter outside Charleston, South Carolina. Following thirty-four hours of bombardment, Fort Sumter fell. The Civil War had begun. The twins, like all Americans, saw the conflict rapidly intensify. On April 19, Lincoln ordered a blockade of the Southern ports; on May 3, Lincoln called for volunteers that would bring the Union Army up to 157,000 men; on May 6, the Confederate Congress declared that a state of war existed between the South and the North.

Then, what Chang and Eng and their neighbors dreaded most came to pass. On May 20, following a convention in Raleigh, the twins watched their beloved North Carolina become the eleventh state to secede from the Union, join the Confederacy, and enter the war.

Neither side would acknowledge that slavery was the cause of the conflict.

A regional account, *History of Surry County* by. J. G. Hollingsworth, gave the Southern viewpoint on the cause of the war, and it certainly was the viewpoint of Chang and Eng:

> The immediate cause of War Between the States was not primarily over the question of slavery. It is true that in the years preceding the struggle sectional differences had arisen over the hostile conception of slavery. The immediate cause of the war was over the right of states to withdraw from federal union. It was the all-important question of state rights. The people of the South upheld the early conception of the union that the states were older than the national union. . . .
>
> The large slave owners of the state were conservative in their views and when the crisis arrived threw their influence on the side of Union loyalty. The slave-holding class in North Carolina in 1860 represented only twenty-five percent of the white population of the state. The Democratic party, chiefly small farmers, merchants, manufacturers, and pro-

fessional men was the noisy element that demanded hasty action and immediate withdrawal from the Union following the election of 1860.

The first convention which was called to consider the state's withdrawal voted against the proposal. But when Lincoln declared the seceding states in rebellion and issued a decree of blockade, the coast of North Carolina was included in the region to be patrolled.

And this inflamed North Carolinians and sent them to war.

The North agreed with the South on the cause for conflict. On July 25, 1861, the United States Senate passed a resolution "that the present war was being fought to maintain the Union and Constitution and not to interfere with established institutions such as slavery."

Even though North Carolina had joined the Confederacy, sympathies in Surry County and in Mount Airy, where Chang and Eng dwelt, were split. There was a good deal of support for the North, although soon much of it would go underground, but still the state had joined the Confederacy, and the majority went along. During the war, the twins' home area contributed 700 soldiers to the Confederate forces and more than 100 to the Union forces. In all, North Carolina contributed 111,000 regular troops, 19,000 of them draftees, to the Confederate Army, and lost 40,275 of these men, half dying in battle, half dying from disease, the greatest loss of lives suffered by any Southern state.

There was some speculation on what would have happened if Chang and Eng, caught in an atmosphere of conflicting loyalties and unable to secede from *their* union, had supported different sides. Actually, to those who knew them, it was never an issue. Judge Graves reported:

In all questions of a sectional character the feelings and sentiments of Chang and Eng were all strongly with the South, with whose people and institutions they had become so thoroughly identified. And in their troubles in the Northern states during the periods of intense excitement caused by the attempted enforcement of the "Fugitive Slave Law" and the still more alarming and angry passions exhibited in the winter preceding "The war between the states," it was with the greatest difficulty that they could control their feelings of indignation. . . .

When the final conflict came, they took sides with their own section, with their neighbors and friends, in defense of what they believed to be their right. Always and under all circumstances true to friends, faithful to all engagements, sincere in all things, warmly enlisted for whatever cause they espoused, they sustained "The Lost Cause" with unflinching fidelity to the last. As soon as their sons were old enough, catching the enthusiasms of their fathers, they enlisted in the Confederate service and proved their courage in the field. At all times noted for their hospitality, their generous and kindly feelings opened the doors of their mansions wider and more cordially to the weary and hungry soldiers than to any other persons . . .

Although North Carolina was a vital supply link to the rest of the Confederacy, it was a minor arena for the warring armies. Only seventy-three skirmishes and eleven battles were fought in the state. And in the northwest corner of the state, the twins saw no enemy invaders for three of the four years of the war. In fact, in the first two years the twins and their families were not directly affected by the conflict, except as everyone on the home front was affected by the nearness of danger and the change in living conditions.

At the outset of the Civil War, Surry County records showed that Chang and Eng were comfortable both in their family and financial situations. On June 1, 1860, the county census taker visited Eng and noted: "*Living under the Eng roof:* Eng Bunker, age 49, male. Value of real estate $1100. Value of personal estate $16,000. Place of birth: Siam. Sarah Bunker, age 40, female. Place of birth: N.C." Then were listed all of

Eng's children to that date: Kate, 17; Julia, 16; Stephen D., 14; James, 13; Patrick, 12; William O., 6; Frederick, 5; Rozila, 1.

Next, the census taker visited Chang and noted: *"Living under the Chang roof*: Chang Bunker, age 49, male. Value of real estate $6,000. Value of personal estate $12,000. Place of birth: Siam. Adelade Bunker, age 37, female. Place of birth: N.C." Then were listed all of Chang's children to that date: Josephine, 17; Chris, 15; Nancy, 13; Mary, 11; Victoria, 9; Louisa, 6; Albert, 3.

In 1862, after a full year of war, the twins were still financially comfortable. The "Tax List for Mount Airy District" listed their individual assets. For Eng: "300 acres, valued at $1,000/ 1 town lot, valued at $300/ 19 slaves, valued at $6,000/ debts and interest [owed him], $1,975/ carriages $30/ household property $150/ other property $125/ plate & jewelry $100." For Chang: "425 acres, valued at $6,000/ 11 slaves, valued at $4,000/ household property $400/ other property $25/ plate and jewelry $100/ gold watch $150."

In 1863, the second year of the war, a document of tax assessments showed that the twins were continuing to prosper. The first entry read: "Eng Bunker Acreage 300 Value $1000 No. slaves 21 Value $17850." Eng was worth $18,850. The second entry read: "Chang Bunker Acreage 425 Value $6000 No. slaves 10 Value $10130." Chang was worth $16,130.

By 1864, the third year of the war, both twins were maintaining their assets, although Eng's slave-holdings were worth almost twice Chang's. For Eng, the tax summation read: "300 acres $1,000/ 1 lot $250/ 21 slaves $17050/ money $1400/ debts [owed him] $1000/C. B. $50/ gold plate $100/ household property $400." For Chang, the tax summation read: "475 acres $6000/ 12 slaves $9500/ C.B. $40/ gold plate $100/ H.P. [household property] $300/ brandy 35 gallons."

But the cold figures did not tell the entire story of the twins' lives during the early war years—the strain on family relationships, the sufferings under excessive taxation and inflation, the pressures of home-front activity, the ever-present danger to those living in the leading blockade-running state.

With the coming of war, Adelaide and Sallie were under additional stress, more and more at odds with one another—the peculiar arrangement that required each of them to live with her husband *and* his brother was a permanent irritant—and they frequently had angry differences.

Like their neighbors, the twins suffered from the higher taxes imposed to help finance the war. They were forced to use newly issued Confederate money and to buy war bonds, both of which sharply depreciated in value as the war wound on and the prospects for victory dimmed. Prices for staple foods soared out of sight. In three war years, the price of flour rose from $18 a barrel to $500; the price of wheat jumped from $3 a bushel to $50; the price of bacon leaped from 33 cents a pound to $7.50. By the time the war was over, the twins were paying $70 for a bushel of salt and $100 for a pound of coffee. Throughout these trying years, substitute foods came into use: parched corn replaced coffee beans, and molasses was used instead of sugar. Since salt was so expensive—but a necessity for the preservation of meat—new factories were built to produce salt by evaporating seawater.

While Adelaide and Sallie were exempt from many of the hardships other North Carolina women underwent—farming the fields for their absent husbands, worrying whether their husbands were alive, suffering loneliness—they still worked hard sewing clothes for the soldiers, preparing refreshments for troop trains, nursing the wounded.

There was constant fear of Union cavalry raids. Efforts were made to mount some protection. According to a local history:

"The entire region began to resound with the tread of men being trained in the arts of war. In at least three places in Surry county military companies were organized and preparation made to get them in ser-

viceable condition. . . . At one time during the struggle efforts were made in the county to organize a
company of cavalry but when application was made
to the Confederate government at Richmond for
equipment the plan fell through because of the scarc-
ity of saddles and swords."

Yet North Carolina's home population contributed mightily to the Southern war effort by blockade-
running. At the start of the war, Lincoln had determined that the most effective means of undermining
the Confederacy would be to blockade its 3,000-mile
coastline with Union vessels that would halt all importing of food, clothing, and firearms, and all exporting of home produce to raise money abroad.

To counter this strangulation, North Carolina's witty, eloquent Governor Zebulon Vance, pro-Union before the war but a patriotic Southerner after secession, established a fleet of speedy, light-draft vessels,
camouflaged gray to run through fog or black to
travel by night. These vessels picked up firearms and
food from British steamers in Bermuda, hurried the
goods 674 miles past Union lookouts, past the protective artillery of Fort Fisher, and upriver to the port of
Wilmington, North Carolina, "the most important
blockade-running port in the Confederacy." On their
trips out, the little vessels slipped through the blockade with their cargoes of cotton to be delivered to
British steamships in Bermuda to build up cash cred-
its in Europe for more imports. One North Carolina
ship, the *Advance*, whose chief engineer was an Irishman who had voted for Lincoln, successfully ran the
blockade eleven times before it was captured.

Since much of the blockade-running throughout
the war originated in Surry County, Chang and Eng
had at least a peripheral involvement in this risky but
successful war effort.

Then, on April 1, 1863, a member of the Bunker
families, the first in either family, got directly involved in the Civil War, and through him Chang and
Eng themselves became more closely involved in the
conflict raging about them. Having just turned eigh-

teen, Christopher Wren Bunker, Chang's second oldest child and first son, enlisted in a Confederate cavalry battalion.

Young Christopher went across the North Carolina state line into Wythe County, Virginia, and offered his services to Company I of the 37th Battalion, Virginia Cavalry, whose commanding officer, Captain E. Young, had organized the company that day and been elected by the men to head it. Captain Young swore Christopher Bunker in as a private "for the war."

Of Christopher's early activity in the Civil War, little is known except for the remark of one descendant who said that "Chris Bunker was only a water boy in the war." Water boy or full-fledged Confederate soldier, Christopher was called up for service on September 14, 1863, and did not return home to Mount Airy until March 15, 1864. Later, his younger sister Nannie noted in a diary she kept that after a two-and-a-half-week furlough Christopher had then returned to the battlefield. "Left again Apr. 3rd 1864."

There is no doubt that, during his second and final stint with the 37th Battalion, Christopher saw active service and was constantly in combat. On April 12, three months after Christopher returned to his unit, his first cousin, Stephen Decatur Bunker, Eng's third child and oldest son, came of age and enlisted in the Southern cause on July 2, 1864. Altogether, Christopher and Stephen had fought on the same side for only one month when Christopher's role as an active participant in the war came to an abrupt end.

The series of incidents that were to lead to the termination of Christopher Bunker's part in the conflict began with the all-out war being waged by a Union commander, General David Hunter, who was invading Virginia towns, attacking nonmilitary targets, burning civilian homes, and treating unarmed Southern citizens like enemy soldiers. The Confederate high command considered Hunter's tactics "barbarous," and General Robert E. Lee determined to put a stop to them. Lee ordered Lieutenant General Jubal A. Early to go after Hunter.

General Early, among whose units was the Virginia Cavalry in which the Bunker cousins were serving, pursued Hunter, driving him westward. Then General Early and his troops marched through the Shenandoah Valley, crossed the Potomac River, and approached Washington, D.C. But General Ulysses S. Grant and his troops quickly came to the defense of the Union capital, and General Early pulled back to Virginia again.

Now, General Early ordered Brigadier General John McCausland and Brigadier General Bradley T. Johnson, who was under McCausland, to invade Pennsylvania and take the city of Chambersburg. Proceeding with 2,600 cavalrymen—Chang's son among them—McCausland moved across the Potomac River, went through Clear Spring, Maryland, and headed toward Chambersburg. Several groups of Union cavalry, operating out of their headquarters at Hagerstown, Maryland, under a West Pointer, Brigadier General William Woods Averell, tried to resist but were swept aside.

On July 30, 1864, the Confederates reached Chambersburg, took over control of the community, and demanded either $100,000 in gold coin or $500,000 in United States currency within three hours if the city was to be spared. The townspeople were unable to meet the ultimatum, and General Johnson disgustedly recounted what happened next:

> Every crime in the catalogue of infamy has been committed, I believe, except murder and rape. Highway robbery of watches and pocket-books was of ordinary occurrence; the taking of breast-pins, finger-rings, and earrings frequently happened. Pillage and sack of private dwellings took place hourly. A soldier of an advance guard robbed of his gold watch the Catholic clergyman of Hancock on his way from church on Sunday, July 31, in the public streets. Another of a rear guard nearly brained a private of Company B, First Maryland Cavalry, for trying to prevent his sacking a woman's trunk and stealing her clothes and jewels. A lieutenant at Hancock exacted and received $1,000 in greenbacks of a citizen; a soldier packed up a woman's and a child's clothing, which

he had stolen in the presence of the highest officials, unrebuked. At Chambersburg, while the town was in flames, a quartermaster, aided and directed by a field officer, exacted ransom of individuals for their houses, holding the torch in terror over the house until it was paid. These ransoms varied from $750 to $150, according to the size of the habitation. Thus the grand spectacle of a national retaliation was reduced to a miserable huckstering for greenbacks. After the order was given to burn the town of Chambersburg and before, drunken soldiers paraded the streets in every possible disguise and paraphernalia, pillaging and plundering and drunk.

Following the destruction of Chambersburg, General McCausland ordered his subordinate, General Johnson, to move on to Moorefield, West Virginia, and wait there, promising to rendezvous with him within a day. Johnson, whose brigade included Christopher Bunker, went south, reaching Moorefield on August 5. Meanwhile, McCausland had been engaged by units of General Averell's 1,300 cavalrymen, fought his way free, and arrived at Moorefield on the heels of Johnson.

McCausland, feeling certain that Union troops were far behind them and that there was no immediate threat, set up his camp three miles outside Moorefield, and ordered Johnson to establish his own encampment on a grassy level area beyond. While this was good grazing land for the horses, Johnson worried that, because it was so flat, it would be militarily indefensible. Still, he obeyed. The tents of his soldiers went up along the road for three-quarters of a mile. McCausland also told Johnson to set up pickets —detachments of lookouts or guards—some distance away on three roads. However, McCausland felt it was not necessary to send out any scouting parties, still certain that Union troops were nowhere near them.

Thirty hours later—it was two hours after midnight on a Sunday morning—as his men slept, General Johnson was awakened by a courier who brought a message from McCausland. There was word that three brigades of Union cavalry, led by General Averell, had been seen passing through Romney, twenty miles away, the night before. Johnson was ordered to get out a scouting party on horseback fast and send it up the road to Romney to verify whether the enemy were really in the area or not.

By three o'clock that morning the scouts, members of the Eighth Virginia Cavalry, passed their lookout pickets and continued up the road to Romney. Suddenly, in the dark, they were surrounded and ambushed, trapped by Averell's cavalry. Losing no time, the Union soldiers stripped the Confederate scouts, removed their own blue uniforms, and donned Confederate gray. Then, two of the disguised Northern soldiers rode toward Johnson's camp. Soon they came on two Confederate sentinels. The gray-clad Union soldiers were routinely challenged. They replied that "they were scouts from the Eighth Virginia." The sentinels passed them, but one of the disguised Union soldiers said he had lost something on the road and wanted to retrieve it. He backtracked into the darkness, then suddenly reappeared with twenty more Union cavalrymen who took the sentinels prisoner. The Northerners moved on until they came across a small reserve detachment on night duty. "Get your horses," the Northerners called out, "you are relieved." As the reserves prepared to leave their posts, they were taken by surprise and overwhelmed.

"Thus," wrote General Johnson later, "scout, picket, and reserve were captured by the enemy uniformed as Confederates, who then rode in my camp without giving any alarm. . . . This great disaster would have at once been retrieved but for the insufficient armament of the command. Besides the First and Second Maryland and a squadron of the Eighth Virginia there was not a saber in the command. In that open country, perfectly level, the only mode to fight charging cavalry was by charging, and this the men were unable to do. The long Enfield musket once discharged could not be reloaded, and lay helpless before the charging saber. With an equal chance the enemy would at once have been driven back. The largest portion of the command remained steady, and after passing Moorefield were held in hand with ease. I reached the Valley with about 300 men missing . . ."

Among those reported missing, on August 7, was Chang's son Christopher Bunker, who had been captured by the Union troopers.

Shortly afterward, a friend of Christopher's brought his blood-stained riderless horse back to Mount Airy. When Chang's Adelaide saw the horse, she went back into the house, pulled a drawer out of a small table, and wrote on the bottom of the drawer, "Christopher Bunker was either killed or captured August 4 [sic], 1864.

As his parents would eventually learn, Christopher was alive but wounded, and now a prisoner of war. Three days after his capture, Christopher was in Atheneum Prison in Wheeling, Virginia. There his vital statistics were recorded: *Age:* 20; *Height:* 5'8"; *Complexion:* dark; *Eyes:* brown; *Hair:* black; *Occupation:* farmer.

After staying in the prison overnight, Christopher, along with other Confederate cavalrymen in his battalion who had been captured at Moorefield, was sent from Virginia to one of the largest of the federal military prisons, Camp Chase, four miles west of Columbus, Ohio.

Camp Chase, on one hundred acres of farmland, was originally established as a training ground for the thousands of Union recruits being prepared to fight in the Civil War. But when Major General George B. McClellan's Ohio regiments began to capture numerous Confederate soldiers in western Virginia, it was decided to convert a portion of the camp into a military prison housing 450 inmates. The first prison, enclosed by a twelve-foot-high wooden wall, contained three single-story frame buildings, each partitioned into rooms with tiered bunks and mess-hall accommodations. In the months to follow, as more and more Confederate captives were shipped north, the facilities were greatly expanded, with two more military prisons crowded with barracks being added. Noncom Confederate officers and political prisoners were kept in the original prison, and enlisted men in the other two.

For a period in 1862, due to overcrowding and a lenient administration, many of the Confederates were allowed to leave the camp on parole and live in nearby Columbus, where they strolled the streets in full-dress gray uniforms, wearing their pistols and swords. As curiosities and romantic figures, these Confederate parolees were entertained by leading Ohio citizens and given much attention by some of the city's women.

"But it was not these practices that provoked the greatest wrath among loyal Unionists," wrote Philip R. Shriver and Donald J. Breen in *Ohio's Military Prisons in the Civil War*. "Rather it was the fact that nearly a hundred Negroes, most of them slaves, had been sent with their masters from Fort Donelson to the prison compound at Camp Chase, there to continue to serve their masters *as slaves*. In the midst of a war brought on by the slavery issue, in the center of a state that had contributed John Brown, Harriet Beecher Stowe, Benjamin Lundy, Joshua Reed Giddings, Benjamin F. Wade, and a legion of others to the abolitionist crusade, it most certainly did not make sense that slavery could exist but four miles from Ohio's capitol building."

After two government investigations, Confederate parolees lost their side arms and freedom, and the outrageous practice of slavery inside the prison walls was brought to an end.

Laxity at Camp Chase was struck a further blow after a sensational escape was made from another state prison, the Ohio Penitentiary, by a famous inmate and his aides. In July 1863, Confederate General John Hunt Morgan and six of his men dug a tunnel down under their cellblock and beneath the courtyard, penetrating twenty feet of earth and four feet of rock, to emerge at the prison wall. Using bed sheets attached to a grappling hook, they scaled the wall and escaped to

Tennessee. This feat inspired the organization of an effort for a mass breakout at Camp Chase. Had the loose administration of the camp continued, the effort might have succeeded. However, the camp commandant decided to tighten his entire security system. To prevent any escapes, the administration hired private detectives who, disguised as Confederate prisoners, spied upon and informed on suspicious inmates. The inmates caught tunneling were hung by their thumbs from the ceiling, or made to wear ball and chain while performing hard labor, or were thrown into a windowless dungeon four feet by eight.

But by the time Christopher Bunker had reached Camp Chase in August 1864, conditions had been somewhat liberalized again. Six months earlier, a new commanding officer, Colonel William F. Richardson, had been placed in charge of the prison. He felt that religious reading matter would be "beneficial to the prisoners and have a tendency to prevent attempts to escape." As a result, Christopher was able to read the Bible. He was allowed to spend his spare time carving boats and musical instruments out of wood. He was also allowed to shop in the sutler's store, and with money that Chang sent him he was able to purchase a wide variety of items, from cigars and underclothes to pocketknives and smoked beef. And he was permitted to receive packages from home.

Still, it was a lonely, primitive life. During his seven months in Camp Chase, Christopher was housed in a small wooden barracks with 197 other prisoners, slept on a straw-covered bunk, and ate meager rations (once being reduced to eating cooked rat).

There was a shortage of clothing, and many of the inmates were in tatters and barefoot. Most of the men were infected with lice. And all were weakened by bouts of typhoid fever, pneumonia, dysentery. Two months after Christopher's arrival, 168 prisoners were stricken with smallpox, some winding up in the pesthouse and then the cemetery. Christopher did not escape the hospital. On September 9 he fell ill and was hospitalized. His records show that he was suffering from "variola"—a virus disease that could have been either smallpox or the less serious chickenpox, since he was listed as not having been vaccinated prior to the war.

Probably the most difficult part for Christopher, and for his fellow inmates as well, was the enforced introspection during those long months in Camp Chase. This was voiced by a Surry County neighbor of Christopher's, William M. Norman, who was a prisoner of war in nearby Johnson's Island, outside Sandusky, Ohio. In his diary, Norman wrote:

> The mind of a prisoner is wandering. He studies over his past life and talks over most everything he has ever done. Political questions are fully discussed and everyone seems to adhere closely to the merits of his own native state, however recreant that state may have proven to her trust. Religious principles come up often for discussion, in which almost everyone expresses his way or his mode of living, or what he considers the true principle of fundamental or practical religion. Farming, too, comes up for discussion and embraces a large scope of argument and pleasant imaginations, as the winding up of such a discussion results in repeating the whole catalogue of the comforts of life and the imagined luxuries he expects to enjoy. . . . The subject of exchange of prisoners is talked of much. It would take volumes to contain all that is said on this point. We are ready to catch at the least glimmering hope or least insinuation on the subject. Everyone has his time set when he thinks an exchange will be effected.

At last, the subject of so many conversations, of dreams and hopes, became reality.

On the morning of February 5, 1865, a Union lieutenant mounted the parapet between the enlisted men's prisons and bellowed, "Attention prisoners!" When he had their full attention, he announced, "Parole exchange of prisoners has been agreed upon between the United States and the Confederate States!"

There were 9,045 Confederate prisoners in Camp

Chase that day, and for the first time joy was unanimous among them.

A month later, on March 4, 1865, Christopher Bunker took the oath of allegiance to the United States, then was transported to City Point, Virginia, where he was exchanged for a Union prisoner of war. Freed more than five weeks before Lee's surrender at Appomattox, Christopher made his way back to Mount Airy and to a warm welcome from Chang and Eng and his mother Adelaide.

For Christopher the war was over. For his cousin Stephen, Eng's son, it was not.

Stephen had managed to escape the debacle at Moorefield, in which so many Confederate soldiers, among them Christopher, had been captured. Less than a month later, on September 3, 1864, fighting beside his comrades with the 37th Battalion of the Virginia Cavalry near Winchester, Virginia, Stephen Bunker was wounded. Apparently, the wound was not serious, for soon he was back in action again—"and bore himself gallantly," Judge Graves noted.

A short time after Christopher had returned home on April 17, 1865, eight days after Appomattox but before the last of the fighting had ceased, Stephen was wounded a second time. With the Civil War ended, Stephen was sent home to Mount Airy to be with his father and mother once more.

According to Eng's grandson Joffre Bunker, it was believed that Stephen Bunker had also been a prisoner of war sometime during his service. Said Joffre Bunker, Stephen's "two sons claim he was a prisoner of the Northern army. They have a bullet about .44 calibre size they claimed the Northern doctor took from his shoulder—I have seen this many times."

Only once were Chang and Eng themselves threatened with physical involvement in the Civil War, and that was in the last month of the conflict when Eng —ludicrous as it may sound—was drafted to serve with the Union forces.

Major General George H. Stoneman, who had

fought under McClellan and Sherman, headed a veteran division of 6,000 battle-hardened men. Each of his cavalrymen carried carbines at well as haversacks containing one hundred cartridges, bacon and coffee, and an extra set of horseshoes and nails. In these last days of the war, Stoneman was ordered to dash into North Carolina and destroy the tracks and facilities of the North Carolina Railroad and the Piedmont Railroad, as well as military stores. He was also expected to liberate Union prisoners from the Confederate prison at Salisbury.

After a successful sweep through the state, General Stoneman reached Mount Airy on April 2, 1865. Pausing in the area, General Stoneman decided to draft some of the locals—no matter what their sympathies—into his division. The names of all males over eighteen in that part of the country were put into a lottery wheel. What happened next was reported by the Philadelphia *Times:* "Into the fateful wheel went the names of Chang and Eng. But one name, that of Eng, was drawn. The gallant Stoneman was nonplussed. Eng must go, but Chang would not. Stoneman dared not take both. So he resigned his claim to Eng."

Of course, the Siamese Twins were known to most of the invading troopers. According to one descendant, "Yankee soldiers had been told not to harm Chang-Eng's places. The Bunker family sat on the porch, and a soldier grabbed one of the daughters—and she slapped him. The other soldiers all laughed and nothing more happened."

It was in this period, while the Civil War was winding down, that Chang and Eng, reconstructed Southerners, were supposed to have been officially forgiven for their personal secession from the Union in the war years by being summoned to the White House for a meeting with President Abraham Lincoln. Just before his death in 1976, Joffre Bunker recalled, "The twins met President Lincoln and he told them the story about the Illinois farmer who owned a yoke of oxen that found it hard to work in tandem"—implying that the twins' physical predicament probably made it difficult for them to pull together on some occasions.

Finally, the Civil War was over. On April 9, 1865, General Lee surrendered the Army of Northern Virginia—but not his sword—to General Grant at Appomattox Court House in Virginia. On April 12, the last major city in the Confederacy, Mobile, Alabama, fell to Union troops. On April 14, the Stars and Stripes were once more raised over Fort Sumter, South Carolina—and that night John Wilkes Booth assassinated President Lincoln. On April 15, Andrew Johnson became President of the United States. On April 26, Confederate General Joseph E. Johnston surrendered to General William T. Sherman. On May 10, President Andrew Johnson proclaimed that "armed resistance to the authority of this Government in the said insurrectionary States may be regarded as virtually at an end" On May 29, President Johnson granted amnesty and pardon to all who had taken part in the "rebellion." The war was ended.

The South was left a shambles, and so were the prospects of Chang and Eng Bunker.

One of the twins' major sources of income during the war years had been the interest from loans that they had made. They lent money to their friends and neighbors, including Mount Airy merchant Robert Gilmer and even Dr. Joseph Hollingsworth. Unfortunately, they had not anticipated the defeat of the Confederacy and the collapse of its currency. According to *The Sun* of New York, the twins "had a good deal of money loaned out on the best securities in the early part of the war when Confederate money went down to about 15¢ a bushel. Their debtors hastened to liquidate their obligations and redeem their securities with the worthless stuff which they [the twins] then could not refuse. Any person wishing to purchase a huge quantity of Confederate notes at very low rates will do well to address Chang-Eng Bunker, Esqs., Mount Airy, Surry County, North Carolina."

But the sound money that the twins had loaned out, which had been repaid with worthless money, was not their greatest loss.

In earlier assessments of their financial worth, the twins' most valuable possessions had been their holdings in human property. According to Surry County tax records of 1864, Chang owned twelve slaves worth $9,500 and Eng owned twenty-one slaves worth $17,050.

Now, a year after the Civil War, in 1866, the Mount Airy tax assessor made new listings of the property owned by the Siamese Twins. Chang was credited with 425 acres of land worth $6,000, as well as "Money $600, G[old] Plate $100, 1 Pistol." Eng was credited with 300 acres of land worth $1,000, as well as "Money $1,500, Gold Plate $100, 1 Pistol."

For each of them, for the first time, one item was omitted from their list of assets. There was no mention of slaves as assets.

With the Union victory in the Civil War, the Southern institution of slavery was abolished and all slaves were liberated. Chang and Eng were forced to tell their thirty-three slaves that they were free. As Bunker family descendants remember the story, all the former slaves cast aside their hoes and shovels, formed lines, and marched off the farms to enjoy their new-found equality and freedom. A few days later, one of the former slaves returned, prepared to resume his old job but as a paid employee. In the weeks that followed, most of the freed slaves came straggling back to the Chang and Eng farms, after discovering for themselves that they had no place to go. No jobs were awaiting them, there were no other houses to live in, no food to eat, and they had no money at all. They were ready to go to work on salaries. Chang and Eng hired as many as they could afford to support. The rest drifted away, desperately seeking employment elsewhere.

The loss of their slaves almost ruined Chang and Eng financially. Not only were they stripped of assets but, to make matters worse, some of these slaves were now paid employees, adding a new expense to the twins' overhead.

In the years after the war, many journalists would report that the twins had been left bankrupt. While this was not true—they still owned their land, their houses and furnishings, and were able to dig a daily living out of the soil—they were desperate to provide security for their large families.

They had also suffered other losses in the year the war ended. Judge Graves presented a somber record:

"Hitherto nothing has been said of death. The families had been singularly fortunate, for except for the little Rosalind who died in infancy, there had been no death until the 27th of February 1865 when Julia A. Bunker [Eng's second child] departed this life before she had completed her twenty second year. She was an intelligent good and pious woman and by her gentleness won many friends. She died quietly and calmly as the good should die and her friends have the hope that she rested. Death having found entrance soon returned, and on the 28th of September 1865 little Georgianna C. Bunker [Eng's tenth child, aged two] was taken to rest with her sister."

Mutually grieved by these losses, the twins knew that nothing could be done about them. But their financial losses were another thing. There was a possibility they could be repaired.

"The slaves which had formed a considerable part of their estate and especially of Eng were freed and their investments were all lost," Judge Graves recounted. "So the brothers at this late period in life found themselves so much reduced in property that they were under the necessity of again going into the laborious business of public exhibition. In the fall of the year 1865 they engaged to travel again ..."

Actually, a onetime wealthy railroad investor and native of Baltimore, along with a youthful Civil War veteran and fellow North Carolinian, were partly responsible for encouraging the twins to return to show business. Simon Bolivar Zimmerman, who had lived in Baltimore, had made a fortune through investments in the ever-burgeoning railroad industry. He had been socially prominent, and had spent his annual vacations at the fashionable spa of Cape May, New Jersey. Before the Civil War he had married and moved to North Carolina. The war had divested him of his fortune and plunged him into bankruptcy. It was Zimmerman who had the idea of recouping part of his wealth by enticing Chang and Eng back into show business and managing them.

For this enterprise, Zimmerman wanted a partner, and he turned to his brother-in-law, eighteen-year-old Henry Armand London, a war veteran. Young London had recently served as a private in the 32nd North Carolina Regiment and had been selected at Appomattox as the courier to carry General Lee's last order of the war, an order stating that Lee was surrendering and that all troops must cease fire. Upon leaving the service, London returned to Chapel Hill to pick up the college degree he had been obliged to postpone when his entire senior class had enlisted. In later years he was to gain renown as a lawyer, state senator, and editor of the *Chatham Record*. But now, in June 1865, he was ready to join Zimmerman in undertaking another career.

According to Henry London's daughter, Camelia London Jerome, in a letter to Dr. Worth B. Daniels, a cousin who was writing a medical paper about the twins in 1962:

"After the War Between the States, my father, who was eighteen years old, and his brother-in-law [Simon Bolivar Zimmerman], went to see the Siamese twins in Mt. Airy to see if they would be interested in making some money (as everyone in the South was broke) and be exhibited again in the North. They were delighted over the idea, so father and Mr. Zimmerman became the advance press agents, going to various organizations and displaying the pictures of the Siamese twins, etc. When they came to Baltimore and the fashionable resort of Cape May, Mr. Zimmerman would stay in his room as he was so afraid he would be seen by some of his friends. They did this for a season and all made some much needed money."

Chang and Eng were fifty-four years old when they set out on this comeback trip through the Eastern and Midwestern sections of the United States. The tour led to a series of short trips out of Mount Airy, not for just one season as Judge Graves stated, but extending over a period of three years.

The Siamese Twins opened at the Smith & Nixon Hall in Chicago on November 1, 1865. In the months preceding the twins' appearance, the theater had successfully featured such attractions as Christy's Minstrels, a play called *The Phantom Traveler* based on the late President Lincoln's dream that he would be assassinated, and Campbell & Castle's Opera. The opera, according to a local history, "was replaced by the famous Siamese twins, Chang and Eng. This attraction . . . proved to be a poor drawing card."

Chang and Eng continued to do poorly in the Midwest. Part of this failure was due to the ineptness of their managers. When the twins' six-month contract ended, they returned to Mount Airy for a brief rest, then resumed their exhibitions under the auspices of a new team of managers. Wrote Judge Graves:

"They soon set out again under an engagement [with] Messrs. Shepherd [*sic*] and Bird. During this trip while in Kansas, Chang had an attack of sickness in consequence of which his hearing was very greatly impaired. This was the first serious attack of sickness either of them had suffered in a long time. Eng was not affected as he had been in 1833 when they both had chills and fever. Then the augue coming on each at the same time and the fever affected them at the same time and in the same manner and they seemed to suffer precisely alike. About the time of Chang's sickness Mr. Sheppard was called to New Orleans and was killed there. This accident terminated their engagement."

Now the twins sought another manager, and chose the man who had earlier replaced Zimmerman. He was Judge H. P. Ingalls, who operated out of Nassau Street in New York City. Ingalls, apparently feeling the twins were too familiar an attraction to carry a show by themselves, booked them into Union Hall in New York City with another act. On February 12, 1866, Chang and Eng appeared along with "Hoonio and Iola, 'wild Australian children,' possessed of long, sharp teeth, very small, curiously-shaped heads . . ."

This was still not enough. As he went on booking the twins, Ingalls sought other means of improving their box-office draw. By the summer he was struck with a brilliant idea for a return performance in New York City. He broached it to the twins almost casually in a letter he wrote them on July 30, 1866:

> I have decided on a opening day which is to be the 31st of August that comes on Monday you had better get here on saturday before if you want to get some things.
>
> I shal commence to advertise you on Monday I shal spare no pains or money to make the show a sucess, you had better send me a picture of your wives & your selves also one of those group & I will have a lot ready when we open I shal try to make the Pictures a big atraction & I think if they are worked up well we can make a big thing of them
>
> Write just as soon as you get this
>
> I think you had better bring two of your children you can chose any of them you like I would like Albert & it mite be well enough to bring a girl be sure & let me here from you by return mail

Ingalls had revived a winning formula. By reminding the public that the joined twins were married to two normal sisters, that this strange marriage had actually produced offspring, that the children might be seen in person with their fathers, the manager was able to pique audience curiosity anew.

Chang and Eng had no objections to publicizing their wives and exhibiting their children again. During earlier American tours, Eng had brought along his sons, Patrick and James Montgomery, or his daughter Katherine, while Chang had been accompanied by his oldest son Christopher or one of his many daughters.

In fact, while in New York City, probably in the spring of 1865, Chang and Eng brought their wives, Adelaide and Sallie, and two of their children, Patrick and Albert, to the renowned photographic studio of Mathew Brady to pose for a group picture that Judge Ingalls might use for his publicity campaign. The bespectacled, goateed Brady—who had photographed Abraham Lincoln, P. T. Barnum, Robert E. Lee, Ulysses S. Grant, Walt Whitman, and Brigham Young, and had lost $100,000 covering the Civil War with his camera—welcomed the twins inside his studio at Broadway and Tenth Street. Brady led his visitors into his glasslined photography room, seated them in a comfortable group, Chang and Eng in the center, each flanked by his wife, with Patrick and Albert at their feet. Minutes later, the camera's shutter snapped, and Chang and Eng had joined Brady's gallery of immortals.

In their travels, Chang and Eng were constantly preoccupied with how things were going back home. On October 31, 1866, from Cincinnati, Ohio, one of Eng's children who was on the tour wrote to a sister in Mount Airy:

"We have been travelling with the Carolina Twins [Millie and Christine, black joined twins] since we left Xenia but I dont know how long they will be with us, [maybe] not longer than this week. Pappa says he hope you are done sowing grain by this time, and have commenced to pull corn put the corn in the loft not the crib it will not be safe Pappa says get the hogs in good order before you kill them. . . . You say corn will be one dollar per bu—Pappa thinks it will be cheaper than that and not to be in a hurry to buy at that price. Let us know when you write again how much corn you have made if as much as last year. and also if the sweet Potatoes are good we think there will be some stealing going on there this fall and winter so tell Montgomery & Patrick to notice every thing."

A year later, in 1867, there was a tragic happening in Mount Airy. Judge Graves recorded it:

"Up to the 16th August 1867 there had been no death among all the children of Chang; but on that day his oldest and favorite daughter who had become a tall fine looking woman with dark and flashing eyes and hair as black as jet died suddenly and most unexpectedly. In apparently as good health as ever she had gone on her favorite gray to visit a sick friend and on her return fell lifeless to the ground about a half mile from home. That is all that is known of her death. It was said she died of heart disease. Some say that there is a sad romance connected with her history and that she died of a broken heart."

The Chang daughter who died so "suddenly and unexpectedly" was Josephine Virginia, age twenty-three.

A month later, Chang and Eng were unhappily on the road again. But now their letters were filled with fewer apprehensions about their crops and more about the good health of their wives and children. To allay their fears, Katherine was forced to write her brother Decatur a reassuring letter:

"You said you was uneasy about home—there is no use for you to be so uneasy for Mama and myself will try and do the best we can & I think the children will do the same. . . . Tell Papa if he does not come home before the end of seven weeks that I do not think he will get many of the grapes to eat but I am going to save him some any how. I can put up a big bottle full in liquor & sugar. I have already put up a jar of peaches in brandy and they are keeping nice. De [Decatur] I do not want you to forget to get me that *under skirt*, but don't get a costly one. Old Aunt Grace [the former slave who had helped raise the children in both families] is here yet and does very well. Bobie is as well as ever and we are all about as usual. We hope this will find you all in good health, and don't be so uneasy about home, for nothing has happened since you left."

Friends and neighbors in Mount Airy also joined

the family, from time to time, in writing to Chang and Eng and reassuring them that their loved ones were well. Typically, before Josephine's death, a Mount Airy merchant and old companion, Robert S. Gilmer, had written the twins at St. Louis: "I was at your house yesterday found your family all well and took a splendid dinner with Engs family and had two or three drinks of excelant brandy I tell you we have abundence of good things to eat in this countary which your table shows abundent proof of yesterday when was at your house—Changs family are all well and in fine spirits . . ."

Meanwhile, Chang and Eng, in their exhibitions, were drawing larger crowds. Discussing the period when Ingalls managed them, Judge Graves wrote:

"In all these engagements they went for a weekly compensation to be paid at the end of each week, partly in gold. As they were at no expense whatever and received very good salaries, usually $50.00 per week, it was to them a source of very considerable profit. They had gained so much that by the end of 1868 Eng was able to buy a very good farm adjoining his home tract by which addition his farm was now made at least as valuable as Chang's."

It was in 1868 that Ingalls contrived to bring Phineas T. Barnum back into the lives of Chang and Eng.

On March 3, 1868, Barnum's New American Museum in New York City caught fire and by the following morning it was a charred ruin. At least $228,000 in curiosities was lost in the flames. A rival showman, George Wood, who was the proprietor of Wood's Museum, approached the dispirited, ailing, fifty-eight-year-old Barnum about a partnership. Barnum was not too interested in being overly active, but at last, after some negotiations, and in return for three percent of Wood's box-office receipts, Barnum agreed to allow Wood's Museum to advertise that it was the successor to Barnum's New American Museum, to lend Wood some of his exhibits, and to act as an adviser to his onetime competitor.

Ingalls was determined to get to Barnum because

he needed him. For some months, Chang and Eng had been talking about taking one more trip abroad, visiting England, Scotland, and Ireland, not only because they thought business would be good there, but because Eng's daughter Katherine was mysteriously unwell and they wanted to consult physicians in London and Edinburgh. Apparently, Ingalls was unsure about managing a trip abroad, and Barnum had been extremely successful in sponsoring foreign tours and was talking about another one late in the year. Ingalls decided that, no matter how much Chang and Eng despised Barnum, he must bring them together with the renowned showman.

With Barnum as his associate, George Wood was opening a renovated Wood's Museum and Metropolitan Theatre at Broadway and Thirtieth Street on August 31, 1868. Ingalls went to Wood and arranged to book the Siamese Twins for the opening night's show, agreeing that they would appear for three weeks. The first night started with a personal appearance by Barnum himself, who delivered a speech. Chang and Eng were also on hand, performing on the bill with General Grant, Jr., and Sophia Ganz, two midgets.

That night, Chang and Eng had their reunion with Phineas T. Barnum. Shortly afterward, Barnum announced two new enterprises he was sponsoring. First, he was sending a group of midgets, led by General and Mrs. Tom Thumb, on an around-the-world tour. Second, he was arranging for the Siamese Twins to make an extensive tour of Great Britain.

In the nine versions of his autobiography and the numerous other books that he published, Barnum made only one passing reference to Chang and Eng —and that concerned his promotion of what proved to be the twins' last trip to Great Britain.

"I sent them to Great Britain where, in all the principal places, and for about a year, their levees were continually crowded," Barnum wrote. "In all probability the great success attending this enterprise was much enhanced, if not actually caused, by extensive announcements in advance that the main purpose of Chang-Eng's visit to Europe was to consult the most eminent medical and surgical talent with regard to the safety of separating the twins."

Barnum, as usual, was exercising his infallible eye for seducing the public. He saw in the twins' predicament a titillation which he knew the paying masses could not resist. Because much of the Western world had seen Chang and Eng, and England had seen them thirty-eight years before, Barnum needed a gimmick. Only this time, the gimmick was real. What Barnum thought was only a ploy was very vital to Chang and Eng. For they still nursed a secret dream—to be separated, at long last. Some say it was Eng who urged the separation, because Chang's drinking had become so torturous for him.

No American surgeon would perform the unique operation of severing their band, but perhaps there would be one in Europe willing to take the chance.

Chang and Eng were ready to face the risk—the risk of being disappointed yet again by a refusal, or the risk of dying in the attempt.

10
CHAPTER
01

The Grand Tour

All the twins' energies were now devoted to readying themselves for their return to Great Britain.

They had been anticipating this excursion with peculiar interest [Judge Graves wrote]. Eng's oldest daughter, Miss Kate M. Bunker, a young lady of brilliant and well cultivated mind had been for some time growing more and more delicate in health; and it was greatly feared by her family and acquaintances that she was beginning to fall prey to a fatal malady. It was hoped that perhaps a voyage across the salt sea might prove beneficial or that some prescription of some of the learned and eminent physicians of London or Edinburgh might be advantageous. With such hopes it was determined that she should accompany her father. She was anxious to go, possibly sharing the hope of restoration, but certainly desirous to see the high civilization of England and Scotland, with many of whose scenes she was already familiar, at least with those renowned in English classics.

Chang's anticipations were not of the same character. His oldest born Josephine with all her loveliness was gone. His next daughter Nannie A. was now a young woman of even greater beauty, and as highly gifted as her cousin; and hitherto she had, from over sensitiveness, been unwilling to travel and go before the public but now she had become willing to accompany her father. And perhaps, it was her kindness of heart which prompted her to go with her father and her uncle and her invalid cousin to visit those countries whose historical associations will always waken fulness of interest in the mind of every intelligent American man or woman. Her father was very anxious for her to go for he knew how much she would improve by the journey and its circumstances. And she was willing to sacrifice a great deal in order to visit those countries of which she had read and heard so much. Her father and her uncle were great admirers of almost everything English—government, literature and institutions. Their favorite authors, Pope, Shakespeare, Kirkwhite, Montgomery had lived and written there and they had read these and others of known character to their families until they had awakened in the minds of their children and especially of the daughters a very great admiration for all that was associated with the fame of the great authors.

On November 28, 1868, a week before their sailing date, Eng and his daughter Katherine, aged twenty-four, and Chang and his daughter Nannie, aged twenty-one, left Mount Airy on a frosty morning headed toward New York and, as Nannie wrote, "bound for Brittain." Two days later they were in Raleigh, where they visited Chang's deaf children, Louise and Jesse, who were attending the Institute for the Deaf and Dumb and Blind. From there they went on to Baltimore, caught a boat, then a train for New York. On the train, Nannie was wide-eyed, noting, "I sat at the window (as I presume all greenhorns do) & gazed at the cities we passed. When we crossed the ferry at Jersey City many people flocked around us crying here are the "Siamese Twins and their Wives.' We arrived in New York & everything looked very grande to me for I had never seen a city lighted up by night before."

According to Bunker family tradition, Chang and Eng did not remain in New York waiting for their ship. Instead, they made a brief overnight trip to Washington, D.C., to call on President Andrew Johnson, who three years and eight months before had inherited his office from Lincoln and who had been acquitted of impeachment charges little more than a half year earlier. In 1975, Eng's grandson Joffre Bunker remembered that the President "sent a message to the queen of England with the twins. It may have been in relation to a pending war . . ."

Just before noon of December 5, the twins and their daughters, along with their manager, Judge H. P. Ingalls, now representing Barnum, ascended the gangplank of the steamer *Iowa*, in New York harbor. They sailed at noon, their destination Liverpool. Both of the Bunker daughters were to keep written records of the trip. Katherine would write a full-length book—"a very detailed and interesting account of all that she saw and felt," said Judge Graves—and submit it to a London publisher. "What he did with the manuscript is unknown," added Judge Graves, "but it is supposed to be in his papers. Still whatever the merits of the composition it would scarcely be expected that the observations on England and Scotland of an American girl without reputation should be published." The fate of the book remains unknown, and its contents have been lost to posterity. On the other hand, Nannie's diary of the sea crossing and her father's and uncle's exhibitions, as well as her own, in Scotland, has survived. Nannie's diary begins with an account of the group's departure from New York in that wintry early December:

On the 5th inst. we—Papa & my Uncle, my cousin and myself sailed from New York in the good ship Iowa for Europe. It was a very cold snowy day. When we got on board we found that a great many people had already arrived, some to see & bid their friends farewell perhaps for the last time & others for curiosity. At 12 o'clock we bade our friends goodbye & launched out on the broad ocean. I felt no alarm as

I watched the land receding as it were from sight. I felt no apprehension at all about sea sickness, but in less than half an hour my head began to feel quite dizzy and I went on deck. Thinking I would get better but instead of getting better I became worse and went down to my room.

At 2 o'clock we were called to dinner. We all sat down to dinner, but I had scarcely tasted my soup before I was compelled to retire to my room. I was soon followed by my friend, Mrs. Hughs, and very soon there were but one or two at the table.

We had some 22 sick passengers & several steerage. The ship was also very heavy laden with this cargo. The Captain, Mr. Henderwick—& the other officers were very kind to us treating us as though we were their own country people. I have read a great deal about the kindness of the Scotch to other sections and I think they deserve all the honors in that respect which they receive.

Meanwhile, on shipboard, moving farther and farther away from home, as Judge Graves later reported, "the country girls grew sad." Katherine, worried about her illness, felt "that possibly she might never return to their home." Nannie, who had never been on exhibit before, "felt a great repugnance to going before the public, arising partly from her pride, partly from an undefined and undefinable feeling which she did not, perhaps could not express." But almost overnight, "these somber thoughts and gloomy feelings were soon dispelled by pleasant associations . . . new acquaintances and the kind attentions from new found friends made their sad hearts feel almost glad as they hastened on the way . . ."

Chang and Eng, of course, had no such concerns. As old seafarers, they enjoyed the voyage from the start. "The twins," wrote Judge Graves, "almost as much at home as at their hotel in the city, passed their time in playing chess, draughts, backgammon and such games, smoking and conversation. And in conversation they *could* make, and *did* make themselves very agreeable and entertaining. Blessed with remarkable rememberance of places, dates, and scenes, their extensive travel had enabled them to gather a great deal of very accurate information of the many places which they had visited and their appreciation of the ludicrous had induced them to keep in mind many laughable incidents which, in their humorous manner, they told very laughably. Probably the rather broken English in which they told their jokes, narratives, their adventures and described occurrences added to the interest of their social intercourse with their fellow passengers."

Nannie, unlike her father, Chang, was unable to find her sea legs. Her saga of woe, confided to her diary, worsened as the pitching and rolling ship got caught in an overnight storm:

On Sunday the 6th December I was still very sick, being totally unable to sit up. The rest of our party were sick with the exception of Papa & Uncle who enjoyed good health during the whole voyage. It was a very nice day for those who were well but then but one other gentlemen besides, Papa & Uncle & the sailors, that were able to go the table, but after this they gradually appeared until nearly all got well before we landed at Liverpool. I did not go on deck today at all but lay in my bunk so very sick. I wished I was on land, but was quite willing to suffer for a few days if I could be landed safely on Britannias shore.

Monday 7th

A very gloomy looking day snowing & raining & very cold. I felt very lonely as everybody seemed to be getting better but myself. Mr. Bixby and Ingalls are still sick but Kate is able to go to the table, on deck or anywhere she likes. Tuesday seemed speedingly long but at night we had a fearful gale. The vessel rocking and pitching so that many of the passengers thought she would certainly go down. One boy of 16 or 17 said "Father, Father, hadn't we be going? I see the Captain going with his carpet bag." I was not at all frightened at first for I knew in whose hands I was & that he could dispose of me as he pleased, but after a time the vessel rocked so badly I could scarcely be in my berth & the lights were extinguished, when all at once there was a mighty crash. I thought the ship had broken in two, but it was only the crockery & glasses dashed from the frames & broken. It was very dark and some were calling for lights. The steward says "What do you want?" I want to see the sea. Go to bed and never mind. The sea, the sea is doing very well, replied the steward.

In a very short time I heard a sucking of water down the stairs. Mr. Ingalls & Bixby room being at the foot of the stairs. The water running down went right on. In a short time was four or six inches deep. The next thing I heard was Mr. Ingalls asking, in a tone of great anxiety, for a light & where the water coming from not receiving any answer he says to Mr. Bixby, "I am going on deck and down below. If the water is so deep here how do you suppose it is down there."

Hearing him talking so anxious I began to get quite anxious too. However, as Papa and Uncle were sleeping quietly I regained my courage & went to sleep. The ship laid to for the night so came through quite safely. Since we came on shore we heard that same gale wrecked the ship Hiberia. I feel very thankful indeed that we did not meet the same fate.

Although the storm had passed and the sky cleared, the ocean was anything but calm, and the rocking steamer continued to be too much for Nannie. As she wrote in her diary:

Kate & all of our family are able to go to the table while I must lie in bed. I do not grumble however.

It is very amusing to hear the passengers grumbling because they cannot stand still & walk about at ease as though they were still on land. . . . Sunday came & there being a parson on board we had divine services. I was not able to go but I could hear all that passed while I lay in my berth. . . . He was not a very able minister, but it was a very solemn thing indeed to witness the sea lashing her proud waves mountain high, our ship pitching to & fro & a few members of God's creation gathered in a circle to worship & adore his great name.

Monday the 14th was a rough day. . . . Time wor

on till one day a vessel came in sight. What a sensation it produced among our passengers. . . . They said she appeared like an old friend. After a few days we saw two others. From this time till we landed we could see them every day or two.

On Friday night they sighted land & there were many glad hearts. I still continued very sick but I went on deck to see again my mother earth. Friday we passed many vessels gliding majestically over the sea. In the afternoon we came to Waterloo [a town on Liverpool Bay]. It looked very beautiful indeed.

It was dark when we neared Liverpool. It was quite a sublime scene to gaze upon the harbors all brilliantly illuminated.

Our good ship anchored a short distance from shore & we remained on board some time after before we could go ashore. Our boat came & we prepared to go, but soon found that we could not go. We were very much disappointed & went down to get ready for tea. We all got in the boat, after bidding our friends goodbye & in a short time were on land!

They had finally arrived in England on the evening of December 18, 1868, after fourteen days at sea. The winter weather was anything but hospitable, but the English customs officers more than made up for it, as Nannie would later recount when she recollected the first moments ashore:

It was very cold indeed. The officers at the Custom House were very kind & carried us to a room where we could warm ourselves. They complimented Papa & us very much, not searching in our trunks at all as they did the others.

Half past 7 o'clock we arrived at the hotel & were informed that we could get supplies in to & a half hours. Imagine our feelings when we found that we could not get it sooner & had to leave on the one o'clock train.

In due time we got supper & all retired to our rooms to get a hasty nap, but none of us could sleep but Papa and uncle. At one o'clock we were called to dress & get ready for the train.

At one we got on the train & left Liverpool for Edinburg. Liverpool is a very nice place. At the hotel it is very unlike America. You cannot get your meals until sometime after you order it & then again you must sit an hour or two waiting for it however hasty you wish to be.

Also you [are served] in a private room which I prefer to the public saloons of America. The cars also are quite different, being divided into separate apartments containing room for 8 only. . . .

Sunday Dec. 20th 1868

We left Liverpool at one o'clock. We were all very tired and sleepy & were soon in the arms of Morpheus whirling on our way to Edinburg.

It was quite eight o'clock before it became light enough for us to distinguish one object from another.

We looked around on the hills of Scotland with wonder and admiration. The solitary peaks rising out of a vast plain without any chain of hills or mountains as is the case in America. Scotland is a beautiful country indeed, quite romantic in appearance.

At precisely 10 o'clock we arrived in Edinburg. We were all very cold, sleepy and hungry.

We were very soon met by the agent Mr. Cassidy, and conveyed to the hotel where we received every kindness we could wish.

Mr. Cassidy is a very portly man very kind and obliging.

We had breakfast & all went to bed & were soon in the land of forgetfulness.

It had been a strenuous time for the four of them since leaving Mount Airy. It was especially trying for Chang's Nannie. After two weeks of unremitting seasickness on the Atlantic Ocean and the tiring train trip to Edinburgh, she was now filled with apprehension over having to make her debut as a public exhibit. For, the very next morning, Chang and Eng and their daughters were scheduled to open their show.

Nannie recorded the experience in her diary entry of December 21: "Was a very disagreeable rainy day. For the first time in my life I was compelled to go before the public. I felt quite embarrassed when the hour came. It was not as I had imagined. We have very few visitors in the forenoon but the number increased quite rapidly during the afternoon & evening receptions."

Certainly uppermost in the twins' minds, besides their scheduled exhibits, was the other major reason they had come to Edinburgh. They had come to see several of the best physicians in the world, having written in advance for appointments. They were more determined than ever to be separated, and hoped that the latest advances in surgery might finally make this possible. And they were equally determined to learn the nature of the ailment Katherine had been suffering.

Katherine's welfare came first, and between shows she was taken to see the physicians on the staff of the Edinburgh Medical College. Judge Graves recorded the results of Katherine's examination:

". . . her symptoms were immediately submitted to them and some of the most distinguished diagnosticians made a personal examination to ascertain the nature and condition of her disease. After examination of their patient they announced that her disease was pneumonary consumption, and that it was so far advanced that, in all human probability their skill would be unavailing and that the only aid which they could hope to render would be simply mitigate the suffering of the invalid. This announcement, which had been anticipated, was received with utmost composure; but surely in one so young it could not have been without regret."

Helpless to do anything further about Katherine, the twins now prepared to learn what could be done about themselves.

They had arranged to meet with Sir James Young Simpson, the renowned Scottish physician who was professor of medicine at Edinburgh University. Simpson, fifty-seven years old, a month younger than Chang and Eng, burly, shaggy-haired, bewhiskered, was the queen's physician when she was in Scotland.

He had been the first physician to use ether in obstetrics, had discovered chloroform as an anesthetic (and used it in delivering children despite opposition from the clergy), had invented a forceps named after him, and had written authoritatively about such diverse subjects as leprosy and archaeology.

Now, on the twins' third day in Edinburgh, Sir James Simpson did not wait for Chang and Eng to call on him. He came calling on them at their exhibition hall. Nannie noted the occasion in her diary on Tuesday, December 22:

> Was also a rainy disagreeable day, but we had a great many visitors. We have the honor of a visit from *Sir James Simpson* at our evening levee.
>
> He is quite a venerable man far advanced in the downward course of life. Very kind & mild in appearance.
>
> He invited Papa & Uncle to attend his lecture rooms the next day. They also made an engagement to visit Professor [Sogine] in order to consult his opinion as regards the propriety of a surgical operation.

The following day, before attending Sir James Simpson's lecture, Chang and Eng went to Professor Sogine's office for a preliminary examination. Nannie faithfully recorded it:

> At ten we called & was quickly ushered into the presence of that eminent surgeon. He examined them & advised that they should remain as they are. We then returned to the Waterloo place (our house) Papa and Uncle & Mr. Ingalls going to Sir James' lecture hall to hear him lecture.
>
> The rest of us remained at home. Professor Sogine is an old man of a mild countenance & is said to be exceedingly cautious in advising & operating as a surgeon. He advised them to remain as they were & also stated that they would find no surgeon in Paris bold enough to undertake the operation.
>
> Sir James Simpson is quite an aged man of a mild heavenly aspect. He honored them with an invitation to breakfast at his house Christmas morning.

Most likely, it was in this week that Sir James Simpson had Chang and Eng to his consulting room and gave them a thorough examination. When he was done, he offered them his opinion on the feasibility of severing their connecting ligament.

Seven weeks later, on February 13, 1869, Simpson made his opinion public by publishing "A Lecture on the Siamese and Other Viable United Twins" in the *British Medical Journal*. His essay began with some remarks regarding united twins in general, and then proceeded to give a standard history of Chang and Eng's lives. He made a few comments about their appearance at present: "Dressed, as they are, in the ordinary American fashion, with the hair cut short, and talking English, as they do, with the American accent, they retain little or nothing of the appearance of Eastern subjects; except their black hair and their features . . ."

At the end of his lengthy paper, Dr. Simpson addressed the "Question of the Surgical Separation of the Siamese Twins":

Chang and Eng have themselves no desire to be surgically divided from each other. But some of their relatives have become anxious that they should be separated, if it were possible to do so, for latterly their two families have been living apart; and they have sojourned for a few days alternately in the two separated homesteads. The operation is certainly possible, and would be attended probably with little, or indeed no difficulty; but it would be so perilous in its character that the twins could not, in my opinion, be justified in submitting to it, nor any surgeon justified in performing it.

The cutaneous, cartilaginous, vascular, and other tissues composing the walls and mass of the band, offer in themselves no special obstruction to its surgical division. The interior of the band, however, contains, I believe, a canal or diverticulum of peritoneum, which passes from the abdominal cavity of the one brother to the abdominal cavity of the other. In modern surgery, we are by no means so afraid of dividing and opening into the peritoneum, as medical men were ten or twenty years ago. In witness of this, we appeal, for example, to the marvelous success attending the now frequent operation of ovariotomy. Still the danger of cutting through a diverticulum of peritoneum is too great to be ever done without very grave and urgent reasons; and none such exist in this case. With them it is not a question of life or death; but a question merely of seemliness and convenience, and perhaps of pleasure and gratification to their relatives. Besides, if it were attempted in the Siamese twins it would be difficult perhaps to close up the exposed peritoneal cavity in each after the division. For, in the lower and inferior portion of the band, or in their umbilical region, the coats are very thin and distended, and this condition runs onwards to the middle of the band.

Simpson went on to describe an unusual experiment he had undertaken to see whether he could learn what the twins' connecting band was composed of:

You are well aware that various attempts have been made of late years, by electric and other strong lights, to make portions of the body more or less translucent. By placing a powerful light behind the connecting band in Eng and Chang, I tried to make its thinner portions transparent, with a view of possibly tracing its contents better than by touch; but I failed entirely in getting any advantage from this mode of examination.

Once again, Chang and Eng were deeply disappointed. Sir James Simpson's medical opinion had proved merely a more sophisticated echo of what they had heard all their lives. The physician's statement that the twins had really not wished to be divided, that it was relatives who had been "anxious that they should be separated," surely could not have represented Chang and Eng's true feelings. Most probably, they had given this version of their situation to Simpson in order to keep their own conflicts private. Chang and Eng may have reflected on Simpson's remark that separating them surgically was not a necessity, was "not a question of life or death," bitterly realizing that neither the doctor nor any normal person could really imagine or understand the anguish of being bound to another for a lifetime. But as ever Chang and Eng appeared to take the bad news stoically and to continue their business of exhibiting as usual.

Christmas Day of 1868 had come to Edinburgh. In her diary, Nannie reported the events of the day, as well as of the days that immediately followed:

Friday 25th December 1868
Papa & Uncl & Mr. Ingalls all came very early this morning as they breakfast at 8 with Sir James Simpson. They anticipat a very nice time indeed.

Mrs. Hughs, Kate & I go to the photographer's a distance of three miles from Waterloo place. It is the 2nd time I have went . . . & I think every thing looks so very nice. We did not expect to remain long but when we arrived at Thomas Douglas's the photographer's that *nobleman* was still in bed, it being after ten o'clock. We waited some time & at last he came in to see us. Mrs. Hughs was very disappointed at his not having a lot of pictures for her.

As we returned I saw a very touching sight indeed, a horse lieing in the road dead all in harness & to a cart. I thought it exceedingly cruel of the driver to drive a poor animal till it died but I suppose some have no thought of the service this noble animal renders them after it is old and worn out. I saw more of this place this day than I ever have before. It is indeed a very picturesque city being built on seven hills & you may stand on the heights & look down several hundred feet below & see people, houses, roads and such seemingly in a deep ravine. We were rather late in getting home & were compelled to dress quite hastily. We did not have so many visitors as we expected [on] Christmas. I thought it very dull, but on speaking to some of the ladies about it they said the Scotch are a very quiet people not having Christmas but New Years's day as the great day.

Saturday, Dec. 26th 1868
We had some very nice people to see us this morn-

ing. One lady far advanced in age & somewhat child-
ish in manner, but an agreeable conversationalist
lectured me on the subject of religion [and] on the
welfare of my soul's salvation & of eternity.

All day we were housed up receiving visitors, a
thing exceedingly irksome to me when I think of the
many beautiful things of antiquity I could see if I
could go out. I never felt so indignant in all my life
as I did this afternoon. One man I will not say gentleman—asked me if my grandmother or grandfather
was a negro. I was so angry I could scarcely speak
but was compeled to say nothing.

Sunday Dec. 27th

Mr. Ingalls & I went to walk. We went out on one
of the heights where we could get a view of the
city. We walked up a steep ascent and looked down
hundreds of feet below on the houses & also we
could look & see houses, fields & the most romantic
landscape I ever saw. We also visited the National
Monument erected in the time of George IV a large
mass of stone with elegantly carved columns surrounded by a yard of the most verdant beauty. Also
we visited another monument where we saw cannons
captured at the Battle of Sebastopole. Standing on this
eminence we could see Holyrood Palace, Queen's
Drive, States Prison, Public College, and many other
buildings & views of note. After this we visited the
monument of Robt. Burns, the celebrated poet &
beautiful structures surrounded by a small enclosure
of fine evergreens. It turned very cold & the wind
was blowing very hard, so we concluded to return
home and it was very near suppertime. We got home
& found we were just in time for our dinner. We all
ate very hearty & it takes us two hours eating & telling
anecdotes is the way we all spend my leisure time.

I think it quite a strange way to spend the Sabbath
but can't help myself. . . .

Tuesday, Dec. 29th 1868

At one o'clock we left the hall & got in a carriage
to go to the Castle. . . . We visited Queen Mary's bedroom in which James the 6th was born, an exceedingly small room in which she was imprisoned and

compelled to live. I looked out of the window from which she let him down to be carried to Stirling to be baptized into the Catholic faith a distance of 250 feet, over rocks and crags & if he had struck one of them would have been instantly dashed in pieces.

After two weeks in Edinburgh, the troupe moved on to Glasgow, which they reached on January 3, 1869. They spent two successful weeks in Glasgow before taking to the road again. Once more Nannie took up her pen to record their activities:

Monday Jan 18th, 1869

Breakfast at Glasgow & at half past ten we left for Dumbarton where we arrived at 12 o'clock. Dined at one & went to the hall had very few visitors during the first exhibition but at night we had quite a good house. It was very cold, raining all the time. At ten minutes past 9 o'clock we left the hall and came back to the hotel. (Called the Elephant). We got supper & made ready to start in the morning for Stirling. I have a very bad cold & felt quite lonely all evening. I hope I will be better in a few days.

Papa and uncle are quite bad off with colds & coughs.

Kate seems quite gay & in good spirits. Zobede [another Barnum freak on the tour] is not quite so jovial as is her wont. I don't think it will last very long for she is a lively hearted creature.

Dumbarton, Scotland. Tuesday Jan 19th 1869

We all arose quite early & made ready to leave for Stirling at 8 o'clock. We ate a hurried breakfast & then bid goodbye to Dumbarton. . . .

We all got on the train & were soon gliding rapidly on our way to Stirling. . . .

We saw several farm houses with poultry in the yard, the first we had seen since we left home. A short distance from Balloch the sky became somewhat clearer & we could see the sun for the first time in three weeks. It seemed like an old friend coming to welcome us once more. We landed at Stirling & in a short time dined & made ready to go to the hall. . . .

After we had been there some time Sir James Simpson of Edinburgh called to see us. He did not stay long & promised to see us at the hotel in a short time. When we arrived at the hotel he was there & presented Kate & myself a beautiful book apiece (a poem by Sir Walter Scott he is very kind). After giving us his best wishes he bade us goodbye.

Dundee, Scotland. Thursday, Jan. 21st 1869.
12 o'clock

We left at 10 Monday for Aberdeen. . . . We had a very pleasant ride indeed. Some of our party were grave others gay. As for myself I am always inclined to be gay when traveling. We arrived at Aberdeen at 12 o'clock & were met by a large crowd at the depot. On getting out of the train they formed a road for us & the crowd gave back on either side so that we could [walk].

The final entry in the diary is a short paragraph about Holyrood House, which she had visited earlier. With that, Nannie's diary comes to a close. But the traveling and exhibitions through Scotland continued from Aberdeen to Arbroath, Montrose, Berwick, Dumfries. On February 7, 1869, the troupe left Scotland and began an extensive tour of England. This part of the trip lasted almost six months. While they spent three days exhibiting in Leicester, four days in Nottingham, two weeks in Manchester, two weeks in Liverpool, one week in Birmingham, and had a stay in London, over half of the tour consisted of one-night stands.

P. T. Barnum's publicity that the twins might be surgically separated in England continued to encourage speculation all along the route. On February 13, 1869, one newspaper, *The Chronicle*, discussed their situation:

"The very question about their separation of itself declares their perfect separateness. . . . Most probably, however, the idea will not be carried into execution. . . . The connexion between their respective blood vessels is such that they must necessarily have any blood disease in common; and it is probable that the last illness of one, from physical as well as from moral causes, would be the last illness also of the other. The separation would present no surgical difficulty, and might be accomplished at any time the accidental illness or death of one brother should require it. But, putting accident aside and dealing with constitutional causes, it is most probable that the brothers, loving in their lives, in death will not be divided."

The article concluded with a mention of the twins' financial problems: "They were slaveholders, enthusiastic Southerners, and lost largely by the collapse of the South. We trust their visit to Europe may in some degree repair their shattered fortunes and may afford them the means of returning in tranquility to their former mode of life."

In most of the cities of England that they visited, Nannie and Katherine, sometimes with their fathers, more often alone, found time between exhibitions to go sightseeing. "Besides visiting those places for the profit of the employee," wrote Judge Graves, "many places of peculiar interest on account of classic or other associations, were visited expressly for the pleasure of the invalid and her appreciative cousin. Their admiration for the rural scenes of England was much greater than their appreciation of the cities. They were particularly impressed with the beauty of the lordly mansions, the beautiful parks, and surroundings of the nobility. And with the charming flower gardens, and the nicely cultivated farms looking more like gardens than anything else."

Meanwhile, along the way, Chang and Eng had been approached by a reputable English impresario named Wallace, who suggested they quit their current tour and undertake a new, more profitable one under his booking. In fact, Wallace had many plans for them, much to Judge Ingalls' dismay. On the last day of their two-week stay in Manchester, May 30, Nannie sat in the Cathedral Hotel and reported on the matter in a letter to her brother Christopher in Mount Airy:

We have concluded to come home in August and not go with the Wallaces for two or three reasons, first because Ingalls wants Papa to go with him and might if we went with anyone else circulate a report that Papa and uncle were not as good as their word and could not stand to their word if they were offered higher wages. & Secondly this Wallace wants to come to America and make an engagement for 12 or 6 months (Papa & uncle want two boys along) so I think in all probability they will get home to remain until next March or April & take you & come over for a continental tour of twelve months. Mr. Wallace has acted like a gentleman in every respect toward us all & Judge Ingalls is very angry because he made a proposition at all. Papa & uncle were once on the verge of closing in & making an engagement with Mr. Wallace, but then they concluded to come home. Papa has just had you two velvet jackets made in black silk and one black with green spots. They cost about $10.00 gold (both). I would have brought them home not made but it would have cost so much duty. The show is doing very big business and has been quite a success. The Chinese Giant Chang [seven feet four inches tall] has been here all the week but I did not get to see him. Mrs. Chang came to see us a few mornings ago. She is a very nice looking person & our folks paid me the compliment of being very much like her. We go away on Monday to Liverpool so I shall not get to see Chang. I shall be glad when we leave here it is so dirty and smoky & they say Liverpool is no better. In these manufacturing places it is so smoky and black one must change collars every day even if they sit in the house . . . 8 weeks from today we start home. I rather dread the voyage but I guess it will be all the better for me to be seasick. Just out of our windows is an orphan school for boys & they are the merriest little fellows I ever saw & so smart. They are up early every morning making a great fuss at play. They are not bigger than Albert & have a band & drums and practice out in the grounds under our windows & march like soldiers. They can surpass the Mount Airy band a long way . . .

The next day Chang and Eng were in Liverpool, and the day after that, June 1, 1869, two of the local newspapers reviewed their act. The first of these, the *Liverpool*, *wrote*:

> In the twins, Chang and Eng, we have the living proof of two human beings having been by each other's side every moment without interruption for the long period of 60 years. The twins visited this town some thirty years ago, and those who saw them will scarcely be prepared to find that they have undergone comparatively little change. . . . The twins were loudly applauded at each of their receptions yesterday, and the only feeling that could have pervaded the minds of the different audiences was one of pure regret—that at any moment one of two beings gifted with a more than ordinary share of intelligence should be "left free to a loneliness he has never even imagined aright from the first consciousness of infancy." The daughters are full-grown, lady-like, and well educated persons, and they evidently share the pleasure which their parents enjoy at witnessing the unmistakeable demonstrations of applause they received from the audiences . . .

The second review, in the Liverpool *Mercury*, also made mention of the twins' attempts to be separated:

> It is said that they . . . came to this country to obtain the best surgical advice which could be procured as to the severance of the singular bond which unites them, but the opinion of scientific men is opposed to such an experiment being attempted. . . . Change and Eng . . . are intelligent men, and converse freely with any ladies or gentlemen who will talk with them; but it is impossible to regard them with any feelings other than of commiseration and pity, for a feeling of pain is awakened in the mind by the very circumstances in which these extraordinary men are placed, and from which their escape is impossible.

While the *Liverpool* reporter had stated that Chang and Eng had "undergone comparatively little change" since their original visit to England, a London newspaper ran a moving account of the twins written by an old friend that gave a different reaction. This article was signed simply "M.F.A.P." It read:

RECOLLECTIONS OF THE SIAMESE TWINS

In 1830 I lived for some weeks under the same roof as these gentle creatures, and in daily intercourse with them. There was then nothing painful in the contemplation of their misfortune. Gay and cheerful in temper, they were ever ready in their best English, to mimic for the amusement of their friends the odd inquiries made of them in public; lithe, supple, graceful and erect, they were capable of exercising and enjoying much freedom and variety of movement.

One of the brothers (we used to call him the laziest) would, if his shoe wanted tying, put his foot on a chair, saying, in a voice of mock authority, "Eng, tie my shoe!" and Eng would hasten to obey.

I remember well one evening when they and I supped with a merry party of half-a-dozen, and something was said of a "hill" in the neighborhood. The bright black eyes of the "boys" sparkled at the word, but not daring to speak their thoughts, they only said, "Is it a mile to the hill?" It was enough; it was resolved to sally forth into the streets under cover of the doubtful moonlight, and by an unfrequented road to reach the hill, stony and rugged on the side we all meant to climb, but which presented a grassy slope of considerable length and steepness on the other. Up we all clambered, the boys as actively as any of us; on the top we all joined hands (our Siamese friends in the centre), and started off, full speed, over the smooth but steep descent; unexpectedly we came upon a hurdle fence, some four or five feet high, before which all the party except the twins suddenly stopped; they, by a uniform impulse, and with the agility of young deer, leapt over it.

At this time their skin was soft and smooth, their complexion a dark rich olive, their hair black and shining, cut short over the forehead, but left long behind, plaited, wound round the head just above the brows, and tied with a long silk tassel which fell over the shoulder.

With this image in my mind I went the other day to the Egyptian Hall, Piccadilly, and was pained to tears by the contrast the reality presented: the features wholly changed, the hair grey, the complexion faded, and an expression of deep melancholy on both faces.

The lecturer, indeed, said they were happy and contented, but I could not believe him. Eng is *now* an inch or two taller than Chang, and the constant leaning on one another has brought about a deviation in the spine of each—slight in the case of Eng, the taller and stronger, very obvious in the shorter and more delicate-looking of the two.

The ligament that unites them has evidently grown more rigid with time; so much so, indeed, that though they can still stand face to face with ease, they can no longer, as in former years, bring their outer shoulders together, and face a contrary direction to that in which they habitually look. I went away sad and sorry, without making myself known as I had intended to do; but I have seen them often since in their quiet home, and under another and brighter aspect, affectionate, cheerful, and happy, retaining even the Christian names of me and mine after nearly forty years of absence, and careful to relate every little circumstance that might show me how well and kindly we had all been remembered. The old love of joking, too, appeared. For instance, on my saying, in reply to a question, that Eng was taller and looked stronger than his brother, Chang took me up with "Yes, but don't you think I am the best-looking?"

Each twin has brought one of his daughters to England; both are unaffected, modest, well brought up young women. They have evidently inherited the gentle nature of their twin parents, and an atmosphere of peace and content seems to hang over them and their surroundings.

Though Chang and Eng are very intelligent, and certainly well up in American politics, their constant residence in a remote part of the States, nearly 200

miles from a town, has apparently kept them un-
spoiled by the world and the world's ways; and to me
they seem to have lost none of the sweetness of the
"Siamese Youths" I knew and loved so many years
ago.

During this same visit to London, Chang and Eng
formed a friendship with Francis Buckland, the renowned English naturalist, author, and eccentric. An
authority on fish, supervisor of his own Museum of
Economic Fish Culture, Buckland shared his bedroom
at various times with a bear, a vulture, an African
mongoose, a badger, a monkey. At the age of four,
Buckland recalled, when Chang and Eng had first arrived in England, he had been so impressed by them
that he had tied two kittens together and called them
his Siamese Twins. Now, learning Chang and Eng
were once more in London, Buckland sent them a
gift of a pair of joined twin salmon born in his museum. With this gesture, the friendship between Buckland and the twins began and ripened. On one occasion, when Buckland had the twins to his house
as dinner guests, he also invited Anna H. Swan, the
seven-foot-five-and-a-half-inch Nova Scotia giantess
(who years earlier had been rescued from a Barnum
Museum fire by use of a tackle and derrick, and who
later married Captain Martin Van Buren Bates, the
seven-foot-two-and-a-half-inch Kentucky giant).

The crowning moment of Chang and Eng's visit to
London was an audience with Queen Victoria, who
had already served thirty-two years of her sixty-three-
year reign as ruler of Great Britain. The reception in
Buckingham Palace may have been arranged by P. T.
Barnum, who, years before, had brought Tom Thumb
before the queen. As one of Eng's grandsons recalled,
"The Queen had invited them to call on her. She gave
each of them a gold watch and chain, engraved with
fine lettering. These I have seen many times. In fact
they are still in the family."

On July 20, 1869, Chang and Eng, their daughters,
and their manager left England, taking an overnight

boat from Hollyhead to Dublin, Ireland. On July 26, they went on to Cork, but at this point they decided to cut their Irish trip short. According to Judge Graves:

"The failing health of Kate began to admonish her father that perhaps it would be best for her to return home, and she too began to be anxious to get back again to her mother and the endearing ties of the home circle. The time of the engagement was mostly out. They had travelled through Scotland during the bleak winter and remained in the cities of England during the spring and in time they had travelled through the delightful country scenes, and during July they travelled over the green fields of the 'Emerald Isle' and having accomplished their undertaking as far as possible now they determined to return home."

The twins made their way to Queenstown, and on July 30, 1869, they boarded the steamer *City of Antwerp*. They reached New York City the second week in August, and by August 15 were safely back in Mount Airy.

The reunion was enlivened by the gifts the travelers had brought home. Chang and Eng always returned from their tours with lavish presents for their wives and children. On an earlier occasion, after a successful tour, the twins had spent $500 in New York for jewelry and other presents for their families and "every slave and servant." This time Nannie was the principal gift-bearer. For her mother, her aunt, her sisters and brothers, her cousins—and for herself—she carried home at least a hundred purchases made in Great Britain. These included candy, gloves, and a pin for her fourteen-year-old sister Louise, and for the others a variety of items such as a jewelry set, several lockets, twelve yards of silk, skirt hoops, a Bible, scissors, nine yards of calico, two skirts, a knife, a lace shawl.

Chang and Eng had a little more than five months' time in the United States before embarking on what Wallace, the promoter they had met in England, planned as the most ambitious tour of their lives. This tour was intended to take them to countries they had never visited before—like Germany, Russia, Italy, Spain—as well as to France for a second visit. In these five months, while devoting some of their time to getting their home affairs in order, the twins encouraged Judge Ingalls to book them for appearances at various annual agricultural fairs in the Western and Northwestern states. They performed at the fairs from early fall into the winter. Then, after a short respite, they set out for New York accompanied by two of their sons, Eng's twenty-one-year-old James Montgomery and Chang's twelve-year-old Albert.

In New York, Chang and Eng joined their new manager, Wallace, and on February 1, 1870, the party of five boarded the steamer *Allemagne* and were soon on their way across the Atlantic to the first destination of their grand tour, Germany. The crossing was uneventful, and on February 19, after eighteen days at sea, they reached Glückstadt, which was the port for Hamburg.

Once on German soil, the party was transported from Glückstadt to Hamburg. There they climbed on a Prussian train and settled back for the relatively short journey to Berlin.

In Berlin, porters took their trunks and pushed ahead of them down wooden stairs to the front of the station, where order was being kept by policemen in spiked helmets. The party found a horse-drawn droshky, perhaps two, and soon was on its way to the boardinghouse.

If the twins' quarters were typical of the rooming houses occupied by other travelers to the Prussian capital, they found themselves in a chilly sitting room with an unlighted fire in the fireplace, the room furnished with a small sofa, a desk, a bureau, several rush-bottomed chairs. In their bedroom there was one bed, a looking glass, and a washstand.

Wallace had booked Chang and Eng for a three-week stand at the Circus Renz. Never in their lives, in America or elsewhere, had the twins performed in a circus. This was to be the first and last such experience.

The dominant figures in Berlin at that time were the seventy-three-year-old Kaiser Wilhelm I, beginning the tenth year of his autocratic rule over an ever-expanding Prussia, and his Iron Chancellor, Prince Otto von Bismarck. Under this pair, who had recently crushed Denmark and Austria, resurgent Germany had become the second most powerful nation on the European continent. France was the first. But that would not continue for long.

Germany was also one of the most austere, conservative, industrious countries in Europe. As the Prussian crown princess wrote to her mother, Queen Victoria, "Our poverty, our dull towns, our plodding, hardworking *serious life*, has made us strong and determined; is wholesome for us. I should grieve were we to imitate Paris and be so taken up with pleasure that no time was left for self-examination and serious thought!"

The twins and their sons visited Unter den Linden, the main shopping street and promenade of the city. The mile-long paved street, bordered by linden, maple, and chestnut trees, was lined with fruit stands and drink shops, stucco houses, large hotels, huge monuments depicting Victory and Frederick the Great mounted on a charger. The sidewalks were crowded with uniformed and decorated soldiers, women carrying baskets of goods, nursemaids and their young charges, businessmen, and street urchins. Nearby, the twins visited the Tiergarten, the huge city park with its paths, shrubbery, trees, and water basin, surrounded by beer gardens and dance halls. Yet, for all that the twins saw—the Raczinsky Palace with its art gallery, Kroll's with its dining saloons and theater, the Brandenburg Gate (Berlin's triumphal arch), the kaiser's palace with its sculptured eagles—they must have found a stolid monotony in the city.

But the monotony mattered little to Chang and Eng. They had not come the long distance to Berlin seeking pleasure. They had come to Berlin for two earnest reasons. One was to fulfill their engagement with the Circus Renz and make money. The other, at the urging of their wives and children, was to see one of the greatest physicians in the world, the renowned pathologist Dr. Rudolf Virchow, who practiced in Berlin and whom they hoped would undertake their separation.

However, before preparing to meet Dr. Virchow, Chang and Eng readied themselves to meet the Berlin public. The *Vossische Zeitung* on Tuesday, February 22, 1870, ran two advertisements concerning the twins. The first announced their Berlin debut with the Circus Renz; the second announced that a book about their lives was available for purchase.

Available at Ernst Litfass, printer at court,
Adlerstrasse 6

LIFE STORY OF THE
SIAMESE TWIN BROTHERS
CHANG AND ENG
WITH ILLUSTRATIONS
Cost: 2½ sgr.

Contents:
Are the twins different men?
Could they be separated?
Climate, navigation, religion of Siam.
Women of Siam.
Travel to America and Europe.
Life in Siam.
Wedding and private life of the twins.
Two families and their children.
The American Civil War.

On February 26, the *Vossische Zeitung* ran a review of Chang and Eng's opening appearance in Berlin: "As men with gray heads they have become mellow in gait and actions. First they appear on a quickly improvised podium which runs all around the area, then, turning this way and that, sometimes taking a bow, they wander through the aisle which is located between the boxes and the stands."

On the following Sunday, Chang and Eng submitted to a physical examination requested by a Berlin

physician, Dr. Berend, who brought along three colleagues named Dr. Friedrichs, Dr. Reichert, and Dr.
Hartmann. According to a report issued nine days
later:

"They all came to the conclusion that the mem-
branous connective part that unites the twins has two
cords, which contain remainders of the former navel
vessels, and that liver and heart of each of the twins
are drawn toward this connective part. Important organs could not be detected in the latter. In spite of
this all doctors present advised against a separation of
this connective part since it could possibly cause the
opening of the abdomen and endanger their lives."

By now, Chang and Eng were the talk of Berlin.
Interest in their abnormality was so great that another physician, Dr. Stryck, delivered a public lecture
on them. Whether Dr. Stryck himself had examined
the twins, or whether he had relied for his material
on the findings of Dr. Berend and his colleagues, was
not made clear. In his talk on March 4, Dr. Stryck
identified the twins' connecting ligament as being "in
the heart region," and stated that because of it "the
twins face each other at a 30 degree angle, lateral."
He went on to reveal that while the twins were in
Edinburgh in 1868 an effort was made by doctors "to
induce a gradual dying of the cord through the application of screws, but without success." He pointed
out that Chang's pulse had "6 to 8 beats more than
Eng's, by the same token Chang breathes faster," that
"the eyes and extremities of both which are located
at the inside are weaker and less developed than those
on the outside," that he believed "a separation possible even if the peritonium should happen to go
through the cord, since one perforates the peritonium, regretfully not without danger, during Caesarian
birth or ovarian dropsy." He said that "the twins
Chang and Eng have been desiring a separation for
the past five years, and the hopes of fulfilling that
wish is said to be part of the reason for their being
here." He concluded with a bit of gossip: that while
Chang and Eng's exhibits caused "little excitement"

in the United States, in England "they received great attention" and had "made their fortune."

When Chang and Eng read about the lecture, they were indignant. They felt that Dr. Stryck's lecture contained "several falsehoods." In a statement to the press, the twins denied that an attempt had been made to separate them using screws, although "a suggestion of this nature has been made by the London surgeon Startin." They also denied that they themselves had been desiring separation for the past five years. It was "their wives and children" who wanted the separation made, "insisting on having the husband [or] respectively the father, to themselves."

Meanwhile, as they continued their daily circus performances, the twins awaited their crucial appointment with Dr. Rudolf Virchow.

They had been briefed on Dr. Virchow's importance, and beyond him, they knew, there was no hope. Dr. Virchow was forty-nine years old the year he saw the twins. He had a remarkable career behind him, and an even more remarkable one ahead of him. The first surgeon to describe leukemia, he was also the founder of cellular pathology. He had been a professor of pathological anatomy at the University of Würzburg. His sympathy for revolutionaries who were threatening the stability of the Prussian government cost him this post, but in 1856 he became the director of the Pathological Institute in Berlin. He denigrated Pasteur's germ theory of disease, and he rejected Darwin's theory of evolution. Nine years before meeting the twins, Dr. Virchow had entered politics, been elected to the Prussian Diet, and started the Progressive party, constantly speaking out against Bismarck (who once challenged him to a duel that never came off). Dr. Virchow introduced anthropology into Germany. He was also interested in archaeology, and in 1874 he became friends with Heinrich Schliemann, the merchant prince and master of thirteen languages who unearthed the walls of ancient Troy and King Priam's palace. In 1879, Dr. Virchow accompanied Schliemann to the site of Troy.

This was the incredible man Chang and Eng were waiting to meet.

However, Dr. Virchow took it upon himself to see the twins before they could see him. Impatient to have a look at the joined brothers prior to examining them, curious to see how they presented themselves to the public, Dr. Virchow made his way to the Circus Renz on Freidrichstrasse one evening, bought himself a ticket, and went inside.

Kay Hunter, in *Duet for a Lifetime*, described what transpired. Awaiting the climactic act of the show, the appearance of Chang and Eng, Dr. Virchow had to endure the high-wire act, the clowns, the bareback riders, the brassy circus band. He found it all disagreeable. At last, a fanfare brought Chang and Eng into the limelight. The two aging men trotted out on the podium, cavorted and bowed, and instead of being greeted with applause they were met with laughter. Dr. Virchow tried to understand the audience's reaction, and then he understood. The two seam-faced, sixty-year-old men, stiffly, awkwardly moving about, seemed ridiculous in this carnival atmosphere. Dr. Virchow's heart went out to them. It was pathetic that they had to perform in this undignified manner and in this place. What might have been charming and amusing when they were younger now appeared infinitely sad. Dismayed, Dr. Virchow quickly left the Circus Renz.

A few days later, Chang and Eng arrived for their critical appointment with Dr. Virchow, an appointment which their wives had looked forward to with so much optimism. Dr. Virchow was the soul of hospitality. He was thoughtful and kind, and tried to allay their anxiety. He had read medical papers about them, and he was well acquainted with their histories. To acquire firsthand information, and to put them at their ease, he chatted with them at length.

Finally, the moment came for the physical examination. Dr. Virchow asked them to undress. Reluctantly, they did so. Now the German physician began his work.

The examination was long and exhaustive, lasting over an hour. The twins were wearied and irritated by the procedure, in particular Chang, who protested fiercely when Virchow pricked his side of the connecting ligament with a needle. Dr. Virchow would later write: "The Siamese allow all examinations of the cord which unites them with the greatest resistance only. Obviously, it is not only sensitivity, but mistrust and fear that the cord might be injured in some way."

When Dr. Virchow inquired politely whether they had fathered any twins of their own, both Chang and Eng looked shocked and upset, and one of them replied curtly that they had had no problems whatsoever with their children. To add to the tension of the meeting, the twins had been offered drinks upon their arrival, and Chang had taken a drink and then had continued to indulge himself freely.

At last, the ordeal was over. The twins awaited the great physician's opinion. He would not give them an immediate answer. He said that he preferred to make out his report and he would show it to them in writing.

Shortly after, while still in Berlin, Chang and Eng received Dr. Virchow's written report. The doctor concluded that, despite the mysterious connecting ligament, their bodies functioned independently. Considering their years, there was little that was wrong with them. The harmony between them was remarkable, but this harmony had "lately been disturbed . . . by the fact that both of them are beginning to go deaf, one more rapidly than the other." Chang was becoming hard of hearing in both ears, but Eng's growing deafness was in only his left ear, the one closer to Chang.

Now Dr. Virchow came to the essential matter, the connecting ligament and its separation. While Dr. Virchow deduced that there was no intestinal link between the twins, he was not sure about the livers, fearing that they might be communal, if only due to the connection of small blood vessels. He would, he wrote, advise against separation. He would not be willing to risk the shock to their systems.

Chang and Eng's last verdict was in. Rudolf Virchow had represented the final dream of freedom for Chang and Eng. With his report, their resources and their hopes were depleted. They would consult no more physicians abroad. They were resigned to living out their days in the same bondage they had known all their lives.

However, Dr. Virchow had one more opinion, and this he made public in an address to the Medical Society of Berlin. There was a single circumstance in which he would advocate risking separation: "It must here be considered, that in case of the death of one, the operation would have to be performed near the body of this one in order to prevent endangering the life of the other brother."

With this last disappointment, there was nothing to do but lose themselves in their work, and Chang and Eng dutifully went on with their performances.

They completed their tour of Germany, and some time in June 1870 their manager, Wallace, started the twins and their sons for Russia. The party traveled to the German port of Stettin, and there took a steamer for St. Petersburg. The voyage on the Baltic Sea was smooth, and at last they entered the Oder River. At dawn they passed the fortifications of the Russian naval base at Kronstadt, and soon, at the crook of the Neva River, they reached St. Petersburg, "a window opening upon Europe," as Pushkin called it.

Alexandre Dumas had been to St. Petersburg not many years before the twins arrived, and had vividly described the city:

"I watched St. Petersburg slowly rising above the water line at the far end of the gulf. Soon I began to notice other domes, lower than the first one, shining here and there, some gilded like the cupola of St. Isaac, others covered with bright stars. St. Petersburg has a multitude of religious buildings—two cathedrals, forty-six parish churches, a hundred other places of public worship and forty-five private chapels, with 626 bells between them!—but the general effect is by no means picturesque, for the place is flat and low-lying."

From the quay, the twins and their party took a droshky, a one-horse carriage, into the city.

That first day in the imperial city, and in all the days to follow, the twins saw the magnificent sights—the main thoroughfare, Nevsky Prospekt, teeming with the very poor and the very rich and the gaudily uni-formed officers of the czar; the Fortress of St. Peter and St. Paul; Troitsky Square; the Alexander Nevsky monastery; the czar's 1,000-room, green baroque Win-ter Palace, with its enormous square; the War Min-istry; the Admiralty Building. Carriages rumbled over the bumpy streets—"oval cobblestones as large as the skull of a Patagonian giant," wrote Dumas—taking the nobility for pastries at Eliseyev's or dinner at Donon's.

The twins' first night in St. Petersburg must have been memorable, if it resembled the first night that Dumas enjoyed. As Dumas described it:

> The vast expanse of the Neva—a river of silver—rolled at our feet; great boats, like swallows, swept noiselessly up and down with billowing sails, leaving a faint ripple in their wake. Not a single light gleamed from either bank, not one star kept watch in the sky. Suddenly a sphere of gold appeared far to our left, rising above a dark green wood, cleaving a mother-of-pearl sky while the waves of foliage were still strongly outlined against it. Slowly this great shining breastplate climbed the sky, but added nothing to the transparency of the night. Only, a long line of molten gold lay trembling on the water, giving a touch of flame to the boats that crossed it, for the brief moment of their passing. At last, majestically, proudly, serene as a goddess, the moon glided slowly down behind the domes of Smolny, which remained sharply outlined against her brilliance for the whole

time it took her to sink from the cross crowning the pinnacle and submerge herself in the depths of the sea on the horizon.

Pushkin, that great Russian poet . . . tried to depict such a night in noble verses. But, fine as they are, they are only the poetry of Man; the nights of St. Petersburg are the poetry of God Himself.

This was the city in which Chang and Eng, so far from Mount Airy, North Carolina, performed. After St. Petersburg, the twins took the railroad (built at a cost of $40 million by a West Point professor, George Washington Whistler, whose wife Anna was the model for *Whistler's Mother*) to Moscow. In Moscow, as well as "the principal cities of the Russian Empire," reported Judge Graves, Chang and Eng also performed.

No record of their appearances or reception has survived, but undoubtedly they were well received, for evidence does exist that the twins met the czar and enjoyed his imperial patronage. The czar in that summer of 1870 was fifty-two-year-old Alexander II, who had been on the throne fifteen years. From the start of his reign, he had been a reformer. Russia's defeat by Great Britain, France, and Turkey in the Crimean War had exposed the nation's backwardness, and Alexander determined to rectify that and modernize his country. Among his more notable achievements were granting the serfs freedom, improving local welfare and education, releasing Siberian exiles, abolishing medieval punishment, and expanding the nation's railroads from 600 miles of track to 14,000 miles. Four years before Chang and Eng met him, Alexander had taken a nineteen-year-old aristocrat, Catherine Dolgoruky, for his mistress. They met regularly in a secret basement room of the palace. Now, when the twins arrived in Moscow, the affair was at its height. Two years later, Catherine bore the czar the first of several illegitimate children and the scandal was in the open.

To illustrate the interest that Alexander took in Chang and Eng and their sons, descendants of the

twins recall that the czar invited them to attend a
theatrical performance in the palace. The twins and
their sons sat with the royal family in the private box,
and Chang's twelve-year-old Albert "held the hand of
one of the Russian princesses throughout the entire
performance." On another occasion, in Moscow, Albert was suffering from a carbuncle on his neck. When
Czar Alexander heard of this, he immediately sent his
personal physician to treat the boy.

Having finished their last engagement in Russia,
Chang and Eng planned to perform in Vienna, Rome,
Madrid, and Paris before returning home. But almost
overnight their plans were interrupted by the sounds
of war. Germany, united and strong, tried to place a
relative of the kaiser's on the empty Spanish throne,
since Bismarck calculated that this would incite Napoleon III to go to war. His plan succeeded. On July
19, 1870, France declared war on Prussia. The twins,
who had canceled their bookings in Vienna, Rome,
and Madrid, still had hopes of reaching Paris. But
hostilities had already commenced, and these would
culminate in a decisive Prussian victory within three
months.

There was no safe place Chang and Eng could go,
except home. Wasting no time, they traveled from
Moscow back to Hamburg, and then took a transatlantic steamer at Glückstadt bound for New York
City. It was to be a tragic crossing.

The bad moment came during their seventh day at
sea. Chang and Eng were relaxing, playing a leisurely
game of chess. Sources differ as to their opponent.
One source says they were playing against Dr. Roberts, the president of Liberia. Another source says
they were playing against Frederick Douglass, the
onetime Negro slave who had become a famous reformer, an adviser to President Lincoln, and the minister to Haiti. When the game ended and Chang and
Eng started to rise, Eng tried to get to his feet but
Chang was unable to move. He had suffered a gradual
stroke, and his right arm, side, and leg were paralyzed.
Medical aid was sought on the ship, but the paralysis

remained. The immobilized Chang was confined to his berth, and the healthy and active Eng was forced to remain inert beside him.

As the ship neared New York, the future of the twins had never looked bleaker.

11
CHAPTER
11

The Last Act:
Three Days in January

When Chang and Eng disembarked in New York late in August 1870, they knew that they would never travel again.

Immediate medical help was sought for the partially paralyzed Chang.

"Arriving in New York," wrote Judge Graves, "the most skillful physicians were called in and they remained a few days under treatment there, but no indications of improvement appearing they left for home..."

Once the twins were reunited with their wives and children in Mount Airy, Chang immediately placed himself under the care of Dr. Joseph Hollingsworth. "All the prescriptions failed to bring about anything like complete restoration," Judge Graves noted, "although after a few weeks there seemed to be some little benefit from the application of cold water. The patient, however, always seemed so averse to the applications of this remedy that he would not consent to a thorough trial of that prescription."

For a while, discouraged, Chang took to his bed,

with the vigorous Eng lying alongside him. At last, Dr. Hollingsworth contrived a means by which Chang could become ambulatory. Chang, according to *The People's Press* of Winston-Salem, on October 14, 1870, was "now able to be up, but his left hand and leg (the side next to his brother) are useless. He goes with a crutch under his right arm, and his left foot is supported by a leather strap which his brother holds up as he hobbles along." Actually, the newspaper erred in describing Chang's affliction. It was Chang's right hand and leg, not his left, that were useless, and his right foot that was supported by a leather strap that Eng carried.

In this period, a depressed Chang took to drinking more and more heavily, often becoming raging drunk. This added to the strain on their relationship and to the frequency of their quarrels.

After one particularly bitter quarrel—during which one of them, probably Chang, pulled a knife and shouted, "I'm going to cut your gut out!"—Eng had dragged his brother to Dr. Hollingsworth and begged the physician to separate them at once. According to the *Philadelphia Medical Times:* "Eng affirmed that Chang was so bad that he could live no longer with him; and Chang stated that he was satisfied to be separated, only asking that he be given an equal chance with his brother, and that the band be cut exactly in the middle."

Dr. Hollingsworth, his grandson later remembered, "became exasperated at them and told them that he was anxious to know what the connecting arm contained, that the whole medical world was awaiting their death to find out their secret, that he felt that the operation would prove fatal to them both, but that in the interest of science he would operate immediately."

Then, laying out "knives, saws," and other surgical equipment, the physician commanded, "Very well, just get up on the table and I'll fix you, but which would you prefer, that I should sever the flesh that connects you or cut off your heads? One will produce just about the same results as the other."

This brought Chang and Eng to a quick decision. They calmed down, finally shook hands with each other, and departed.

Sometimes when they saw Dr. Hollingsworth, Chang would say, "*We* can't live long." The doctor would reassure Chang, and then promise both of them that if either one died, he would be quick to sever them so that the living twin had every chance to survive.

On the other hand, Judge Jesse Graves, who was close to them in these years, played down their differences and insisted that they got along well, considering the circumstances. In the last paragraphs of his unpublished manuscript, he wrote:

> During all this time Eng was entirely unaffected, still retaining his usual health and his vivacity of spirits in a wonderful degree when his situation is considered. It was not expected that Chang would ever recover and Eng must have been under constant apprehension of his death at any time, and although the experiments which have been reported had never been made yet they had been examined by the most skillful surgeons and physicians of the world whose opinions were almost unanimous that separation could not be made without fatal result and he must have known that the death of his brother would be the immediate signal for his own dissolution. As the disease of Chang continued its effects began to be apparent in its operations upon the mind, which although not so much impaired as to disqualify him from the management of his business affairs, yet did at times exhibit painful aberration from its original clearness and strength. . . . During his long continued confinement as an invalid as almost universally happens Chang became somewhat peevish but certainly not more than is common in such cases. The most of the time he was very much resigned and patient, very rarely exhibiting any loss of temper.

To the end of Judge Graves' manuscript was appended a postscript written in a feminine hand, possibly by one of the twins' friends or family, trying to make certain that the world understood that in their worst travail the twins still got along:

"Eng's treatment of his brother was very kind and forebearing during all the long period of his sickness, showing great tenderness and affection for him and endeavoring by every means in his power to alleviate his suffering. His kindness was received with the warmest appreciation by Chang, whose disposition was very different from the morose, ill nature so falsely ascribed to him."

Despite the difficulties imposed by Chang's afflictions, the twins continued to be busy with their families and their prospering farms.

In 1870, Chang and Adelaide had nine of their children at home: Christopher, 25; Nancy, 23; Susan, 20; Victoria, 17; Louise, 14; Albert, 12; Jesse, 10; Margaret Elizabeth, 8; and Hattie, the baby. Hattie had been born less than two years before, on September 12, 1868, indicating that Chang had been sexually active a year before his stroke.

Chang's farm was doing well. He had three young black laborers, as well as his eldest son, Christopher, taking care of his house and 200 acres of farmland. (Chang also owned 350 acres of adjoining unimproved woodland.) He gave his three laborers room and board, and paid them a combined salary of $350 for the entire year. On his farm, Chang had 1 horse, 3 mules, 6 head of cattle, 8 sheep, and 30 pigs. In 1870, Chang's farm produced 50 pounds of beeswax, 200 pounds of butter, 300 pounds of honey, 2 bushels of peas and beans, 20 bushels of Irish potatoes, 80 bushels of sweet potatoes, 50 bushels of winter wheat, 50 bushels of rye, 300 bushels of oats, and 1,500 bushels of Indian corn. Also, Chang was able to sell his orchard products for $200 and his slaughtered animals for $650. In a year, the farm earned him $2,037.

Altogether his holdings were worth $23,000, a considerable sum in 1870.

That same year, Eng and Sallie had six of their children at home: Katherine, 25; James Montgomery, 21; Patrick, 20; Frederick, 13; Rosella, 11; and Robert, 5.

Eng's situation was comfortable, although he had nowhere near the assets that his brother possessed. Besides Grace Gates—Aunt Grace—working as a housekeeper, Eng had one black and one white laborer, along with his son James Montgomery, tending to his house and 100 acres. He also owned 150 acres of unimproved land. His two laborers and Aunt Grace received room and board and a combined salary of $100 a year. Among Eng's assets were 2 horses, 3 mules, 8 head of cattle, 10 sheep, and 20 pigs. In the year 1870, Eng's farm produced 3 pounds of beeswax, 25 pounds of wool, 72 pounds of honey, 150 pounds of butter, 2 tons of hay, 25 bushels of Irish potatoes, 60 bushels of winter wheat, 75 bushels of rye, 300 bushels of oats, and 875 bushels of Indian corn. He earned $100 from his orchard products and $150 from animals slaughtered. His income from the farm for the year was $1,535.

Eng's total assets in 1870 were valued at $7,000, less than a third of his brother's worth.

While the twins were no longer able to help out on their farms as they used to do, they still tried to remain active. One of their outdoor pleasures was riding in their buggy—not only the one-mile ride every three days to change houses and partners, but also pleasure excursions with their children. In April 1873, one such ride had serious consequences. The result was reported in the *Surry Visitor:*

"On last Saturday the Siamese twins (Eng and Chang Bunker), who reside three miles from Mt-Airy, started to town in a buggy, with little Lizzie, the daughter of Chang, driving. Before they had proceeded far, the horse ran away, and Lizzie, becoming frightened, jumped from the vehicle, breaking her left hand in two places, while the horse sped on and overturned the buggy, throwing the Twins out and injuring them severely."

Although Chang and Eng no longer corresponded
with friends as they used to, they continued to harbor affection for their one-time manager James Hale,
and stayed in touch with him. Returning from their
last trip to Europe in 1869, they sent a gift to him in
New York. When Hale, who had been out of the city,
returned a month later and found the gift and the note
that accompanied it (which made no mention of
Chang's stroke), he promptly wrote to the twins:

> I am very much obliged for your kind invitation
> to visit you this winter, and regret much that I cannot
> have the pleasure. I hope some of these days that better
> times will come and that I can afford the money and
> time to do so . . .
> I should like very much to have a look at your
> family of 26 (and perhaps 28) and wonder how the
> deuce you manage to be contented on a plantation,
> where you see comparatively little company, after
> you have spent so many years in the bustle and confu-
> sion of crowds.—I know how heartless and unfeeling
> the *world* generally is, and how much comfort
> a man ought to take at home with his family—
> still, yours has been such a life of excitement, that I
> should almost suppose your present quiet would be
> *too much* comfort. Do you ever intend to visit New
> York and the large cities again—many very many
> would be glad to see you, and I dont doubt you
> could make it profitable if you were disposed. If you
> *do* come, the humble home I have is at your disposal.

The twins did not accept the invitation. They
never saw Hale again. He lived on and on, working
as a proprietor of a coffee house, a bookseller, a
steamboat agent, head of a private mail delivery service, and finally as a notary public in New York until
his death at the age of ninety in 1892. Nor did the
twins ever visit New York again. They were through
with "the bustle and confusion of crowds."

They were also through with publicity. Yet, occasionally, they did receive a member of the press. In
1874, the Wilmington *Morning Star* carried a story by

"A Lady of Wilmington" who had visited Chang and Eng in the summer of 1873:

> The houses of the twins are plain country houses, coarsely, but neatly furnished. Their families live a mile apart, this being caused by the incompatibility of temper on the part of their wives, who have been often estranged from each other for weeks at a time. Arriving first at Eng's house, we inquired if the Twins were at home, and being told that they were at the "other house," we went thither.
>
> Upon approaching the house we saw, for the first time, the Siamese Twins, who were standing on the piazza. After alighting from the carriage, assisted by one of Chang's sons, we were cordially met by the Twins. This cordiality surprised us, as we had heard in Mt. Airy that [Chang] frequently insulted visitors, and often positively refused to see them. Upon entering we were ushered into a very large room, which seemed to be the parlor (although it contained a bed), plainly but neatly furnished. The walls were hung with many pictures of the Twins taken in different positions. On one side of the room was a double chair made from the wood and bark of the elm. These the twins occupied after handing us chairs.
>
> To secure the good humor of [Chang] who has always been charged with being the possessor of a disposition less amiable than that of his brother, we spoke in high terms of their beautiful place, of the improvements, the fine crops, etc., and seeing that they were affable and communicative, we plunged *in medias res* and obtained a cursory history of their lives.

The Lady then spun out a long, and often inaccurate, biography of Chang and Eng from their days in Siam to their "retirement from public gaze and comment" in North Carolina. She next went into their families and present condition:

> The oldest of [Chang's] daughters [Nannie] is dying now of consumption. The next daughter (deaf and dumb) married a teacher from the Deaf and

Dumb Asylum in Raleigh, from which institution she graduated last June. [Chang] had, a few years ago, a stroke of paralysis and since then his irritability had become almost unbearable. They both indulge freely in intoxicating beverages, and when under this influence would threaten to sever violently the ligament which so mysteriously bound them. Many think that this exceeding peevishness was caused by the great fear each had of death as a consequence to himself of the death of the other. *Apropos* of this, in answer to the question whether they anticipated longevity, they replied, shaking their heads with a sadness which betokened earnestness and sincerity, that they did not, being already sixty-two years old, and [Chang] not knowing at what moment he would have another stroke of paralysis, which would, most certainly, prove fatal. They were excessively sensitive to the curious gaze of visitors, and we were compelled to bring all our feminine tact into play to enable us, at opportune moments, to cast furtive glances at them, and in this manner we obtained a satisfactory view of the monstrosities. Their *tout en semble* was, to us, exceedingly repulsive: *Monstrum horrendum informe.* The Twins were clad in the rough garments of farmers, this apparel being composed entirely of homespun. After we had been at the house of the Twins about an hour, they brought, with the hospitality, which we flatter ourselves, had been acquired since their residence in the South, large glasses of cider which they had made for our refreshment. This we enjoyed vastly, not only because we liked the beverage, but because by this little display of appreciation we could still hold captive their good humor. When we handed our goblets to be refilled they smiled pleasantly, showing that our appreciation was heartily recognized. They spoke in English very broken, and it was only by listening *auribus erectis* that we could catch and intercept all that they said. They talked a great deal too, often making voluntary remarks and sometimes introducing new topics. Our time, which was limited, passed very quickly, and after remaining two hours, we rose to leave. At this movement, they insisted upon

our remaining to tea, and when we informed them
that we were compelled to decline this hospitable
invitation, they importuned to us to remain longer;
but even this we were forced to decline because of
other engagements made in Mt. Airy. They escorted
us to the carriage door, and again assuring us that
they were "sorry we could not sup with them,"
bade us adieu.

Chang and Eng would give no more interviews.
The year 1873 had almost passed into history. Except
for a financial panic on Wall Street, it had been an uneventful year in the United States. Ulysses S. Grant
had begun his second term in the White House. In
small towns throughout the country, farmers were
uniting into alliances. A school for nursing was
founded at Bellevue Hospital in New York City.
People were reading a best-seller, *Around the World
in Eighty Days*, by a Frenchman named Jules Verne.
The corrupt New York City politician William "Boss"
Tweed was sentenced to twelve years in prison on
204 charges of fraud. The president of Cornell
University refused to allow his football team to travel
to Cleveland to play the University of Michigan, stating, "I will not permit 30 men to travel 400 miles to
agitate a bag of wind." The winner of the first Preak-
ness Stakes and the $1,800 purse was Survivor.

And now it was 1874.

A nineteen-year-old young man named Shepherd
Monroe Dugger was visiting Mount Airy. Later, he
remembered a meeting that occurred in January
1874: "The 12th day of January, Mr. Ed Banner, of
Mt. Airy, whose five brothers were my neighbors at
Banner Elk, N.C., took me to see the twins at Chang's
house. They received me very courteously indeed . . ."

He was the last outsider to see the twins, and write
about them, before the end.

◆ ◆ ◆

Chang and Eng had just gone to Chang's house, to
spend three days with Chang's wife Adelaide and

Chang's children, when their neighbor Ed Banner and his young guest Shepherd Monroe Dugger came calling.

After their visitors had left that Monday night, Chang began coughing, "a dry cough with scanty, frothy sputum." Then he began to suffer chest pains. A member of the family was sent to Mount Airy to summon the family physician. The twins' regular physician, Dr. Joseph Hollingsworth, was not at home, but his brother and partner, Dr. William Hollingsworth, who sometimes attended the twins, responded at once.

Upon arriving at Chang's house Dr. Hollingsworth examined Chang and found that he was suffering an attack of bronchitis. He also found that Eng had been unaffected and was in the best of health. The doctor ordered the ailing brother to keep warm and stay indoors until he recovered.

During the two days following, Tuesday and Wednesday, Chang remained confined, while his brother deferred to his every wish because of the sudden illness and because they were in Chang's residence. By Wednesday, there was some improvement. The bronchitis had subsided, and Chang felt slightly better.

On Thursday, January 15, Chang's condition was stable. The arrival of evening signaled the time when they should move to Eng's house, since they had already spent three days in Chang's home. Now, as they had without fail for many years, they were expected to spend the next three days under Eng's roof.

Chang was ready to make the change, but Adelaide objected. She pointed out that he was still coughing, still suffering chest pains, and that he was simply too sick to travel. The doctor had cautioned him not to go outdoors. And outside, it was freezing, the coldest night of the winter. Eng concurred. He saw no reason to adhere to their routine practice. There could be, after all these years, an exception to the rule. Chang was too ill and the weather too chilling. He proposed they stay on at the Chang residence until Chang had fully recovered.

But Chang would not have it. He stubbornly persisted in his demand that they stand by their agreement—three days in his house, then three in Eng's. He was so adamant about it that, finally, Adelaide and Eng gave up trying to dissuade him.

Chang and Eng both dressed warmly, and then they went out to face the bitter cold. They climbed into their seats in the open carriage and settled down for the one-mile drive to Eng's house. It was over a road that "was very rough and frozen." The air was like ice and everywhere frost lay on the ground. Eng drove the horse hard as they bounced along. Chang huddled uncomfortably beside him.

When they reached Eng's house, Sallie had a hot supper waiting for them. Throughout the meal, Chang shivered, complaining that the short trip had chilled him and that he felt very cold. A roaring fire was going in the parlor fireplace, and Chang wanted to sit before it and warm himself. Eng, feeling well and with many things to do in his own home, did not want to sit in front of the fire. He "grumbled" about it, yet had no choice but to comply. The twins sat before the fireplace a long time, Chang refusing to leave but, at a late hour, he at last agreed to retire with Eng to their bed.

While Eng fell right off to sleep, Chang slept fitfully. When they awoke in the morning, Chang said that throughout the night "he had had such severe pain in the chest, and so much distress, that he thought he should have died."

It was Friday, January 16, and it was a long day for both the twins. Early in the day, an inquiry came by messenger from Adelaide asking how her husband was feeling. Chang sent word back to his wife that he was feeling better. But, in reality, as the day progressed he began to feel worse. Eng, now on his own ground, tried to perform some work indoors, but it was impossible. Chang hobbled along with him in obvious pain and in a foul temper.

Finally it was night. Some time after supper, they both agreed to go to sleep. There was a small bedroom they used, frequently sharing it with one of Eng's younger children. But this night they were alone in the room. They seemed ready for sleep. The others in the household also went to bed.

Eng fell off to sleep, but Chang was restless. In a little while Chang was fully awake, rousing Eng beside him, groaning that he was finding it difficult to breathe. Together the twins left their bed and made their way to the porch outside the house, so that Chang could inhale the cold air. They drank some water while on the porch, went back indoors, and retired to their bed again.

Eng dozed off at once, but Chang could not.

Midnight came and went, and now it was Saturday, January 17. Shortly after midnight, Chang shook Eng awake. He wanted to get out of bed and start a fire in the parlor fireplace. Eng refused to budge. He said the bed was warmer than sitting up in a chilly room. He insisted that Chang lie back and try to go to sleep. Protesting, Chang obliged.

Their rest was brief. Soon Chang was up, shaking his brother by the shoulder, insisting he could not breathe lying down, that he had to get up. Eng had no choice but to rise and accompany his ailing brother out of bed. Together, they shuffled to the parlor fireplace, laid some fresh logs in the grate, and soon had a blaze going. Then they sank into their double-sized chair before the leaping flames. Eng smoked his clay pipe.

After a short interval, Eng began nodding off. Rousing himself, he insisted that they must go back to bed. Chang refused, saying ". . . it would kill me to lie down" and that it hurt his breast "to recline." They continued to sit in front of the fire. At one o'clock in the morning, Eng again asked Chang if they could go to bed. This time Chang agreed.

They made their way to the bedroom, got into the massive bed, and lay silently in the darkness. Soon Eng dropped off into a deep exhausted sleep.

There was no sound in the house for an hour or

more, then several of the children heard a voice call out from the twins' bedroom. But no one answered it immediately.

At last, at four o'clock in the morning, one of Eng's sons, eighteen-year-old William, decided to look in on his father, and found him soundly asleep and breathing heavily. He went around the bed, turned up the lamp to study his Uncle Chang, and gasped. Chang was not breathing.

The lamp had awakened Eng. "William, I feel mighty sick," said Eng. Then he asked, "How is your Uncle Chang?"

"Uncle Chang is cold," William answered. "Uncle Chang is dead."

Immediately, reported the Philadelphia *Times*, Eng "in the greatest alarm turned and looked at the lifeless form beside him. He exclaimed, 'Then I am going!' and was at once seized by violent nervous paroxysms."

The boy ran out of the bedroom to awaken the rest of the household and tell them that Uncle Chang had died. Quickly, Sallie sent one of the children racing off on the three-mile trip to Mount Airy to summon Dr. William Hollingsworth, no doubt realizing that her own husband was still alive and that the doctor's brother had promised that if one of the twins died he would quickly operate to sever the living twin in an effort to save him.

All members of the household had crowded into the terrible bedroom. Eng lay there, very much alive, and Sallie bent over him. Eng told her what he and Chang had done before and after midnight. Then Eng said to her, "I am very bad off." Actually, he was rational but terrified. "He complained of agonizing pain and distress, especially in his limbs," the *Philadelphia Medical Times* would report. "His surface was covered with a cold sweat. At his request his wife and children rubbed his legs and arms, and pulled and stretched them forcibly. This was steadily continued."

He wanted to defecate. He rubbed his arms. He half sat up, saying he was choking.

He then lay back again. He had not once mentioned his brother, but now he reached out and drew Chang closer to him.

He stared at those around him. "May the Lord have mercy upon my soul," he gasped.

Those were his last words. He lapsed into a coma-like "stupor." It was an hour since Chang's death had been discovered.

Eng suffered no convulsions, no more visible agony. He continued to lie there in a stupor for an hour more. And then he died.

Shortly after, Dr. William Hollingsworth, carrying his surgical instruments, arrived. But there was no need for the surgical instruments.

It was over for the Siamese Twins.

Sixty-three years before, on a houseboat in a canal of a distant land, they had come into this world together, as one, and now, on a remote farm in North Carolina, in the dawn of a Saturday morning, on January 17, 1874, they departed this life together, as one.

❖ ❖ ❖

There was no telegraph in Mount Airy, so the news was carried to Greensboro, North Carolina, where it went out over the wires to the rest of the United States, eventually to be relayed to Great Britain and Europe.

The New York *Herald* featured it as the front-page lead story. The headlines read: THE DEAD SIAMESE TWINS. A LIGATURE THAT JOINED THEM IN LIFE AND DEATH.

In Mount Airy the weekend was busy, as were the days to follow, days filled with mourning, indecision, curiosity, speculation, and controversy.

On Saturday, in the hours after the twins' deaths, Adelaide had been informed, and with her children she hastened over to Eng's house. Dr. William Hollingsworth wanted to perform an autopsy on the twins' bodies, but this the wives would not permit.

Adelaide and Sallie next prepared their husbands'

bodies so that friends and neighbors could come by to pay their last respects. The daughter of a neighbor recalled that her father as a youngster had visited Eng's house and seen the bodies. "He said he could still remember going with his mother in a buggy that night to see them. They were laid out on a trundle bed."

That Saturday night, inside Eng's house, there was a meeting. Adelaide and Sallie were conferring with Dr. Joe Hollingsworth, who had returned to town, and his brother William. The discussion concerned how the widows should dispose of their husbands' bodies. There had been some talk of a funeral the next day, Sunday, but the widows did not want a funeral until their entire families could be gathered together. Four of their sons were away from home, including the two oldest boys, Chang's Christopher, who had been working in Sacramento, California, and was now in San Francisco, and Eng's Stephen, who was also in a Western city. The sons had to be notified and told to return home before there could be a funeral. The Drs. Hollingsworth, however, had another concern. After Chang and Eng were buried there would surely be vandals or graverobbers who would attempt to steal the corpses and sell them to promoters for public exhibition. Since the burial site could not be protected forever, this horrendous act was bound to occur sooner or later. The Drs. Hollingsworth made what they regarded as a sensible suggestion. Let Adelaide and Sallie circumvent the possibility of theft by themselves legitimately selling their husbands' corpses for exhibition. In this way, they could at least profit by the act and gain some security.

Both appalled and confused by what their advisers had to say, Adelaide and Sallie decided that they would prefer to let the senior son in both families, Christopher, help them make the decision when he arrived home. The Drs. Hollingsworth agreed this was wise. Meanwhile, the physicians pointed out, the bodies had to be preserved and temporarily buried

in a place that could be protected. They had no
means of embalming the bodies, so the four of them
determined that the corpses would be hermetically
sealed in a walnut casket, which would be placed in a
tin coffin, which in turn would be enclosed in a
wooden box. This triple coffin would be kept in the
cellar of Eng's house, where it could be guarded until
final disposition of the bodies was made.

Immediately after the meeting ended Saturday evening, a local tinsmith, William Augustus Reich, was
told to make a tin coffin large enough to hold the
twins' casket.

Meanwhile, a rumor was spreading through Surry
County that the funeral would be held on Sunday and
that the public would be able to view the bodies.
When Sunday came, a large crowd of people, including some clergymen, assembled outside Eng's house to
see Chang and Eng and then attend the funeral. The
door to the house was opened, and the crowd poured
inside. There, after filing past the bodies, they were
informed that there would be no funeral for the time
being, that the funeral had been postponed. This announcement succeeded in dispersing the crowd.

During the height of the crush, William Augustus
Reich delivered the tin coffin. The next morning,
Monday, January 19, he wrote a letter to his sister:

Dear Darling J

I write you a few lines this morning. I expect you
heard the Siamese Twins are dead. I got an order late
Saturday evening for a large tin coffin. I made it. I
worked nearly all night, finished it about noon yesterday. Cut out yesterday afternoon & soldered them
up. It was a sight the people that was there. It was a
long time before I could get my foot in at the door,
so crowded. It was like a camp meeting so many
people horses and carriages. It was most night before
I got through soldering them up. They are not going
to bury them but keep them in the house. I expect
they are afraid somebody would steal them. The

Siamese Twins is the greatest human curiosity in the world & who ever thought I would be the man to solder them up. I had to cut into 34 big sheets of tin to make the coffin. I have a notion to charge $20 do you think that would be about right? Their death was sudden & unexpected—on Friday night late yet they were unusually cheerful & went to bed all right. A little before day on Saturday morning Eng found his brother dead. He called for the family to get up, said he felt himself failing complaining of pains in his limbs & died about two hours after the other one. Chang the smallest one that died first had something like palsy about a year ago & I believe he got it again & died with it & as soon as he was dead the disease passed right into the other one. All the doctors went out Saturday morning prepared to cut them apart, but they were both dead when they got there. I heard somebody say that Chang had always been accustomed to liquor, but had not used any for a few days & perhaps caused a reaction. They had intended going out showing shortly had they lived. I wrote a letter to Edward Blum & he will probably put something in the paper about it. They were both real business men & had large families. . . . The Siamese twins were nicely dressed in black with slippers on I helped lift them in their coffin it was a strange sight. I must close with our best love I remain

Affectionately xxx
AUGUSTUS

It was a sight to see the people that came to my house to see me make the coffin. It was the greatest job I ever done. . . . I send you a drop of solder that dropped on the coffin as I was soldering them up yesterday.

On Monday, the very day that the tinsmith was writing his letter, Chang's daughter Nannie—aged twenty-six, seriously ill with the tuberculosis she had contracted from Eng's Katherine— was writing a more crucial and urgent letter to her older brother Christopher in San Francisco:

Dear Brother Cris

It is with deepest sorrow I write the sad news of poor papa's & Uncles death. They died on Saturday Morning the (17th) inst. Papa about a quarter before 5, o'clock & Uncle about 2 & a half hours after.

Papa took deep cold and it settled on his lungs eight days before he died. Dr. Bill told him he must stay in the house & take care of himself or he would have pneumonia he coughed awfully & could not lie down much. On thursday evening it was bitter cold & the Dr. was here & told them to remain here, but they would go, and that night he was very low, next day he coughed and was in much distress about his lungs seemed to breathe with great difficulty. They went to bed late friday night & rested a little—then they got up a while & set by the fire afterwards they lay down again & tried to rest between four & five—papa commenced coughing & congestion of the lungs come on & he died immediately, he called William but before he could get there and turn up the lamp he was gone. Uncle had been as well as usual all this time but when William lighted the lamp Uncle said William I feel mighty sick he—uncle did not know papa was dead—from that moment he seemed to suffer the most intense pain, calling on them to rub & pull his arms until life was extinct.

And now Cris comes the hardest the most awful part to be told—We dare not bury their bodies—but have put them in a tin coffin lined with wood & a wooden case outside and will today put them in the cellar at Uncles house until you, De Pat & Mont comes home—and then we fear they will not be safe. Dr. Joe says their bodies would not remain in the grave three nights if they were put there, that the best friends we have can be bought. (some we may think our friends may not be so) And he & Dr. Bill both said for one or two thousand Dollars almost any one would make an effort to secure their bodies. And for us to do this thing until the grown boys could get home. Cris will you come—do please All wish it—And I feel sure you will never get your property until you do come and besides, there is no one capable of managing the affairs here and times here will be awful until you do come for we fear that some one will go to Uncles house & do mischief—There is the most awful excitement in the Country that has ever been known—Dr. Joe says he has never known the like & that we may watch. On sunday they thought they would be buried and a Crowd such as has not met for any purpose lately met there and they could not clear the rooms sufficiently for the family's to go in and see them until they told them they would not be buried. Dr. Joe and Dr. Bill told Mary that there is no doubt but what a reward for the bodies has already been put out (*secretly*) & for us to try to watch & keep them until you and the boys from Uncles can come home. They say we never can keep them that some one will steal them from us. I could not tell you all they advise it would take too long besides I don't know that my letter will go to you. The excitement is certainly awful and Dr. Joe says the farther it goes the greater it gets. he leaves home for the North this Morning and he says he will write to us and advise us what to do to the best of his ability— Not that he expects to profit by it *but*, as a friend to both families—Now I will tell you what he says—In the first place if we could bury our dead, conscious that they would rest as we placed them, it would be just and proper, but we cannot do this, some paid demon would drag them from their resting place in less than three nights And when once gone we could not help ourselves, that they would make Merchandise of the bodies in spite of all we can do, or could do. In the next place he said—as it is entirely and wholely impossible for us to keep & guard them always; it would be no disgrace, show no low principle for the two families to accept any profits from their bodies they could—that *some* one *would* receive something— Why not their families and not strangers? Cris this looks & seems awful to me but the Drs. put it in such force to our reason & our minds that we do not know what to do about it; We await your arrival for we feel sure you will come, and they will try to guard and keep them safe until you can come which we hope will not be many weeks. Besides all this, R. S. Gilmer says from the nature & manner of papa's will we are not sure of this home of ours, that this Mrs. Doty in New York also has a will by which she *may* be able to turn us all out of the house & home and Mama is troubled about that. She is anxious that you should come home and wind up the affairs. Drs. Joe & Billy & Mr. R. S. Gilmer said you could do better than any one else.

Mary received your letter from San Francisco she will write you in a few days ... Cris come if you can & as soon as you can, & write to us if you are or are not coming. We may Telegraph to you.

Yours as Ever
N.A.B.

As Nannie had informed her brother, the tin coffin holding the bodies of the twins was buried in the cellar of Eng's house later that Monday. The coffin was carried downstairs into the cold basement, lowered into a shallow grave, and entirely covered on the top and sides with powdered charcoal two feet deep.

The warnings by the Drs. Hollingsworth that someone might try to steal the corpses to put them on exhibition were probably not unwarranted. Offers from Eastern Entrepreneurs to purchase the bodies of Chang and Eng were soon coming in to Adelaide and Sallie. One of them, from Brooklyn, New York, dated January 29, 1874, read:

Mrs. Kang & Ang,

We wish to negotiate with you about the Bodys of the twins. it is a Crase subject but we wish you to answer by Return Mail the lowest price Cash. Confidential on our part. You will oblige us Very Much.

Name your price. we would not think of proposing the subject but we think it will be for the Benefit for the Country as others may be so unfortunate.

We Remain Respectfully Yours
Rozell Horton.

There was much gossip in Mount Airy about the possibility that the Bunker widows might sell the bodies of their husbands for profit, and a correspondent of the New York *Herald* on his way to Mount Airy quickly learned of it and filed a story:

THE BODIES OF THE SIAMESE TWINS
AT THE DISPOSAL OF THE HIGHEST BIDDER

What the proposed final disposition of the bodies of the Siamese Twins is to be I am not informed, but report here says that they are to be embalmed and disposed of at an enormous price to some museum or medical college, or placed on exhibition at a sum equivalent to the value set upon them by the Mount Airy managers, who, of course, will realize a handsome percentage out of the transaction. All of this, however, is to be subject to the decision of the members of the families, who have been notified of the death of their parents, and are expected home at an early day.

No effort whatever was made to perform an operation on the ligament with regard to ascertaining whether there was an artery passing through it or not, as that would have materially interfered with prospective greenbacks, and present speculation would have been nipped in the bud. Embalmed and preserved as they are, the bodies of the twins will have a market value from which money can always be realized by those having possession of them. The ligament cut in the interest of science, the curiosity would be destroyed and consequently the separate dead bodies would be of no value.

While the selling of the bodies of her father and uncle continued to agitate Nannie Bunker, there was another matter referred to in her letter to her brother that also troubled her. Although a family friend, Robert Gilmer, had just read the last wills left behind by Chang and Eng, he had cautioned Nannie that there existed an earlier will in which Chang had given the bulk of his estate to a love of long ago, Catherine M. Bunker, now Mrs. Doty. The apprehensions of Nannie, and the other members of the twins' families, about this previous will proved to be groundless. Mrs. Doty never sought her outdated inheritance. The most recent wills in Gilmer's possession were the ones recognized and acted upon. Curiously, although both twins had had to be present at the signing of Eng's will in 1868, Chang did not sign his final will until 1871.

Eng's will, signed over five years before his death, read:

I Eng Bunker of the county of Surry and state of North Carolina being of sound mind and memory and knowing the uncertainty of all human events especially life do make and declare this to be my last will and testament to wit as follows.

First I do by this my last will and testament constitute and appoint my beloved wife Sally Ann Bunker my due and lawful executor who after paying all the necessary expenses of a decent burial for myself shall pay all my just and lawful debts out of my personal estate.

Item. I bequeath and devise to my wife Sally Ann Bunker on account of the love and tender affections I have for her all my lands to have, hold and enjoy during her natural life and should my beloved wife Sallie Ann Bunker die before my minor children become of age then it is my desire that the lands remain unsold in order that my minor children may enjoy the rents and profits of my lands and may have a house during their infancy and after the death of my wife and after my infant children shall come to age then the said lands may be equally divided among all my children.

Item. I will, bequeath and devise all my household and kitchen furniture and horses, cows, pigs and all cattle of whatsoever kind that is now on the farm. Also all farming utensils to my wife during her life and after her death should she die before my infant children come of age, it is my desire that the above named personal property remains for the benefit of my infant children and none of the above mentioned property be sold until after the death of my wife and until the minor children shall become of age.

Item. I will and bequeath all of my money that may be on hand or due the estate at my death to be divided among my children equally and it is further my desire that after the death of my wife and after my minor children shall become of age that all my property both real and personal be equally divided among all my children.

In testimony whereof I have here unto set my hand and seal this 27th day of November A.D. 1868.

ENG BUNKER

Chang's will, signed May 15, 1871, two years and eight months before his death, was similar to his brother's will. Chang left all his lands to his wife, or if she died before their children had come of age, then the lands were to be held to support his offspring and later divided among them. However, Chang's will differed from Eng's in one respect. He had made a special provision for two of his children:

"I will and bequeath that after my death all my personal property of whatsoever kind and descript shall be divided equally among all children and wife—except my two dumb children Louisa E. Bunker and Jesse L. Bunker who shall have five hundred dollars each more than any of the rest of my children on account of their affliction . . ."

In the days following the death of Chang and Eng, the frenzy of excitement generated by their demise persisted throughout Surry County, the state of North Carolina, and most parts of the United States. The same questions were being asked by everyone: What would happen to the bodies of Chang and Eng? What were the actual causes of their deaths? What did the famous ligament that bound them together really consist of?

The speculative answers to these questions were reflected in a front-page story in the New York *Herald*, written from Mount Airy and telegraphed from Greensboro on January 24, 1874, by a Manhattan reporter assigned to visit the scene and deliver a first-hand picture of what was going on. The *Herald* reporter arrived in Surry County five days after the twins had died. He began his interviews and investiga-

tions at once. The newspaper gave his long and detailed story a sensational play by headlining it in bold-
face type:

THE SIAMESE TWINS
A Herald Man at the
Hyphenated Brethren's Home
THE DEATHS OF CHANG AND ENG
What Was the Cause of
Death, Sympathy
or Shock?
"AND I MUST DIE TOO!"
Was There an Essentially Vital
Union Through the Ligament?
HOW THE BODIES LOOKED

The Siamese twins had so long become a part and
parcel of this community, and of whom it evinced
no small pride, as the twins, like any other natural
curiosity, gave it notoriety, brought visitors and
tourists to its hotels, added dignity to its standing as
a town and gave *éclat* to its society, that their totally unexpected deaths, on Saturday last, the 17th inst.,
produced a gloom from which the people here have
scarcely yet recovered. Upon the arrival of the
HERALD representative here yesterday this feeling
of regret was markedly observable in the tone and
manner in which every one, even the negroes, spoke
of the dead twins. For twenty-seven years they had
been residents of the county, were familiar and intimate with nearly every citizen in it, were universally beloved and respected, and, owing to their well
known hospitality and liberal spirit, their loss is just
now as universally regretted.

As he had neared his destination by buggy, the
Herald reporter wrote, a fog had begun to descend.
Out of the fog there materialized a man on horseback,
dressed in gray. As the rider drew closer, the reporter
stopped him.

"How far is it to Mount Airy?" the reporter asked.

"About five miles," the rider answered.

"Do you know if Dr. Hollingsworth is at home?"

"That is my name, sir. But there are two Dr. Hollingsworths; which of them do you want to see?"

"I want to see the one who attended the Siamese twins when they were living," the reporter said.

"Then I am the one. My brother, Dr. Joe Hollingsworth, who also assisted me, went North yesterday. My name is William Hollingsworth."

"How soon will you be back in town?" the reporter asked.

"Not till midnight," said Dr. Hollingsworth.

This information dismayed the reporter, since he had planned to leave Mount Airy at six o'clock the next morning in order to reach the Greensboro telegraph station by the following day. The reporter realized that his only opportunity to interview Dr. Hollingsworth might be right this minute on the road. Immediately, from his seat on the buggy, the reporter began to ask his questions, while the physician on horseback answered them. The reporter later wrote:

> Dr. Hollingsworth then explained that Chang had an attack of paralysis shortly after returning from Europe last year, that he had been suffering from pneumonia, or severe lung cold, for the past month and that he (the Doctor) believed that it was exposure before he had sufficiently recovered from this malady that precipitated his death. On Friday Eng was as well as usual—Chang not apparently very much worse. Eng was in excellent spirits and seemed remarkably cheerful and sprightly. Chang, on the other hand, from the debility caused by his paralysis and cold, together with a certain stupidity resulting from the use of too much stimulant, was fretful, sullen and snappish when spoken to, which of late was his accustomed conduct. All the family retired at the usual hour. Eng's wife and children slept up stairs; the Twins slept down stairs. It was five o'clock in the morning when one of Eng's sons heard, as he thought, a call from his Uncle Chang. Responding as quickly as possible, he came down stairs and going to the side of the bed upon which his Uncle Chang

lay found him lying, apparently in a deep sleep, but was startled by the ghastly and singular appearance of the features, which wore an expression of pain, if not agony, and were much darker than he had ever seen them before.

After a closer examination the boy discovered his uncle was dead, and uttering an oft-repeated cry of "Uncle Chang is dead!" alarmed the whole household, all of whom speedily came pouring into the room in their night dresses.

While the boy still believes it was his uncle's voice that called everybody else feels convinced that it must have been Eng, his father.

The tumult caused by the death of Chang, the hurry and noise in sending for the doctor and for Chang's wife and children, must have so terribly shocked Eng that his nervous system became completely prostrated, and he never uttered a word except the single expression heretofore reported in the HERALD—"And I must die, too."

It was two hours after Chang died, said Dr. Hollingsworth, that he had arrived on the scene, only to find Eng dead as well.

"How long do you think Eng had been dead when you arrived?" the reporter asked.

"Not more than ten or fifteen minutes."

"Do you think his death was caused by any vital connection or artery passing from one to the other through the ligament that united them?"

Dr. Hollingsworth's answer was firm. "I am confident that Eng's death was produced by no such cause."

"Do you not believe the existence of some such vital connection through the ligament?" the reporter persisted.

"I do not, because I have attended them when one was sick and the other was in good health, and when there was as much as twenty beats difference to the minute in their pulsation."

"What, then, in your opinion, caused Eng's death?"

"The great shock and terror inspired by such a

union with death," said Dr. Hollingsworth, "added to which was the belief which prevailed between them that when one died the other would. These combined to destroy his mental faculties and paralyze his physical energies, and he succumbed to the dread visitation."

"You do not think, then, that if the ligament had been severed his life would have been saved?"

"I do not," said the physician. "I rather think that any operation, unless performed immediately upon his discovery of Chang's death, would have hastened Eng's death."

"What appearance did they present at first after death?" the reporter inquired.

"Chang was a little discolored, but not much. Eng looked as natural as if he was asleep. In fact I thought he was sleeping until I ascertained that he was actually dead."

"Is their appearance much altered since?"

"Not materially," said Dr. Hollingsworth, impatient to leave.

"Have they been interred?"

"Well, only temporarily." Dr. Hollingsworth indicated he had to be on his way. "Good evening, sir," he said, and with that he rode off.

When the *Herald* reporter reached Mount Airy and learned that the Bunkers' residences were some miles out of town, he realized it was too late to attempt to interview the widows or children. Instead, he made inquiries about Chang and Eng's friends, and was finally directed to a close friend of the twins named Isaac Armfield, who had been at Eng's to help Sallie and Adelaide the day after the twins died. Isaac Armfield proved ready to cooperate with the visiting journalist.

The reporter, dissatisfied with Dr. Hollingsworth's opinion as to the cause of Eng's death, now decided to bring up the subject again. "Mr. Armfield, is it not your opinion that Eng died from the shock or fright occasioned by his brother's death?"

"No, sir, it is not," said Armfield with certainty. He had his own view of Eng's death, and now he voiced it fully. "I am as well satisfied that blood flowed from one to the other through that connecting ligament as that the same blood flows in my right and left arm."

"Then you think it was the death of Chang that precipitated the death of Eng?"

"Yes, sir. After Chang's death, the blood from Eng's body flowed into his, but there being no responsive vitality it would not flow back, so that Eng died from exhaustion and loss of blood, and not from any shock or fright."

"Why, then, does the Doctor persist in saying that it was from a shock or fright that Eng died?" the reporter wondered.

"I don't know," said Armfield, "but I heard Dr. Bill Hollingsworth say that he would rather have the bodies of the dead twins than the whole of Surry county."

"What appearance did the twins present after their death?"

"Chang was nearly black in the face and looked as if he had died in a fit or in great agony. Eng looked as if he had been asleep."

"Do you know whether Eng made any expression of pain before he died?"

"Yes," said Armfield. "I inquired particularly about that, and found that he called repeatedly to those around him to rub and pull his arms and legs, that he was cramped—a sure indication of loss of blood or that the circulation was impeded from some cause, and this confirms me in the opinion that the death of Chang superinduced that of Eng."

Satisfied with Isaac Armfield's theory about Eng's death, the *Herald* reporter decided to call it a night and get some sleep. But the next morning he was up early, determined to confront Dr. Hollingsworth once more, this time in the physician's office. Realizing that in their talk on the road, he had failed to identify himself as a journalist from New York, the reporter did so now as he sat down with the doctor. This information had an immediate inhibiting effect on the physician. As the reporter wrote later, "I found him more guarded in his expressions and very reticent in giving opinions."

Instead of leaving for Greensboro that morning to file his story as soon as possible, the reporter decided to stay on in Mount Airy and try to learn more about the activities that had occurred following the twins' deaths. Tramping around town, interviewing everyone and anyone who had known the twins, the reporter finally had the remaining information that he needed:

The living twins were quite a source of profit to several of the prominent men in Mount Airy, and why not now turn the dead bodies to some account in the shape of greenbacks? Thus it was that on Saturday, the day on which the twins died, a consultation was held by these gentlemen, who had been connected in various capacities with the families of the deceased, at which it was decided that it would be unwise, injudicious and impolitic to bury the twins at the present time, for various and sundry considerations. This much, and more, perhaps, agreed upon, the wives of the twins were taken into the conference, and they were soon won over to the plausible and prospectively profitable propositions of the Mount Airy friends of the family.

On the following day (Sunday) a large crowd of sympathizing friends and acquaintances of the twins' families assembled at the residence of Eng, where the dead were laid out, in the anticipation of attending the funeral. A clergyman also put in an appearance to perform the last sad rites of Christianity over the bodies of the respected deceased. Contrary to the general expectation, however, no funeral took place, the assembled multitude being informed that it was postponed in deference to the wishes of the members of the families who were at home. Several of the sons of Chang are absent, and some of the daughters of both, and it was given out that they were to be consulted before a final disposition of the bodies would be agreed upon. In the meantime something had to be done with the bodies, and, with a celerity that was remarkable, all the utensils of temporary interment were forthcoming. . . .

Here, in a civilized land, were two mysterious deaths, and yet no inquest was held. I asked again and again why the Coroner had not been notified and why a post-mortem examination had not been held, and the general reply was that nobody considered it necessary, as the doctor had satisfactorily explained to the public and the families of the deceased the cause of the deaths. Thus the matter rests in mystery, in order to afford interested parties an opportunity to either sell or otherwise dispose of the bodies.

During their lifetime the twins belonged to no religious denomination and rarely attended divine service, nor was there any clergyman sufficiently intimate with them to have any knowledge of their religious views. One of their wives is a member of the Baptist Church, the other of the Society of Friends, the children being nearly all Baptists. One of the daughters of Chang, I was told, was highly incensed at the boxing up process performed on the dead body of her parent and uncle and the denial of Christian buried to them, and several of the junior members of the family were vehement in their expressions of indignation at the disgraceful course pursued by their Mount Airy friends and their own mothers.

On the very same day the *Herald* reporter had sent his detailed story to New York from Greensboro, he came across a second story about the Siamese Twins. It gave some clue as to what was going on behind the scenes in the disposition of the twins' bodies. The reporter filed that story, too:

Upon my arrival here this evening from Mount Airy I was informed, on the most authentic authority, that Dr. Joe Hollingsworth, while *enroute* for the North, stated here that his mission there was to dispose of the dead bodies of the twins on the most favorable terms he could negotiate. This accounts for the veil of mystery which has been thrown over the deaths of the twins and furnishes the clew to the object in suppressing the real cause of the death of Eng, by attributing it to the shock or fright occasioned by Chang's death.

The sum asked for the privilege of a post-mortem is stated to be $8,000 or $10,000.

The rumor that the Bunker widows were actually bargaining to sell off the corpses of their husbands to the highest bidder was widely accepted for many weeks. As far away as London, *The Lancet* was stating that while the widows were against an autopsy, they were ready to sell their husbands' bodies for $8,000 to $10,000 to competing medical men or showmen for the purposes of autopsy or exhibition. All of this was later proved completely untrue.

What was true was that a group of eminent surgeons in Philadelphia, in the interests of science, had approached Adelaide and Sallie Bunker in an effort to persuade them to permit an autopsy. An exchange of money in return for a postmortem was never suggested by the physicians and never demanded by the widows.

This effort to examine the bodies all began with one man—Dr. William H. Pancoast, son of a renowned surgeon and himself a professor of general, descriptive, and surgical anatomy at Jefferson Medical College in Philadelphia.

On learning of the twins' death, as Dr. Pancoast later recalled, his interest as well as that of his colleagues was "excited . . . as to what might be the nature of this connecting band" and he held "a hope that a postmortem examination would be made to investigate its structure, so as to decide whether or not they could have been safely separated. It was held to be a duty to science and humanity, that the family of the deceased should permit an autopsy."

Moreover, Dr. Pancoast felt that Chang and Eng owed something to the medical profession worldwide, and their families should be aware of this. Dr. Pancoast believed that for years the twins had used the leading physicians in America, England, and Europe to obtain free examinations and advice (mainly for publicity purposes, Dr. Pancoast cynically contended), and now it was time that the world of medicine should be paid back.

The fact that the precious bodies had not been embalmed appalled Dr. Pancoast, and perhaps this more than anything else provoked him to act.

"In conversation with some of my present colleagues of the faculty of the Jefferson Medical College," he said, "it was thought advisable to make inquiry at Mount Airy, the home of the twins, distant about 400 miles. . . . I telegraphed to the Mayor of Greensborough (that city being the nearest point of telegraphic connection to Mount Airy), by the aid and through the courtesy of Mr. Wm. S. Stokley, Mayor of this city, and General Henry H. Bingham. I inquired if a post-mortem examination had been made, and, if not, if one would be permitted; offering the use of the anatomical rooms of the Jefferson Medical College for that purpose, and my own services in making an autopsy. Should the family not permit the bodies to be removed, I volunteered to go to Mount Airy to make the examination."

When the mayor of Greensboro received Dr. Pancoast's telegram—actually signed by Mayor Stokley of Philadelphia—he felt that he could do nothing to help. He wired back that he had "neither knowledge nor power in the matter." Immediately after this, Dr. Joe Hollingsworth arrived in Greensboro on his way North. Somebody, knowing that Dr. Hollingsworth had been the twins' physician, arranged for him to see the telegram signed by Mayor Stokley on Dr. Pancoast's behalf. At once, Dr. Hollingsworth decided to detour to Philadelphia. He addressed a telegram to Mayor Stokley: "Inform Dr. Pancoast that I shall be in Philadelphia to-morrow night at the American Hotel. I attended the Siamese Twins."

In Philadelphia, word of Dr. Hollingsworth's visit quickly leaked to the newspapers. The Philadelphia *Press* ran the following on January 22, 1874:

Dr. Joseph Hollinsworth, of Mount Airy, North Carolina, at one time family physician to the Siamese twins, has arrived in this city. His object in coming here is to consult with Dr. Wm. H. Pancoast, demonstrator of anatomy, Jefferson Medical College, relative to a post mortem examination of the bodies of the twins. Dr. Hollinsworth over two years ago attended the twins, but since that time has given them no medical advice. They lived in an out of the way place, and he was not present when either died. His brother, also a physician, was there after Eng died. . . .

Dr. Hollinsworth saw the family soon after the death of the twins. He says the wives are not willing for a post mortem examination.—They want first to consult the children, who live in various portions of the State. The bodies are now buried beneath their house, but are in a state of preservation. They are being guarded by the family . . .

While inaccurate in its spelling of Hollingsworth's name and about his relationship with the twins, the account was correct in one respect. Dr. Hollingsworth had indeed arrived in Philadelphia and was ready to meet Dr. Pancoast on this Friday evening.

Later in the evening Dr. Hollingsworth called upon Dr. Pancoast at his house at 11th and Walnut Streets. Also attending the initial meeting was Professor S. D. Gross, Pancoast's superior on the faculty.

There are two versions of what occurred in that meeting. Although the twins' families always insisted they had never wanted money for the bodies, one Philadelphia newspaper stated that Dr. Hollingsworth had asked Dr. Pancoast and Dr. Gross for $10,000. According to this account:

"Your correspondent waited upon the doctor this evening at the American Hotel, and was informed by that gentleman (Dr. Hollingsworth) that the proposition had been made to the faculty, but they, considering the figure too large, were negotiating with the faculty of a New York college relative to a joint contribution to a sum necessary for the purchase. . . . The doctor also said that as the families of the twins were averse to any mutilation of the bodies, he thought that they could hardly be induced to allow the remains to be embalmed. . . . Since the families are not in affluent circumstances they might conclude to allow a large pecuniary consideration to alter their present decision."

Writing of this same meeting, the authoritative *Philadelphia Medical Times* said simply that "a letter was written to the wives of the twins, proposing that Dr. Pancoast should come on to embalm and examine the bodies."

The letter to Adelaide and Sallie was written by Dr. Joe Hollingsworth, and sent to his brother with a request that Dr. Bill deliver it to the widows and discuss it with them. While they awaited a reply, several more meetings were held, with other members of the College of Physicians in attendance. It was agreed that if the widows gave their consent, an informal commission consisting of Dr. Pancoast, Dr. Harrison Allen, a professor of comparative anatomy at the University of Pennsylvania, and Dr. Thomas H. Andrews, on the staff of Jefferson Medical College, would visit Mount Airy. So eager were the doctors to make the trip that they were prepared to pay their own expenses.

Now began a period of waiting for a decision from Adelaide and Sallie. On January 26, a Philadelphia newspaper reported:

"The letter that was expected from Dr. Wm. Hollingsworth of Mount Airy, N.C., has not been received, but Dr. Joseph Hollingsworth and Joseph [*sic*] Pancoast of Jefferson Medical College expect it to arrive in a day or so. The entire particulars as to the designs of the twins' families relative to Chang and Eng's bodies will at that time be known. Telegrams and letters are reaching Dr. Pancoast from all parts of the country from leading scientists asking for new facts about the autopsy, some of them stating that they will give financial assistance if necessary to carry the examination through successfully."

Almost a week passed before the matter was resolved. Apparently, in Mount Airy, Dr. William Hollingsworth's influence on Adelaide and Sallie was sufficient to carry the day.

The commission was invited to come to Mount Airy.

On Thursday night, January 29, the commission parted company with Dr. Joe Hollingsworth, who promised them that his brother would meet them in Mount Airy. He himself continued his journey north.

The *Philadelphia Medical Times* shortly after reported on the events that happened next:

> The Commission arrived at Mt. Airy on the evening of Saturday, January 31, and proceeded to the residence of Eng the following morning, in company with a photographer and Dr. William Hollingsworth, who is the family physician in the absence of Dr. Joseph Hollingsworth. The widows of the twins received the Commission hospitably, and a conference was at once entered into, at which the "Mistresses" Bunker, the Commission, Dr. Hollingsworth, and the widows' legal adviser [Robert S. Gilmer] were present. It was then agreed that, under consideration of embalming the bodies of the twins, permission would be granted to exhume and examine the structures distinguishing them, provided that no incisions should be made which would impair the external surface of the band. Subsequently it was agreed that limited incisions would be allowed on the posterior surface of the band.

The commission members quickly saw that the conditions in Eng's house were not conducive to a thorough autopsy. They pleaded with Adelaide and Sallie to permit them, after embalming was completed, to send the bodies to Philadelphia, where Dr. Pancoast could perform the autopsy under optimum conditions in the Mütter Museum of the College of Physicians. Adelaide and Sallie were finally convinced.

"We succeeded in inducing the family to trust us with the bodies," said Dr. Pancoast, "under a written agreement which engaged Dr. Allen and myself to return them to such agent or agents as the family should select. This gave us permission to make such post-mortem examination as would not disfigure the cadavers, and to examine the strange band that united them, on what was called its posterior part, but in no way to deface it in front, nor to divide it asunder."

The *Philadelphia Medical Times* elaborated further on the agreement and what followed in Eng's house:

An agreement in writing was then drawn up, expressing the above restrictions, but extending authority to the Commission to remove the bodies to Philadelphia, provided that they be kept there in a fire-proof building, and held subject to the commands of the families when informed of the completion of the embalming process.

The object of the visit of the Commission, having been noised about the country, had attracted a crowd of curious people, who were willing enough to give the necessary aid in exhuming the bodies. . . . The bodies were buried in the cellar of Eng's house, in a shallow grave, which had been covered with tumulus of powdered charcoal. This being removed revealed several planks covering an outer wooden box, which, in turn, enclosed a tin encasement to the coffin. After unsoldering the tin box, the coffin was carried to the second floor of the house, to a large chamber. The lid was unscrewed, and the object of the search of the Commission was exposed to view. It was certainly an anxious moment. Fifteen days had elapsed since death, and no preservative had been employed. It was an agreeable surprise, therefore, that no odor of decomposition escaped into the room, and that the features gave no evidence of impending decay. On the contrary, the face of Eng was that of one sleeping; and the only unfavorable appearance in Chang was a slight lividity of the lips and a purplish discoloration about the ears. The widows at this point entered the room, and, amid the respectful silence of all present, took a last look at the remains.

Once Dr. Pancoast and his colleagues were alone again, they went efficiently about their business. Chang and Eng were stripped of their clothing and their bodies propped to standing position, while the photographer took full-length pictures of their naked bodies and close-ups of the connecting ligament. Since the day was overcast and the light from outdoors poor, the picture-taking process went on for some time. During this, Dr. Andrews jotted notes, some typical ones reading:

"*Examination made Sunday, February 1, 1874, fifteen days and eight hours after the death of Chang.*

"The bodies were found in the coffin in a good state of preservation: there was a slight cadaveric odor about Chang . . .

"The fingers of [Chang's] right hand—the paralyzed side—were forcibly flexed, although *rigor mortis* was absent . . .

"In both subjects the hair of the head was gray.

"On *the pubis* of each subject the hair of the *left side* was *gray*, that of the *right side, black*."

With the photography done, the moment had come to start embalming the bodies. Dr. Pancoast made lengthy incisions in the body of each twin, starting at the outer side of the median line of the abdomen.

"We first injected the bodies with a solution of chloride of zinc, which I took with me, of the ordinary strength that I have been in the habit of using for the preservation of subjects for dissection," recalled Dr. Pancoast. "We opened the right primitive iliac artery of Eng, and the left one of Chang, injecting the antiseptic fluid upwards and downwards, as the bodies lay before us in their natural or customary recumbent position."

After the embalming process was finished, Dr. Pancoast continued his incisions "upward and inward towards the band." Superficial examination of the connecting band showed that it was too complex in structure to be studied further in these nonmedical surroundings. The physicians unanimously agreed that they had gone as far as they could go in Eng's house, and that their autopsy would have to be resumed in Philadelphia.

The incisions in each body were carefully sewed

up. The bodies of Chang and Eng were once more clothed in their black suits and slippers and lifted back into their walnut casket. After reassuring Adelaide and Sallie, and saying farewell to them, the members of the commission had the coffin loaded onto a wagon, and then they followed it to Mount Airy. There, the coffin was placed in the tin box again, and the lid was carefully resoldered.

The doubly enclosed bodies were driven to Salem, North Carolina, and from there were shipped by express to the Mütter Museum of the College of Physicians in Philadelphia. Drs. Pancoast, Allen, and Andrews then started for Philadelphia themselves, returning to the city on February 5, a week after they had left it.

Three days later, the bodies of Chang and Eng were delivered to the Mütter Museum, where they were locked up and kept under guard. That evening a meeting of the College of Physicians was called. The commission members were heartily congratulated, the expenses for their trip reimbursed, and an appropriation of $350 was voted to pay for the photographs and plaster casts of the twins which would be kept by the museum.

On Tuesday, February 10, the bodies of Chang and Eng were once more removed from their casket, disrobed, and placed on operating tables. Dr. William Pancoast directed the official autopsy. This surgery, it was hoped, would reveal to a waiting world the nature of the ligament that had joined the twins for sixty-three years, would disclose the chances they might have had to survive separation, and would provide better understanding of their lives and deaths.

Eight days later, on Wednesday, February 18, in the Hall of the College of Physicians, the leading surgeons and medical professors gathered to hear reports of the autopsy from Dr. William Pancoast and Dr. Harrison Allen. The only reporter permitted inside was a representative of the *Philadelphia Medical Times*.

Dr. Pancoast led off. When he had given his report, Dr. Allen gave a more minute anatomical description, demonstrating his points by touching the bodies laid out before him. After they spoke, the audience was allowed to examine the bodies for themselves.

As to the actual composition of the band, and the must disputed question whether the twins' livers intruded into it, Dr. Pancoast had this to say:

> The livers we have found to approximate each other and to push through the respective peritoneal openings into the band. We extended our incisions to the margin of the band in front. By placing my hand in the peritoneal cavity of Eng and my colleague placing his hand in the peritoneal cavity of Chang, we pushed before us processes of peritoneum, which ran on to the median line of the band; and we could feel our fingers in the lower portion of the band, behind the median line, with a distinct layer of peritoneum between them, demonstrating at once the prolongation of the peritoneum into the band, and the complete separation of one peritoneal cavity from the other at this median line.

> . . . the surgical anatomy of the band consists in the skin and fascia which cover it, the two separate peritoneal pouches which meet in the middle, the large peritoneal pouch, the vascular connection, to whatever extent they may exist between the two portal circulations, and the remains of the hypogastric arteries in the lower portion of the band. Thus the main difficulty in any operation for section of the band would seem to be in regard to the peritoneal processes and the portal circulation.

Dr. Allen noted that Chang's half of the band was weaker, in keeping with his general condition:

> You notice that the tissues [of Eng] are well supplied with fat; and this condition is very plainly in contrast with that of Chang. Eng's side of the band is well-nourished; Chang's end of the band presents an entirely different aspect. Chang was an invalid, and the weaker half of this organism, with less strength in the abdominal walls, and in every way less tissue, than was possessed by Eng. You can mark that distinction very plainly in the two halves of the band, prov-

ing, if we had no other means of proof, that there could not be any very intimate communication of the vessels between the two.

The *Philadelphia Medical Times* reported on the next day's findings:

> On Thursday, February 19, the Commission continued the autopsy upon the Siamese Twins, and reported some important discoveries. They found that the two livers, which were supposed to be joined only by blood-vessels, were one body; the parenchymatous tissue being seemingly continuous between them.
>
> The so-called *tract of portal continuity* is apparently liver-tissue, but the point has not yet been proven by microscopic examination. It will be remembered that Chang was said to be possessed of one more pouch than Eng. When the liver was removed, however, an upper hepatic pouch was found also proceeding from Eng, so that the band contained four pouches of peritoneum, besides liver-tissue. These disclosures show that any attempt during life to separate the twins would in all probability have proved fatal.

Medical opinion, then, was unanimous in its answer to the question "Could the twins have been divided?" The answer was a flat no, they could not have been divided.

The reasons for this were best summed up in Dr. Pancoast's written report, completed a year after his verbal autopsy report:

> As far as I can learn, it was the general opinion of our profession, both in Europe and America, that any of the proposed methods of section of the band would have involved great risk to life; that upon moral and even physical considerations, it would have been well if the twins could have been separated; but that, upon such information as could be obtained of the anatomy of the band, it was thought to contain structures of such vital importance that the twins'

lives would unquestionably have been endangered from shock and subsequent inflammation. . . .

The result of this autopsy must, however, in the case of any similar monster, in connection with the autopsies of analogous cases, not only bring to the surgeon's consideration as parts likely to be severed, the peritoneum and cartilages, and some arteries and nerves of lesser importance, but must also suggest the possibility of danger from the presence of the liver, if there be but one doing duty for both bodies, or from some connection between separate livers, and also from the existence of connected or united diaphragms.

As far as I have been able to find opinions expressed in regard to the propriety of an operation, it was not the fear of vascularity of the band that impressed surgeons with the danger of the procedure, but the known risk of shock and inflammation attendant upon opening or cutting into the peritoneal cavity; and, in addition, the uncertainty as to the constituents of the band, and the fear lest some additional and unforeseen complication might occur in the operation, which would increase the risk already recognized.

The post-mortem examination has revealed that the vascularity of the band would have been no obstacle, and that even the circulation in the tract of union of the livers was slight. . . . But cutting through the united diaphragms would have made an additional and grave complication, and the shock to the sympathetic nervous system would have been serious. In addition to peritonitis, diaphragmitis might have occurred, with inflammation extending to the pericardium and pleura, and a new disturbance to the heart might thus have been added to the original shock. . . .

From a consideration of the anatomical structure of the band, as described and illustrated, I think that the surgeons who refused to operate upon the Siamese twins, in their adult state, were right in their decision. I do not believe it would be judicious to operate by section of the band upon any other such exactly similar adult monstrosity, should it present

itself. The experiment of applying a strong ligature
around the band, when the idea was under discussion
of cutting through it by the progressive ulceration
caused in this way, proved that it could not be done
safely, as the pressure of the ligature caused so much
sickness and nervous impression that it had to be
removed. This, I think, is proof of the greater dangers which would have been produced by any violent
separation. Apart from such experiments, the twins
could easily endure those of a much rougher character. For instance, when returning from Europe,
they allowed themselves to be pulled about the deck
of the vessel by a rope passed around the band. . . .

In regard to the question of separating the dead
brother from the living, I think it should have been
done, and that it would have been the part of wisdom
in Eng, when he found his brother so ill, to have engaged his surgeon to remain constantly at his house.
It would have given him a chance for his life, and as
the section would have been made through the dead
parts of the band on Chang's side, the peritoneal
cavity of Eng need not have been opened. Of course
the result would have been uncertain, but I have the
wish that it had been essayed. . . .

In concluding the surgical consideration of the
uniting band of the Siamese twins, I believe that
every practical surgeon will coincide in the opinion:—

I. That as a necessary deduction from the anatomical demonstration of its constituent parts, no
operation of section of the band, for the purpose of
separating the twins in adult life, could have been
performed and their lives preserved.

II. That it would have been judicious surgery,
upon the death of Chang, to have at once applied a
strong ligature around the band, as far as possible
from the body of Eng, and then to have cut through
the band between the ligature and the body of
Chang.

III. That whether or not the operation would have
been successful in the childhood of the twins, is prob-
lematical; but that it would have been the part of
wisdom and humanity to have made the effort, using

all the precautions employed by Dr. Fatio in his case in 1689, with such additional ones as might have been suggested.

As to the cause of their deaths, Dr. Pancoast and Dr. Allen shared the opinion that Chang had died of a cerebral clot, and Eng had died of sheer fright. In Dr. Allen's "Autopsy Report," he stated:

> With reference to the cause of death of the Siamese twins it may be briefly said that, in consequence of the restrictions by which we are bound, no examination of the brains was made. It cannot, therefore, be proved that the cause of Chang's death was a cerebral clot, although such an opinion, from the suddenness of death, preceded as it was by hemiplegia and an immediate engorgement of the left lung, is tenable. Eng died, in all probability, in a state of syncope induced by fright—a view which the over-distended bladder and retraction of the right testicle would appear to corroborate.

To this, Dr. Pancoast added: "As to the question, 'What caused Eng's death?' I am not able to tell. The post-mortem which has been made does not show the condition of his lungs. Probably the valves of his heart were in a disorganized condition, and probably also the shock upon that weakened organ caused death."

A different speculation as to the cause of Eng's death was ventured by a third physician, Dr. Summerell:

> The actual work of autopsy and dissection was assigned to a man by the name of Nash. . . . He had always found it true that the *arteries* of a dead body were completely empty of blood—and that the veins were more or less filled with it. This is a well known fact. In making the dissection in this instance, he noted that the vein of No. 1 (that died) were full of blood—that his *arteries* contained some blood—that the arteries of No. 2 contained a small amount of blood—that *his* veins contained less than the amount to be expected.

The anatomicists present, after examining the dissection, formulated a report on their anatomical findings—but were at a loss to pronounce the cause of No. 2's death. After much learned discussion on their part, Nash, who was a very rough but also quite privileged character broke in on their conversation, and bluntly informed them that there was no room for discussion—that the cause for No. 2's death was plain—that he *bled to death*. There being direct arterial connections between the two, when No. 1's blood flowed into his veins after death—a vaccum occurred in his arteries—this immediately caused a flux from the arteries of No. 2—which soon caused his death also—practically from hemorrhage.

But most likely, Dr. Allen's opinion was the correct one: On finding himself attached to a dead brother, Eng had literally been scared to death.

Besides the fascination which the autopsy held for the medical profession, the public interest was tremendous. When the doctors decided to publish their findings in the *Philadelphia Medical Times* exclusively, the newspapers were enraged. The Philadelphia *Times* ran a story about the twins many years later, in which it described the newspaper feud:

"This put the newspaper men on their mettle. C. Cathcart Taylor, then city editor of the *Press*, performed some marvels of enterprise in a vain effort to capture the precious document. One of the morning newspapers did obtain possession of the report, and Taylor in his chagrin, published two columns of denunciation in the *Press* next day, claiming that the doctors had sold the document for cash. But after all the autopsy report was not worth all the fuss. It described the condition of affairs the doctors found, but no conclusion was reached as to whether or not the twins could have survived a separation by the knife."

Meanwhile, the news of the twins' death had generated a convulsion of false stories about their lives. For example, the Baltimore *Sun* mangled the stories of their courtship and marriage, said that they had fought all the time, and that their wives had been English chambermaids.

Zacharias Haynes, Chang's deaf son-in-law (married to Louise), was so furious at the Baltimore newspaper that he wrote an angry letter which appeared on February 14 in a Raleigh, North Carolina, paper. His reply to the *Sun* read in part:

Editor of the Daily News: Please allow me space in the columns of your paper to correct some malicious falsehoods, which appeared in the correspondence column of the Baltimore *Sun*, and were copied by several other papers, in relation to the late Siamese twins. I feel totally incapable of giving the intelligent writer such a reply as the falsehoods demand. . . .

They were married in 1843, five miles from Wilkesboro, N.C., to ladies native of Wilkes county, N.C., and not to chamber maids from England; so there is not a word of truth put forth in the assertions of the *Sun* concerning their courtship and marriage. . . .

They were very even-tempered themselves, and did not seem to be quarrelsome with each other, and no one but a donkey would, for a moment give credit to the atrocious lies concerning the fight in Barnum's museum. . . .

The correspondent of the *Sun* charges them with being so rapacious that it prevented showmen from making any proposals to them. This is utterly untrue. They never exacted anything great from their employers, and then if either side was favored their employers were the ones. More than one instance has occurred where their employers were unsuccessful, through bad management or otherwise. Then they would not exact their full wages. They were considered by all who knew them to be generous-hearted men, and the good people of Surry county will testify to this fact.

Z.W.H.

Preceding the autopsy, Chang's son Christopher had left San Francisco for Mount Airy. Reaching home and finding the bodies gone, he went on to Philadelphia, where he met Eng's son Stephen.

Like Zacharias Haynes, both sons were infuriated by the rumors and scandal which surrounded their fathers' deaths, and were determined to return the bodies to North Carolina and give them a decent burial. The Philadelphia *Press* wrote:

> The sons deny the report that the family intend to make speculation of the remains by exhibition. They evince much filial feeling on this point, and it is to be hoped that the correction of the report may be as wide as the publication of the false statement has been. So deeply do they feel in the matter that they inquired anxiously if the embalming process could not be undone and the bodies allowed peacefully to decay, and on being assured the process could not be reversed, and decomposition must now be a very slow process, they expressed evident regret.
>
> They also spoke strongly about the report that the commission went South with a large sum of money, and that the transfer was the result of a business bargain with the widows of the twins. They said this report was generally credited in their section, and that all the family could not disabuse the minds of friends and neighbors on the subject. They desired Drs. Pancoast and Allen to give them a formal written denial of this rumor, to be shown to the people, and, if necessary, to be published; which request, of course, the commission at once complied with.

Another newspaper wrote of Christopher: "He demanded the return of the bodies. His attitude was decidedly unfriendly, and the College of Surgeons, really having little further use for the bodies, consented to his demand that they be returned to North Carolina for burial."

Finally, it was arranged for the bodies to be sent by Adam's Express to Salem, North Carolina.

Having satisfied the curiosity of the medical profession, Chang and Eng were brought back to their home soil at last—but not in their entirety. Dr. Allen received this letter, probably from Christopher and Stephen, dated April 1, 1874:

Dr. Allen

Enclosed you will find the receipt for bringing the bodies of Papa & Uncle from Salem to our home. You will please send the money by post-office order.

My Mother and Aunt was very sorry that we did not bring the lungs & entrals of our Fathers with the bodies home, and as we did not bring them, you can keep them until further orders from the families.

Respectfully G R [*sic*] & S D Bunker

While the Mütter Museum still has the joined livers of the twins preserved in formalin, it is not known what became of the "lungs & entrals."

When the bodies of the twins arrived in North Carolina, it was not considered safe to bury them immediately owing to the danger from graverobbers. A local newspaper reported: "For a year they were kept in the cellar of [Eng's] house, the casket covered with charcoal and heavily guarded by the family day and night. After a year they were buried on the lawn near [Chang's] house."

In 1897, a mere twenty-three years after their deaths, the American Medical Association declared that had the twins been alive then, they could have been safely separated:

"Today, as was clearly revealed in a number of addresses made before the recent gathering in this city [Philadelphia] of the American Medical Association, a different verdict would be reached by reason more especially of the revelations regarding the use of antiseptics in surgery made by Lister. Among the physicians who went to Mt. Airy, North Carolina, to bring the dual body of the Siamese monstrosity to this city and who assisted in the subsequent autopsy was Dr. Thomas H. Andrews, now police surgeon of Philadelphia. He who joined in the decision of Dr. Pancoast twenty-three years ago now unhesitatingly declares that Chang and Eng could have been separated, were they alive at the present time, without endangering the life of either."

Perhaps Adelaide and the many children who still survived heard of this new opinion. One wonders what they thought and felt knowing that had Chang and Eng lived on after such an operation, they might have been "normal" husbands and fathers.

Since the deaths of Chang and Eng, there has been an average of five conjoined twins born somewhere in the world annually. Most have been stillborn or have died shortly after birth. Of the survivors—and only about three hundred conjoined twins in all history have lived beyond a few days—many have been successfully separated. Some of these were joined in a manner similar to that of Chang and Eng, by a ligament or band, while others were connected in more complicated and often bizarre ways.

One of the first recorded modern cases of Siamese twins who at least briefly survived surgical separation were the Orissa sisters, Radica and Doadica, born in a village in India in 1889, and imprisoned for being embodiments of the devil. When one of them contracted tuberculosis, a French surgeon separated them. Doadica died immediately, but Radica survived, if only for a short time.

The first such twins to be separated and live for a year or more were a pair of sisters, Nancy and Ellen, born in Cleveland, Ohio, and joined at their breastbones by a one-and-a-half-inch band. They were successfully separated in 1952. A year later, Carolyn and Catherine Mouton, with connected lower intestines and joined at their lower spines, were successfully cut apart by a team of fifteen doctors in New Orleans. In March 1955, a pair of two-year-old conjoined twins born in Siam (Thailand), Prisna and Napit Atkinson, were successfully separated in Chicago.

In 1965, two six-year-old Italian girls, Giuseppina and Maria Santina Foglia, joined at the base of their spines, were separated in Turin. After the operation, Giuseppina asked, "Is it really me? Am I really myself?" And then she said to her sister, "You're so far away!"

In September 1974, a twenty-five-member surgical team at Children's Hospital in Philadelphia undertook the separation of two sisters from the Dominican Republic, Clara and Altagracia Rodriguez, who were connected at their abdomens and pelvic areas. After a ten-and-a-half-hour operation, the girls were successfully severed, and remain healthy and independent.

In 1976, a pair of Wichita, Kansas, girls, who shared a liver as had Chang and Eng, survived a four-hour operation in which the doctors were able to divide the common organ and give each child a separate functioning liver.

Had these surgical feats been possible in 1811, when Chang and Eng were born, there would not exist today the term "Siamese twins," and the brothers would have been two little-known duck-egg merchants in Siam, rather than the rare and quixotic caprice of Mother Nature that gave the world six decades of awe and wonder.

▸◂ ◂▸◂ ◂▸◂

Adelaide and Sallie Bunker had been married thirty-one years when Chang and Eng died.

In the years their husbands had been with them, the sisters had been very much in the limelight, constantly publicized, regularly visited by the press and curiosity-seekers. With their widowhood most of that public interest diminished, and the sisters retreated into privacy. They would not receive the press or strangers, and lived in relative seclusion.

But Adelaide and Sallie were not alone in the small, close-knit community of Mount Airy, North Carolina. They had numerous friends and neighbors who were helpful. Above all, they had their large families. Eight of Adelaide's ten children were alive during many of her years without Chang. And seven of Sallie's eleven children were alive during her years without Eng.

In the early period of their widowhood, Adelaide and Sallie still had young children to raise and educate. Two of Sallie's seven children were only fourteen and eight, and four of Adelaide's eight were sixteen, twelve, ten, and five years old. Adelaide was the one who believed in education, and she saw to it that her youngsters, as well as Sallie's, attended the one-room log cabin schoolhouse the twins had established on the dividing line between their farm and the Greenwood farm. Also, Adelaide and Sallie kept up their interest in the nearby White Plains Baptist Church, which their husbands had helped build on land they had donated. Neither sister was wealthy, but both had been left financially secure. Actually, Adelaide was much the better off of the sisters, because she had encouraged Chang to take more land and fewer slaves when the twins divided up their assets.

Sallie survived eighteen years as Eng's widow. On April 29, 1892, when Benjamin Harrison was starting his fourth year as President of the United States, Sallie died at the age of seventy. She is not buried beside her husband, as is commonly believed, but for some unknown reason still rests on Eng's farm beneath a gravestone that is now hard to find.

Adelaide remained the sole survivor of the original foursome. Her son Patrick would long after remember her as "a handsome woman and a fine Christian," and he thought she had a "wonderfully good disposition." A friend would remember her as being "cute.'" Only one tragedy marred these years. In 1909, her deaf son, Jesse, aged forty-eight, was killed by a bolt of lightning.

In all, Adelaide lived forty-three years without Chang. Often, from the window of the downstairs parlor, she would gaze out at the grave of Chang and Eng in the front yard beside the large holly tree. The world beyond was rapidly changing, and still Adelaide lived on. President Woodrow Wilson was in the White House, and the First World War was long since under way. Little more than six weeks after the United

States entered that war against the kaiser's Germany, on May 21, 1917, Adelaide Bunker died. Her long obituary in the local newspaper read, in part:

Mrs. Adelaide Bunker, widow of Chang, one of the Siamese Twins, died at her home three miles southwest of this city last Monday morning at 6:30 o'clock. Had she lived till October she would have attained the great age of 94. She had been in declining health for several years, though, up to two or three years ago, she continued to have a supervision over the household duties. She lived to a great age and died because her physical powers were exhausted. It could not be said that she died of disease. . . .

Mrs. Bunker was the grandmother of 39 living grandchildren, some are probably dead. There are 18 living great grandchildren.

Those who knew her speak of her as a good woman. She was a good neighbor, for 65 years a loyal and consistent member of White Plains Baptist church, but her true womanly character was shown in her devotion and loyalty to her children.

When it was time to bury Adelaide, one of her sons-in-law, Caleb Hill Haynes, who had married her daughter Margaret Elizabeth, suggested that she be laid to rest in the graveyard of the White Plains Baptist Church, since the church had meant so much to her for most of her life. Further, Haynes suggested, since Chang's farm, where the twins were buried, could one day become someone else's property, it might be well to disinter Chang and Eng and rebury them in the church graveyard with Adelaide. The family members agreed to these proposals.

And so, in May 1917, the walnut coffin containing the joined bodies of Chang and Eng was unearthed and lifted out of the plot beside the holly tree on the front lawn of Chang's house. Apparently, the bodies of the twins were briefly exposed to sight, for one witness recalled that "when they were dug up to be reburied there were very few bones—a little hair—and a shoe heel with nails in it." Then the coffin was closed.

As the coffin was being moved from Chang's property to the White Plains Baptist Church cemetery, a white dove flew down and alighted on the coffin. The dove rested on the coffin until it reached the cemetery, and then it flew away. Those attending the funeral looked upon the dove with "awe and regarded it as an omen from God."

Five of Adelaide's six living children were present to see their mother buried and their father and uncle reburied.

Today, the state of North Carolina has a metal sign posted outside the White Plains Baptist Church. It reads:

SIAMESE TWINS
ENG AND CHANG, THE
SIAMESE TWINS, BORN IN
1811 IN SIAM. SETTLED
AS FARMERS IN THIS
NEIGHBORHOOD. DIED 1874.
GRAVE 100 YARDS WEST.

And one hundred yards west, in the crowded cemetery to the rear of the church, stands the white granite headstone on its granite base. The headstone gives the names of four persons, although only three lie buried beneath it. Chiseled into the headstone is the inscription:

B

ENG BUNKER	CHANG BUNKER
May 11, 1811	May 11, 1811
Jan. 17, 1874	Jan. 17, 1874
HIS WIFE	HIS WIFE
SARAH A. YATES	ADELAIDE YATES
Dec. 18, 1822	Oct. 11, 1823
Apr. 29, 1892	May 21, 1917

SIAMESE TWINS CHANG AND ENG
BORN IN SIAM
BUNKER

Between them, the two couples had produced twenty-one children. What finally happened to the offspring of these unique matings?

Of Eng Bunker's eleven children, four died during his lifetime. The first to die was a daughter, Eng's sixth child, Rosalyn. One day in 1852, when Rosalyn was four months old, she was left at home with a female slave to watch over her. The slave was negligent, and little Rosalyn accidentally fell into an open fireplace. She died of third-degree burns. Thirteen years later, in a single year, 1865, Eng lost two more daughters. Julia, nineteen, died in February, cause unknown, and Georgianna, two years and five months old, was scalded by boiling water in September and died of the burns. The last to die was Eng's first and oldest child, and one of his favorites, Katherine, who expired at twenty-seven from tuberculosis.

With possibly one exception, Eng's remaining seven children lived on into their seventies and eighties. The oldest child Eng had left behind at his death was Stephen, a veteran of the Civil War who was in charge of his father's farm. Eventually Stephen married, and after his death in 1920 at seventy-three, his widow Susan applied for and obtained a Confederate Civil War pension from the state of North Carolina. Surry County folk say this marriage had produced a son, Woo Bunker, a night watchman for a hosiery mill, in retirement in 1976.

Eng's fourth child was a son, James Montgomery, who left Mount Airy after the Civil War to become a farmer in Kansas, where he died in the 1930s in his eighties.

Eng's fifth child, a son, Patrick Henry, also left home after the Civil War and migrated to Kansas with his brother James. Patrick Henry married, and gave Eng four grandchildren. Patrick Henry's wife later asked for a divorce, as well as custody of the children and ownership of the farm, and she was granted everything she wanted. Patrick Henry fell on hard times, and in his old age became an inmate of the county poor farm in Medicine Lodge, Kansas, where he spent his last years fishing and reminiscing about his famous father and uncle, until his death in 1938 at the age of eighty-eight.

Eng's seventh child was a son, William, who made his home in Mount Airy his entire life. He married, had children, and died in 1932 at the age of seventy-seven. William had a granddaughter, Gladys, a nurse and a lieutenant colonel in the United States Army, who visited Siam (Thailand) and was royally received because she was related to the legendary Chang and Eng.

Eng's eighth child, also a son, was Frederick, who was sixteen when his father died. He moved to Missouri and, according to a descendant, was killed in a barroom fight in St. Louis, date unknown.

Eng's ninth child was Rosella, who was fourteen at his death. She married a man named Ashby, and was the only Eng daughter to raise a family. One of her sons, George Ashby, grew up to become president of the Union Pacific Railroad. She died in 1941 at eighty-two.

The youngest of Eng's children—only eight years old when Eng died—was Robert. He came to be known as Big Bob. He married and had two children, a daughter, Kate, who became a schoolteacher, and a son, Robert, known as Little Bob. When Little Bob married and had twins, Big Bob asked him to name them Eng and Chang, and this was done. After Big Bob died in 1951, at eighty-five—he had predicted he would be the last living child of the twins, and he was—Kate inherited Eng's old house, began to restore it, and became the keeper of the flame. Big Bob had not permitted any alterations, repairs, or painting in Eng's house. Once, when someone found that a few nails in the front-porch floor had worked loose and had been pounded back in, Big Bob indignantly pried them loose again. Little Bob died in 1975, and one of his twins, the modern-day Eng, inherited the family tobacco farm, while his twin, the modern-day Chang, is a career man in the United States Air Force.

As to "the other side of the creek"—which was how

the two families referred to one another—Chang's heirs were more affluent than his brother's but fared no better or worse in their lives. Of Chang's ten children, only one was lost while Chang was still alive. This was, of course, his oldest child and favorite daughter, Josephine, twenty-three, who apparently suffered a heart attack while riding home on her horse one August day in 1867 and fell to the ground dead.

Chang's oldest surviving child, Christopher, was nearly twenty-nine when his father died. He had hurried home from California at the time to take charge of the twins' burial. Christopher, the cavalryman who had been captured at Moorefield and imprisoned in Ohio, always took his service for the Confederacy very seriously. He rarely missed a Confederate reunion. After the war he had run his father's farm whenever Chang was away, and later he built a house on land of his own nearby. Unfortunately, he became estranged from his mother Adelaide, and most of his brothers and sisters, after Chang's death. What happened was this: In 1879, Christopher was taken to court in a property dispute. Christopher won the case, but in so doing incurred $525.15 in costs. He felt, under the terms of Chang's will, that this sum was an estate expense, not his alone. Adelaide would not have it. Christopher sued his mother, naming his brothers and sisters as co-defendants. The case was fought in the courts for twenty-six years. In 1905, the North Carolina Supreme Court held for Christopher. He won, but because of an error, he did not collect. In the meantime, the legal action had alienated him from the family.

In 1882, when he was thirty-seven, Christopher married twenty-two-year-old Mary Haynes. They had a son, Christopher L., who in turn married Emma Snow, a local Mount Airy girl. Christopher senior told his son and daughter-in-law that he would will them his 1,000-acre farm if they had children, but if they did not, the property was to go to the Baptist Children's Homes of North Carolina. Christopher died in 1932, at the age of eighty-eight, without grandchildren, and much of his estate—worth half a million dollars three decades later—went to the Baptists, who used a portion of the inheritance to build Bunker Cottage at the Kennedy Home in Kinston, North Carolina.

Chang's third child, Nancy or Nannie, who had accompanied her father to England on his final visit there, had contracted tuberculosis from her ailing cousin Katherine, who also was along. At her father's death in 1874, Nannie had frantically written her older brother Christopher begging him to come home from San Francisco. But before he could reach Mount Airy, and the day before the autopsy report was read to the College of Physicians in Philadelphia, Nannie died at the age of twenty-six.

Chang's fourth and fifth children were both daughters. Susan died in 1922 at the age of seventy-two; Victoria died in 1896 at the age of forty-four.

Chang's sixth child was also a daughter, the deaf Louise who was specially provided for in her father's will. Her husband, Zacharias Haynes, who was deaf as the result of an early scarlet fever attack, taught at the North Carolina Institution for the Deaf and Dumb and Blind, in Raleigh, for thirty-two years. Louise had married Zach when she was eighteen. They had nine children; one became a North Carolina state legislator, another a teacher in the Kentucky School, and another a bank executive. The latter, who was six feet four and looked Oriental, cheerfully answered to the nickname "Chink." It is Chink's son Milton Haynes, a handsome young restaurant manager, who now owns the twins' expense account book. Chang's Louise died in 1934 at the age of seventy-eight.

Chang's seventh child was a son, Albert, who had gone to Russia with his father and uncle on their last trip abroad. He was attending college in Guilford, North Carolina, and was not quite seventeen, when he learned of his father's death. After Christopher returned home from the West to take over the family affairs, he found he was executor of his father's estate. It was his duty to distribute Chang's estate among his brothers and sisters and his mother. Albert strongly objected to the way Christopher did this. His elder siblings had gone through college with their expenses paid by their father. Albert was still in college, and needed money to finish. He felt that he should be given this money in addition to his share of Chang's estate. His older brother Christopher disagreed and refused to give him the extra money. This led to a permanent break between the two brothers.

Albert, however, won in the end. It was he who eventually inherited Chang's house on the hill from his mother Adelaide, with whom he had lived until her death. In later years, Albert enjoyed sitting at the window and staring out at the corncrib when it was filled after the fall harvest. At such times, he would say with satisfaction, "We're set"—meaning set with food for the approaching winter. He proved to be an astute businessman, and owned several profitable farms.

Albert remained a bachelor until the age of sixty-five, when he suddenly married a young woman who had been a music major at Meredith Baptist College for Women. They had three bright daughters. One afternoon when Albert took one of his daughters into Mount Airy, someone asked him, "Cap'n, is this your granddaughter?" Albert snapped back, "No, by God, it's my young'un." When he was eighty-five years old, Albert drove another of his daughters to Duke University to enroll her there personally. He died in 1944 at the age of eighty-seven.

Chang's next child was a son, Jesse, born deaf and dumb like Louise. He studied at the Institution for the Deaf and Dumb and Blind in Raleigh, married, had a family, and owned a farm. He was the one who, in 1909 when he was forty-eight, was struck by lightning on his farm and killed.

Chang's ninth child was his daughter Margaret Elizabeth, who was ten when her father died. She was twenty-six when she married Caleb Haynes. She had eleven children, and several became extremely successful. One of her children headed a textile company, another an underwear company, and a third became the most famous of Chang's grandsons. This was Major General Caleb Vance Haynes, of the United States Air Force, an aide to President Wilson at the Versailles Peace Conference, chief of the American Bomber Command in China during the Second World War, and holder of the Silver Star and Distinguished Flying Cross. Margaret died in 1950 at the age of eighty-seven.

The last of Chang's ten children, Hattie, was five years old when her father died. She lived until 1945, when she died at the age of seventy-seven.

According to Bunker descendants now residing in North Carolina, there "are probably at least one thousand living grandchildren, great-grandchildren, and great-great-grandchildren scattered across the country." Many of these faintly resemble the Siamese Twins, possessing the same black hair and dark eyes, as well as the twins' shrewdness, cleverness, and honesty. Most Chang and Eng descendants also have other characteristics in common: a real love of the land on which they were raised; a belief in keeping their word, and an explosive temper when others do not keep theirs; and a sensitivity about having descended from the Siamese Twins.

This sensitivity is not apparent in all descendants, but it exists side by side with the word "freak." One Bunker relative recalled:

"The wife of a Bunker male descendant innocently bought a figurine of the Siamese Twins that she saw somewhere. When she brought it home, her husband was furious. In earlier years, many of the descendants were very defensive about the twins being their fathers or grandfathers. And with good reason. They were always being asked perfectly insulting questions, were openly leered at, and the like. The Bunker women especially were affected by this. Upon more than one occasion, a Bunker girl—and they were attractive and in many cases beautiful girls—found a swain had disappeared after the young man's family discovered he was courting a Bunker."

Besides a thousand or more descendants, what remains of Chang and Eng? Pieces of their original custom-made furniture exist, and many personal relics, too. The double chair in which they sat has survived. However, the bed in which they slept—and died—was lost in a fire that destroyed Eng's old house in 1956. Still in the hands of relatives are the twins' fortune music box, their gold watches and chains, their amethyst seal reading "Chang-Eng," their silver cigar case, their wind-up white metal watch, their Canadian cigarette case embroidered in flowers, their two travel trunks, and their copy of *The Psalms of David* signed "C.E.."

But something more significant remains. In the dictionaries of the world lies their immortality:

Siamese Twins. 1. congenitally united twins . . . 2. any twins joined together in any manner.

They have become part of the language, every language. With the birth of any Siamese twins anywhere, *the* Siamese Twins are resurrected in memory.

In North Carolina, they sleep their eternal sleep together. In the world, they live, perhaps forever.

ACKNOWLEDGMENTS

The kindness, goodwill, and cooperation of many people go into the making of a book like this. We owe one and all our undying gratitude.

Our greatest debt of thanks for research assistance must go to Walter Kempthorne, of Riverside, California. His tireless correspondence and interviews, his initiative and persistence as a literary detective, truly made this book possible. Almost equally, we give our thanks to his wife, Elizebethe Kempthorne, whose scholarship, fact checking, and editing contributed so much to our biography of the original Siamese Twins. And for devoted assistance to Mr. and Mrs. Kempthorne in North Carolina, we give our thanks to Ruth Minick, Secretary of the Surry County Historical Society.

While all the materials we received proved valuable, a handful of papers were of incomparable help. For these, our special thanks to the staff of the Division of Archives and History of the State of North Carolina for use of primary biographical material on the twins and a great number of unpublished letters; to the library staff of the University of North Carolina at Chapel Hill for use of Chang and Eng's income account book; to Milton Haynes, of Wilmington, North Carolina, for use of the twins' expense account book; to Mrs. Emma Bunker, of Mount Airy, North Carolina, for use of Nannie Bunker's diary; and to Mrs. Grace Haynes Hill, of Mount Airy, for the use of Judge Jesse F. Graves' unpublished biography of the twins and Nannie Bunker's photograph album.

We are indebted also to numerous other individuals who gave so selflessly of their time and energies to collaborate with us in our preparation of this biography of Chang and Eng. These persons, variously, gave us advice, suggestions, information, contacts, and provided us with original journals, pamphlets, lithographs, paintings, photographs, all of which aided in the development of our book. We are lastingly grateful to the following for their help.

Jonathan Daniels, Hilton Head Island, South Carolina; Dr. Worth B. Daniels, Washington, D.C.; George London, Raleigh, North Carolina; Mrs. Kate Cross, Mount Airy, North Carolina; Mrs. Dorothy Haymore, Mount Airy; Joffre Bunker, Mount Airy; Mrs. Alfred H. Haynes, Raleigh; Lucile Haynes, Washington, D.C.; Mrs. Henry Galt Siegrist, Bordentown, New Jersey; Mr. and Mrs. Kester Sink, Mount Airy; Mrs. W. O. Absher, Wilkesboro, North Carolina; Mrs. Ruby Warren, Trap Hill, North Carolina; Mr. and Mrs. James Stinson, Wilmington, North Carolina; Dr. Fred C. Hubbard, North Wilkesboro, North Carolina; Mrs. Eugenia Tufts, Costa Mesa, California; Mrs. E. J. Clowser, Rome, Georgia; Mrs. Dorothy Coffin, Laguna Hills, California; Mrs. Mack Brown, Trap Hill; Reverend Frank McKenzie, North Wilkesboro; Joe H. Carter, Jr., Anderson, South Carolina; Mrs. Kate Hoster, Bradenton, Florida; Mrs. Frank Carter, Mount Airy; Daniel Adams, Los Angeles, California; Kay Hunter, Botesdale, England; Mr. Norman Shields, Badwell Ash, England.

Our thanks, too, to the following researchers we employed:

Mrs. Michele Lawing, Raleigh, North Carolina; Mary Harasek, Ramsey, New Jersey; Inez Bremer, Rijswijk, The Netherlands; Enid Klass, New York, New York; Michael Gardener, Boston, Massachusetts; Mrs. Rosalind Toland, London, England.

We owe very special gratitude to a number of institutions, and to their dedicated personnel, who accumulated for us invaluable materials and photographs we were able to use. The following offered most useful aid:

The University of North Carolina, Chapel Hill, and Dr. William Powell, Dr. Carolyn A. Wallace, Mrs. Ellen Neal; Division of Archives and History, Department of Cultural Resources, State of North Carolina, Raleigh, and Paul P. Hoffman; Surry County Historical Society, Mount Airy, North Carolina, and Ruth Minick; National Archives, Washington, D.C., and the staff in charge of Civil War records; State Archives, Richmond, Virginia; *The State* magazine, Raleigh, North Carolina; Bridgeport Public Library, Bridgeport, Connecticut, and Mrs. Caroline Lydon, David W. Palmquist; Duke University's William R. Perkins Library, and Patricia Hummer; Mütter Museum, the College of Physicians, Philadelphia, Pennsylvania, and Mrs. Lisabeth Holloway, Mrs. Ellen Gartrell, Mrs. Elizabeth Moyer, Gretchen Worden; the Mount Airy *News,* Mount Airy, and Jesse Burchette, Wanda Smith, and the entire staff; Peabody Museum, Salem, Massachusetts, and Kathy Flynn; Library of Congress, Washington, D.C., and Shirley Lebo, Dr. Oliver Orr; National Library, Bangkok, Thailand, and Niansiri Talaluck; Circus World Museum, Baraboo, Wisconsin; Wilkes Community College, Wilkesboro, North Carolina, and Dr. J. Jay Anderson; Mugar Memorial Library, Boston University, Boston, Massachusetts, and Dr. Howard B. Gottleib; the Society for the Preservation of New England Antiquities, Boston, Massachusetts; Massachusetts State Archives, Boston; National Institutes of Health, Bethesda, Maryland, and John Blake; the New York Historical Society, New York, New York; Chicago Historical Society, Chicago, Illinois; Seattle Historical Society, Seattle, Washington; the Free Library of Philadelphia, Philadelphia, Pennsylvania; New York Public Library, New York, New York; University of California Library, Berkeley; Essex Institute, Salem, Massachusetts; the Mount Airy Public Library staff, Mount Airy; the Legislative Library of the North Carolina General Assembly, Raleigh.

BIBLIOGRAPHY

Absher, Mrs. W. O. "Yates—Wilkes County, N.C." *North Carolina Geneology*. Vol. 18, No. 2 (1972).

Andrist, Ralph K. *The Erie Canal*. New York, Harper & Row (© 1964).

[Anon.] *An Account of Chang and Eng, the World Renowned Siamese Twins*. New York, T. W. Strong, 1853.

Ashton, John. *When William IV Was King*. London, Chapman & Hall, 1896.

Barnum, Phineas T. *Struggles & Triumphs* . . . Buffalo, N.Y., Warren, Johnson, 1873.

Barrett, John G. *The Civil War in North Carolina*. Chapel Hill, University of North Carolina Press, 1963.

Beckett, Gilbert A. *The Siamese Twins*. London, J. Cumberland (n.d.).

Besse, H. *Diploteratology* . . . Delaware, Ohio, Gazette steam book and job office, 1874.

Blassingame, John W. *The Slave Community*. New York, Oxford University Press, 1972.

Bowring, John. *The Kingdom and People of Siam*. London, Oxford University Press, 1969.

Burton, Margaret, and Osbert Sitwell. *Sober Truth.* London, MacDonald & Co., 1944.

Carter, William F., Jr., and Carrie Y. Carter. *Footprints in the Hollows.* Surry County, N.C., Surry County Historical Society/Surry County Schools/Mount Airy City Schools, 1975.

Chamberlin, Joseph E. *The Boston Transcript/A History of Its First Hundred Years.* Freeport, N.Y., Books for Libraries Press, 1930.

Clair, Colin. *Human Curiosities.* London, Abelard-Schuman, 1968.

Clemons, Samuel L. *Pudd'nhead Wilson and Those Extraordinary Twins.* Baltimore, Md., Penguin Books, 1969.

——, *The Writings of Mark Twain*, Underwood Edition, Vol. XIX. Hartford, Conn., American Publishing Co., 1901.

Columbia Encyclopedia, New York, Columbia University Press, 1963.

Crawford, John. *Journal of an Embassy . . . to the Courts of Siam and Cochin China.* London, Henry Colburn, 1828.

Cutler, Carl C. *Greyhounds of the Sea.* Annapolis, Md., United States Naval Institute, 1961 (©1930).

Davis, Burke. *Our Incredible Civil War.* New York, Holt, Rinehart and Winston (©1960).

Drake, Samuel A. *Old Landmarks of Boston.* Boston, Roberts Bros., 1889.

Drimmer, Frederick. *Very Special People.* New York, Amjon Publishers, 1973.

Dugger, Shepherd M. *Romance of the Siamese Twins . . .* Burnsville, N.C., Edwards Printing Co. (1936?).

Dumas, Alexandre. *Adventures in Czarist Russia.* New York, Chilton (©1969).

Durant, John. *Pictorial History of the American Circus.* New York, A. S. Barnes, 1957.

Edwards, Frank. *Strange People.* New York, Lyle Stuart, 1961.

Emblen, D. L. *Peter Mark Roget.* New York, Crowell, 1970.

Encyclopaedia Britannica, 15th ed. Chicago, Benton, 1974.

Ferris, Helen. *Here Comes Barnum.* New York, Harcourt-Brace, 1932.

Fitzsimons, Raymund. *Barnum in London*. New York, St. Martin's Press, 1970.

Fowler, John. *Journal of a Tour Through the State of New York in the Year 1830*. New York, Augustus Kelley, 1970.

Gaddis, Vincent, and Marget Gaddis. *The Curious World of Twins*. New York, Hawthorne Books, 1972.

Gale, Robert L. *Plots and Characters in the Works of Mark Twain*. Hamden, Conn., Shoe String Press, 1973.

Garnett, Richard, and Edmund Gosse. *English Literature*. Vol. IV. New York, Macmillan, 1904.

Gosling, Nigel. *Leningrad*. London, Studio Vista, 1965.

Gould, George M., and Walter L. Pyle. *Anomalies and Curiosities of Medicine*. Philadelphia, Saunders, 1897.

Grun, Bernard. *The Timetables of History*. New York, Simon & Schuster, 1975.

Hale, James W. *An Historical Account of the Siamese Twin Brothers, from Actual Observations . . .* New York, Elliott and Palmer, 1831.

Harris, Neil. *Humbug*. Boston, Little, Brown, 1973.

Harrison, Wilmot. *Memorable Paris Houses*. London, Sampson, Low, Marston, 1893.

Hartnoll, Phyllis, ed. *The Oxford Companion to the Theatre*. London, Oxford University Press, 1967.

Hayes, Johnson. J. *The Land of Wilkes*. Wilkesboro, N.C., Wilkes County Historical Society, 1962.

Hirst, Barton C., and George A. Piersol. *Human Monstrosities*. 4 vols. Philadelphia, Lea Brothers & Co., 1891–93.

Horan, James D. *Mathew Brady*. New York, Bonanza Books (© 1955).

Howarth, Patrick. *The Year Is 1851*. London, Collins, 1951.

Hunter, Kay. *Duet for a Lifetime*. New York, Coward-McCann, 1964.

Johnson, Guion (Griffis). *Ante-bellum North Carolina*. Chapel Hill, University of North Carolina Press, 1937.

Joyce, Michael. *Edinburgh/The Golden Age*. London, Longmans, 1951.

Keese, William L. *The Siamese Twins and Other Poems*. New York, E. W. Dayton, 1902.

Kellogg, Sanford C. *The Shenandoah Valley and Vir-*

ginia/1861 to 1865/A War Study. New York, Neale Publishing Co., 1903.

Kirk, Rhina. *Circus Heroes and Heroines*. Maplewood, N.J., Hammond, Inc., 1972.

Langer, W. L., ed. *An Encyclopedia of World History*. Boston, Houghton-Mifflin, 1968.

Lefler, H. T., and A. R. Newsome. *The History of a Southern State/North Carolina*. Chapel Hill, University of North Carolina Press, 1973.

Leigh's New Picture of London. London (n.p.), 1834.

Long, E. B. *The Civil War Day by Day/An Almanac. 1861–1865*. Garden City, N.Y. Doubleday, 1971.

Lytton, Edward George Earle Lytton Bulwer-Lytton, 1st Baron. *The Siamese Twins*. New York, J. & J. Harper, 1831.

Melville, Herman. *The Confidence Man: His Masquerade*. San Francisco, Chandler Publishing Co., 1968 (facsimile of 1857 ed.).

Moreheid, N. J. *Lives, Adventures, Anecdotes, Amusements, and Domestic Habits of the Siamese Twins*. Raleigh, N.C., E. E. Barclay, 1850.

Morison, Samuel E. *Maritime History of Massachusetts, 1783–1860*. Boston, Houghton-Mifflin, 1921.

Mosse, W. E. *Alexander II and the Modernization of Russia*. London, E.U.P., 1958.

Munk, William. *The Roll of the Royal College of Physicians of London*. Vol. III (1801–1825). London, R.C.P., 1878.

Muscatine, Doris. *Old San Francisco*. New York, G.P. Putnam's Sons, 1975.

Neale, Fred A. *Narrative of a Residence at the Capital of the Kingdom of Siam* . . . London, National Illustrated Library, 1852.

Nevins, Allan, ed. *The Diary of Philip Hone*. New York, Dodd, Mead, 1927.

Norman, William M. *A Portion of My Life*. Winston-Salem, N.C., Blair, 1959.

Odell, George C. D. *Annals of the New York Stage*. Vols. I–XV. New York, Columbia University Press, 1927.

Powell, William S. *The North Carolina Gazetteer*. Chapel Hill, N.C., University of North Carolina Press, 1968.

Quennell, Marjorie, and C. H. B. Quennell. *A History of Everyday Things in England*. London, Batsford, 1933.

Richardson, Joanna. *La Vie Parisienne*. London, Hamish Hamilton, 1971.

Sellers, Charles C. *Charles Willson Peale*. Vol. II. Philadelphia, American Philosophical Society, 1947.

Shedlin, Michael, and David Wallechinsky. *Laughing Gas*. Berkeley, Calif., And/Or Press, 1973.

Sherman, Robert L. *Chicago Stage*. Chicago (n.p.), 1847.

Shriver, Philip R., and Donald J. Breen. *Ohio's Military Prisons in the Civil War*. Columbus, Ohio State University Press, 1964.

Stimpson, George. *Information Roundup*. New York, Harper, 1948.

Sutton, Felix. *Masters of Ballyhoo*. New York, Putnam, 1968.

Tavernier, Bruno. *Great Maritime Routes*. New York, Viking, 1972.

Thompson, C. J. S. *The Mystery and Lore of Monsters*. London, Williams & Norgate, 1930.

Truax, Rhoda. *The Doctors Warren of Boston*. Boston, Houghton-Mifflin, 1968.

Tuckerman, Bayard, ed. *The Diary of Philip Hone*. New York, Dodd, Mead, 1889.

Van Noppen, Ina W. *Stoneman's Last Raid*. Boone(?), N.C., North Carolina State University Print Shop (© 1961).

Vella, Walter F. *Siam under Rama III, 1824–1851*. Locust Valley, N.Y., J. J. Augustin, 1957.

Vizetelly, Henry. *Berlin under the New Empire*. London, Tinsley, 1879.

Wallace, Lee A., Jr., comp. *A Guide to Virginia Military Organizations 1861–1865*. Richmond, Va., Virginia Civil War Commission, 1964

The War of the Rebellion: A Compilation of the Official Records of the Union and Confederate Armies. Washington, D.C., U.S. Government Printing Office, 1895.

Watt, Robert, *Bibliotheca Britannica*. Vol. II. Edinburgh, Constable, 1824.

Webster's Biographical Dictionary. Springfield, Mass., Merriam, 1972.

Wells, Helen. *Barnum, Showman of America*. New York, David McKay, 1957.

Werner, M. R. *Barnum*. New York, Harcourt-Brace, 1923.

Wheeler, John H. *Historical Sketches of North Carolina/ from 1584 to 1851*. Vol. II. Philadelphia, J. B. Lippincott, 1851.

Whitehill, Walter M. *Boston/A Topographical History*. Cambridge, Mass., Harvard University Press, 1968.

Who's Who in America, 1956–57. Chicago, Marquis.

Who Was Who in America, 1943–50. Chicago, Marquis.

Who Was Who in America, 1951–60. Chicago, Marquis.

Youngson, A. J. *The Making of Classical Edinburgh*. Edinburgh, Edinburgh University Press, 1966.

MAGAZINES

American Heritage, August 1962; *American Phrenological Journal*, 1853; *Asiatic Journal*, December 1829; *Berliner Medicinischen Gesellschaft*, March 14, 1870; *British Medical Journal*, February 13, February 20, March 20, 1869; *Life*, August 11, 1952; *The Mirror of Literature, Amusement, and Instruction* (London), November 28, 1829; *The New Yorker*, September 2, 1933; *Philosophical Transactions*, 1830; *The Progressive Farmer*, November 1939; *Punch*, March 13, 1869; *The State Magazine*, September 9, 1939, December 13, 1952, May 30, 1965, September 15, 1970; *Transactions of the American Clinical and Climatological Association*, *Vol*. 73, 1961; *Transactions of the College of Physicians of Philadelphia*, Ser. III, Vol. I. 1875; *The Universal Pamphleteer*, London, n.p. (1829?).

NEWSPAPERS

Argus (France), February 9, 1836; *Asheville* (North Carolina) *Times*, May 31, 1926; *Aurora and Pennsylvania Gazette*, October 24, 1829; *Berkshire Chronicle* (England), November 28 and December 5, 1829, May 1 and 3, 1830, February 13, 1869; *Berlin Vossische Zeitung*, February 22–March 14, 1870; *Boston Daily Advertiser*,

August 17 and 22, September 1, 8, and 18, 1829; *Boston Daily Courier*, August 22, 1829; *Charivari* (France), February 20, 1836; *Charlotte* (North Carolina) *Observer*, October 11, 1931, July 29, 1934; *Cheltenham Chronicle* (England), May 13, 1830; *Constitutionel* (France), December 12, 1835, January 15 and February 20, 1836; *Le Corsair* (France), December 12, 1835, January 23, February 3, and February 23, 1836; *Le Courrier Française* (France), January 15, 1836; *Daily Alta California*, December 6, 1860–February 18, 1861; *Dublin Morning Post*, August 30 and September 1830.

Edinburgh Evening Courant, July 17 and 24, 1830; *Elkin* (North Carolina) *Tribune*, May 20, 1957; *Fayetteville* (North Carolina) *Observer*, November 1939; *Galignani's Messenger* (France), December 6, 1935, January 2 and February 17, 1836; *Gazette de France*, January 8 and 15, February 13 and 24, 1836; *Gratis* (France), February 26, 1836; *Greensboro* (North Carolina) *Daily News*, 1951, January 10, 1954; Greenville (North Carolina) *Daily News*, November 4, 1951, January 10, 1954, February 6, 1955; *Greenville* (North Carolina) *Patriot*, October 30, 1852; *John Bull* (England), January 10, 1830; *Journal de Paris*, January 7 and February 26, 1836; *Kentish Gazette* (England), 1835.

Liverpool Chronicle, June 26, 1830; *Liverpool Courier*, June 30 and September 15, 1830; *Liverpool Daily Post*, May 31, 1869; *Liverpool Mercury*, July 2, 1830, June 1, 1869; *London Court Journal*, October and November 1829; *London Morning Herald*, November 1829; *London Morning Post*, December 1829; *London News*, November 22, 1829; *London Times*, November and December 1829, 1835, February 11, 1869; *Morning Courier & New York Enquirer*, September 22 and 30, October 13, 1829; *Mount Airy* (North Carolina) *News*, January 3, 1956; *Newburyport* (Massachusetts) *Herald*, August 14, 1838; *New York Advertiser*, September 29, 1829; *New York Evening Post*, October 13, 1829; *New York Herald*, January 1874; *New York Sun*, December 10, 1870; *New York Times*, October 15, 1860.

Paris Advertiser, December 12, 1835, January 27 and February 17, 1836; *Philadelphia Gazette*, May 6, 1831; *Philadelphia News*, January 1874; *Philadelphia Press*, January 22, 1874; *Reading Mercury* (England),

November 31, 1829; *Reading News* (England), May 15, 1830; *Roxbury* (Massachusetts) *Gazette*, October 30, 1847; *Sacramento Daily Union*, December 1860–February 1861; *The Scotsman*, July 31, 1830; *Le Temps* (France), January 6, 15, and 23, February 13 and 17, 1836; *Vert Vert* (France), January 23 and 30, February 13 and 23, 1836; *Wilmington* (North Carolina) *Morning Star*, 1873; *Windsor Herald* (England), May 7 and 10, 1830; *Winston-Salem* (North Carolina) *Journal & Sentinel*, August 1, 1926, May 18, 1930, February 13, 1938, April 9, 1950; *Yadkin Valley* (North Carolina) *News*, June 16, 1892.

INDEX

ABOUT THE AUTHORS

IRVING WALLACE is one of the most widely read novelists in the world, with estimated worldwide sales of twenty books, in all editions, at 112 million copies. His first great international success was with *The Chapman Report*, followed by *The Prize*, *The Man*, *The Seven Minutes*, *The Word*, *The Fan Club*, *The R Document*, *The People's Almanac* and *The People's Almanac #2* (both with his son, David Wallechinsky), and *The Book of Lists* (coauthored with David and Amy Wallace)—all major bestsellers.

AMY WALLACE, Irving Wallace's daughter, is a graduate of the Berkeley (Calif.) Psychic Institute, and has developed such psychic skills as clairvoyant reading and psychic healing. Besides *The Two*, she has coauthored *The Book of Lists* and *The Psychic Healing Book*.

IRVING WALLACE

Adventurer, masterful story teller, man of the world. Irving Wallace is a master of both fact and fiction. His novels are acclaimed worldwide. His non-fiction, written along with his children, is a potpourri of fascinating, little known information which educates while it entertains.

Fiction:

☐ 11720	**THE FAN CLUB**	$2.25
☐ 10908	**THE MAN**	$2.25
☐ 10090	**THE R DOCUMENT**	$2.25
☐ 12160	**THE TWO**	$2.50

Non-fiction:

☐ 11150	**THE BOOK OF LISTS** with D. Wallechinsky and A. Wallace	$2.50
☐ 01137	**THE PEOPLE'S ALMANAC 2** with D. Wallechinsky	$9.95
☐ 02428	**THE SUNDAY GENTLEMAN**	$1.95

Bantam Book Catalog

Here's your up-to-the-minute listing of over 1,400 titles by your favorite authors.

This illustrated, large format catalog gives a description of each title. For your convenience, it is divided into categories in fiction and non-fiction—gothics, science fiction, westerns, mysteries, cookbooks, mysticism and occult, biographies, history, family living, health, psychology, art.

So don't delay—take advantage of this special opportunity to increase your reading pleasure.

Just send us your name and address and 50¢ (to help defray postage and handling costs).